The Complete New Tarot

THEORY—HISTORY—PRACTICE

Onno Docters van Leeuwen
Rob Docters van Leeuwen

STERLING PUBLISHING CO., INC.
New York

English translation of the text, layout and editorship:
Robert A. W. Docters van Leeuwen, Ph.D., M.Sc., Dip. Ed.
Perth, Western Australia

English translation of the Tarot poems: Margitta S. Docters van Leeuwen,
Perth, Western Australia

English translation review: Bruce A. Beaton, B.A. (Hons), M.App.Psych.,
Perth, Western Australia
Illustrations and inside work: Onno Docters van Leeuwen,
The Hague, The Netherlands
Copyrights currently held by Kosmos-Z&K Publishers Ltd, The Netherlands
Advice and assistance to Onno Docters van Leeuwen:
Art van Remundt, The Hague, The Netherlands
A deck of 80 Tarot cards, as described in this book, has been designed by
Onno Docters van Leeuwen and is available from the authors.

Library of Congress Cataloging-in-Publication Data available

10 9 8 7 6 5 4 3 2 1

First published 1995 under the title *De Tarot in de herstelde orde, theorie,
geschiedenis, praktijk* by Servire
Servire is part of Kosmos-Z&K Publishers, The Netherlands.
Kosmos-Z&K Publishers, St Jacobsstraat 125,
3511 BP Utrecht, The Netherlands
© 1995, 2001 Onno and Rob Docters van Leeuwen

First edition in Dutch 1995
Second, revised edition in Dutch 1996
Third and fourth edition in Dutch 1997
Fifth edition in Dutch 2000

Published in English by Sterling Publishing Co., Inc.
387 Park Avenue South, New York, NY 10016
© 2004 by Onno and Rob Docters van Leeuwen
Distributed in Canada by Sterling Publishing
c/o Canadian Manda Group, One Atlantic Avenue, Suite 105
Toronto, Ontario, Canada M6K 3E7
Distributed in Great Britain by Chrysalis Books PLC
The Chrysalis Building, Bramley Road, London, W10 6SP, England
Distributed in Australia by Capricorn Link (Australia) Pty. Ltd.
P.O. Box 704, Windsor, NSW 2756, Australia

Printed in China
All rights reserved

Sterling ISBN 1-4027-0087-3

Dedicated to:

Bernadette
Erica
Yvonne

CONTENTS

PREFACE

Small causes can have far-reaching effects. In 1970 my wife and I gave my brother Onno a book about the Tarot. Why we gave it and why I thought that something had to be done with it I did not know. . . .

Later, it inspired him to make sculptures of the Major Arcana. That in its turn caused this book to be written. It has taken my brothers Onno and Rob many years of persistent research and struggle to achieve the right form for this work. I am certain that its influence will be profound and that it will be a resource for many people.

There will be those who do not want to venture into reading this book. They may not want to accept the premise that chance is a force that makes sense, and that the meaning of life can be made visible through the proper application of oracles like the I Ching and the Tarot. But in the natural sciences, the experiment provides the proof. The laws of physical nature are not easy to discover; much study is required and the right questions have to be formulated. The same is true for laws of a spiritual nature. This book offers you the chance to study and formulate the right questions about your life. Every time you do a Tarot reading and interpretation, you are carrying out an experiment. Whether it convinces you or not, whether it contributes to the meaning of life as you see it, is up to you.

I offer this book to you realizing that the Tarot is only complete when it is used properly.

Arthur W. H. Docters van Leeuwen, M.Law

INTRODUCTION

It has become apparent that the authentic order of the Tarot, as it has been passed along through the centuries—through the Tarots of Marseilles, Court de Gébelin, Etteila, Levi, Mathers, Papus, Wirth, and Waite—is still obscured. In this book we will restore its true order. Using the Rider-Waite deck, so brilliantly structured by Arthur Waite and beautifully illustrated by Pamela Coleman Smith as our inspiring starting point, we will show how much more useful the restored Tarot is, and how much more fully you can understand it in this completed version.

This restored order brings the Tarot closer to its origin and expands its use as a philosophical instrument. The two blank cards, traditionally added to each deck of playing cards, are revealed, explained, and are visibly active in the Tarot. The new order reintroduces two Major Arcana, as depicted on the cover of this book: (+) Truth, and (–) Intuition. They are the yang and the yin, the animus and anima, the male and the female aspect of God. This reverses the mutilation of the Tarot that took place early in the Middle Ages, and brings the number of Major Arcana to the original 24 once again.

The Tarot can now be correlated with cosmological and philosophical principles 1: God, Tao; 2: Yin and Yang; 3: the Holy Trinity; 4: the Four Emblems; 5: the Pentacle; 6: the Star of David, Seal of Solomon; 7: the Divine Octave; 8: the eight-spoke Vedic sun-wheel and the lemniscate; 9: the enneagram; 10: the binary zero and one; 12: the zodiac; and 24: the hours in a day.

The return of the essential archetypes of Intuition (Juno) and Truth (Jupiter) brings the Tarot back to its original order, in which the Star shoves the Moon away from the top of the life cycle; and pretense and decay in the world make way for hope and incarnation.

The restored order shows simply and clearly the hierarchy and hermetic structure of the Tarot. The four elements of the cards in the Minor Arcana are now related to similar groups of cards in the Major Arcana. This universal and hermetic structure makes it possible to see the Tarot as an integrated and logical set of laws and principles. Neither the Tarot nor humankind benefits from secrecy and inaccessibility. Through this restoration, the Tarot will be more distinctively active.

Onno and Rob Docters van Leeuwen

The Hague, The Netherlands   *Perth, Australia*

The world hangs by a thin thread
And that is the psyche of man.
—*Carl Gustav Jung*

What Is the Tarot?

The world, it is you.
—*J. Krishnamurti*

CHAPTER 1

What Is the Tarot?

The source of the Tarot

The Tarot is made up of a total of 80 cards with 81 different images consisting of:

24 Major Arcana
16 Royal Arcana (sometimes called Court Cards)
40 Minor Arcana
1 back of every card, which is the same

In the Near East the Tarot has had a long and mysterious history. During the crusades the Order of the Knights Templar learned to work with the Tarot through oriental esoteric schools. Subsequently, they introduced the Tarot to Western Europe. About A.D. 1300 the Church of Rome banned the Tarot, and it is only now, in the late 1900s and 2000s, that the Tarot has become widely known.

There are many different versions of the Tarot. The Tarot of Marseilles is thought to be the oldest. It stems from about A.D. 1500 (figure 1.1), but it is generally agreed that the Tarot had been

1.1 Three cards from the Tarot of Marseilles: The Juggler; The World; and The Hanged Man.

developed from much older philosophical systems, and that it originated in the Near East.

Tarot cards embody arcane information

The words *arcanum*, *arca*, and *arcane* come from the Latin *arca*, which means chest or case. The word *arcanus* means closed, hidden, or secret, and arcanum means a secret or mystery. An arcanum is an entity that encompasses all these qualities—it is a body of information known only to a few.

The word arcanum was added to the Tarot later, as a consequence of the loss of the knowledge of the original meaning of each card in its abstract and objective reality.

Tarot cards depict archetypes

Objectively speaking, the Tarot is just a collection of cards with pictures, which at first glance come across as a little strange. They are not easy to comprehend, and their meaning is—especially in the beginning—enigmatic. For this reason, a Tarot card traditionally is called an arcanum.

One way or another, though, the pictures of the arcana of the Tarot look familiar to us, even if we have never seen them before. They clearly have to do with "life" and the "world." The pictures on the Tarot cards are *archetypes*. An archetype is a concept defined by Carl Jung (psychologist, 1875–1961) as a fundamental, collective pattern familiar to everybody because it is part of the collective unconscious of humankind (figure 1.2).

1.2 The image of a mother with her child is an archetype (Albrecht Dürer, copper engraving from 1503).

> *These collective patterns I have called archetypes, a term formulated by St. Augustine. An archetype signifies a typos (impression), a delineated group of archaic origin, whose form and content contains mythological structures.*—C. G. Jung (*Tavistock Readings*, London, 1935).

Archetypes in our unconsciousness correspond with fairy tales, symbolic objects, constellations, religious rituals and godheads, and artistic expressions. Some examples of archetypes are: the witch; the hero; the divine child; the mother; the world-egg (see chapter 2); the heart; the apple; the oak; Taurus; Aquarius; the Christian ritual of baptism; the Druidic ritual of symbolic emasculation of the old year by cutting the mistletoe from the oak on which it grows; the Greek goddess of fertility Demeter; the Celtic Sun-god Balin; the fertility and horse goddesses Epona and Rhiannon; the Roman god of trade, Mercury; the Egyptian ape-god of wisdom and inventor of writing, Thoth; the Hindu elephant-god of wisdom, Ganesha; the *Pieta* by Michelangelo, and so on.

Archetypes often appear in dreams; for example, a mother's breast is a symbol of safety and nourishment; fire indicates purification; ice and snow represent a psychologically cold situation. Each Tarot arcanum contains a coherent set of archetypes represented in a composition of symbols. This is the reason why Tarot pictures have so much spiritual power. You become more aware of the meaning of an arcanum by observing it in a contemplative way. Also, without even meditating on them, the essence of, for example, Death, The Star, The Devil, or The Lovers passes the filter of "linear thinking;" everyone knows immediately the message the cards are passing along.

Collective-psychological information in the Tarot

Many matters of daily life are organized in a standard way. Very often their sources are practical laws and structures that have developed over time. For example, everywhere on earth the family is a core element and cornerstone of society. The relations and interactions in the family are of collective-psychological origin and humankind's common cultural heritage. We encounter these social archetypes especially in the Royal Arcana (Court Cards) of the Tarot, which portray this collective-psychological information.

The Tarot as cosmology

A cosmology is an attempt to explain coherently the cosmos, men, women, and their world, the events therein, and the relations between these elements. It seeks to explain events as well as to

1.3 The Mexican Sundial (about A.D.1500) is a calendar, but also a horoscope. Its base structure features various circles divided into four quarters and built up from cards containing meaningful figures. As cosmology, the Mexican Sundial clearly shows kinship to the Tarot.

understand and predict them. The Tarot is a pictorial cosmology, consisting of meaningful archetypal illustrations. The Biblical account of the creation is an example of a verbal cosmology. The *I Ching*, a Chinese oracle book from the twelfth century B.C., is an ideographic cosmology, consisting of stylized ideograms composed of whole and broken lines. All ritual dances—for example, the Dervish dances—have a cosmological meaning.

Architectonic, three-dimensional cosmologies have been preserved longest. The astronomical edifice Stonehenge in England is well known, as are the temple complex Borobudur in Indonesia, the great pyramids of Egypt, and the temple complexes in Mexico. These architectural monuments were designed, used, and managed by priest-scientists. It was not until the Renaissance that the vocations of "priest" and "scientist" were separated.

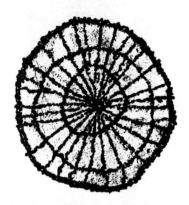

1.4 Sun symbol made by Aborigines in Australia (circa 30,000 B.C.). It is remarkable that this rock engraving consists of 81 segments! The Tarot–including the common back of the cards–also consists of 81 pictures.

Later, cosmologies were also summarized in two dimensions. We know that in the Egypt of the Pharaohs the zodiac consisted of 24 signs. On other continents similar cosmological structures were developed, such as the Mexican Sundial, and Asian mandala structures (figures 1.3–1.6). *Mandala* is the Sanskrit word for "circle." Mandalas appear in the mind during very deep meditations and are spiritual gates through which the soul transgresses from our limited world into the realm of Eternal Being.

Because the oldest cosmologies were traditionally passed on in secret initiation rites by word of mouth only, most of this knowledge has been lost during the fall of the old cultures. Therefore, it is difficult to unravel the knowledge laid down in these architectural and pictorial systems.

In this book we will restrict ourselves to uncovering, clarifying, and objectifying the cosmological knowledge assembled in the Tarot. The arcana in the Tarot have not only psychological significance, but many other meanings as well. *The Tarot has great significance as a frame of reference for every developmental process and the individual stages of that process.*

Information through pictures and symbols

1.5 Borobudur is a cosmic-symbolic temple complex built in the form of a three-dimensional mandala. A dynasty of priests began the erection of this pictorial initiation into Buddhism in 775 and completed it in 840.

From the beginning of humankind, sculptures and drawings have been used to summarize and convey information. Approximately 60,000 years ago, cave murals were made depicting animals and hunting scenes. Archeologists believe that these cave murals had a magic-religious and educational meaning. Since early times, humankind represented psychological and emotional content in sculptures, pictures, and mythologies, such as the drawings of Greek myths on vases and bowls, and alchemistic allegorical representations.

Over the years, the meaning of frequently used sculptures and pictures shifted. In the ninth millennium B.C.E. in Asia Minor, small tokens enveloped in clay—the earliest precursors of writing—were used to record possessions. An image gradually acquired the meaning of the principal sound-phoneme in its name. Next, these sound-representing images were stylized into icons. More and more, groups of pictures were used to represent groups of sounds, and thus words. In this way, gradually, from about 3000 B.C. writing developed. Clear examples are the Minoic writing developed on Crete, Mayan writing in Central America, Egyptian hieroglyphs, and Chinese characters. Later, the stylized images were simplified further into symbols without a retrievable meaning, except for the phonemes they represented. Thus, alphabets sprouted from archaic cosmologies. The Rune alphabet is a significant example (figure 1.7). These 24 letters were recorded directly from cosmological and abstract principles. Hence, the runes are related to the Tarot by substance and function.

1.6 *Mandala* is the Sanskrit word for "circle." Mandalas appear in the mind during very deep meditations and are spiritual orientation structures (gates) in which the soul passes from the limited world of becoming into the realm of Eternal Being. Mandalas contain objective symbols and archetypes. In this mandala, all depicted gods represent particular archetypes. The outer rim contains a series of gods, representing undivided ego-energy.

Apart from alphabets, people also continued to use images as a means of transferring information. Also in the world of today, stylized images, called pictograms or icons, are often applied to convey information quickly and effectively. Traffic signs are a clear example.

The Tarot in its totality—and each arcanum in itself—is an integrated collection of archetypal, psychological, philosophical, and societal symbols. The information comprised by an arcanum is therefore much more complicated than that of a traffic sign.

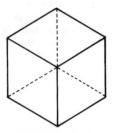

THE EMPTY RUNE

1.7 The form of the 24 runes is based on the empty rune, a cube. The cube traditionally symbolizes solidity, durability, and truth. The New Jerusalem (Revelations 21:16-17) is described as a cube, based on the number 12.

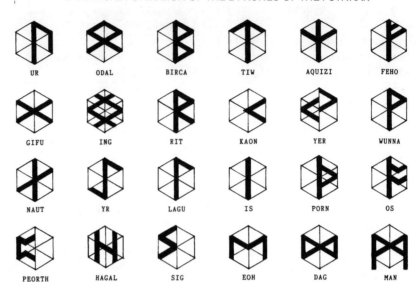

UR	ODAL	BIRCA	TIW	AQUIZI	FEHO
GIFU	ING	RIT	KAON	YER	WUNNA
NAUT	YR	LAGU	IS	PORN	OS
PEORTH	HAGAL	SIG	EOH	DAG	MAN

The Tarot as philosophical tool and alphabet

The Tarot is a loose-leaf collection of philosophical and psychological images with formal rules to explain this information.

Every arcanum in the Tarot:
- contains several philosophical principles, practical knowledge, rules, "facts of life"
- relates in various ways with all other arcana, and aggregates with them to form a complete entity
- is a building block to create complicated philosophical information which, like letters of an alphabet, are used to build words and sentences.

One could, as P. D. Ouspensky, Russian philosopher and esoteric from the beginning of the twentieth century, puts it, speak of it as a *philosophical machine* or *instrument*. Such a device contains:

- ordered philosophical information;
- a collection of rules and principles which can be used to distill answers to questions from that philosophical information.

Ouspensky describes in his book, *A New Model of the Universe*, a philosophical machine designed by Raymond Lully in the 13th century:

. . . His machine consisted of concentric circles with words in a particular order, which indicated ideas from different worlds. When a question was formulated by placing selected words in a particular position, other words (on the circles) gave the answer . . .

OTAR

7

THE CHARIOT

1.8 A Tarot card is a complex pictogram. Shown here is The Chariot.

Working with a philosophical instrument

A philosophical instrument is used as follows:

1. The diviner and the questioner focus on using the philosophical instrument for advice.
2. The questioner formulates the problem in the form of a question.
3. The diviner allows the questioner to draw cards, according to a particular rule, from a bank of philosophical information.
4. The cards with information are then laid out in an ordered pattern predetermined by the general content of the question.
5. Finally, together with the questioner, the diviner interprets the philosophical information comprised by the ordered cards.

Asking for advice by means of a philosophical instrument is called divining or consulting an oracle. Tarot, runes, I Ching, and astrological readings all proceed according to this scheme.

Synchronicity

All philosophical tools like astrology, runes, I Ching, and the Tarot are based on the principle of synchronicity. Everyone has examples of coincidences taking place without a clear cause. For example, we meet a person in a busy mall shortly after we thought about him or her.

The psychologist Carl Jung (figure 1.9) called this phenomenon of coincidence *synchronicity*. He defines synchronicity as the simultaneous occurrence of a certain psychological content, such as a dream, idea, presumption, thought, or emotion, and one or more factual events presenting themselves as *significant parallels* of the existing inner situation. In the esoteric document *Kybalion: A Study of the Hermetic Philosophy of Ancient Egypt and Greece*, this principle is pointed out by Hermes Trismegistus: *It is above as it is below.*

Carl Jung and educator J. B. Rhine studied the phenomena of coincidence extensively. Jung stated that synchronicity is not limited by distance, and that the order of timing can be reversed in synchronistic phenomena. We can have precognition shortly before or after something has happened outside our boundaries of observation.

Synchronicity has no regard for demarcations of time and space. Emotional commitment influences coincidences positively. If we decide to buy a purple car, for instance, we see purple cars driving by again and again. We attract those incidents. In a similar fashion we can, through an incorrect psychological attitude, become involved in accidents. Through emotional commitment, our psyche and the objective environment tune in to each other. This is one of the psychological backgrounds of the Biblical saying *"Knock, and the door will be opened,"* and *"Seek, and you shall find."* Through emotional commitment we can tune in to the world so

1.9 Carl Gustav Jung (1875–1961), psychiatrist and philosopher, introduced many fundamental principles, such as the distinction between introverts and extroverts, the concept of archetypes, and the concept of synchronicity. Jung studied alchemy, the Tarot, astrology, the *I Ching*, and the interpretation of dreams.

that synchronicity can occur. Alternatively, the objective world may, via synchronicity, through the unconscious, generate certain psychological situations or content.

During his practice as a psychologist, Jung found that occurrences of synchronicity were related to archetypes. Sensory and extrasensory perception apparently are connected via common links. When we work with the Tarot, there is a substantial chance for synchronicity to emerge because of the archetypal content of the Tarot.

According to Aldous Huxley (writer/philosopher/psychonaut, 1894–1963), synchronicity is omnipresent. Normal consciousness may provide a window to synchronicity in some cases. However, synchronicity as a phenomenon that determines all coincidences can only be perceived and experienced in a state of elevated awareness.

Synchronicity and the Tarot

The Tarot is a loose-leaf book. The order of pages in a bound book is fixed, but the sequence of Tarot cards changes every time the deck is shuffled. This change of sequence is essential. Being loose-leafed, the Tarot is continuously in tune with All and Everything. G. I. Gurdjieff (Russian philosopher, 1872–1949, and teacher of Ouspensky) says very pertinently: *Your environment is a reflection of your state of being.*

Every time a deck of Tarot cards is consulted, it synchronizes with the questioner's psychological condition and reproduces it in pictures and archetypes. Every time the Tarot is shuffled and parted, the sequence of cards concurs synchronistically with the current situation. The Tarot cards harmonize with the questioner and his or her situation.

The fact that the Tarot cards are shuffled does not mean that the Tarot does not have an order. Just as the zodiac appears in the sky in a particular sequence, but at the same time moves with the whole cosmos, causing each horoscope to be different, so the Tarot is a depiction of a changing universe. This is the reason that the Tarot, despite its rigid inner structure, is loose-leafed and therefore always in transit, through the process of shuffling. We'll talk more about synchonicity in Chapter 8.

The Tarot, ordinary playing cards, and roulette

The ordinary card game and roulette are games of chance derived from the Tarot. The Church was very much against the Tarot, because as a philosophical instrument it gave people direct access to cosmological and practically useable philosophical knowledge. In the early Middle Ages, the clergy stripped the Tarot of its powerful meaning in an attempt to keep deep philosophical insights in the hands of the Church. The Tarot was relegated to being only a chance machine with which people could play games at a material level. This was no threat to the Church, although the Church continued to oppose the "picture book of the Devil." People remained fascinated with the ordinary playing cards derived from the Tarot.

IL PAPA

THE HIEROPHANT

DE PRIESTER

1.10 Adulterations and restoration of the Tarot: The Pope in the Milanese Tarot by G. Sironi (1892) compared to The Hierophant by Waite (1910) and The Priest in *The Tarot Completed* (1999).

Adulteration and restoration of the Tarot

Over the centuries a considerable number of impurities and subjectivity have been introduced into the Tarot, which disguise the original meaning of some arcana and decrease or deform their power. For example, in the Middle Ages, The High Priest was pictured as the pope in formal habit (figure 1.10). As a result this arcanum mistakenly became associated with the pope and his environment. Metaphorically, this implies infallibility, opulence, and perhaps even corruption, inquisition, and other papal matters. However, the content of this arcanum had nothing to do with the pope as such, but with a high priest, a person of elevated standing—initiated and evolved—and at an abstract level, communal morality.

In the Tarot decks of the eighteenth century, the Emperor is often pictured in full armor, looking more like a warrior or a general than an emperor. This evokes the wrong associations. An emperor has an army with which to protect the country, but metaphorically he is the royal human who rules over matter. For example, the Egyptian pharaoh or the Chinese emperor connects the heavenly order with the earthly one, and expresses this order in matter by giving shape to his country and people.

In the twentieth century in the 007-Tarot, made for the James Bond movie *Live and Let Die*, the Major Arcanum Justice is portrayed as a blindfolded woman with a sword. Originally, however, Justice was an old man, a blind seer who judged objectively and truly, as the old sages did (figure 1.11). In most tribes, justice is still administered this way. We find the archetype of the wise, judging seer in Tiresias from *Oedipus Rex* by Sophocles.

RTOA

1. 11 Subjectivity in the Tarot: Justice in the 007-Tarot compared to Justice by Waite and Justice in the (Dutch) Tarot in the Restored Order.

Sir Arthur Waite (1857–1940) accomplished a great work in his Rider-Waite deck, by thoroughly purifying the arcana of subjective content. He removed the Hebrew alphabet, as well as planetary symbols, the zodiac, and moralistic symbols on garments and in the background. Furthermore, he gave the arcana objective names. For example, he changed the name of the Major Arcanum "The Pope" to the more universal "The High Priest." In this book, the names of the Major Arcana have been returned to their core meaning wherever possible. The Major Arcanum the Pope, for instance, has the essential meaning *Knowing-and-Being*. Hence, by leaving out the adjective "high," the name The Priest indicates more purely the content of this arcanum (figure 1.10).

The completion of the Tarot

Arthur Edward Waite's "Rider Tarot Deck" is the most often used version of the Tarot. Although he thoroughly purified the Tarot, his version still consists of 78 pictorial cards and the centuries-old and traditional two blank cards. *Because of the absence of pictures on those two cards, it is our belief that the Tarot is incomplete and cannot function properly as a philosophical instrument.* Even though the meanings of very old traditions are often concealed, we have determined—from other versions of the Tarot that will be discussed later in this book—that the two blank Tarot cards should bear the archetypes Jupiter (Truth) and Juno (Intuition). The Tarot is only complete when these two missing archetypes have returned to it, in their appropriate places (figure 1.12).

After these two Major Arcana had been concealed—made blank—the proper order in the Major Arcana could not work properly. In his analysis of the Tarot cards in his encyclopedic work *The Secret Teachings of All Ages,* Manly P. Hall states:

> *The diverse opinions of eminent authorities on the Tarot symbolism are quite irreconcilable. The conclusions of the scholarly Court de Gébelin and the bizarre Etteila—the first authorities on the subject—not only are at radical variance but both are equally discredited by Levi, whose arrangement of the Tarot trumps was rejected in turn by Arthur Edward Waite and Paul Case as being an effort to mislead students. The followers of Levi—especially Papus, Christian Westcott, and Schuré—are regarded by the "reformed Tarotists" as honest but benighted individuals who wandered in darkness for lack of Pamela Coleman Smith's new deck of Tarot cards with revisions by Mr. Waite.*

Elisabeth Lasloë succinctly summarizes the problems regarding the order in her book *The Secrets of the Tarot:*

> *It would be difficult to restore the original order in the Tarot, an order about which the most learned occultists do not agree.*

The loss of the right order was not only caused by the disappearance of Juno and Jupiter, but also by a misunderstanding of the archetypal content of the Major Arcana—The Priestess, The Priest, The Empress, The Emperor, Temperance, and Death:

The esoteric Priest is archetypically attracted to an inwardly (and outwardly) wealthy woman, The Empress, to carry out his spiritual assignment in life. The archetypal marriage between them led to changes in and discussions about the numbering of these two cards.

The ethereal Priestess is attracted to a strong, worldly man, The Emperor, also to carry out her tasks in a protected environment. The archetypal marriage between The Priestess and The Emperor also led to changes in the numbering of these two cards.

Under the influence of Christianity, insight into the process of dying and the content of the archetypes Death and Temperance became blurred. In virtually all Tarot decks, Death wrongly comes before Temperance. The right order is that the process of dying starts with the soul leaving a living person. Then, as a consequence, the person's body physically dies. Therefore, the Major Arcanum Temperance ought to be placed *before* Death.

JUPITER

JUNON

TRUTH

INTUITION

1.12 The two missing Major Arcana in the Tarot: Jupiter (Truth) and Juno (Intuition).

JUPITER.
JUPITER.

JUNON.
JUNO

JUPITER.

JUNON.

JVPITER

JUNON

O ZEYΣ

H IEPEIA

OSIRIS

ISIS

JUPITER

JUNON

JUPITER

JUNO

The authors of this book have designed a deck of Tarot cards in which the two restored Major Arcana, Truth and Intuition, are integrated and the order of the Major Arcana is restored. The authors explain the obfuscation, restoration, and completion of the Tarot in Chapter 6 of this book.

The Major Arcana in the Tarot as a "strip"

When the arcana are in the right order, a "strip" develops with a clear beginning, middle, and end. Knowledge of the strip is necessary to be able to put an arcanum into the context of the total, cyclic, ordered Tarot.

OTAR   OTAR   RTAO

1.13. The series of three Major Arcana: The Empress, The Chariot, and The Hermit (from the Dutch Tarot in the Restored Order) together portray a successful development.

We can compare this with a picture book that, for instance, tells the story of Little Red Riding Hood. When we see the picture in which she leaves the road to pick flowers, we know that the next picture will show us the big, bad wolf that is going to talk to her to discover her plans. We know this because we are already familiar with the story. If the order of the scenes is wrong, confusion may arise about the story's plot and wrong conclusions may be drawn.

For example, in the restored Tarot deck, The Chariot is preceded by The Empress (who is pregnant) and is followed by The Hermit. In this way the arcanum The Chariot indicates a situation in which a development, The Empress, via success, The Chariot, leads to a deepening, The Hermit (figure 1.13).

A clear understanding of the order of the Major Arcana is very important. For this reason, in the Middle Ages the Tarot cards were numbered. Number 7—the lucky number—happens to be the arcanum The Chariot, and number 13, Temperance. Unnumbered versions of the Tarot also exist, for example, the Visconti Sforza deck from the fifteenth century. It is certainly possible to understand a card very well without its being numbered.

The arrangement of the Tarot and its quadruplicity
The 56 arcana of the Minor Arcana and Royal Arcana are divided into four groups: Pentacles, Wands, Cups, and Swords. This classification is related to the four elements Earth, Fire, Water and Air, which in turn represent certain properties.

Quadruplicity is an archetype that occurs universally. It is the logical condition for the evaluation of something in all its aspects. If you want to judge in such a way, you must use a fourfold aspect. If, for example, you want to indicate the total perimeter of the horizon, you name the four directions. There are always four elements, four primordial qualities, four colors, four castes in India, four ways for spiritual development in Buddhism. The ideal completeness is round, the circle, but the natural minimal division is fourfoldedness.

— C. G. Jung

We find the Tarot's quadruplicity in ordinary playing cards, which are a degraded version of the Tarot. Pentacles became Diamonds, Wands became Clubs, Cups became Hearts, and Swords became Spades.

The three books of the Tarot
The Tarot is made up of three "books:" the Major Arcana, the Royal Arcana, and the Minor Arcana.

- The *Book of Major Arcana* consists of 24 cards, each comprising a complex, archetypal depiction of a major philosophical principle (figure 1.15).
- The *Book of Royal Arcana* comprises 16 cards grouped in four royal families, each with their own coat of arms or color: Pentacles, Wands, Cups, and Swords. Each family is made up of four members: the father, the mother, the elder son or daughter, and the younger son or daughter. The father in the family is the King; the mother is the Queen. The eldest child is the Knight. Sexually mature, he leaves the family to fulfill his task in life. The youngest child is the Page. Still immature, he lives with his parents. These cards are all part of the Royal Arcana (figure 1.10).
- *The Book of Minor Arcana* consists of 40 cards in four groups of ten. They are numbered 1, 2, 3, 4, 5, 6, 7, 8, 9, and 10. The card numbered 1 was later given the name Ace. Each group is linked to one of the symbols in the cards (figure 1.17).

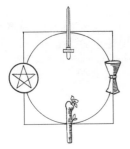

1.14 The four Tarot emblems.

1.15 The book of 24 Major Arcana. At a most elementary level, this book is the cyclic story of man who is born, goes through life, dies, goes to heaven, and incarnates again.

Pentacles (Earth)	materialism, condition for growth
	Tradesmen
Wands (Fire)	growing power and love for work
	Farmers and commercial people
Cups (Water)	emotions, feelings, sacrifices
	Clergy, religion, artists
Swords (Air)	intellect, selection, regeneration
	Aristocracy and scientists

The order of Major Arcana in the Tarot

The most usual order in the Tarot is the one indicating a life cycle. This cycle invariably starts with card 0, The Fool, and ends with card 21, The Universe. All cards thus form a cyclic strip, with the end introducing the beginning of the next cycle.

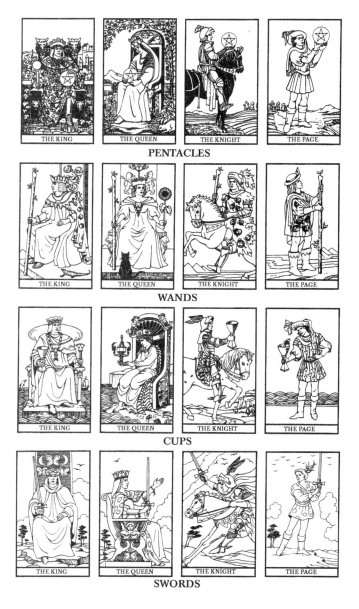

THE KING THE QUEEN THE KNIGHT THE PAGE

PENTACLES

THE KING THE QUEEN THE KNIGHT THE PAGE

WANDS

THE KING THE QUEEN THE KNIGHT THE PAGE

CUPS

THE KING THE QUEEN THE KNIGHT THE PAGE

SWORDS

1.16 The Book of the Royal Arcana: four royal families, each with its own emblem or coat of arms.

1.17 The Book of the 40 Minor Arcana consists of four groups of ten cards and portrays people, guided by the Royal Families, implementing the principles depicted in the Major Arcana.

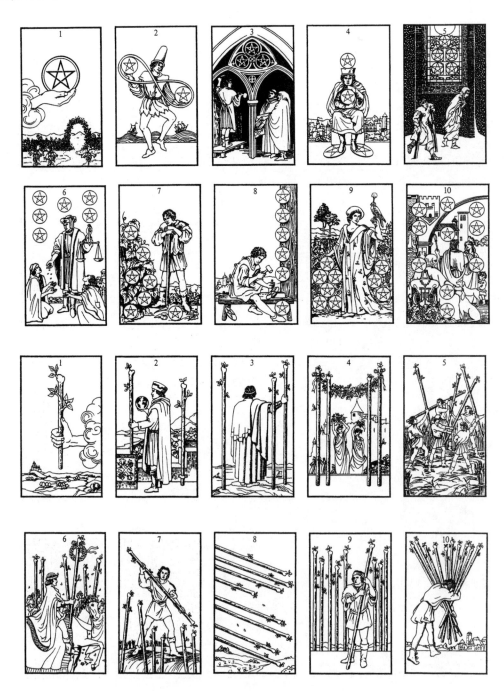

The eighty-first card

Together, the 24 Major Arcana, the 16 Royal Arcana, and the 40 Minor Arcana form a group of 80 cards with 80 pictures that represent archetypes, laws, and principles. These 80 cards all have the same background (figure 1.18). Thus, in total the Tarot comprises 80 + 1 = 81 principles.

The square of nine is 81. In Hinduism this square is graphically reproduced in a mandala consisting of 81 squares, symbolizing the

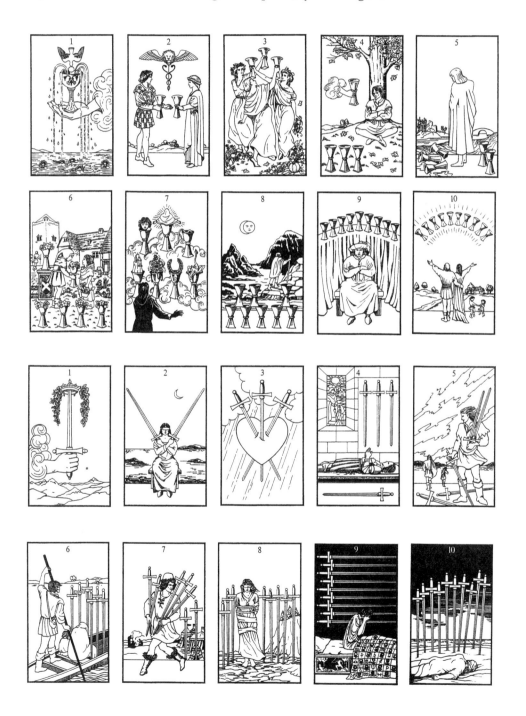

1.18 The Tao, or the way, is pictured as a path without a beginning or an end, thus symbolizing eternity, the cosmos.

universe. It is used as an aid in making prophecies (figure 1.19). The number nine has a peculiar characteristic. The outcome of any multiplication by nine, when reduced to a single digit, is always the number nine: for example, 64 x 9 = 576, 5+7+6 = 18, 1+8 = 9. The nine therefore can be seen as a number that always returns to itself and thus symbolizes eternity.

We also refer to the Tao, as it was described by the Chinese philosopher Lao Tse in about 400 B.C. In his *Tao Te Ching* he described a complete philosophy in 81 aphorisms. Its main concept is Tao, which literally translated means road, but its true meaning is much more profound. Tao is the source without a name, the beginning and end of all things. Lao Tse describes Tao as follows:

> *Return is the movement of Tao.*
> *Softness is the way in which Tao works.*
> *All things begin from Being.*
> *Being originates from Not-Being.*

Using the Tarot

Working with the Tarot requires a respectful and open attitude. Involvement with the questioner is a second, important factor. Working with the Tarot is only possible if you are fully conversant with the meanings of the arcana and their correct order, their interrelations, and the methods used to consult the Tarot as a philosophical instrument. With this knowledge and with skill in using the Tarot, you can achieve clear insight into situations and problems.

1.19 The Tao symbol in the mandala consisting of 81 squares (Kangra, Himachal Pradesh, eighteenth century). The 81st principle is the circle on the square in the middle. Tao is also depicted as T in figure 7.3.

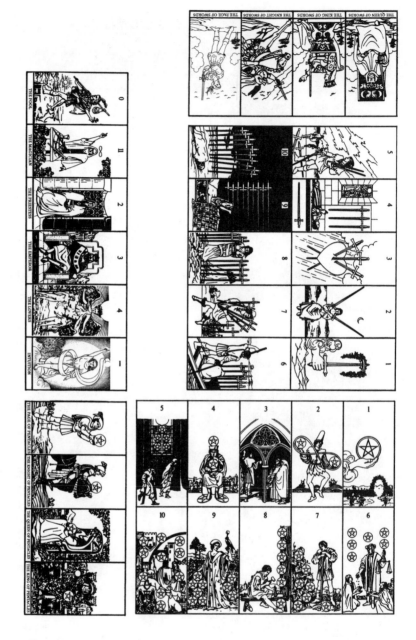

1.20 The three books of the Tarot are organized in the structure of a mandala. The core of this mandala is a swastika representing the four Aristotelian elements.

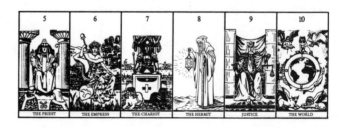

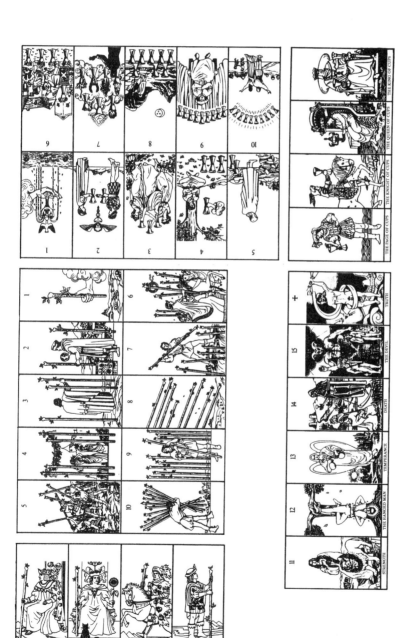

The 24 Major Arcana of the Tarot as the Path of Life

Stonehenge, a 5,000-year-old
monument in Wiltshire, England.

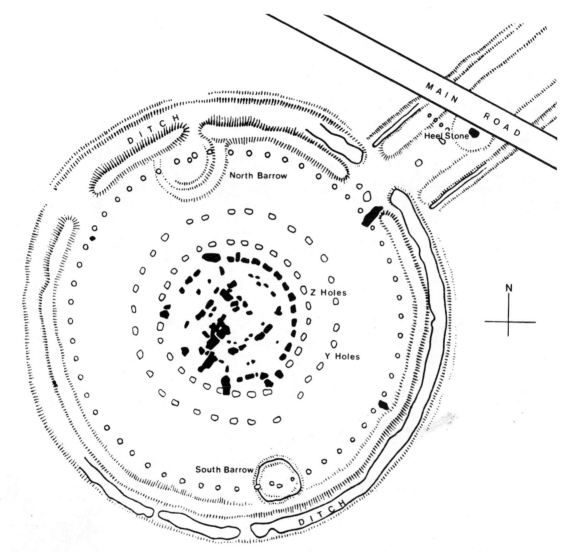

In this way in prehistoric times
Sages laid down and passed on
Knowledge about the universe.

Diagram of Stonehenge, ca. 2000

THE 24 MAJOR ARCANA OF THE TAROT AS THE PATH OF LIFE

The 24 Major Arcana of the Tarot as the Path of Life

The circle as a symbol of creation

Most accounts of creation start with a description of desolate emptiness (though not empty in the true sense), which is called One or All. The circle—or the line that returns into itself—the symbol of the whole universe, represents the All Encompassed.

We find the circle everywhere in the world, in all cultures: in prehistoric, megalithic edifices; in cave paintings; in philosophical systems; and in exercises for meditation. Architectonic-cosmological ring structures are very impressive: through their forms they try to convey special knowledge.

The Chinese drew the primordial beginning, the Wu-Chi, as an empty circle. We find the circle of creation also in the Brahma's cosmic egg, in the Japanese and Chinese Tai chi symbol, and in the Ensó of Zen Buddhism (figures 2.1–3).

2.1 Zen circle. In Japanese Zen the circle (Ensó) is one of the most profound symbols. When we are liberated from illusions, we appear to ourselves in the most luminous light and are able to understand ourselves.

The Tai Chi consists of a primordial circle divided in light and dark, Yang and Yin, male and female. This expresses the duality of everything.

The *I Ching*, a centuries old oracle book (1200 B.C.), states that creation starts with a line, ———, a ridgepole. This line, which is in itself a unity, has the potential to bring duality into the world: the line divides in two: — —. Below and Above appear, Left and Right, Front and Back, White and Black, Man and Woman, Good and Bad, Space and Time. These resulting contrasts are the

2.2 Brahma's egg.

2.3 The Tai Chi as a symbolic, cyclic representation of the first partition in creation. Yang's light penetrates Yin's darkness.

building blocks of our reality. In nuclear physics it happens at a subatomic scale: the formation of electron-positron pairs. Confucius was China's most important philosopher, teacher, and political theorist, who lived from 551 B.C. until 479 B.C., and whose ideas still influence all East Asian civilizations. Once, standing beside a river, he said: "In this way everything passes like this stream, without cessation, day and night." The one who understands this does not focus on objects passing by in the outside world, but on the constant, eternal law, the foundation of all change.

This law is the same as the paradoxical Tao described by Lao Tse—the natural way of things, the One in the multitude of things.

Evolutionary processes

In the development of nature, one event proceeds from another. The theory of evolution states that, in a time span of millions of years, one animal species develops from another.

The development of a human being differs fundamentally from that of other animals. Evolution of mankind takes place along two lines: the line of knowing and the line of being. In a proper development these lines run parallel and support each other. However, if one of the two lines overtakes the other, the whole process comes to a standstill. Often such a period of stagnation is followed by a period of retrogression and deprivation.

Positive and negative powers

Evolutionary processes do not take place without problems. Everyone's life has to follow a particular, well-defined course. Coincidental events are often called the hand of God, or karma. These influences, like those of angels, give direction to our path through life.

We may actualize ourselves through objectively proper actions. Naturally, it is of great importance for us to make the right decision: every mistake takes us away from self-realization—a loss of terrain that has to be regained at a later stage or in another life, often with struggle and suffering.

What is a proper—and what is a wrong—decision? What is "good" and what is not? The execution of witches by means of burning at the stake, for example, justified in the Middle Ages by Christian belief, is now seen as an offense against humanity. The times we live in seem to mask our insight about what is objectively appropriate. However, it is not really the time, but the lack of clear consciousness—our Knowing-and-Being—that is causing this lack of insight. Often we become aware of the objective value of our actions later, when we are able to look back upon our decisions and their consequences. Apparently, we are not aware of all aspects of reality: we lie to ourselves without knowing or wanting to know.

Gurdjieff states that we are actually asleep while we are conscious—existing on a rather primitive level. In a treacherous way, our level of awareness changes continuously. Gurdjieff discussed this extensively with his students and did exercises in consciousness with them, in which they had to remember everything that happened and everything that they observed during a day. Lack of vigilant awareness—in essence, the forgetting of our Self—makes us lose contact with our real task in life, causing errors of judgment and wrong decisions. Notwithstanding all this, every human's conscience gives an objective and immediate insight into what is appropriate and what is not. Conscience is the interpreter of the soul, which, deep inside us, is striving for actualization—transforming the realization of what we wish to become into actuality.

One mistaken decision often leads to a chain of wrong decisions, and sometimes to a chain reaction of years of erring and unnecessary suffering. The longer the wanderings take, the more extensive the damage and suffering is when the wrongly constructed edifice of life has to be broken down. It serves our interest to see and admit a wrong decision as quickly as possible.

Making choices in life
When it has become clear that a particular decision was wrong, an analysis of the situation often follows. In general, incorrect decisions are induced by impulses or instincts, due to lack of contact with the conscious self—because humankind is asleep or does not listen to the voice of its conscience. But admitting of an incorrect decision or inappropriate behavior is not in itself a guarantee of improvement. Often, mistakes are made again and again: "The spirit is willing but the flesh is weak" (Matthew 26:41).

2.4a–b Two illustrations from the book *Dogma and Ritual of Higher Magic*, written by Eliphas Levi (Alphonse Louis Constant, 1810–1875).

King Solomon's seal. The macroprosopos and the microprosopos. God of light and God of reflection, the compassionate and the avenger, the white Jehovah and the black Jehovah.

The hand of a priest makes the sign of God's Truth and at the same time projects as a shadow the shape of the Devil.

There is a substantial difference between Knowing and Being. It is even more difficult to develop both in a balanced way. If Knowing is emphasized over Being, people have little power to do things and are useless beings. If, on the contrary, Being wins over Knowing, they have the power to do things, but lacking knowledge and insight, do not know what to do: they are mechanical people.

Sleep-walking on our path of life we can cause all sorts of damage to ourselves and others. What we acquire in this way is false and without purpose: all exertions have been useless. In order to Do, that is: actualizing the Good, one has to Be.

Everything has two sides. Many religions personify "bad" powers that distract us from reaching our goal and softly whisper us into wrong actions or cause harm. However, the good and the bad are two aspects of one power: *Diable est Deus inversum*—the Devil is God inverted. We have to choose continuously between these two powers. Good and bad do not exist independently from each other (figure 2.4a–b). For this reason the bad cannot be destroyed: being the opposite of good (Truth), the bad (The Devil) will emerge again and again. In Major Arcanum 7, The Chariot, a person surpasses this dualism.

The bond with the Luciferan Ego as a co-determining power in the cyclic process of life is portrayed in the Tarot by the Arcanum The Devil. In the Tarot life cycle, The Devil immediately precedes Truth, also called Jupiter. In this way the Tarot indicates that bad and good as principles are next to, and linked to each other.

> *Man does not proceed from error to truth, but from truth to truth, from lower truth to higher truth.*
>
> —Paramhansa Yogananda

Cyclic processes

Many processes in our lives have recurrent dynamics: a simple example is the alternation between day and night. There are also more complicated processes. Not only do we know the daily path of the sun across the sky and the recurrent sequence Spring-Summer-Autumn-Winter, we are also familiar with phenomena such as the movement of the planets and the regular return of comets. We are familiar with the rotation of the crankshaft of a piston engine and alternating current. In all these cases, the system returns to a stage at which it has been before, sometimes at a higher level of existence. A circle represents these processes well, as the circle also returns to itself. For this reason these processes are called cyclic.

The beginning and end of a cycle flow over into each other. Therefore we can search for the beginning just as well in the future as in the past. Creation, evolution, and the path of life in some way all return to themselves.

To a novice the Tarot seems to be a collection of loose cards with symbols and figures. However, in reality the Tarot has a *structured, cyclic order* in which 24 Major Arcana are linked with Royal and Minor Arcana. In this way the Tarot offers *a frame of reference for each developmental process,* in particular our cyclic path of material and spiritual development.

The phases of the cycle of life

Many processes in nature and in a human's life follow a pattern in which rising, blooming, declining, and renewal follow upon each other. Today's winner is defeated tomorrow. Such processes in life return to themselves and have a cyclic nature (figure 2.5)

Cycles in Daily Life

Two-phased cycles	Day and Night
	Yin-Yang
	The warm and the cold half of the year
	Coming into being and decay
	Life and Death
Four-phased cycles	Spring-Summer-Autumn-Winter
	Birth-Production-Dying-Regeneration
	New moon, First quarter, Full moon,
	Last quarter
12-phased cycles	The 12 months in a year
	The 12 signs in the zodiac
	The 12 Nidanas of Buddha
24-phased cycles	The 24 hours in a day
	The 24 phases of the moon
	The 24 Major Arcana in the Tarot

2.5 Cycles in daily life.

All cycles are closely related. Not only humans, but other entities also go through cyclic processes: a growing tree converts minerals, carbon dioxide, and nitrogen into wood and leaves. After many years the tree dies and decays, and releases the same minerals, carbon dioxide, and nitrogen back into its environment.

Rocks wither under the influence of weather and wind to pebbles and sand, which is transported by rivers and deposited as layered sediments further downstream. During millions of years of compression, chemical reaction, and heating, the sediment is converted to hard rock. When geological force brings this rock to the surface, the circle is closed and the weathering process starts again. The Tarot depicts human life processes in 24 Major Arcana.

The purpose of the cyclic processes of life

Each cyclic life process is always marked by a clear beginning and end; in between all sorts of situations and circumstances take place that push the process forward according to the objective laws of cause and effect, also called karma.

During a cycle there is always production. Materials acquire a higher degree of order through which a different function may be exercised: matter transmutes. The degree of order acquired during this life process is partially lost in the end phase, but the objective, true foundation formed in the cycle stays intact. This process goes on and on; and through constant repetition a higher degree of

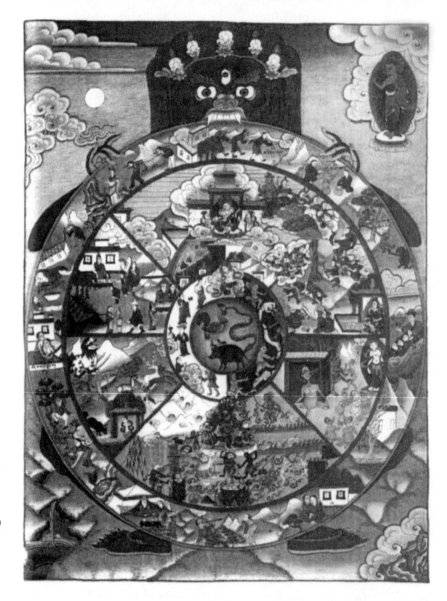

2.6 The Buddhist wheel of life and death. Mahakala (time) shows the wheel of time as a symbol of the sequences in life: becoming born, being in the world, death of the body, return of the soul to the other existence and the return to earth in another body and in other circumstances.

order is achieved. Similarly, by repeating the purification processes, the alchemists of old tried to obtain the Stone of Wisdom.

Through actualizing ourselves we create objectively "good" entities. The fruits of life live on, bring about more benefits, and

THE 24 MAJOR ARCANA OF THE TAROT AS THE PATH OF LIFE

are also called "good karma." This may come in the form of well-raised offspring, books, organizational structures, inventions, creations, new or restored relationships, and so on. The objective good is indestructible. We each have the task of actualizing the Buddha and Christ in ourselves by detaching and living in Truth.

The goal of the cyclic process is the realization of our Self. In this process of growth the essence of our Self has to express itself; which is the soul's assignment. Our ego wants to elbow forward and, in this way, obstruct the expression of our essence. In subsequent cycles during our lives we each can make explicit our essence and actualize the Self more and more. Because of mistakes during this process, many cycles may be necessary before this goal is attained. Karma, at least, can be seen as the realization of our assignments in Self-actualization.

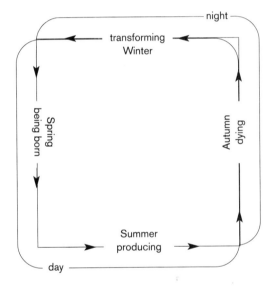

2.7 Diagram of the fundamental life cycle. It consists of four main processes: 1. Birth and growth; 2. Production; 3. Decay and death; 4. Transformation and reincarnation.

The cycle of life as a frame of reference

In all cycles to which living organisms are subjected, two main phases can be distinguished: emergence and decay. Decay is a very important process that starts with death, and generates the building materials essential for new life. In nature we differentiate between four main phases—birth, reproduction, death, and regeneration—as the four seasons. In general, these four phases, including their intermediate stages, are characterized as the Tarot life cycle (figure 2.7). The Tarot represents these four stages with Pentacles, Wands, Cups, and Swords (figure 2.8).

The path of life in 24 stages

When the 24 Major Arcana are laid down in the right order, they depict the fundamental life cycle (figure 2.9). This arrangement of cards is a symbolic and archetypal frame of reference for the fulfillment of our Soul's task. In each pass through a cycle we realize our essence more completely.

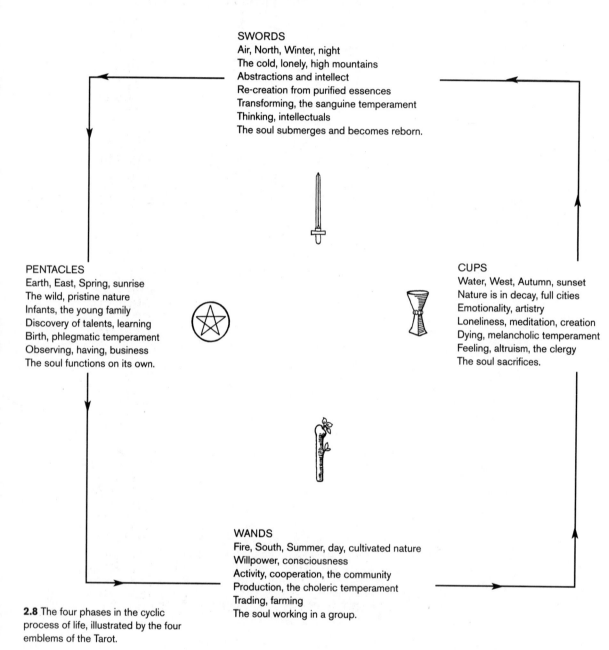

SWORDS
Air, North, Winter, night
The cold, lonely, high mountains
Abstractions and intellect
Re-creation from purified essences
Transforming, the sanguine temperament
Thinking, intellectuals
The soul submerges and becomes reborn.

PENTACLES
Earth, East, Spring, sunrise
The wild, pristine nature
Infants, the young family
Discovery of talents, learning
Birth, phlegmatic temperament
Observing, having, business
The soul functions on its own.

CUPS
Water, West, Autumn, sunset
Nature is in decay, full cities
Emotionality, artistry
Loneliness, meditation, creation
Dying, melancholic temperament
Feeling, altruism, the clergy
The soul sacrifices.

WANDS
Fire, South, Summer, day, cultivated nature
Willpower, consciousness
Activity, cooperation, the community
Production, the choleric temperament
Trading, farming
The soul working in a group.

2.8 The four phases in the cyclic process of life, illustrated by the four emblems of the Tarot.

THE 24 MAJOR ARCANA OF THE TAROT AS THE PATH OF LIFE

2.9 The 24 Major Arcana in the restored Tarot show a life cycle as a story in pictures. The series of images is read counterclockwise. In this figure the cardinal and the fixed cross are drawn. The arcane The Star and The Chariot form the vertical (male) axis, and the Priestess and Temperance the horizontal (female) axis of the cardinal cross. The arcane The Universe, The World, Truth, and Intuition as corners form the axes of the fixed cross.

Time always passes through the Major Arcana of the Tarot in the same order. On very old Tarot cards we already find this order indicated with numbers. Seen in this way the Tarot is a pictorial view of the path of life that initiates humankind into a higher form of existence.

The Major Arcana are to be read counterclockwise. Humans feel most comfortable with left-turning circular movements. In a counterclockwise circular movement the strongest side of the body, the right, is on the outside. Competitions such as running, skating, car races, and so forth, are always held counterclockwise, as are all old board games. At an abstract level a left-turning movement stops time, and creates space for meditation and reflection.

In the Tarot some Major Arcana traditionally indicate the counterclockwise movement. The Fool enters the path of life going left (upper left in figure 2.9). The Empress, symbol of progress, production and pregnancy, looks right and forward. Somewhat further down the track, The Hermit, having achieved wisdom in the meanwhile, looks left and back on the path covered. The figure in the arcanum The Star represents forward movement and looks forward. If we were to put the Major Arcana in clockwise order, The Fool would walk backwards, The Empress would look back, The Hermit would look forward, and The Star would point to the past. This right-turning movement would be in conflict with the traditional position and movement of the figures on the cards.

Arcana as gateways along a timeline

We can think of any evolution or personal development as a chain of events, or actualized points in a cloud of possibilities, which together form a multi-dimensional time-space of eternity-points. Each eternity-point in time-space comprises a complete situation.

Everything we do or learn adds new actualized eternity-points to our personal evolutionary timeline—also called an eternity-line or fate-line through infinite time-space. We can combine eternity-points with a similar characteristic—for example, beginning situations—by mentally drawing an eternity-plane through these points. That eternity-plane then acts as a multiple gateway through which intersecting timelines may pass.

In the Tarot every arcanum can be considered an eternity-plane or eternity-segment with a point or gateway through which someone's evolution-line, or timeline passes (figure 2.10). The Fool represents an eternity-plane with gateways beyond which new life adventures start.

An eternity-plane consists of an infinite number of intersections of timelines. In the eternity-plane that we could call "The Fool," each eternity-point is a situation of beginning and a different intersection through that same eternity-plane. So, for instance, the effect of the arcanum The Fool in a life situation is different for everyone.

Most points of an eternity-plane are never actualized, and remain unused as potential eternity-moments, or possibilities.

The Tarot is an objective group of eternity-planes describing concrete situations in the past as well as situations that may be actualized in the future—potential intersections of timelines with Tarot eternity-planes.

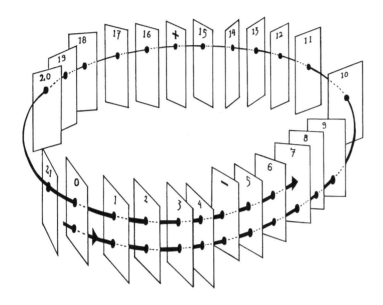

2.10 Diagram of a timeline through infinite time-space, passing through the 24 eternity-planes of the Major Arcana of the Tarot. Each intersection of the time spiral with an eternity-plane is a concrete situation that is symbolized in an arcanum of the Tarot.

A person actualizes an eternity-moment by making a choice between the various options that present themselves in such an eternity-plane. Through that choice a new eternity-moment is actualized and added to the existing timeline of that person.

Ouspensky states in his book *A New Model of the Universe:*

The sequence of moments of actualization of each possibility forms the timeline. Each time-moment has an infinite existence in eternity. The actualized possibilities stay forever realized in eternity, while the not-actualized possibilities remain infinitely not-actualized and cannot be actualized.

Each arcanum is a segment of, or plane in, time-space full of actualized and (many more) non-actualized situations, through which people's timelines run. If, for example, someone's timeline passes through the eternity-plane of The Fool, the person actualizes the beginning of a new life cycle, which will give that life shape for quite some time (figure 2.11).

The life cycle as a spiral

Superficially, it seems that processes run in cycles, but in reality every time a cycle is passed through, something has changed. For instance, a person who starts a new job will not do exactly the same things as in his last job. We change our life situation through the decisions we make and the actions we undertake. Hence, each

2.11 A new life cycle starts.

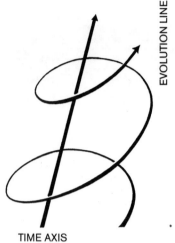

EVOLUTION LINE

TIME AXIS

2.12 The life cycle is one winding of the "life spiral" that winds itself around a time axis through time-space. This picture is in three dimensions; in reality the life spiral happens (for living beings) in four dimensions.

2.13 The life spiral intersects eternity-planes in time-space. In this diagram two Major Arcana are drawn as "major" eternity-planes.

consecutive cycle has a different level and content. For this reason a life cycle can be considered a spiral which moves through time-space; this is called the time- or life-spiral.

Déjà-vu and other psychic experiences probably happen when one winding of someone's life spiral is close to another winding of the same or another's life spiral. Experiences may then "tunnel" from one winding to another through time-space, in a way similar to the random movement of electrons. A prior life in a particular country may be the explanation of a strong déjà-vu experience when visiting a strange country for the first time.

The Tarot bundles eternity-moments in a path of initiation

The Major Arcana in the Tarot together form an objective knowledge structure, which groups eternity-moments in time-space in 24

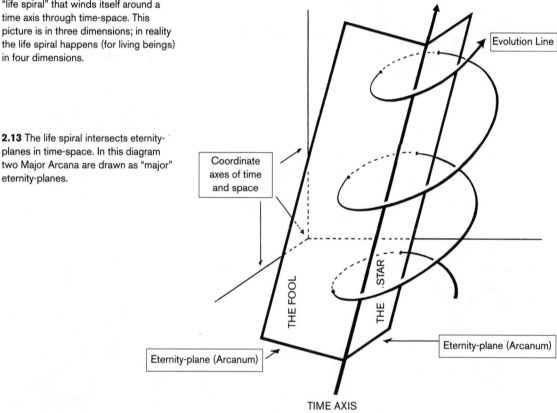

Evolution Line

Coordinate axes of time and space

THE FOOL

THE STAR

Eternity-plane (Arcanum)

Eternity-plane (Arcanum)

TIME AXIS

eternity-planes. Each person's evolutionary line runs more than once through the arcana or eternity-planes, at different levels (figure 2.13).

The Major Arcana as the Path of Life

When all arcana are laid out in a circle, it is striking how smoothly their individual, influential principles overlap. The Major Arcana depict a path of initiation, the psychological journey of a human being through two fields of activity, subdivided in four different work domains. Each arcanum is an intermediate station after which the journey's characteristic landscape alters.

Within the life cycle we can distinguish four major stations. They mark the boundaries between the four different areas of work in this cycle: birth and growth, self-expression through consummation and production, retirement and death, renewal and regeneration. Figure 2.14 summarizes this journey of the soul in diagram form.

2.14 Arrangement of the Major Arcana as a psychological journey of the soul through two fields of activities and through four work areas.

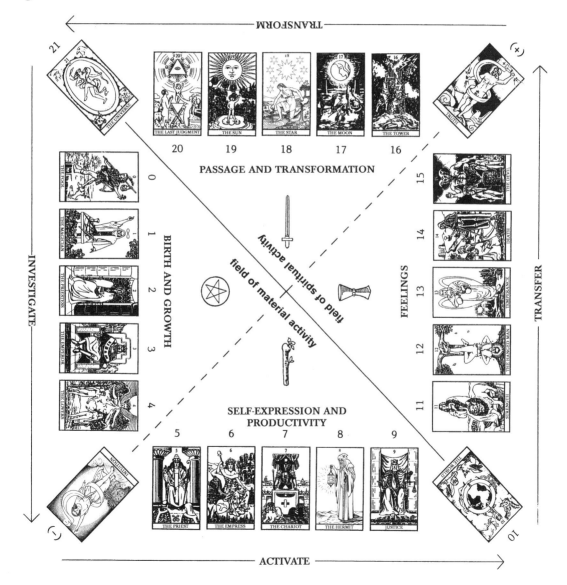

THE FOOL

0 The Fool

The story of the path of life starts with a picture of a young person who, newly incarnated, moves on in a sunny morning landscape. Pure and innocent, unconscious of anything that is going to happen, blank as a white sheet of paper, without knowledge—not conditioned but also without direction—The Fool steps into life. The lost son takes in everything that happens on his still sunny path. *Astrologically this arcanum corresponds with the energetic, enthusiastic, and initiative-taking zodiacal sign of Aries.*

This arcanum bears the number 0, zero. The zero is a circle, which symbolizes the universe. The Universe is the last and previous arcanum in the story of the life journey. Every human being passes through a number of important cycles in his life. This arcanum means a new beginning—for example, moving to a new environment, starting a new job, being in a new city for the first time. It is a period of discovery, instability, and many emotions. The Fool is also the questioner, the person who asks the Tarot for advice.

The Fool symbolizes the soul in a newborn baby, the potency that chooses for life. He is welcomed as a prince by those who live around him. He is the proverbial zero. Open to everything, he has not achieved anything yet.

The value of The Fool is in his purity and potency: full of energy, and with many unknown resources, he is at the beginning of his life. He is always portrayed with a swag over his shoulder. This contains the characteristics and talents he has received for this journey. The Fool does not know the contents of his swag. The chance of missteps is very present and symbolized by the abyss. However, because of his pure cosmic consciousness, angels protect him. The dog accompanying The Fool symbolizes the awakening of the instincts and functions as messenger of the unconscious. The dog also restrains The Fool from maturing.

The Fool takes to the road and is going to try out many new things. In this way he discovers his body, functions, possibilities, and environment. Striding forward, The Fool arrives at the next arcanum, The Magician.

Before me lies an open road
Behind me the end of time
Although I know not what awaits
New adventure is mine.

1 The Magician

THE MAGICIAN

The arcanum The Magician symbolizes the first conscious Doing, walking for the first time, writing, swimming, making love, buying a house, and so on. Through these activities The Magician acquaints himself with his body, prospects, and talents and becomes a conscious human being. The contents of the swag are now displayed on the table of the altar. What is on the table is dedicated to the Lord in Heaven. The Magician sacrifices his powers through the conscious use of his capacities and talents. He acquires knowledge through living and learning; he has the might of enlightened willpower. Doing things changes The Magician's situation completely. "There is only one type of magic and that is consciously Doing" (Gurdjieff). *Astrologically, this arcanum correlates with the activity of Aries.*

The Magician is the youth who, full of energy and life, wants to push forward and succeeds in doing this. He is the performer who knows how to fascinate his audience with his originality. His right hand points up and his left hand points down. This attitude symbolizes the fundamental hermetic principle: *It is above as it is below.* The divine creative forces are guided from above to below and from below to above in the magic act that is the Great First Doing.

The contents of the Fool's swag consist of a pentacle, wand, cup, and sword. These symbolize the talents in the material, work, emotional, and intellectual realms of life. He wants to achieve the best and initiates intimate interactions with these materials and tools. In this way The Magician works at himself and changes his environment.

Living and learning, The Magician discovers laws related to his world. Now he is open to learn from his mother, grandmother, and teacher, and arrives at the arcanum The Priestess.

Through my wand magic flows
Earth and heaven I join
What the sword has brought to flow
I will gather in my cup.

TORA

THE PRIESTESS

2 The Priestess

The Priestess is seated between two pillars that symbolize space and time with the book, the Torah, the law, in her lap; she personifies Sophia, the divine wisdom. Learning and using practical and inner knowledge is now a prerequisite for further growth. The Priestess symbolizes the mother and the teacher who reveals what is still hidden. Through interactions with her the young traveler enriches his knowledge of life. She confronts him with fundamental skills and knowledge and science, laid down in laws and principles.

Astrologically, this arcanum corresponds with the sensitivity and trust of the zodiacal sign of Taurus. The two horns on the crown of The Priestess demonstrate this correlation.

The Priestess is mild; she does not tell everything she knows and sees. It would not be helpful for her to tell everything because everyone needs practical experience. In this arcanum in particular, dying, and more generally, the harsh reality of life—which is the *real* expression of the soul in time and space—is still concealed. This is indicated by the curtain between the two pillars (Kings 7:13–51). By living, that is, moving through time and space, we all gain the knowledge of life.

The arcanum The Priestess represents the female aspect, the anima, in man and is the complement of the not yet completely mature male arcanum The Magician. She gives insight into dreams and other archetypes that manifest themselves when the controlling will is subdued.

The Tarot itself, as a revelation of fundamental knowledge of life via archetypal symbols from the collective unconscious, is closely related to the arcanum of The Priestess. When the arcanum of The Priestess is entered, self-reflection starts, with her as a mirror. This phase of learning brings youth to a high level of practical mastery of the material world. Having passed through this phase, the traveler has the material world in his hands and reaches the next arcanum, The Emperor.

With the softness of my being
I will care for the fools
I shall learn to live without dread
Full of heart, no empty phrases.

3 The Emperor

The arcanum The Emperor brings the traveler to a phase in which, clothed with power, he rules over a domain in which he is responsible for the success of business; he is mature and in a masculine phase of development. He is in command of the situation. In the previous arcanum, The Priestess, the traveler became acquainted with the four elements and learned to rule over matter. This knowledge is used and applied by The Emperor. *Astrologically, this arcanum corresponds with the solidity of the sign Taurus.*

Ruling means choosing and deciding in such a way that people fare well. With parental authority, The Emperor imposes his will, encourages his people, and inspires them to work. The Emperor changes chaos into order, judges, administrates and lets grow and blossom. In short, within the realm of laws and principles with which he too must comply, he determines what happens. As the boss in his empire he gives the royal example. However, outside the boundaries of his realm he has no power. Historical examples of this archetype are Alexander the Great (356–323 B.C.) and Charles the Great (Charlemagne, A.D. 742–814).

The Emperor takes on the identity of the male organizer. He accepts the substantial responsibility in the certainty that he can accomplish the tasks. He is seated majestically on a cubic throne, which symbolizes the Stone of Truth and Wisdom. This means that he derives his position from striving for truth and the refinement of matter. He is protected by armor: if necessary he will defend the interests of the country through conflict. The ram's head on his left shoulder points at the male and able-bodied planet Mars. The emblem of Mars—the spirit (symbolized by the cross) placed above matter (the circle)—is found in the imperial globe that the Emperor holds in his left hand.

In the arcanum The Emperor, the realization of virtues, order, refinement, and material growth is placed first. "Respect everyone, love your fellow-believers, fear God, and honor the Emperor" (1 Peter 2:17). In this way man gets ready to communicate and to commit. Through errors of judgment in The Emperor, the traveler delves into the process of choosing what is good and what is bad, thus becoming fit for the arcanum The Lovers.

THE EMPEROR

Those who do not accept my power
Shall despair and lose their way
Ruling over Earth's values
My authority speaks all her tongues.

THE LOVERS

4 The Lovers (Choice)

Talents are brought to fulfillment and the traveler arrives in a paradisiacal garden: the arcanum The Lovers. In this philosophical arcanum, we are able to choose consciously. A responsible, committed choice between alternatives, however, is only possible if we can distinguish between them. This arcanum deals with these polarities—it is also called The Choice. *Astrologically, this arcanum is correlated to the overview and skills of the sign Gemini.*

In the previous four arcana, youth rammed like a bull through the porcelain cabinet of life, with zestful fire and mediocre consciousness, gaining experience and, unknowingly, harming others. Now, matured, we are able to build love relationships consciously with a partner. In The Lovers the traveler passes through this problem, enlightened by Lucifer and seduced by his disguise as the snake.

In this arcanum two archetypes, Adam and Eve, stand before the Tree of Life and the Tree of Knowledge, and the archangel Lucifer lures them to knowledge and insight. Now they are confronted with a choice. This is the moment where absolute consciousness starts: the process of choosing deepens. Spiritually and materially a choice is made between life and death. From this point on, love relationships are influenced by physical perception.

Subsequent to the choice Adam and Eve have made, they yield to one another. *For this reason a man will leave his father and his mother and unite with his wife, and the two will become one. So they are not longer two, but one. Man must not separate then, what God has joined together.* (Matthew 19:5–6). They search for themselves in the other and the other in themselves; they supplement each other and bridge the differences through love. The parties form a whole that is more than the sum of the parts. Later, from this unification, new life will spring. From this joining starts a family, a community. In The Lovers, a more direct contact with the soul develops—through conscious choice, emotional commitment, conscience, and inner truth—and it starts guiding our life. The traveler arrives at the arcanum Intuition.

To be joined in life
To forever be one and the same
To learn to receive and to give
To know mine is thine.

(–) Intuition (Juno)

INTUITION

With Intuition, the first phase of the expression of the soul's task on earth (Pentacles) ends, and the second phase of the life cycle (Wands) begins. As the inner voice of the heart is increasingly listened to in the process of choice, commitment, and conscious coexistence, intuition dawns—symbolized by the bright light on Juno's breast. The traveler makes contact with the deep, inner dimension of Self, the Inner Truth. The arising Intuition resonates with the soul, humankind itself, and the purpose of life, which is the realization of the Self. Opposites are unified through proper choices between alternatives. Intuition is crowned with a golden diadem that contains the pearl of practical, inner wisdom—Sophia. *This arcanum corresponds with the communicative aspects, and the desire to understand that is so strong in the zodiacal sign of Gemini.*

In this phase of development, a person becomes aware of the feminine expression of the soul (Yin). It is indicated with the minus symbol. This archetype includes the anima, and therefore must not be confused with the "Universal Mother," or "The White Goddess," which we meet in The Empress.

Communities are characterized by production, manufacturing, and the delivery of services. Efficiency requires quick decisions based on experience (The Emperor) and insight (Intuition). Now, the traveler more and more consciously follows the inner voice. The Gospel of Mary Magdalene says: "Lord, on who has a vision, does he see with the soul or the spirit?" The Redeemer answered and spoke: "He sees neither with the soul nor with the spirit but with the conscious, which is in between the two." In this stage Intuition seduces the ego to follow her—this seduction is the reason why traditionally Intuition is portrayed with one leg uncovered. The traveler must overcome vain personal insights.

In earlier Tarot decks, Intuition was called Juno. She is the protector of marriage, and the wise—but also feisty—spouse of Jupiter. She is the queen of gods; her cart is pulled by peacocks, symbols of the Higher Self. Those who try to seduce her husband can count on being brought down. In the religion of ancient Egypt, this arcanum was known as the goddess (H)athor or Isis. She was honored as the protector of lovers and later often depicted as the nurse of kings.

Joan of Arc (1412–1430) is a figure in world history who personifies the psychological archetype depicted in Intuition—a peasant girl who believed that she was acting under divine guidance and claiming direct communication with saints via visions or voices. She led the French armies to a momentous victory at Orléans, which marked the turning point in the English occupation of France during the Hundred Years' War.

In Intuition, the traveler makes contact with the soul, the divine source. Moral values in the family and society are becoming very important; their stabilizing influence promotes continuity, growth, and evolution. The traveler reaches the arcanum The Priest.

Arrange my feathers
Smooth my robes
Hear my songs
Because my singing goes beyond the fancies
That force their way into your life.

THE PRIEST

5 The Priest

The traveler, socially committed through free choice, becomes a complete human being and part of a community. As in every social group, values, norms, and solid rules are of prime importance; these have to be laid down and accepted first. This occurs in the arcanum The Priest. In the Middle Ages this arcanum was also called The Pope. It personifies common morality. The moral rules of society are, metaphorically speaking, the keys to God's Kingdom on earth. "Everything is pure for those who are pure, but for them who are tainted and unreliable, nothing is pure. Their thinking and conscience are soiled" (Titus 1:15). Western society tries to found itself on Christian norms and values. *This arcanum corresponds with the contemplative and nurturing aspects of the zodiacal sign Cancer.*

The word religion—*religare* means "re-binding"—points at how we connect with our primordial source, our divine origin. In religion we acknowledge our heavenly heritage and the means of maintaining this connection.

The Priest is the spiritual father of the community. Examples are the minister, doctor, lawyer, and Santa Claus: they confront us and shape our social conscience and communal morality. The Priest protects and perpetuates the family as a societal core building block and conducts rituals to establish social alliances, such as the institution of marriage. It is important for us to see that in this arcanum the traveler is not only guided in moral affairs by The Priest, but that he or she, as The Priest, also leads. The Priest is supported in his activities by Intuition—the spiritual, higher anima Christi—as well as the wealthy and worldly Empress. Society puts The Priest on a pedestal and places a tiara on his head, to symbolize the threefold dignity of priest, king, and teacher. The danger in this, however, is perverted spiritual materialism.

The Priest, as a spiritual and moral guide collaborates closely with the matriarchy. To actualize our Self we should not renounce, repudiate, or ban the anima within us (which is the case in fundamentalist Christian and Islamic religious communities). In the next arcanum, The Empress, the traveler flourishes in a material sense.

I preach to you the rules
Which you all ought to know
God's seal shines on your forehead
Henceforth, you may be known
As human souls.

THE 24 MAJOR ARCANA OF THE TAROT AS THE PATH OF LIFE

6 The Empress

THE EMPRESS

The Empress, portrayed as a pregnant woman in lavish circumstances, is the universal symbol of fertility and prosperity. The traveler can now work in a socially meaningful and safe climate: a very fruitful, productive and prolific period commences.

Matter has a tendency to condense around Spirit. This process starts in The Empress and finds its fulfillment in The Chariot. The victorious person in The Chariot is The Empress' unborn child and the result of the allegorical union of The Priest and the Empress. The Empress is Mother Earth, who makes the seeds germinate, gives life, and inspires. In some decks we find her, the inspiring primordial mother, named "Grande Mère." *Astrologically, she is linked with the strong personality and motherly nature of the sign Cancer.*

In the arcanum The Emperor the traveler governed by using mental powers. He erected houses and made decisions over life and death. In The Empress it is the other way around. Her scepter carries a golden apple signifying matter, the fruits of work, and the female breast. The globe is supported by a circular Tao cross: matter rules the spirit. The Empress, the beautifully dressed Summer-Queen, is the gate through which growth and life enter the world. The waterfall pours forth into the pond, representing the unification of the male and the female. Through The Empress a new living being grows. She inspires the male to invent and produce. The overflowing river symbolizes the yearly rain and floods. Plants are growing and flourishing richly at her feet, wheat ripens in the foreground; it is the time of the horn of plenty. The white dove on the Empress' love shield—an ancient archetype signifying the soul—symbolizes the Holy Spirit and peace.

The Empress, also an ancient archetype with many names, is Demeter, the Greek barley and corn goddess of vegetation and fruitfulness. She is the Roman goddess of flowering Flora. Her floral crown is set with ten diamonds signifying the ten celestial bodies. She is Rhiannon, the richly dressed Celtic horse and fertility goddess who could invoke life and death via the songs of her accompanying birds. She is the Celtic fertility and horse-goddess Epona, who was also worshipped by the Roman army and depicted riding a white mare with a foal. The Empress is also called Urania, the ninth muse, and the Triple Goddess of love, fame, and power. The creative forces and material prosperity in the developmental phase of The Empress induce the manifestation of the soul through the fruits of work in the arcanum The Chariot.

Filled, overflowing I want to be
I want to marry fire to my earth
I offer you my summer wine
So life brings forth life.

THE CHARIOT

7 The Chariot

We manifest our creation and harvest recognition for our work. We are at the pinnacle of our power. This arcanum appears as the summit in the life cycle, inasmuch as the sun is at the highest point at noon. It is the moment of the entry of Jesus Christ into Jerusalem. This manifestation invokes conflict: If someone comes forth in essence, someone or something else cannot be there and will have to retreat. In the phase of The Chariot, hostility and rebellion are controlled. *Astrologically, The Chariot corresponds with the warmly radiating and high-hearted zodiacal sign Leo.*

Through the expression of the soul we overcome dualism, cross the boundary between time and space, have an overview and control the situation. Jesus said: "When a person is one he will be full of light, but when he is divided he will be filled with darkness" (Gospel by Thomas Logion 61). The Chariot is pulled forth by two sphinxes. Supported by the veracity of his work, the traveler moves on under the influence of two polar forces, which are controlled by his willpower. He does not use reins. Emerging from the cube, which is the Philosopher's Stone on which The Emperor was seated as well, is the Son, the revelation of his Father: "The Word became a human being, and full of grace and glory, lived among us . . . " (John 1:14).

The creation expressed by humankind has eternal value and, in a particular way, changes the face of the earth and mankind forever. This is indicated by the zodiacal belt around the middle of the human being in The Chariot. He wears a crown with a sparkling star: the crown chakra is open and in contact with The Star of promise, hope, and incarnation.

His fellow humans expect that this creation (invention, technology, thought, etc.) will bring them further along. A tunic of knowledge and feelings of appreciation are protecting the man in The Chariot. He carries a wand with a grain of wheat on top: the seed of manifestation; these days it is the marshal's baton. His emblem on the carriage is the unification of opposites, the wheel and the axle, the zero and the one in the binary number system. The two moon phases—the waxing and the waning moons on his shoulders—together form the head of Janus. As the fifth essence he shapes the world and gives it meaning, the fourfoldedness (the four poles of the canopy, see also The Chariot by Eliphas Levi, figure 5.11a).

In a still agricultural landscape, in the background a town develops: society expresses itself through greater complexity and assumes urban forms. Having reached the top we calm down and become older and wiser. In this way the traveler becomes a counsel of the community and arrives at the arcanum The Hermit.

In my right hand lies the power
In my left hand battle rests
Let reflection wait for me
Here and now I am, eternally.

8 The Hermit

THE HERMIT

An older and wiser man retires from active life. He does not fight any more, but detaches himself and becomes aware that time goes by. The sun is setting and it gets colder around him. He is now an elder in the community, someone who has been around and, as a counsel with experience, gives advice to others in difficult situations. As an elder the community treats him with respect, because "he who does not honor old age is not worth old age." He lives in a quieter way or is on a pension, takes part in governing bodies and committees and interprets social norms in his own way.

The Hermit is listened to because not long ago he drove The Chariot himself and has extensive experience at his disposal. Because of his assistance and advice to new rulers and conquerors—the king's counsels in the game of chess are placed left and right of the royal couple—*this arcanum correlates well with the authority and dignity of the zodiacal sign of Leo.*

Symbolism in this arcanum is sparse. The hermit is a somewhat dignified person who looks back on his path in life. "Old age cures us of our youth." So far he has done things without caring much about backgrounds or consequences. Lonely, he now exists between material and spiritual levels of existence: an inhospitable province. He meets himself. The living staff that supports him is a hazel rod. The hazel, especially its sweet nut, is a symbol of wisdom; the expression "in a nutshell" is related to this symbolism.

The Hermit has the urge to reflect on what he has done and why, how he made appropriate and wrong decisions, what was wise and what was not. In this way he enters an inner path of self-realization. His lamp of insight casts its light, for others and himself, on all the arcana he has gone through. On that road, outward appearances and sex are unimportant. The Hermit is dressed in a habit and leans on a flowering staff—his spiritual potency. Humankind now deals with life in an abstract way. Society accepts his wisdom and judgment, and the traveler enters the arcanum Justice.

Turn within and see
The years gone by
Is in the light that parts
Value to be realized?

9 Justice

In the arcanum Justice, we are in a situation in which justice is administered. We can act as judges, but we must also be judged ourselves. Now we harvest what we have sown. The balance weighs our acts and determines the punishment; the sword executes the judgment; the sages in the community officiate as judges. They determine the truth, symbolized by the square jewel in the crown and the square buckle on the throat chakra, and ascertain who has acted rightly and who has the right to what.

In Justice, an independently operating authority sets up absolute standards for actions and behavior. In this arcanum direction is given to the development of humans who stray from their path of life either by their own fault, or the fault of others. *Astrologically, this arcanum correlates with the analytical and purifying sign of Virgo.*

In this stage of life, society creates an authority that can judge man if he is not able to do so himself. Not everyone is allowed to punish, because that would mean taking the law into his or her own hands and hence abandoning justice and order. For that reason only authorities may handle the sword. At the end of the productive phase of Wands, man cannot agree on how to divide the harvest. To that end an objective measure is necessary: this is symbolized by the scales. "For God will judge you in the same way you judge others, and he will apply to you the same rules you apply to others" (Matthew 7:2).

Society has developed into a complicated societal structure, a city that is kept together by a justice-administering authority. The arcanum Justice represents the assessment of our work, weighing and apportioning, karma. As a result, the karmic wheel turns further. New potentialities open up. The traveler enters the arcanum The World.

Balance in life there must be
That is what I demand
Skilled in upholding the law
Man earns his just reward.

10 The World (Wheel of Fortune)

THE WORLD

The life cycle continues according to the laws of cause and effect within omnipresent synchronicity. Therefore, this arcanum is also called The Wheel of Fortune or The Karmic Wheel. Possibilities are opening for emotional and spiritual development; a new corner has been turned. A feature of the moving wheel is the continuing up and down movement that also takes place in the cycles of our life. "Whoever makes himself great will be humbled, and whoever humbles himself will be made great" (Matthew 23:12). For this reason important changes happen in this arcanum. *Astrologically, this arcanum is correlated with the searching, ordering, and earthly sign of Virgo.*

The wheel is a well-known fate archetype. In Greek mythology the goddesses of fate spun the life thread of every human being on spinning wheels. They were so powerful that even the supreme god Zeus had to obey them. "Jesus, peace is with him, has said: The World is a bridge. Cross it, but do not sit on it." (Agrapha— discovered in 1910 on the southern, main portal of a mosque at Fathpur Sikri in India).

The word TARO is written on the wheel, the recurring course of travelers through the universe of life and death. The snake (materialism) is going down, the jackal (renewal) is moving up; the sphinx keeps the balance at the top. In the four corners of the card, the four Biblical living, winged creatures are portrayed: the angel, the bull, the lion, and the eagle (Ezekiel 1:5–13 and Revelation 4:6–9). They honor God and have insight into the Book of Life. *Astrologically, they form the fixed cross in the zodiac: Aquarius, Taurus, Leo, and Scorpio.*

The arcanum The World rounds off a phase of the life cycle in a similar fashion to Intuition. Here, the productive phase, Wands, comes to an end. The traveler now sets out on a more emotional, spiritual course in which the material and productive approach will have to be sacrificed as he or she arrives in the phase of Cups.

Now the consequences of actions and newly gained karma have to be borne. Held responsible by The World, our wanderer enters the arcanum Strength.

Rota round your life's path
When fate gives a sudden turn
Can you still guard yourself
Against the turning of the wheel?

ORTA

II

STRENGTH

11 Strength

In Strength it is dusk, the night side of the path of life, and the more emotional phase of Cups commences. In this arcanum we start to detach; our convictions and soul are becoming ready to bring the sacrifice. We are now fully responsible for (and openly shape) our inner convictions; in the process we put what is most valuable—life, career, or possessions—in the balance. The harvest is weighed; life and death are balanced against each other. *Astrologically, this arcanum is correlated with the benevolence and synthesis of the sign Libra.*

In this stage human beings are spiritually very strong and able to withstand great pressures that try to destroy what they stand for. This is symbolized by the impressive lion that accompanies the traveler. Both are connected by a garland of flowers. This symbolizes the influence of the archangel Raphael who gives us inner strength to withstand harmful forces and illnesses.

The power of conviction keeps us on our feet. We now act in a responsible way, based on our beliefs. We stand for our convictions, even if nobody asks us to do so! It is the confidence of the political refugee who gives up all existing certainties for an insecure future, the employee who resigns for a principle, the believer who is persecuted.

In its masculine form the symbolism in this arcanum is correlated with the Biblical story of Daniel, who was thrown into the lions' pit because of his service to God. The lions (the royal symbol of society) did not harm Daniel, since God sent an Angel who closed the lions' muzzles (Daniel 6:1–23). Also, Logion 7 in the Gospel of Thomas is relevant in this regard: Jesus said, "Blessed is the lion who will be eaten by a human; cursed is the human who will be eaten by the lion—and the lion will become human."

The Indo-Germans consecrated the highest worldly spirits saying *joe-gho-tom*, meaning sacrifice. From this expression the word "God" developed, the name that is now used to indicate the highest spiritual entity, The Creator. Those who want to serve God have to sacrifice themselves and in this way become one with God. The sacrifice is always to society, and happens in the midst of it. Jesus Christ was crucified in Jerusalem. His and our sacrifice and suffering is painfully real and belongs to worldly reality.

Thus, in the end the traveler is the immolation of his or her own beliefs and convictions, and arrives at the arcanum The Hanged Man.

In essence—without chattel
I give splendor to "human nature"
And inspire every chance
To surrender.

THE 24 MAJOR ARCANA OF THE TAROT AS THE PATH OF LIFE

12 The Hanged Man

The situation is serious. The person in The Hanged Man clings to his life and knowledge and has become a conscious victim of his own values. Karma now necessitates the forfeit of one's life for an Idea. Materially, he loses everything he has worked and fought for. Money drops out of his pockets; matter accumulated by him returns to earth. His awareness alleviates the suffering, because he sees the purpose of his sacrifice. "Do not be afraid of those who kill the body but cannot kill the soul; rather be afraid of God who can both destroy body and soul in hell" (Matthew 10:28). He is convinced that a liberating resurrection will follow. *The Hanged Man is astrologically correlated with the creative sacrifice of the sign Libra.*

The Hanged Man's ordeal is not only painful because it is accomplished in a conscious way, but because it is also an initiation in which he is enlightened and at the same time aware of what is happening: the eyes of the Hanged Man are open. His head points at the earth, and is surrounded by an aura of rays. Others are gaining in a material and spiritual way, for he shows what is of indisputable importance in the world.

This arcanum is connected with creativity in the arts and sciences. Creativity requires self-sacrifice. Through unification with God in the sacrifice, inspired creations evolve. Mozart, Michelangelo, Rembrandt, Van Gogh, Bach, Einstein, and the Curies sacrificed their lives, metaphorically as well as literally, because of the esoteric idea that this had to be done. In the arcanum The Hanged Man all values are turned upside down. The traveler now has a disenchanted vision of the world and himself. This is a result of a very tight alliance with and belief in his own world. The cup is turned upside down and poured out; the Hanged Man's money falls out of his pockets. What was valid in the past is no longer of any value. This conscious suffering is necessary for the soul to crystallize further.

The Hanged Man is suspended from a cross made from living wood: growth is accompanied by pain. He hangs upside down from the leg on which he stood when he defended his truths, now he cannot do anything but sacrifice. The shape of the tree—the Tao cross—symbolizes this; it is the sign of surrender, the sacrificial table, the altar. The mushrooms refer to the plutonic nature of the turnaround, which takes place in The Hanged Man's inner self, and his elevated state of consciousness during this process. The falling leaves refer to autumn, the season in which life sacrifices itself. While illuminating The World, The Hanged Man enters into the process of transferring his soul from life on earth to life on the other side, in an otherworld. The traveler is touched by the angel of death and arrives at the arcanum of Temperance.

THE HANGED MAN

Around my head a gentle light fingers
Now that summer has been defeated
During my last days I hang
Darkness is my balance.

TEMPERANCE

Raphael Sanzio (1483–1520). An angel receives Christ's blood. This painting points at the esoteric profoundity and meaning of the transition that takes place in the arcanum Temperance.

By nature I am transient
Flowing in and streaming out
Sometimes an offer, sometimes the
  spoils
Am I weighed down or do I drift?

13 Temperance

Life on earth is over—the process of dying commences. The wanderer is now in a stage of transition. The dimensions of time and space unite, which makes further life on earth impossible. At the perimeter of the material and immaterial, the body is abandoned and the soul excarnates. The archangel Raphael receives and preserves the human's essences. A dying human being has no more material wishes, is calm, modest and temperate. *Temperance is astrologically correlated with the mysterious zodiacal sign that strives for self-discipline but also can kill itself during a transmutation: Scorpio.*

What remains after death returns to the primordial water of continuous time-space, which we know unconsciously and of which we are reminded by certain archetypes: the angel standing with one foot on land and one in water, for example. The Tarot describes the processes of dying and resurrecting in the series of arcana that starts with Temperance and finishes with The Last Judgment (20). Through many well-documented near-death experiences, Western circles are also more open now to the idea that the soul continues to exist after death and goes through subsequent stages, after which it is reborn on earth.

Reincarnation is a central point in many religions. *The Tibetan Book of the Dead* and Dante's *Divine Comedy* describe the stages after death in the same way as the Tarot. Through death the soul first arrives at a peaceful intermediate stage: the clear light radiates, above rocky mountains. Soon the soul will live through a complete, timeless insight into the past life or lives. Then, the essence either sets about in a new way that ends in reformulation of the task in life, and on to rebirth as the start of a new life cycle, or we become what is described as the final goal in many religions—enlightened and one with the divine. The traveler now passes into time. The soul enters a new path; the material body enters the next arcanum, Death.

14 Death

After "giving up the ghost," material death follows. This may pertain to a human being but also to a company, a piece of art, or an instrument. The cells of the human remains fall apart; the deserted castle goes to ruins; the device in unfamiliar hands breaks down; the army without a general is defeated. In general, this arcanum describes how, through dying, attainment is scattered over the earth and inheritances are divided. The law for all living beings is that durability does not exist. *Astrologically, the arcanum Death—of which the secrets of life and death are a central feature—correlates with the sign Scorpio.*

New wheat can bear fruit only when the old has died off. Hence, death is often portrayed with a scythe, with which humans are harvested by mowing them down like wheat, and so, killing them. Death goes with material chaos. It is a natural process, for humus has to be spread evenly to bring about new growth everywhere.

We are all signaled by Death with its hourglass when it says that the time has arrived. Every human has to let go of material existence: young or old, rich or poor, high or low. Death makes even the Emperor fall. In death we are all the same. Death is an attesting arcanum. *Memento mori* (remember that you are mortal) is the only fact in which humankind finds certainty concerning the future. The purpose of this knowledge is to make us see that with respect to other people, life, and ourselves, we have to be humble. The process of purification begins, selects, and annihilates the uselessness in the soul and transforms and bundles the worthwhile for the purpose of a new life cycle. The two towers and the light at the horizon point to the prospect of the new separation of time and space, the soul's future reincarnation. You came from God and to God you will return.

The 13th and 14th arcana belong together. First, in Temperance the soul passes on; then the body, deserted by the soul, is taken by Death. The spiritual inheritance of the life that has been lived on earth is still bound to the soul, which is depicted by the next arcanum, The Devil.

He who fears me cannot avoid me
Insurmountable is his fate
To be consumed by earth
Or be absorbed in heaven's
* atmospheres*

THE DEVIL

15 The Devil

Although after death the soul is detached from the body, it is still bound to the life lived. Strong material identifications, like structures of thought and emotions, still exist around the soul after death, along with psychological baggage such as emotional relationships. Property, as well as now-useless work that made it impossible for the soul to grow, bind the soul to the past life and hinder the acceptance of death. *Astrologically, this arcanum is linked with religion and the God-searching and experiencing aspect of the sign Sagittarius.*

The soul is still chained to the king of lies and half-truths (boasting). The half cube on which the devil is seated symbolizes this. Humans who place themselves above their divine task become prisoners of their own limitations and weaknesses. In the arcanum The Devil, the soul is confronted with its misdeeds. The Devil is like a policeman who points to a stop sign or a boundary, which one cannot pass beyond without further ado.

The torch in the left hand of The Devil is pointed downward. It symbolizes the Luciferan fire, which is sent to earth and incorporated in human rational logic, and corresponds to the apples in the tree of Good and Evil in the arcanum The Lovers. This fire stands for the human initiative in the choice between good and evil and also indicates that Evil—The Devil—bears and executes his own destruction.

The soul, now existing in the continuity of time-space, has an overview of the life it lived, but it no longer has a choice—it cannot "sleep" or escape in any other way. It is bound to the identifications devised during its life. In consequence, misdeeds stand out and are a stone on the heart. The hell-worlds created by the soul are brought home to it. The soul has to identify them as reflections of its own work, in which humanity is turned upside down—the way the pentacle on the head of The Devil is turned upside down. Dante's *Divine Comedy*, and *The Tibetan Book of the Dead* describe these events accurately. As soon as the soul sees through the limitations of its ego and recognizes the experienced hell-worlds as reflections of its identifications with matter, it steps through the devil's mirror held in front of it—through the black upside-down pentacle into the clear light of the white upright pentacle. Self-knowledge is knowledge of the Lord God. In the next arcanum, Truth, the traveler starts to see.

To my anvil you are moved
Flames and sulphur on your decks
Bound to my chains
You must turn your course.

(+) Truth (Jupiter)

TRUTH

Truth liberates. The soul awakens. The nightmare of being in the phase of The Devil is over. The soul of the human being is now confronted with the absolute and objective truth with regard to itself and Creation. In a flash the human soul has acquired total understanding and experiences being one with Creation. *The Tibetan Book of the Dead*, and many near-death experiences describe this as being in the whole space shining with brilliant light. *Astrologically, this arcanum is correlated with the sign Sagittarius, in which the arrow is aimed at Truth in the urge to know and understand everything.*

Many souls can face Truth, the brilliant white light, only for a short while. The more completely a soul has realized itself, the more it will feel at home in this light of divine truth. A soul who can surrender to unification with this bright light comes out of the circle of reincarnation, life, and death, and is enlightened and forever one with this arcanum. This soul is free.

In the Tarot of Marseilles and the Tarot of Besançon, Truth—the male expression of the soul, Yang—is represented as Jupiter, King of the Gods and husband of Juno. In the Tarot, Truth and Intuition are also seen as a divine couple. Jupiter keeps the conscience awake so that mercy, justice, order, benevolence, and friendliness can rule on earth, and spuriousness and falsehood can be punished. His symbol is the double ray of lighting. In Norse mythology he is Thor, the god of thunder. In Tibet this ray of lightning is symbolized in the *dorje*, the ritual object of the Buddhist priest.

The archetype of the eagle is traditionally depicted as an omnivoyant observer and companion of Jupiter. Placed in this corner of the life cycle, it symbolizes the mystic death of the lower self. Truth is the other side of the lie.

Through acknowledgment of the objective truth about oneself, the soul can leave behind the mundane life lived on earth, and throw off the cloak of mind structures: in the arcanum Truth the soul rediscovers its divine origin and task. The soul comes to active and spiritual reformulation. The edifices of outdated mind structures have to be struck to pieces by Truth's lightning rays. This happens in the next arcanum, The Tower.

Should my servant show you the light
Bear witness with your own eyes
Moved by love
Never swayed by hate.

THE TOWER

16 The Tower

Our errors detain us. The ego's willpower and conceit are the walls of The Tower that imprison us and the chains that bind us in the arcanum The Devil. The opportunity for deliverance is in us, attainable when we see this imprisonment and acknowledge the truth. Truth leads irrevocably to demolition of psychological falseness and pulp. The soul loses its complete outfit and returns to its essence in the winter phase of the life cycle. *Astrologically, the sense of science and order of the sign Capricorn symbolize this arcanum.*

In life each human builds a fortress, tower, house for the soul; a prison of experiences, memories, skills, events, and science: we call these mind structures. Part of the structure is sincere, in harmony with the soul and able to stand up against the ravages of time; part of it is false. The egotistical behavior of humans leads to the tower of Babylon. This tower is hit by the lightning of Jupiter (also Zeus, Thor, Wodan, Truth, God) and tumbles down. "If the Lord does not build the house, the work of the builders is useless" (Psalms 127-1). Faults are now restored. The bankruptcy is clear and thorough. The crookedly built ship is wrecked in the hurricane; the bad project dies; the cheat is uncrowned. The process represented by The Tower is extremely painful for the soul. A person loses face, the mask tumbles to earth.

The Tower is also a jail, symbolized by the bars in the windows, and its destruction—through acceptance of the truth—means release. "You will know the truth and the truth will set you free" (John 8:32). That is why in this arcanum traditionally two people are portrayed, one fallen dead on the rocks, the other alive and gliding free through space. "The house is destroyed, it consisted of semblance only. Unharmed I proceed, liberation is my part" (Buddha).

After the demolition of false, adverse thoughts and crystallizations, the soul moves closer to the reformulation of the task in the next life through a process of condensation and recreation. In the next arcanum, The Moon, essences are gathered for the new beginning.

Those who have read this verse so far
Know that the tides are turning
What you may learn from the light just
  seen
Is what you are most fearing.

17 The Moon

THE MOON

In the previous arcanum—also called the second death—the material soul structure is destroyed, but not the heavenly one. What remain are vestiges of the soul. What happens now is an "alchemistic" process in which illusions vanish and the remaining fragments of the soul are collected and concentrated. Whereas in the arcanum The Empress the spirit bonded with matter, in the arcanum The Moon the spirit lets go of matter completely, and comes to a new, independent consciousness. *Astrologically, this arcanum is in the sign of the lonely and persevering climber, Capricorn.*

The arcanum The Moon shows the primordial sea full of souls and soul fragments from which a crayfish emerges. This symbolizes the part of the soul that turns out to be real and indestructible. From the swamp, fluorescent soul flames arise as in a distillation. The Moon is the cold receptacle, the vacuum that attracts the fragments of the soul and condenses them. The dogs of death guard the entrance and exit of the realm of the dead and the ghosts, and mark the end of the purification that the soul goes through.

An incorruptible spiritual body gets through the stages of The Tower and The Moon with comparatively little damage, but from a badly founded spiritual body only a few proper fragments survive, which coalesce into a new structure.

The arcanum The Moon is a period of fixed hope and desolate despair. While waiting, the new goal in life is formulated, after which the reorganized soul patterns will align themselves.

When the night has reached the deepest darkness, the hope of a new day arrives. Now the two towers are close: the separation of time and space are near. The soul's new path will soon cross the imaginary line between those two towers and commence a new incarnation.

The hope of a new life and a new chance to go through it again is announced by the next arcanum, The Star.

Abundance is my biggest trump
I am impartial
Those who hang on my every word
I will test through and through.

18

THE STAR

The bird in the background symbolizes the Holy Spirit. The soul-streams that flow from the two vessels represent two aspects of the Holy Spirit: animus and anima. At conception the soul-streams find the desired incarnation and gender and unite into one human being. At the same time the two gametes combine and life starts to develop in The Sun.

18 The Star

The star is the universal symbol and archetype of inspiration, life, and hope. It provides direction, the light at the end of the tunnel, the star of Bethlehem, the morning star Venus. For the ancient Egyptians it was the Dog Star Sirius, which, by appearing at the horizon, announced the yearly flooding of the Nile and fertilization of the fields. Now, the process of dying and healing that started with Temperance comes to an end. After the purification in The Moon, The Star announces reincarnation: a new life or plan is drafted, a new soul is poured out. This is also celebrated at Easter in the resurrection of Jesus Christ.

The figure in The Star is a delicately featured male with a balanced animus and anima. Esoterically, the figure in The Star is the archangel Lucifer—"light-bearer"—before his fall. In Greek mythology he is Ganymede, who was so beautiful that Zeus abducted him to become his cupbearer and lover. Ganymede gained immortality as the star constellation Aquarius, the water-carrier. *Astrologically, the archetypes in The Star in a remarkable way match the sign Aquarius, who from two vessels empties the Holy Spirit over land and water. Aquarius symbolizes the conscious human in contact with the guiding principle of divine inspiration.*

The eight stars in this Major Arcanum represent the eight tones in a complete octave. The 12 points in the big star represent the 12 zodiacal signs. The seven small stars symbolize planets. In astrology the planets bring the principles in the zodiac to the work-place: the astrological houses. The number seven symbolizes the consolidation of the soul, which now commences its incarnation.

The archetypal bird in the tree of life symbolizes the Holy Spirit; the Egyptians called it Ka. It is also one of the Celtic goddess Rhiannon's birds, evoking life through its song. The soul-bird in the tree is about to fly away to commence a new task in life.

From a golden (male) and silver (female) vessel, Water of Life soul-energies pour out over water and earth. The angel Raphael in Temperance conserved this soul-energy at the moment of passing away. Through the descent of the soul into matter, a human, gender-defined being starts to express itself and gradually assume form and behavior.

In The Star, the renewed soul formulates and directs itself to guiding principles. This provides the soul with self-respect, which brings new, potentially fruitful situations within reach. The soul resonates with like vibrations in environments on earth and chooses one to unite with. An unemployed person at this stage will suddenly be offered several opportunities for work from which to choose. In the next arcanum, The Sun, the soul will draw matter towards itself and form a new, fetal body for a new existence on earth.

Soul derived from Heaven
I reside in my house which awaits
In lustrous splendor
To flow Heaven's path on Earth.

The Sun is the arcanum of power and growth. The purified soul begins the actualization of the goal that was chosen in The Star. As the new task is fixed and the environment for incarnation chosen, the soul can group matter around itself and flesh out into a new child. Having been conceived it manifests itself and grows in its mother's womb. *Astrologically, this Arcanum, which is an extension of The Star, fits the arising new man in the sign Aquarius.*

The soul's stage in The Sun is also described in *The Tibetan Book of the Dead*. The soul looks for a home from which it can actualize the new goal. As the soul reaches a higher degree of integrity, the purer the synchronistic resonance will be, and the more suitable the chosen environment for incarnation. *The Tibetan Book of the Dead* shows how to choose the proper womb.

The sun signifies universal and personal life power, without which neither life nor consciousness is possible. In a horoscope it is the sun that, as a dominant, spiritual field of activities, gives shape to the manifestation of the soul. In this phase of the life cycle there is Light in the darkness. The spirit assembles and develops matter. The fetus develops its temple—the human body.

The child means new possibilities for the soul. The new human is a benefaction to humankind just as the sun shines for everybody. The child is placed on a cloud and thus is elevated above the earthly world; the child is carried in the womb. The sunflowers symbolize the four elements; the material, which is at the disposition of the incarnated soul, will group around the soul to form a material body.

The wall covered with flowers represents the ruins of the arcanum The Tower. They typify the safe and paradisiacal state of the growing, new human being. The situation can be compared with a parachute jumper who has already jumped out of the plane, but has not yet landed. The new beginning, the birth on earth, happens in the next arcanum, The Last Judgment.

THE SUN

More magnificent than stars
I am anchored very high
With my radiant shine
I greet you from afar.

THE LAST JUDGMENT

20 The Last Judgment

The spiritual and material preparation of the soul has been completed. Now, the last heavenly judgment of the human being takes place: the beginning, the birth of the new human being/soul on earth. In The Star the soul chose the place where it would start its path through life—this way it determined its future assignment. In this arcanum the umbilical cord with the past—the previous lives—is cut. The new human being has a completely new chance, because the previous life has been digested and is no longer valid. It is time for atonement and forgiving: the old has served its turn and the new start has commenced. *Astrologically, The Last Judgment is related to the deliverance and willingness to make sacrifices of the sign of Pisces.*

The soul now goes through the eye of the needle, the hole of the hourglass. The form of the trough—also a manger—accentuates this process. The continuous time-space in which the soul sojourned since it passed away from its human dwelling, splits now into the four separate dimensions—the soul has become a physical reality.

Guardian angels announce the birth with blasts of trumpets. The archangel Gabriel is related to all who accompanied the soul in, through, and out of death, and to all who mediated between the world of the living and the world of the dead. Gabriel calls forth the transformed soul from the world of the dead. The newly born, the New Human has resurrected! "Freedom is what we have" (Galatians 5:1).

The child is part of the generative trinity: Father, Mother, Child. The parents receive the new child in rapture, admiration, joy and love, as a gift from heaven: for the parents this birth means as many new possibilities as for the child itself.

The Last Judgment completed, it starts a new life cycle—this process is rounded off in the last major arcanum, The Universe.

Summoned by the child
I rise from cornfields green
I long to hear about insurrection
And of life's victories.

21 The Universe (The World)

THE UNIVERSE

The Universe is all the arcana in one. The Universe creates everything, is everything, knows everything; it is cosmic consciousness. The arcanum The Universe symbolizes the moment of naming that bestows Reality onto an entity—the moment when a child is given its name. It is the horoscope of a new life, a new enterprise. The oval shape symbolizes the vagina, the womb, the empty circle, the Wu Chi, the gaping hole in the Edda. *Astrologically this arcanum is correlated with the all-knowing and all-forgiving qualities of the sign Pisces.*

In The Last Judgment the series of transformations and judgments is completed. The Universe is the seal that closes this path of life and connects it with the present and the future. At the four corners of this arcanum we find the four mystical creatures that also appear in the arcanum The World. The angel, the bull, the lion, and the eagle represent respectively the evangelists Matthew, Luke, Mark, and John. They are the custodians of the four corners—in fact, quarters—of the Universe, who in this way together mark the creating All, and form the fixed cross. The wreath of laurel is the old symbol for triumph and excellent, divine achievements. The oval also symbolizes the life cycle depicted in the Tarot. We find the oval symbol for the Universe in Indian philosophy laid down in the Vedanta, as radiating womb and as Brahma's Egg, the testicle in which semen is formed; and in Egyptian hieroglyphs as the cartouche in which the names of kings were written. The infinite universe is also pictured as ouroboros, the snake that eats its own tail. The dancing figure is the androgynous human, eternally alive, giving shape to all forms by its divine dance. The position of the legs hints to liberation (through incarnation). Liberation also happens in Truth when the soul is unshackled from its lies. The soul also sets itself free—to a degree—in The Hanged Man, namely by releasing itself from the bond it had with the thing that was sacrificed in this stage of the life cycle. By contrast, the situation is now joyous, harmonious, and creative.

The straight and the twisting snakes in the hands of the dancing deity symbolizes the binary polarity, the zero and the one—the straight and crooked principle, useless if separated, together creative and efficient—as a bow and arrow. The cast arrow in its nature destroys darkness and creates Light. So this arcanum personifies the All, the whole Tarot, in eternal movement.

Emerged from nothing
Through darkness of birth
I grow to be all
Within me is
God's Self-radiating Universe.

The names of the arcana The World and The Universe

The names of the two arcana The World and The Universe have been chosen to put an end to the confusion about their meanings. In former times arcanum 10, "The World," meant The Earth, the microcosm, and was mostly called The Wheel of Fortune. Arcanum 21, The Universe or the macrocosm, was usually called The World. The origin of this confusion stems from the fact that the meanings of the words "world"' and "universe" partially overlap.

The World may mean "the earth," as in "the world we live in," but it also has a more abstract meaning signifying an environment: the world of animals, for example, or the world of the gods. It may also mean "the entire universe." In the expression "God created the world in six days," world has the meaning of the earth and everything on, below, above, and around it.

In general, the word "world" expresses a thought in which the earth and its inhabitants play an important role. The Arcanum 10, The World, denotes the archetype "the turning globe on which humankind lives and is part of, together with the animals, plants, and minerals, and to which the universal laws apply" (figure 2.15).

ROTA

2.15 In the medieval woodcut (right) an angel puts The World into movement with seven archetypes of mankind.

The arcanum The Universe means the entire creation, the firmament, that which comprises everything, the macrocosm. Arcanum 21, The Universe, therefore signifies everything on earth and in heaven—the grand entity of which the earth is a small part—everything that is and will be, can be thought of, and has not been thought of yet (figure 2.16).

THE 24 MAJOR ARCANA OF THE TAROT AS THE PATH OF LIFE

THE UNIVERSE

2.16 The Indian God Shiva creates through dancing the universe in all its forms. Life is part of death, and death is part of life. The fire, carried and cast by Shiva, symbolizes the destructive and creative forces in the universe.

The 12 Principal Arcana

Having discussed all 24 Major Arcana, we can consider them comprehensively. The first half have a worldly, the second half a heavenly, tendency. The 24 Major Arcana can thus be considered paired-up conceptions of 12 Principal Arcana.

Each Principal Arcanum is abstract. Each Principal Arcanum works out into a pair of major arcana that are juxtaposed in the life cycle: one represents an incoming, receiving, and material principle, the other the outgoing, giving, and spiritual complementary principle. Each pair of two Major Arcana together describes a principle or state of the soul that can be summarized in a motto or theme (figure 2.17).

FORMATION OF THE TWELVE PRINCIPAL ARCANA IN THE TAROT

Worldly aspect	The soul's activity	Spiritual aspect
The Fool 0	I WANT	11 Strength
The Magician 1	I OFFER	12 The Hanged Man
The Priestess 2	I TRANSCEND	13 Temperance
The Emperor 3	I RULE	14 Death
The Lovers 4	I COMMIT	15 The Devil
Intuition (–)	I SEE THE TRUTH	(+) Truth
The Priest 5	I ESTABLISH VIRTUE	16 The Tower
The Empress 6	I COLLECT	17 The Moon
The Chariot 7	I MANIFEST	18 The Star
The Hermit 8	I ILLUMINATE	19 The Sun
Justice 9	I DO JUSTICE	20 The Last Judgment
The World 10	I AM ALL	21 The Universe

2.17 The Major Arcana of the Tarot can be combined into 12 pairs. These together form the Principal Arcana of the Tarot. In this diagram each Principal Arcanum is named by a motto summarizing the soul's aspirations in this phase of its path.

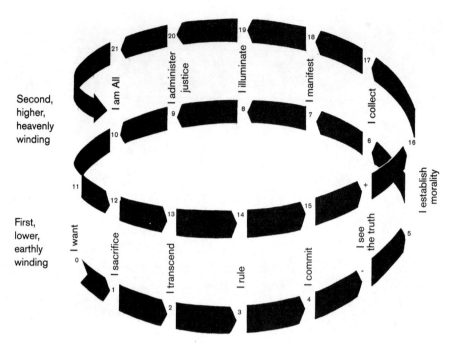

Second,
higher,
heavenly
winding

First,
lower,
earthly
winding

I want · I sacrifice · I transcend · I rule · I commit · I see the truth · I establish morality

I am All · I administer justice · I illuminate · I manifest · I collect

2.18 The Tarot-helix. The first winding comprises the first 12, materialistic and work-oriented Major Arcana. The second winding contains the 12 spiritual and mentally oriented Major Arcana. In this spiral the complementary arcana are aligned vertically, and connected by the catch-phrases that symbolize the 12 principal arcana.

The Tarot-helix as the Path of Life

The essence of the Tarot is a cycle of 12 pairs of Principal Arcana. However where ego and "The All" are not unified, each Principal Arcanum splits into a pair: a worldly-material, and a heavenly-spiritual major arcanum. Every time the life cycle arrives at a higher level, it appears to be a life spiral with two windings, in which the major arcana in the first turn are coupled with the major arcana in the second turn, as is the case with the double DNA helix.

The first winding in the Tarot spiral is the worldly version, the second winding, the heavenly version. Hence, the Tarot-spiral is a double helix.

The Principal Arcana are located between each pair of coils (figure 2.18). Having passed through the 12 Principal Arcana first in a rather material way, an existential augmentation happens, after which the same 12 Principal Arcana are lived through on a higher and more spiritual level of existence.

The life cycle formed from the 12 Principal Arcana is an eternal spiral movement in which humankind can achieve increasingly higher levels of existence (evolution). The Major Arcana offer us insight into our path of life and expand our understanding of the cycles through which we all are going (figure 2.20, page 96). On the next pages the Principal Arcana are discussed in such a way that they present themselves as pairs with a motto in the life cycle of the Tarot.

2.19 The Phoenix, symbol of the ever-renewing soul.

TAOR

ORTA

THE FOOL

STRENGTH

0 The Fool

Starts a task on his own and is not held accountable for his doings. He lacks information and training and *wants to discover everything with all the vigorous power of life*. He incarnated with his parents because he resonated with their vibration and this level of existence seemed best to accomplish his task in life.

11 Strength

Persons in Strength start a task on their own and are held accountable for their actions. They are full of an idea that has captivated them. They are called and want to do this with all the power they have, even if it would bring them down. Those in their environment think they are fools because they see only the risks involved, and do not share the belief of Strength.

The arcanum The Fool is materialistically oriented, with the purpose of realizing material growth. In Strength material growth is of no importance, on the contrary: the issues at stake are principles and ideas, the defense of emotional points of view at the cost of material advantage. Both aspects of the Principal Arcanum I WANT—The Fool and Strength—lead to a sacrifice.

THE MAGICIAN

THE HANGED MAN

1 The Magician

Puts his possibilities, skills, qualities, and talents on the table and offers his energy, capacities, and potentialities in exchange for money. In the same way, sacrifices by primitive tribes ensure the kindness of the ancestors. The Magician receives something in return for his sacrifice that keeps him alive or improves the quality of his life.

12 The Hanged Man

In The Hanged Man we *offer our life* for the realization of our potentialities. He, for instance, is the artist or inventor who persistently continues to work on his "brainchild," which often requires great sacrifices. He forfeits his money and possessions for the sake of the contemplated goal. It is not important to him that he get something in return other than the achievement of the spiritual goal. The calling and acceptance of conditions, knowing that this is the way it has to be, relieves the torment.

The sacrifices of The Magician and The Hanged Man possess the same magic, in the sense that these sacrifices change something in an absolute and permanent way. The Hanged Man's actions, however, are of a more spiritual caliber and guide to the highest sacrifice. Both aspects of the Principal Arcanum I SACRIFICE lead to a transition from one dimension to another.

TORA

RATO

THE PRIESTESS

TEMPERANCE

2 The Priestess

Educates and guards the laws and knowledge of life. She forms human conscience as interpreter of the soul, through initiation. As a teacher *she leads a child from one level to the next*. Gradually, she imparts higher wisdom and the principles of life to the child, but hides the idea of mortality. The Priestess guides the change from child-hood to adolescence. The child matures and is introduced to life.

13 Temperance

Safeguards the soul in the process of dying and carries it to the other side, the other-world. The life on earth has come to an end. A person's real sacrifice has opened him/her up for death. Temperance captures the soul in the grail. *The essence of a human transcends to an astral level of existence where time and space converge.* Temperance accompanies the transit from life to death. A human being now "gives up the ghost"—the soul leaves the body.

The Priestess initiates into life, but remains silent about man's mortality. Temperance is the law of conservation of spirit, and guides a human in death. In both arcana an initiation—a transfor-mation—takes place. Man becomes familiar with laws. The Priestess represents the laws of life, and Temperance symbolizes the laws of death. Man cannot avoid these laws any more than he can evade gravity. Being in command of these laws is only possible through knowledge of them. In this way the Principal Arcanum I TRANSCEND leads to a confrontation with ruling powers.

THE EMPEROR

DEATH

3 The Emperor

Rules over matter, and life and death, when these are within his circle of power. He is the father of the people around him in ultimate form. He is also the sublime youngster who has mastered all subjects and skills; he is the young King Arthur. Through his interest in his fellow humans, his skills, and culture, he attracts all sorts of people who want to serve him, and want to be governed and guided by him.

14 Death

Rules over life: death brings even an emperor down. In this way Death rules where the power of The Emperor ends. Death cannot be other than merciless, as this change already has been prepared in Temperance. No matter how painful and even dramatic the departure may sometimes seem, the soul's flight and the ensuing decomposition of its material dwelling of the soul are inescapable. "It is put to an end."

The Emperor leads and kindles with enthusiasm. Death imposes changes and separates the spirit from the body. The Emperor may be a good or a bad ruler. When Death rules, it may be welcome or not, but its will is inevitable. The Principal Arcanum I RULE leads to the making of choices and commitment to a chosen direction.

TRAO

AOTR

4 The Lovers

People can *choose and commit* to give a particular direction to their life in the future. Puberty is over; a period of free choice commences. Humans are fully grown and ready to develop intimate spiritual and sexual relationships. The person now starts a love relationship, in which other things matter more than attaining material goods. Humankind chooses for commitment and is, through this commitment, able to reproduce, not only with the material body, but also through the confluence of two souls.

15 The Devil

Humankind has no choice any longer. We are bound to our deeds and actions of the past. The soul has committed itself to the material aspects of life (desire, lust, lying, and vanity based on accomplishments): *a relation with* has become *enslaved by*; the democracy becomes a dictatorship. As material things are only tools the soul uses to fulfill its task in life, material achievements are only half of the truth of what has been achieved. Humankind now has to give up the material part.

In the Principal Arcanum I COMMIT, two aspects of commitment are depicted. There is a new engagement in freedom, or an enchaining duty in slavery that has to be broken in order for the soul to reach truth.

INTUITION   **TRUTH**

(–) Intuition (Juno)

Intuition is the practical truth that comes from within; it works in the worldly quarters of Pentacles and Wands. By entering into relationships and making choices, we make contact with inner truth. The source of intuitive wisdom is opened. We can pursue our task in this incarnation more effectively, provided we listen when making choices and commencing relationships.

(+) Truth (Jupiter)

The objective truth from beyond makes its liberating and purifying influences felt in the heavenly quarters of Cups and Swords. *The naked truth comes to light* when the soul recognizes The Devil in itself and relinquishes egoism. When all identification with the material world has been resolved, our inner eyes are able to meet the objective truth in freedom.

Truth and Intuition appear in mythologies as the divine couples Osiris and Isis, Zeus and Hera, Jupiter and Juno, Wodan and Freya. They refer in various ways to the soul of humankind, working at earthly levels toward Truth. Jupiter expresses himself in the inescapable flash of higher insight, sometimes accompanied or preceded by an acute physical disorder. Juno manifests herself as the inner voice that is heard only if we listen for it. Those who do not listen will quickly encounter problems in daily life. It is important to strive for higher insight as well as to listen to the inner voice. A disruption between these polarities may have very serious physical and psychological consequences, which have to be dissolved by a real change of values. Intuition can be listened to; Truth must be listened to and followed in order to prevent difficulties for ourselves or others. In this way morality is founded and confirmed.

ATRO

ROAT

THE PRIEST

THE TOWER

5 The Priest

Receives blessing from above and propagates this through confirmation of moral norms and values. The Priest harbors the conscience of working humans in *common morality*. Now, acceptance and refinement of the Truth takes place, heard through Intuition. Humankind, now touched in its essence, contemplates and works on its development. Spiritual structures are sealed and incorporated in social guidelines.

16 The Tower

This is the place where untrue norms and values, in short, *immorality* in humans, is destroyed by Truth. The Tower bears the same symbolism as the Biblical "Tower of Babel" and the Greek myth of Icarus who arrogantly flew too high, causing the sun to melt his waxen wings. He smashed to earth—in spiritual bankruptcy. The insight given by Truth rips off the covering. Only essential soul structures remain.

The Priest and The Tower are two aspects of the same Principal Arcanum I ESTABLISH VIRTUE, namely the acceptance or dismissal of moral mind structures. The lower cannot understand the higher, but the higher is able to understand the lower. For this reason, the soul can gain complete insight into its actions and commitments only in The Priest and, at the end of its path of life, in The Tower.

THE EMPRESS   **THE MOON**

6 The Empress

She is abundance, life, and growing power; *she collects and gives material form to life.* The Empress is the fertile imagination and profuse nature. Matter has the tendency to condense around spirit. The small idea becomes reality. The crowned and reigning empress makes everything grow and flourish, invites to sexuality, potency, conception, and creativity.

17 The Moon

Without life, the Moon attracts life and the force of growth. Seeds germinate, and plant life grows better when the moon is full. Without wealth, it absorbs form and power. The Moon represents the phase in which work and creations are destroyed, new efforts fail, and we can only hope that in the end the damage will be less bad than we expected. *The Moon is like a vacuum that attracts life and collects spiritual essences.*

The Empress and The Moon are two aspects of the Principal Arcanum I COLLECT, in which spiritual material is regrouped, based on different goals. In both cases this material is of essential value. In The Empress matter acquires a higher degree of order, because significant ideas acquire a tangible form. In The Moon spiritual and material forces are brought together. Regrouping of the spirit in matter leads to a renewed manifestation.

OTAR   AROT

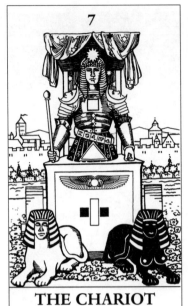

THE CHARIOT   **THE STAR**

7 The Chariot
Symbolizes the manifestation of the conception, which has been developed in the preceding arcana. Humankind (or the idea that has been given shape) fully manifests, and victoriously takes the lead. The personal, spiritual ideal formulated in The Star now propagates. The environment senses the ideal, which gives the manifesting person or idea the power and control to disseminate that idea. Humankind is now a "star on earth," the living, directing hope, to which everyone looks up.

18 The Star
Conception, descent of the Holy Spirit. The abstract idea manifests itself as a new insight. It is the moment of integration into a new, spiritual concept of the essences that have been collected in The Moon. The soul sees its next task in life: "the light is turned on." New ideas are poured out over the earth through the *manifestation of new life.* The spirit manifests through enthusiasm.

The Chariot and The Star both are aspects of the Principal Arcanum I MANIFEST. The essences that were collected in the preceding arcanum are now integrated into a new soul structure. This manifests itself as a guiding principle, in the material as well as in the spiritual world.

8 The Hermit

Having grown old and wise, he illuminates the world through his experience. The soul begins moving away from earthly life. People were victorious, have reached their goal. They have acquired much experience and become older. They "part from life." In The Hermit we are alone and lonely. Now, the Hermit makes it his objective to help others. As counselor he sheds light on and clarifies the situations of younger people.

19 The Sun

The naive child is still in the womb. The soul aims at living on earth. A person *"sets out to live."* A new human develops by means of the solar-intelligence, the power necessary to be born on earth later, and then to be a light to others. *The unborn child illuminates the lives* of others through offering potential prospects and perspectives.

The Hermit and The Sun are two aspects of the Principal Arcanum I ILLUMINATE, in which the world receives spiritual power, light, and insight. In this Principal Arcanum our own development and helping others go hand in hand.

JUSTICE

THE LAST JUDGMENT

9 Justice

The completed work is judged in a worldly way. Worn out items are thrown away. When we "detach from life," a situation arises in which we have to face facts. Humankind is weighed and a judgment is determined. After this discernment, we are freed from dead weight (a heavy conscience); and relieved that we can dedicate ourselves to spiritual matters.

20 The Last Judgment

Heavenly justice determines where the new soul-creation will be born on earth, how the new human will be "used"; now the new idea will become reality. The incarnating soul's assignment to start the new life is ready. The Last Judgment marks the end of the sojourn in heaven. Humankind is physically reborn.

Justice and The Last Judgment are both aspects of the Principal Arcanum I ADMINISTER JUSTICE. In worldly life, Justice settles the part of the life lived thus far, after which a new start is possible. In heavenly life, in The Last Judgment, heavenly justice is done to the completed past life cycle. At the moment of birth the memories of the past life as well as knowledge of the future are fenced off. New humans will not dwell on what has been, nor lose themselves in what will come.

THE WORLD   **THE UNIVERSE**

**10 The World
(The Wheel of Fortune)**
This is the place where human-kind, *a microcosm* in itself, may fulfill its tasks. The World is planet Earth. This is where our life manifests in four dimen-sions and becomes reality. Here turns the wheel of birth, life, death, rebirth. For each human being all possibilities and oppor-tunities for spiritual growth are present in The World.

**21 The Universe
(The World)**
This is the one, immutable All, *the macrocosm,* where every-thing happens and has happened. The Universe repre-sents complete creation: not only all solar systems, but also all spiritual worlds, hence the complete time-space where everything already has been formed and everything already has happened. It reflects not only the "empty" horoscope, which can be filled in many ways, but also the Akasha chronicles in which the knowl-edge of all time has been stored.

The World (The Earth) and The Universe (The All) represent two aspects of complete creation: the earthly level on which we are carrying out our soul-assignment and the universal heavenly level to which our spiritual growth is connected.

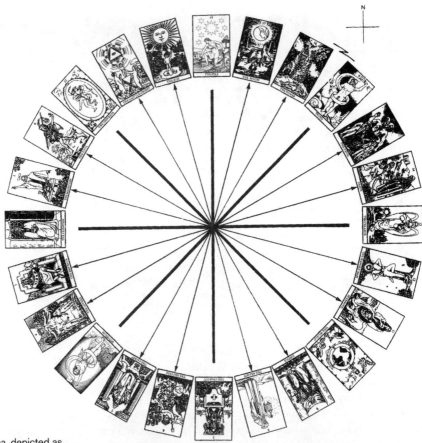

2.20 The 24 Major Arcana, depicted as a Vedic wheel with spokes. The twelve pairs of juxtaposed arcana form the twelve Principal Arcana. Heavy lines emphasize the fixed and the cardinal cross. The eight spokes correlate with the eight spokes in the sun-wheel of the Vedic god Suria at Konarak in India and serve as a cosmological basic structure in all great world cultures.

The 40 Minor Arcana and the Structure of the Tarot

"June" from "Tres Riches Heures" by the Limburg brothers, 1415.

Master, wife, knight, peasant
Spouse, youngster, child
Along these steps
Humanity climbs into unity.
—*Old nursery rhyme*

CHAPTER 3

The 40 Minor Arcana and the Structure of the Tarot

Three levels of work

In daily life we can work at a task on three levels. There is a conceptual level where, as a designer, we form thoughts, ideas, and plans. The second level of activities is managerial; as a leader we organize people and guide them in the realization of those abstract concepts. At the third, concrete level, we as workers bring the concepts into reality and thus actualize ourselves. This three-part division is also present in the Tarot. The Tarot bundles its archetypes as follows:

1 At the conceptual level: the Major Arcana.
2 At the governing and managerial level: the Royal Arcana.
3 At the actualizing level: the Minor Arcana.

The Minor Arcana serve the Royal Arcana, and the Royal Arcana serve the Major Arcana.

WORK LEVEL IN THE TAROT

Group of Arcana	Level	Type of Activity	Level of Work
Major Arcana	Conceptual	Ideological	Mental
Royal Arcana	Governing	Social	Leading
Minor Arcana	Actualizing	Social	Executing

3.1 The three groups of arcana, the corresponding three levels on which one can be active, and the nature of the work.

The symbolic structure of the Tarot

The Tarot comprises 24 Major Arcana, 16 Royal Arcana, and 40 Minor Arcana—in total, 80 principles. All Tarot arcana possess a penetrating symbolism, which passes the filter between rational thinking and the unconscious without hindrance. The arcana are connected to each other through their symbolism. As the Royal Arcana form the link between the Minor Arcana and the Major Arcana (figure 3.1), the nature of this link can be explained only after the Royal Arcana have been discussed—which happens in Chapter 4.

The life cycle is present in all three groups of arcana. Each group has its own type of communication (figure 3.2). The Major Arcana depict the life cycle mainly in archetypes. The emblems of the royal families are symbolic-archetypal; their mutual coherence has a collective-psychological nature. The Minor Arcana depict the life cycle mainly in a symbolic and metaphorical way.

TYPES OF PICTORIAL COMMUNICATION IN THE TAROT

Group of arcana	Types of messages		
	Mainly	To some degree	Less
Major Arcana	Archetypal	Symbolic	Psychological
Royal Arcana	Psychological	Archetypal	Symbolic
Minor Arcana	Symbolic	Psychological	Archetypal

The Major Arcana describe the life cycle in archetypes. The royal family's coats of armor are symbolic-archetypal. The relations between the Royal Arcana are of a collective-psychological nature. The Minor Arcana explain the Life cycle mainly in a symbolic way.

The symbols on the cards of the Minor Arcana originally consisted of an amount—one up to ten—of each of the four Tarot emblems. The quantity indicates the archetypal value of the number (figure 3.3). For example, the image of *two Cups* means *emotional duality* or, put in a more detailed way, *the harmonious or conflicting sharing of emotions and feelings*. In 1910, for the first time, Waite clarified the meanings of the numbers of the emblems in the pictorial Minor Arcana.

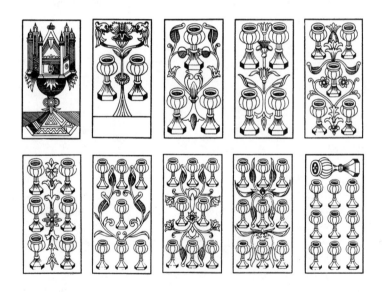

The four Tarot emblems and their symbolic meaning

A strong connection and flow is found in the Tarot between creating concepts, and governing and executing them. Between the Major, Royal, and Minor Arcana clear symbolic relationships exist: they are linked into a strong structure via the four archetypal Tarot emblems. The four sectors in the life cycle, Growth, Production, Death, and Regeneration are represented in the Tarot by Pentacles, Wands, Cups, and Swords. These emblems are related to various

THE FOUR TAROT EMBLEMS CORRELATED WITH THE MAJOR ARCANA AND FOURFOLD ARCHETYPES

Tarot emblem	PENTACLES	WANDS	CUPS	SWORDS
The Major Arcana	The Fool	The Priest	Strength	The Tower
	The Magician	The Empress	The Hanged Man	The Moon
	The Priestess	The Chariot	Temperance	The Star
	The Emperor	The Hermit	Death	The Sun
	The Lovers	Justice	The Devil	The Last Judgment
	Intuition	The World	Truth	The Universe
Phase in cycle	Birth	Production	Death	Regeneration
Power	Belief	Hope	Love	Understanding (Gnosis)
Element (Aristotelian)	Earth	Fire	Water	Air
Metal	Gold	Copper	Silver	Steel
Element (alchemistic)	Salt	Sulphur	Mercury	Air
Elemental	Gnomes	Salamanders	Ondines	Sylphides
Direction	East	South	West	North
Season	Spring	Summer	Autumn	Winter
Zodiac	Taurus	Leo	Scorpio	Aquarius
Moon phase	New Moon	First Quarter	Full Moon	Last Quarter
Day phase	Morning	Midday	Afternoon	Night
Celtic Sabbath	Walpurgis	Lammas	Halloween	Candlemas
Archangel	Gabriel	Raphael	Uriel	Michael
Race	Black	Yellow	White	Mixed
TARO	A	R	T	O

3.4 The four Tarot emblems correlated with the Major Arcana and fourfold archetypes.

archetypes, each having a fourfold nature (figure 3.4).

Decimal number symbols

From time immemorial humans have used their fingers when counting. Numbers are still often called digits. Together with the alphabet, humankind also developed icons and later symbols for numbers. Most important are the numbers one to ten. Our decimal number symbols are of Indian origin. The Brahmi symbols (100 B.C.) are quite similar to our numbers. Arabic number symbols are almost identical to the Western (figure 3.5).

Around A.D. 800 the Arabic mathematician Al-Khwarizmi wrote the book *The Numbers of the Indians*. An Arabic mathematical treatise from the tenth century contains the remark that it is helpful, when writing numbers, to put a little circle when the particular column (decimal space) of a number does not contain a value. This little circle—our zero—is called *sifr* (empty) in Arabic. From this developed the words zero, and also *chiffre*.

In medieval Spain the Arabic decimal system was introduced during the invasions by the Moors from 800 to 1200. The decimal number system was introduced in the rest of Europe by the Crusades, where it replaced the Roman numeric system in the next centuries. It would take until about 1700 before the Hindu-Arabic number system was generally accepted as the mathematical standard throughout Europe.

COMPARISON OF OFTEN-USED NUMERIC SYMBOL SYSTEMS

	1	2	3	4	5	6	7	8	9
Europe									
Arabia									
Tibet									
Kashmir									
Bangladesh									
Thailand									

3.5 Our number symbols have their origin in India and Arabia.

Number symbolism

Number symbolism, or numerology, has fascinated humankind since ancient times: each symbol is assigned a numerical, and also a symbolic, value.

Number symbolism is based on the teachings of Pythagoras and his discovery of the intervals in music. He found that pitch depends on the length of the string and that pitch can be expressed in numbers. The numbers one to four determine intervals in music and with four points, the simplest spatial figure, the tetrahedron, can be constructed. For this reason the Pythagoreans assumed that

THE 40 MINOR ARCANA AND THE STRUCTURE OF THE TAROT

any order is founded by a mathematical principle and that the numbers one to four are the basis of the numerical schema that form the base of the cosmos (figure 3.6).

NUMBER SYMBOLISM IN THE MINOR ARCANA

Number	Meaning
1	A new series of ten work stages begins.
2	The values within the frame of work are determined.
3	The dynamic start is rounded off in the first, preliminary moment of rest in the series of ten stages.
4	Temporary stagnation and contemplation about the objectives that are to be pursued.
5	Establishing a bridge between reality and ideal. The real nature of the emblem, the task, is now fully understood.
6	The task is resumed with pure intentions. Masculine and feminine principles are integrated; the Star of David.
7	Execution of the task is now in full swing and starts to pay off.
8	The task is near completion.
9	The harvest of all actions becomes reality.
10	The task has been accomplished; a transformation has been completed.

3.6 Number symbolism in the Minor Arcana of the Tarot.

In the Tarot the numbers one to ten also have an important meaning, as given in figure 3.6. The specific meaning of numbers pertaining to the separate arcana are discussed in the next chapters.

The Minor Arcana

We can each realize our individual essence by means of the cyclic process illustrated by the Tarot at the conceptual level of the 24 Major Arcana. Each of the four quadrants in the Tarot life cycle is divided into 10 specific stages. In this way a continuous series of 40 stages is formed that are called the Minor Arcana. Together they symbolize the life cycle at the level of actualization. The archetypal content of the arcana is formed by integration of the symbolism of the four Tarot emblems with the symbolic meaning of the numbers one to ten.

The Minor Arcana describe, by means of the number and the archetypal symbols, the phases of a particular task. After every ten stages, success is achieved and a transformation completed. Next, a transition to a new work situation can occur.

The 40 Minor Arcana as a "strip"

The Minor Arcana form a series of 40 symbolic work situations. We encounter these when we carry out a task or assignment, or proceed through the spiritual development of a person, a business, or an idea. The Minor Arcana symbolize people who are ruled by leaders and monarchs and who accomplish tasks appointed to them. In older versions of the Tarot, the Minor Arcana do not bear a picture. Arthur Waite and Pamela Coleman Smith greatly contributed to the Tarot by providing the Tarot cards of the Minor Arcana with archetypal pictures that clarify their meaning.

By laying out the Minor Arcana next to each other in a row from left to right, starting with Pentacles 1 and ending with Swords 10, we obtain a story in pictures, a strip in four chapters. In this book the story is made visible on the next two pages by printing the 40 Minor Arcana in four horizontal rows (figure 3.8). The reader is invited to arrange the 40 Minor Arcana in a similar way in four rows of ten cards—this will assist in understanding the discussion of the Minor Arcana.

The stage cards in the Minor Arcana

The pictures on the Minor Arcana sometimes show scenes on a stage. On these cards the depicted persons are not an integral part of the environment and do not stand on rough soil, but on a flat platform, while the environment is a background like a stage set. Such cards are called stage cards (figure 3.7):

Pentacles:	2 - 4 - 6 - 8
Wands:	2 - 4 - 9 - 10
Cups:	2 - 5 - 8 - 10
Swords:	2 - 5 - 7 - 9

Stage cards are more abstract and symbolic than other cards and emphasize specific phases in the traveler's way through life. Stage cards indicate clearly, by means of a scene, what specifically to do—or not to do—in life for the soul to grow. They emphasize the exterior and established forms in our deep-rooted ways of recurring, daily routines.

Non-stage cards in the Minor Arcana are related to situations that may arise from the mental attitudes depicted in the stage cards. They are directly connected to growth of the soul or the stagnation of this growth.

We will be using the Minor Arcana of Pentacles as an example:

- The stage card Pentacles 2 indicates that the wanderer needs to learn to control matter through experimentation. With success he arrives at the situation described in the non-stage card Pentacles 3, in which the next task is to create a masterpiece.
- Stage card Pentacles 4 describes what, in contrast with the preceding card, decidedly should not be done—to withhold knowledge and material possessions, for example—because such behavior would result in the situation described in the non-stage card Pentacles 5: spiritual isolation and straying into poverty.

- Stage card Pentacles 6 describes what erring humans have to do to liberate themselves from the preceding situation, namely develop humility, through which, as depicted in the non-stage card Pentacles 7, the wanderer will experience true love for work.
- Stage card Pentacles 8 shows that only regularity and persistence will yield a profit and bring material and spiritual growth and well-being.

3.7 The stage cards of Pentacles.

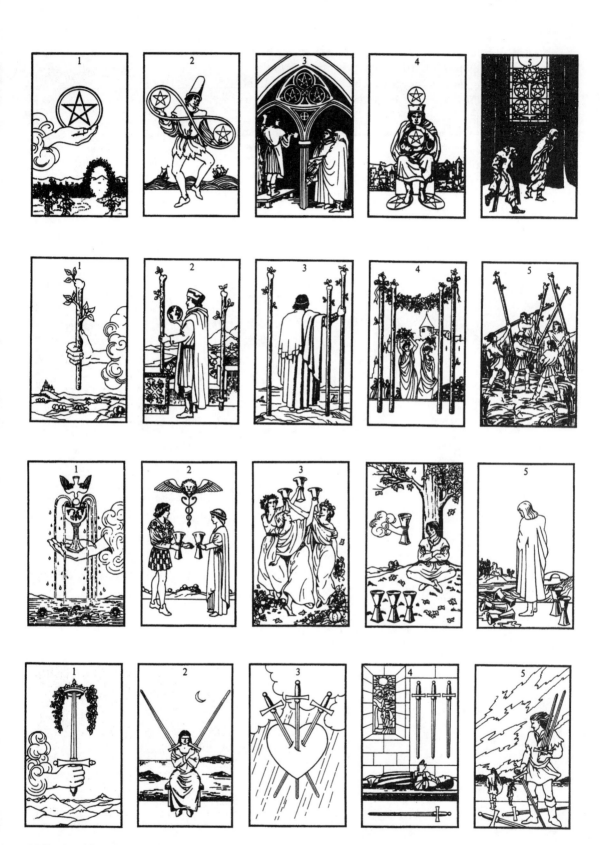

3.8 The forty Minor Arcana of the Tarot.

THE 40 MINOR ARCANA AND THE STRUCTURE OF THE TAROT

  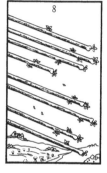  

The stage cards in the Minor Arcana

Pentacles One
The power of the Earth
This new phase starts with birth. The Pentacle is offered, symbol for earth, talents, and money, and also the body that is formed from matter. "You came from God and to God you will return" (James M. Pryse).

Here we are being given all the opportunities necessary to achieve the physical and psychological harmony required to commence our path in life.

Pentacles Two
Playful discovery game
We do not know yet what to do with the Pentacles, their material capacities, their body, and talents. In the first instance, we play with them and learn in amazement their endless possibilities, symbolized by the lemniscate. This playing is passionate and restless, like ships on the high seas. While playing, we are learning and becoming aware of what we can and cannot do.

Pentacles Three
First Assignment
The number three indicates that the skills acquired in Pentacles Two are now more or less integrated into one whole. Spiritually guided by a priest and materially guided by an architect, we may now carry out our first assignment and put into practice what we have learned. Thus we manifest ourselves as working humans for the first time. Meanwhile, we learn more and attain particular achievements. In the guilds this is the way from fellow to master.

Pentacles Four
Pride
In this stage we are proud and crown ourselves for the accomplishments achieved in Pentacles Three, even though that was only a humble beginning. We now show our achievements, have power over them and rest on them. We brood on ideas without asking for advice or discussion. We do not want to share our knowledge and money with others. This immature attitude, which we also find in puberty, creates a discrepancy between the person and society—the city is far away in the background—resulting in isolation.

Pentacles Five
Isolation
By hanging onto and not sharing knowledge and goods, we lose access to the circles where life is sung to the fullest, do not acquire anything new, and are at the point of "losing it." Out in the cold, impoverished and unhappy, the woman pictured personifies the soul. In this way we learn that those who give what they have are worth their life.

Self pity, identification with our own "bad luck," and over-exercise to get out of the doldrums, prevent us from seeing that there is help around the corner. This is symbolized by the tree of life in the lighted window, which the individuals are passing. This situation will go on until their eyes are opened.

Pentacles Six

Mercy

Humankind has learned its lesson. We have become humble, starting to forgive and share. Our animus and anima kneel and offer their palms, the gesture of submission. Their empty hands are filled. The person that weighs and gives is also the one who gives and receives. Progress takes place. Mindful of our mistakes, we will resume our work. The three figures are the symbolic representation of one person. The woman to the right of the giver receives four talents for her work in the fields. At his left a man kneels who earned his wage in an industrial area.

Pentacles Seven

Working with Love

Now working with love, humankind nurtures growth and flowering. We really work and the love for the work makes it flourish. This arcanum indicates a working relationship with things, plants, animals, and humans, and symbolizes service. Pentacles Seven depicts the way we emotionally deal with building up Pentacles—talents, matter, and money.

Pentacles Eight

Work with Perspiration

Mastership is achieved through steady work with regularity, order, and a sense of responsibility. This arcanum points at the same work relationship that is described in Pentacles Seven. The person in the picture creates one Pentacle for each day in the week, but has, unnoticed, created an extra, eighth pentacle through his own skills and work rhythm. The Eight of Pentacles reflects the recurring and mechanical aspects of our development of the Pentacle (money as the tangible result of labor).

Pentacles Nine

Profit

Owing to steady and responsible work, we have acquired more goods and money, which seems to increase to some degree by itself. We do not have to work very hard anymore. The anima in us feels safe and nice. The fruits of work are visible and the time is near when we will rise to a higher level of existence. Pentacles Nine portrays an accomplished human being whose soul, symbolized by the falcon, enjoys almost complete freedom. The falcon, aware of the "divine goodness" of its master or mistress will always return. Dealing with matters of money and talents is now about to be rounded off spiritually.

Pentacles Ten

Prosperity

We have come into riches. The opulently ornamented wall tapestry at the left protects the inhabitants from heat and cold and reveals a rock island in a sea of emotions; there is stability. The family lives in harmony and is in tune; this is indicated by the two pillars of space and time on the rock island. The decoration on the back of the father's chair shows new moons: it is the right time to sow. The father watches as a new family is going to be established by his son or daughter, who is about to marry and live in the castle, safe behind the wall. The bridegroom bears the wand with the mystical grain that will express itself in The Chariot. The little bridesmaid is the youngest daughter who assists her aging father. Cooperation within the community is gaining real importance. The second phase in life begins.

Wands One

The Power of Fire

A new phase starts. Having integrated with matter in the previous phase we are now offered a flourishing wand; it is a symbol of potency, fertility, growth, and flowering. The flowering wand represents the magical wand, but it is also a tool, a weapon, and a measure or gauge.

Wands Two

Balanced Command

We use the powers, skills and all other means at our disposal in a well-balanced way. Regularity and balance bring harmony. The work plan is made up, the land to be developed is mapped. Employees are about to be appointed.

Wands Three

Alertness

Summer is in full swing. We look from our world into the future. The ships in the distance may be traders of our own and other communities…or are they pirate vessels?

As honest trade can easily degenerate in ruthless competition, we now have to be alert, prepared, and protected; on the right arm of the person in the picture, a coat of arms is just visible. The first signs of the parasitism that uses up the vital energy and great productivity of the community are developing; weeds may start contaminating the wheat. The situation develops into harvest or conquest.

Wands Four

Completed Work

There is plenty of everything. This arcanum relates to the many festivities that take place in the beginning of May, such as the old Gaelic festival of the Beltane Fires on May 1. It also symbolizes summer feasts and dances in preparation for the harvest or war, as well as the coronation of the May Queen. Another example is the era of the "Roaring Twenties" that preceded the Great Depression. Through festivities the community becomes unified, which is necessary in order to be able to complete the exertions that are at hand in Wands Five.

Wands Five

Combat

The five laborers are trying to form a pentacle with their wands. Harvesting is in full swing, the wheat is being cut down.

A certain measure of violence accompanies all harvests It may be a situation in which a community or society is conquered or a territory is expanded.

What manifests itself always pushes something else aside. Hence, a battle is unavoidable and often happens in a chaotic way. This turmoil precedes the victory or manifestation.

  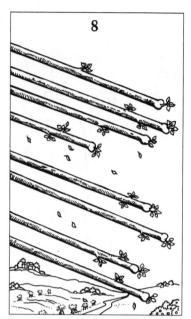

Wands Six

Victory

The victor enters the town on horseback. The harvest is in; the manifestation has been accomplished. Fellow men are looking up to the conqueror. The wand and the wreath symbolize fertilization and conception. Consciousness has taken form. In Wands Six the upper triangle touches the lower one. The spirit and the material will merge into the Star of David.

Wands Seven

Contemplation

The heat of the battle presses us to continue the fighting, although it is not necessary any longer. We are already in a safe, high position; what was desired has been achieved. We gradually start to see this.

This arcanum points to the fact that the law of inertia also works at human levels.

Wands Eight

Capitulation

We reflect on achievement. There has been enough: the movement has come to a standstill. We put down the arms or the harvesting tools and gather friends and enemies around the table to consider the situation. In Wands Eight a fundamental change of attitude takes place. The third phase of life is approaching.

THE 40 MINOR ARCANA AND THE STRUCTURE OF THE TAROT

Wands Nine

Recovery and Result

This arcanum depicts the situation in which a person, tired and wounded in the battle—a bandage wound around his head—uses his dominant position to put the discarded arms to use for constructive and peaceful purposes. The power, knowledge, and goods secured in battle (harvest) are protecting his position; this is indicated by the fence of wands. This potential will be used for building and restoration. "And they shall beat their swords into plowshares, and their spears into pruning hooks" (Isaiah 2:4). Damaged or broken relationships are now restored. The chaff is separated from the wheat: there is quality control.

Wands Ten

Stockpiling

We collect the experiences or powers (harvest) and brings them to the city or community. Corn is stored in silos as stock for the approaching winter, knowledge is condensed into books. This material will ensure the future, not only of ourselves, but also of others. The city is a gathering place. In general, the forces of fire are now being accumulated to serve the sacrifice that will be brought in the cold nights of the forthcoming winter. Carrying our own goods burdens us. This card also means literally paying taxes for the benefit of the community.

Cups One

The Power of Water

A new phase: The cup or grail symbolizes the body in which the soul, the essence of a human, has found its place. The archetypal cup with the "blood of Jesus" is handed out. In this phase we give of ourselves out of love, sacrificing ourselves and our ego. From the cup springs the water of life. The cup also symbolizes the prize someone wins as reward for a superb achievement, which is always preceded by great self-sacrifices. The sacrifice and the prize generate new life—power and new emotions—represented by the bubbles that are rising from the lake as vapor. Lotus flowers float on the surface of the primordial sea.

Cups Two

Loving Exchange

This arcanum portrays the pure exchange of the sacrifice, such as happens in real friendship and brotherhood. Humankind has passed the sexually inclined stage of The Lovers. There is now a situation of friendship in which people in intimacy mutually exchange their inner life, their emotions, and love. This arcanum points at the essence of all real communication. This event is sanctified and therefore generates healing power, symbolized by the Hermes wand—two snakes crowned with a winged lion's head. "For where two or three come together in my name, I am there with them" (Matthew 18:20).

Cups Three
Spiritual Prosperity
This arcanum illuminates the joy of giving. It is more blissful to give than to receive, and delightful to be able to create. In the first instance the offer leads to a feeling of well-being. The three muses Euphrosyne, Thalia, and Aglia—patrons of gaiety, comedy, and glitter—are inspiring the artist. They enjoy the work the artist creates, often undergoing great sacrifices. There is festivity going on because of that sacrifice. In a more negative sense, the offer is feasted away, for example, by religious leaders who are converting the gifts and other sacrifices of their disciples to exorbitant luxury, as well as the commercialization of art, culture, nature, science, and sports.

Cups Four
Doubt
When real sacrifice begins, we often have doubts. There is a choice between the deepening of the sacrifice with the possibility of losing one's freedom and life, or hanging onto less extreme but more agreeable sacrifices. The situation is similar to the one depicted in Pentacles Four, where a human hangs on to the Pentacles gained. The penultimate sacrifice is the offering of one's life. This is symbolized by the fourth cup, which is offered from a cloud—the inspiration is from heaven. We wonder if this fourth cup has to be taken. Jesus said in the Garden of Olives: "Abba, Father, all things are possible to Thee; remove this cup from me; yet not what I will, but what Thou wilt" (Mark 14:36). In the end, we accept the cup—we simply have to do it.

Cups Five
Emotional Bankruptcy
In this stadium the person gains the insight that most of the sacrifices were useless: three of the five cups have toppled and their contents spilled. The soul, which is still shackled to the body, sees that many of its sacrifices did not bring it closer to its goal in life. Understanding the relative futility of all exertions carried through leads to a profound depression. It is perceived that real sacrifice requires complete submission. The Five of Cups portrays Neaniskos, the naked youngster, dressed in the shroud.

Cups Six

Submission

We are ready to fulfill the complete sacrifice now that its value is understood: We offer a flower in a cup. The sacrifices of children are genuine, pure, and essential, as is the childlike friendliness of elderly people depicted here. "Truly, I say to you, unless you turn and become like children, you will never enter the kingdom of heaven" (Matthew 18:3). This arcanum asks for the last sacrifice: material death.

Cups Seven

Contemplation of Life

Life has finished. The soul leaves and the body dies. During the process of dying, which can also be interpreted in a metaphorical way—for instance, as the discontinuance of a relationship or job—we look back. Projected in time-space, the excarnated being sees all the cups that were accepted during life—for example, a lover, a home, or a castle. One cup bears a skull: the sacrifice of our life and body. The soul recognizes that this ultimate sacrifice is crowned with laurels.

Cups Eight

Separation

Having contemplated all the sacrifices that have been fulfilled in our life, we cannot do anything but turn away from them and leave them behind. As was mentioned before, the cup is also the body in which the soul has lived for a whole life. The soul now abandons the body and all related material aspects. We move up to an astral level of existence where time and space unite and the sun and the moon coalesce into one while serving as guide. The way we go now is unknown: all we see is water—emotions and massive mountains of rock— eternal truth.

THE 40 MINOR ARCANA AND THE STRUCTURE OF THE TAROT

Cups Nine

Tied to Earth

At this point in our journey, we meet ourselves. From a materialistic viewpoint we have left "our" cups behind. However, our soul is still attached to them and the orgiastic events they represent. Our thoughts about our sacrifices in the past form a wall, which ties us to our past. Although in front of this barrier we can "live" in the past in a self-contained way, it impedes our progress to the "radiant light," the Truth, God. In this arcanum the soul is in the stage of being bound to earth. We now must become aware that we have to let go of material and spiritual bonds.

Cups Ten

Exalted Passage

The soul sees that in order to be able to progress it has to completely surrender all sacrifices, achievements, and actions. The moment it takes this step, the cups, which had become a wall, elevate themselves to form a gate to the Truth. Truth, which illuminates our life, forms a rainbow of hope behind which the Summer Land is visible. Our animus and anima now understand how they completed their tasks and karma together with their kindred spirits. The soul passes through this gate, into Heaven.

The Minor Arcana of Swords

Swords One

The Power of the Spirit

For those who have not united with God in Heaven, with the Self-Radiant Light, the last new phase in the cycle of life begins. The Sword pointing upward symbolizes divine justice and life; a sword pointing downwards would mean death. In this phase our life cycle is crowned with the divine judgment of the life and how it has been lived. This will direct the soul to renewal and prepare it for incarnation in a new life.

Swords Two

Inevitable Judgment

In Swords Two divine judgment is applied in a pure and unemotional way; our karma is adjusted. In the background is the restless primordial sea that contains the souls of all, living and dead. The divine judgment is fair and serves the interests of all other souls.

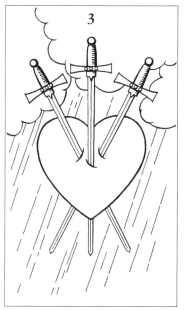

Swords Three
Grief

Divine judgment is true and severe. Now is made a radical end to all remaining emotional ties of the soul to material life. This is also called "the second death." In this card all remnants of the feelings of the heart are killed. This judgment liberates the soul of its laden conscience. The situation also relates to the significance of mourning and Jesus' death at the cross, which was heart-rending for Mary. "Day and night I cry, and tears are my only food" (Psalms 42:3).

Swords Four
Transmutation

After its second death, the soul is in a comatose state, symbolized by the coffin. It is a situation of pupation of the soul; outwardly passive, inwardly profoundly active. In this arcanum the soul is shown the entirety of things. The stained glass window depicts a situation of mercy and forgiveness. In this stage of submission, the light of Christ illuminates the soul. Through contemplation and stillness soul patterns coalesce to a new whole.

Swords Five
Remembering the Self

Through waiting and contemplation, soul patterns have condensed into a structure with which the soul can work. Through the reflection and meditation in Swords Four we have overcome ourselves and our inner enemies and identifications, which sap our energies—they are personified by the defeated persons walking away in the background. We take up—in a moment from heaven—soul energy in the form of swords of heavenly justice. In this way a new goal and plan for life originates as a crystallization of soul power. This is the moment of conception: the soul starts its reincarnation.

Swords Six
Crossing the Great Water
When enough soul power has been collected, the execution of the new plan starts with the crossing of the great water. The soul has just entered upon an incarnation journey and has not yet assumed a clearly defined form. To arrive there, the soul in the boat is moved forward by the ferryman Charon. The little child depicts the soul, the vague shape next to it is its future physical body. This card shows the process of the soul's incarnation; the fetus develops in the womb on earth. With unclear perspectives, we leave one situation and transcend into a new one.

Swords Seven
Loving Growth
This card shows the soul during the process of reincarnation. The child in the womb of the family that it has chosen (a family meeting and their tents are visible in the background) collects heavenly justice in a loving way. The figure in Swords Seven, the unborn child, looks towards the mother in the arcanum Eight of Swords, from whom it has taken life powers in a playful manner. At this stage the fetus exists partly in heaven, partly on earth, and is not fully grown. The unborn needs not only matter from the body of the mother, but also the love and nurturing of the parents.

Swords Eight
Bound to Growth
This arcanum sketches the bound position in which both the pregnant mother and the unborn child are placed. Neither of the two can move and see what is happening. The mother does not know whether the child is a boy or a girl, or how the child will develop. But she has to keep supporting it in a material way; with one foot she stands in fertile mud, the symbol of Mother Earth. The soul needs matter to serve as a lodging place on earth.

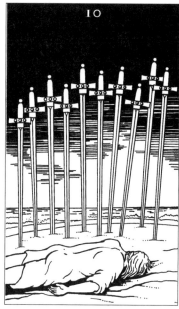

Swords Nine

Awakening

The countdown starts; stopping or returning is not possible any longer. Just before a new life cycle starts—just before birth—the inner eye sees once more all the events that have happened in the past and have led to the new beginning. The panel on the bed vaguely shows a battle scene from the past. Shocked, the soul asks itself what it has done in its previous life and what the new life or plan will lead to. Humankind awakens. The zodiacal and planetary signs on the blanket indicate the stars under which the new birth will take place. The new life is becoming a fact.

Swords Ten

Birth

The clock has sounded twelve. The old cycle is totally over; a new life cycle starts. This last card of the Minor Arcana shows the archetypal newborn child. The umbilical cord, its connection with the mother, has been cut. Almost as if drowned in the ocean of souls and in the womb, the new human being is washed ashore at the land of life. The ten swords behind it form a fence, which protects it from the past, the memories of prior lives. We start again like a blank sheet of paper. We cannot, and are not allowed to go back. The ten Heavenly swords separate life on earth from the other level of existence, from where it came (visible in the background). They do this by splitting space-and-time into four separate dimensions, in which the soul is to achieve its new task.

The 16 Royal Arcana and Their Function in the Tarot

Chieftain,
Cairo, 2800 B.C.

All things require the natural state of Innocence.
In this way, the old kings, rich in virtue and
In harmony with time, nurtured and nourished all beings.
—*I Ching*

CHAPTER 4

The 16 Royal Arcana and Their Function in the Tarot

The collective-psychological family structure in the Tarot

In the preceding chapter we briefly discussed the presence of psychological and social symbol structures in the Tarot. These are centered around the most important cornerstone of society, the family, consisting of the father, mother, and one or more children. In the Tarot this base element is bundled in a group of archetypes that are called the Royal Arcana. The Royal Arcana describe the collective-psychological aspects of our existence.

In total, there are 16 Royal Arcana. They are subdivided into four groups of royal families—four is the number of matter. Each royal family in the Tarot comprises four family archetypes:

The King	The father
The Queen	The mother
The Knight	The eldest child
The Page	The youngest child

The Page may be a male or a female because a child is neutral.

Above all, the Royal Arcana have a psychological bearing. The archetypal family structure clearly shows up in the classical family table arrangement. The father and mother sit opposite each other. Their attention is directed to those aspects of the family for which they bear immediate responsibility: The father looks outward, the mother inward. The eldest child sits at the father's right side and can come to his aid. The youngest child sits to the left of the mother so that it can be educated and fed by the mother directly. The father and mother are focused on each other. Besides, the father occupies himself mainly with the eldest child on his right and the second eldest child to his left; the mother with the youngest child to her left and the second youngest child to her right (figure 4.1 and 4.2).

Function and organization of the Royal Arcana

Society has a hierarchical structure. Every human being has to obey superiors and guide subordinates. This is reflected in the Tarot as well.

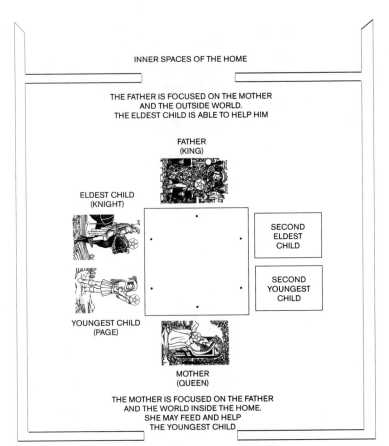

INNER SPACES OF THE HOME

THE FATHER IS FOCUSED ON THE MOTHER
AND THE OUTSIDE WORLD.
THE ELDEST CHILD IS ABLE TO HELP HIM

FATHER
(KING)

ELDEST CHILD
(KNIGHT)

SECOND
ELDEST
CHILD

SECOND
YOUNGEST
CHILD

YOUNGEST CHILD
(PAGE)

MOTHER
(QUEEN)

THE MOTHER IS FOCUSED ON THE FATHER
AND THE WORLD INSIDE THE HOME.
SHE MAY FEED AND HELP
THE YOUNGEST CHILD

THE ENVIRONMENT OUTSIDE OF THE HOME

4.1 Functional and collective-psychological, classical table seating plan. The father and mother are seated opposite each other and survey those parts of the environment of the family for which they bear direct responsibility.

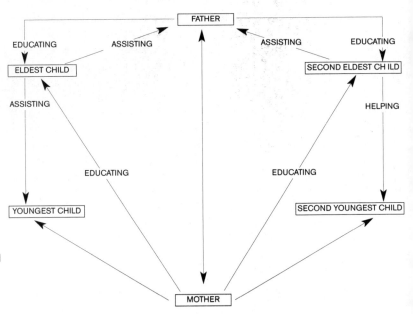

FATHER

EDUCATING   ASSISTING   ASSISTING   EDUCATING

ELDEST CHILD   SECOND ELDEST CHILD

ASSISTING   HELPING

EDUCATING   EDUCATING

YOUNGEST CHILD   SECOND YOUNGEST CHILD

MOTHER

4.2 Interaction structure in the classical table seating plan.

The members of the royal families represent governing and leading principles. They pass on the abstract principles of the Major Arcana to the level of execution in the Minor Arcana to facilitate further evolution. Each member has his/her own task.

Kings: Are visionaries, governors, paternal and national leaders, directors, and judges.

Queens: Are planners, counselors, and motherly, social caretakers.

Knights: Propagate the royal message and defend the family if necessary.

Pages: Are at home, being raised and trained in the tasks they have to carry out later in life. They assist the other members of the family and have a mystical inclination.

The Royal Families in daily life

KINGS represent the land and government at meetings of the great dignitaries. They chair meetings; they are directors, and members of societies active at high levels of society. They transform the world through abstract thinking and approach matters regarding humans in a rational way. Thus, they emphasize the element of *air*.

QUEENS represent the town and its government. They are also leaders, chair meetings, and are members of associations with influential friends. They accentuate the element of *water*—emotionality, art, and an empathic approach to humankind.

KNIGHTS represent the element of *fire*—productivity, assertiveness, and conflict. They carry out decisions and make sure that everything happens as planned. They are also the armed forces, police, and action groups. They are usually extroverts.

PAGES represent the element of *earth*—which is material growth and development. They visit and study at schools and universities, are focused on learning situations, new plans, and ideas, and function as students in group settings.

The Tarot emblems of the Royal Families

Each royal family in the Tarot has a coat of arms, an emblem that was painted on the family's shields so that during a battle they could recognize each other. Hence, the emblem on a coat of arms symbolizes the family's general characteristic.

In the Tarot each of the royal families is psychologically linked to the Tarot emblem they carry on their coat of arms (figure 4.3).

Their emblem connects them to a particular quadrant of the life cycle, as well as connecting them with the ten Minor Arcana that carry the same emblem.

TAROT EMBLEMS AND THEIR MEANINGS

Tarot emblem				
	PENTACLES	**WANDS**	**CUPS**	**SWORDS**
Royal family	King	King	King	King
	Queen	Queen	Queen	Queen
	Knight	Knight	Knight	Knight
	Page	Page	Page	Page
Psyche	I have	I am	I feel	I think
	Wanting	Daring	Keeping silent	Thinking
Inclination	Perceptive	Intuitive	Emotional	Rational
Area of tasks	Writing	Professional	Artistic	Abstracting
Societal class	Businessmen	Tradesmen	Clergy	Intellectuals
Type	Phlegmatic	Choleric	Melancholic	Sanguine
Path of life	Rebellious	Ascension	Suffering	Incarnation

4.3 The four Tarot emblems correlated to the four Royal Families and four-fold essential characterizations.

The royal family of PENTACLES is closely related to the element *Earth*. The collective-psychological meaning of this emblem is connected with money, talents, and material affairs. To this emblem are related the metals iron, which is the most abundant on earth and gives red-brown oxides, and gold, which is the metal that has been known the longest. The background color of these cards is yellow, the color of the sun and gold. Pentacles are related to the color *black*, which creates the strongest contrasts. The complexion is dark; eyes and hair of the royal family of Pentacles are usually dark-brown or black. They have phlegmatic, down-to-earth, businesslike characteristics.

The royal family of WANDS is closely related to the element *Fire*. In daily life this means professional productivity in social contexts. The metal of Wands is copper. It has a fiery color and its oxides display a variety of the color green, which is the color of life. On Tarot cards the human figures are placed in cloudless summer landscapes. Wands are related to the color *red*, which is blood, life in action. The royal family of Wands often has fire-like, red or orange-colored hair, a predominantly olive complexion, and green eyes. Their character is choleric and easily excited; their main interest is in their career.

The Royal family of CUPS is related to the element *Water.* Its members concern themselves with the emotional and sensitive aspects of daily life. Cups are related to the soul. On all Royal Arcana water is pictured as a stream, river, or sea. The metal is pure silver. The color associated with Cups is *light-brown.* The hair color of the members of this royal family is often light-brown, the eyes blue-green or dark blue. The royal family of Cups has a melancholic character, is sensitive, emotional, and quickly tired.

The Royal family of SWORDS is related to the element *Air.* This family is intellectual and mentally oriented. The skies on these cards are turbulent, alive; in all these court cards birds—symbols of the free-thinking spirit—are cruising through the air. Its related metal is steel. The color of Swords is *white,* a reflection of the Self-radiating Light, God, as encountered in the Major Arcanum Truth. The royal family of Swords has a very fair complexion, with fine, white or light-blond hair. Their eye color ranges from blue to light gray. Their character is sanguine, resolute, and cheerful.

The Knights in the Royal Arcana
In the Tarot the knights and their horses reveal remarkable parallels with the knights in Revelations 6:

Knight of Pentacles	Black Horse (Revelations 6:5)	Task: To determine
Knight of Wands	Sandy Horse (Revelations 6:4)	Task: To fight
Knight of Cups	Pale Horse (Revelations 6:8)	Task: To kill
Knight of Swords	White Horse (Revelations 6:2)	Task: To conquer

Humankind in the Royal Arcana
The Royal Arcana depict ourselves: human beings of flesh and blood, with principles and tasks that have to be carried out, but also with shortcomings. The fewer shortcomings, the more "royal" a person can be. The context of our activities is in social groups where we lead, obey, exchange, and deal.

The following discussion of the Royal Arcana is related to the order of the Major Arcana in the life cycle in the restored order, and to the wave-shaped power variation therein (figure 4.10). Further details about the symbols in the Royal Arcana are discussed in Chapter 10.

PAGE OF PENTACLES

KNIGHT OF PENTACLES

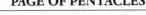

The Page of Pentacles

A young person with brown/black hair and brown eyes. A resourceful child with a careful, dedicated character.

The Page of Pentacles represents the earth-aspect of the element Earth. This youngster is friendly, cautious, and well-mannered. Spiritually, these individuals are investigators with great perseverance. They hold the Pentacle up in an examining way and see more in it than their mother does. They bring the message of the discovery of the earth's secrets. Because of youth's readiness, they are more agile than the other family members.

The Page of Pentacles is seen outside the boundary of its parents' land, in free, grand, and pristine nature.

The Knight of Pentacles

A young rider with almost-black hair and dark eyes. A responsible, functional materialist with a thoughtful, industrious attitude.

The Knight of Pentacles represents the fire-aspect of the element Earth. These individuals make certain that things happen and are practical people with conventional values and ideas. They are materialists, patient, handy, and inventive, but with a somewhat sluggish nature. They are inclined to discount the feelings of others and could be labeled as pushy.

The Knight of Pentacles rides on a black horse and oversees the family's plowed fields, in the middle of untouched nature.

The plowed fields around the Knight of Pentacles continue to the right, into the landscape where the Page of Pentacles is standing. This symbolism indicates that the Knight of Pentacles not only protects the family's property, but also his young brother, the Page of Pentacles.

QUEEN OF PENTACLES

KING OF PENTACLES

The Queen of Pentacles

A dark, attractive, affluent woman, intelligent and quiet. A good spouse and homemaker with grace and dignity. Good at raising children.

The Queen of Pentacles represents the water-aspect of the element Earth. Her perspective on material matters has an emotional connotation. She is clever, a sensitive nature-woman with psychic talents. The Pentacle she keeps in her lap resembles a crystal ball in which the future reveals itself to her.

The Queen of Pentacles' throne is placed in a Spring garden at the border of free nature, and is decorated with cupids and goats, symbols of love and the god Pan. The hare points at the regeneration of nature in Spring.

The King of Pentacles

An important, mature man with dark hair and dark eyes, married, intelligent, with strong character and sensual power. A successful businessman.

The King of Pentacles represents the air-aspect of the element Earth. He approaches earthly matters from an intellectual point of view, like a gentleman-farmer. A simple man, who works in a systematic and crafty way, he is loyal, patient, and persevering, and as a result his wealth increases. He may have a permanent position in a large enterprise.

The King of Pentacles' throne is decorated with bull's heads, symbolizing power and fertility, and is placed in a lush, growing garden. In the background is his castle or property.

KING OF WANDS

QUEEN OF WANDS

King of Wands

An honest, reliable, sympathetic, virile man, usually married, with red-brown hair and green eyes. Conscientious and entrepreneurial with a noble, liberal character.

The King of Wands is the air-aspect of the element Fire. An honest, friendly and ethical person, loyal and generous, he honors family traditions. He is active, enterprising, and authoritative. His heraldic device is "I will maintain."

In his right hand the King of Wands holds the flowering stick signifying spiritual potency. On his throne the lion stands for society, and the ouroboros for the universe. Next to him sits a fire salamander, indicating his genius.

Queen of Wands

An attractive woman with blond or chestnut red hair and green eyes, an inspiring, magnetic personality. She is active, practical, intelligent, and independent.

The Queen of Wands represents the water-aspect of the element Fire. Beautiful, generous, and friendly, with a practical inclination and independent opinions, she is very motivated towards her home and position.

In one hand the Queen of Wands holds the flowering wand of fertility and inspiration, in the other a sunflower symbolizing the health of those who are in tune with their heavenly task. Also on her throne are two lions beside the tree of life. At her feet is the sacred cat, a reference to her self-awareness.

KNIGHT OF WANDS

PAGE OF WANDS

Knight of Wands

An attractive, energetic, redheaded young person with green eyes. Impetuous and impulsive, he is an individualist with startling charm.

The Knight of Wands emphasizes the fire-aspect of the element Fire. Strong and audacious, he is the one who reveals and actualizes the assignment, the father's secret weapon, and the purging of the Temple (Mark 11:15–18).

The Knight of Wands rides on a sandy-colored horse and passes several pyramids in the background; they symbolize eternal manifestation. "I came from sunset to here and am going to sunrise. I am causing sunrise and sunset" (Celtic mythology).

Page of Wands

A very intelligent young person with red-brown hair and light green eyes, who has remarkable verbal talents and wisdom.

Against the backdrop of the pyramids, the Page of Wands proclaims the message of the procreation, the inception of the new plan, a new life. The Page of Wands approaches the element Fire in an earthly way. Resourceful, enthusiastic, and ambitious, he reacts quickly and emotionally, in love or in hatred. He symbolizes Jesus, who censures the Pharisees and the Teachers of the Law (Luke 11:37–54).

PAGE OF CUPS

KNIGHT OF CUPS

Page of Cups

A rather feminine young person with an artistic and sensitive inclination, brown hair and light green eyes. A philosopher with a vivid imagination and a loyal and accommodating character.

The Page of Cups represents the Earth-aspect of the element Water. A calm, gentle, artistic, and philosophical person, he is from time to time, a dreamer. He also delivers spiritual messages.

The Page of Cups studies and shows a fish in a chalice. This symbolizes intuition, the unconscious. In folktales a fish often fulfills wishes and returns personal possessions laden with emotions that were lost in the primordial sea. In the background we see the primordial waters of the unconscious.

Knight of Cups

A romantic, creative, and intelligent person with light brown hair and blue eyes. He brings love, ideas, gifts, and opportunities; he disseminates the sacrifice. In the Grail Legends he is Parcival.

The Knight of Cups emphasizes the fire-aspect of the element Water, which is steam. Ingratiating, romantic, and intelligent, he is also a dreamer who may quickly go out of balance.

The Knight of Cups rides a pale-colored horse (Revelations 6:8). He is about to cross a river on the way to the white cliffs of pure truth. This arcanum also refers to the conveyance of the Grail to Cornwall.

QUEEN OF CUPS

KING OF CUPS

Queen of Cups

A very sensitive, loving, intelligent woman with light brown hair and blue eyes. A self-sacrificing, loving spouse or mother.

The Queen of Cups represents the water-aspect of the element Water. Rich in fantasy, artistically gifted, intuitive and psychic, she is gentle, sometimes dreamy. Being intellectually strong is not very important to her.

The throne of the Queen of Cups is placed on a peninsula at the border of the sea in front of white cliffs; it is decorated with water cupids, representing the sympathetic side of love. In her hands she holds the ciborium, a closed chalice guarded by angels, containing the essence of life.

King of Cups

A man of the arts and sciences, religion, and psychological matters, he is influential, sensitive, and responsible, with creative characteristics. He has light brown hair and light blue eyes.

The King of Cups is the air-aspect of the element Water. He is a sensitive, skillful negotiator and a psychologically inclined listener who understands. He knows the low and high tides of life. His throne is placed on a square rock in an agitated sea, signifying truth unperturbed by emotions and the collective unconscious.

This arcanum points to the archetypal Fisher King in the Grail legends and the Biblical figure Joseph of Arimathea. In the background, his ship is on a journey to the tin mines in England. On board are Mary Magdalene and the Grail. The dolphin jumping up from the sea carries the alchemical gold, which is love that comes from the heart.

KING OF SWORDS

QUEEN OF SWORDS

King of Swords

A sagacious, gray-haired man with steel-blue eyes, wise and acute, with great analytical skills. He may be a counselor, a scientist, also a judge. He possesses power over life and death.

The King of Swords represents the air-aspect of the element Air and is the intellectual *par excellence*—solemn, rational and logical, conscientious and strict. As a man of order and rules, full of respect and command, he simply *is*.

The throne of the King of Swords is placed on a rough rock, symbolizing truth. Behind him in some decks is a banner as a tower in a lonesome plain with a threatening winter sky. His facial expression is austere, but also compassionate. The decoration of butterflies on his throne refers to air and transformation.

Queen of Swords

A serious and sensitive woman with flaxen hair and gray-blue eyes. An academically trained mother or grandmother with great individual power, wit, and a noble comportment.

The Queen of Swords represents the water-aspect of the element Air. She is a lonely, intelligent, and witty woman, smart and extraordinarily sensitive. The archetypal female judge, she is very good at achieving compromises between warring parties, and in this way attains her goals.

The throne of the Queen of Swords is placed on a rock in a lonesome plain. Her facial expression is grave and sad. Clouds are gathering. In this card, as in that of the King, the motif of the butterfly on her throne and crown means renewal.

KNIGHT OF SWORDS

PAGE OF SWORDS

Knight of Swords

A brisk young person with blond hair and blue eyes, a master of well-considered presentation and action. The perfect noble knight who courageously wields the sword.

The Knight of Swords emphasizes the fire-aspect of the element Air, symbolizing the battle that is associated with mental affairs. Dynamic, intelligent, and subtle, he has great presence and is engaging and astute, a born negotiator who solves situations that have run into a deadlock. He can be and act on his own. The Knight of Swords rides on a white horse at full speed, brandishing the sword of heavenly justice.

Page of Swords

An active young person with dark blond hair and light-green eyes, he is alert with a clear mind, insight, and discretion.

The Page of Swords emphasizes air-matters in an earthly way. He or she is a compelling, vivid, and versatile person. The lemniscate of the 12 returning migratory birds symbolizes eternal change, *panta rhei*— "everything flows." The Page brings the message of improvement, birth, and growth.

A tall person, the Page of Swords holds the sword in a calm way. The landscape is less desolate, the weather improves, the wind has abated, and the clouds are disappearing; soon the sun will warm the scene.

4.4 The Royal Arcana of Pentacles.

Psychological relations between the members of the Royal Families

By placing the images of the four members of one royal family together, we gain an insight into the psychological relationships and interactions within each family.

The Royal Family of Pentacles

The King sits face on and looks in the direction of the Queen and their two children: the Knight and the Page. The Queen looks in the direction of the King and Knight. The King and Queen are affectionate to each other. All watch the Page, who is the darling and the most promising member of this family.

The Knight and the Page are both moving to the right. The Knight rides across his father's plowed fields; he does not fight outside his own territory. The Page wants to move farther and discover the wild and pristine nature outside the father's property.

There is a strong bond between the father and the mother, on the one hand, and between the eldest and youngest child, on the other. The Knight stands attentively behind the Page and is primarily worried about the well-being of his younger sibling.

The Royal Family of Wands

The King of Wands is depicted from the side; the Queen is seated face on. The King is watching achievements that were accomplished in the past; the Queen is facing the present and the future. The two children have turned away from each other. They move in opposite directions to carry—each in his own way—the family emblem, the Wand.

The Knight pulls the reigns to steer the horse forward. The Page has turned away from the Knight and looks towards the future, like their mother. The Page has assumed the role of the proclaimer, expressing the family's ideas. The queen looks covertly and with pleasure to the achievements of the Knight. In this family there is not a clear bond between the father and the mother, or between the Knight and the Page. All members of the family of Wands are going out freely and independently to work and to produce.

4.5 The Royal Arcana of Wands.

The Royal Family of Cups

The King and Queen are looking toward each other. They are affectionate, a "sea of feelings" surrounds them. The Queen is very spiritual and has an emanation of transparency. The closed Cup with angels forms something like Cancerian claws: it refers to the protection of the soul, which is inside the Cup.

The Knight has a spiritual and psychic inclination and "carries forth" the Grail. Of all family members the Page is the most acutely aware. He is depicted in almost frontal view: the Knight and Page are walking in each other's direction and offer each other the Cup. The Queen and King are on swampy ground. In general, the royal family of Cups is strongly introverted.

The Royal Family of Swords

All members of the Royal family of Swords act independently. The family forms an entity, but its members have a large degree of individuality. The King is depicted frontally and looks the reader straight in the eye. What is straight cannot be crooked. The Queen is shown in profile: the marriage is emancipated.

The Knight of Swords carries the sword of heavenly justice undaunted and energetically. The Page is alert and vigilant in his own right. The Page and the Knight have a working relationship: they are going out in the world together. The Page, a very powerful and active person, covers his sibling to the rear.

The wave-like power variation in the Royal Arcana

When the Royal Arcana is arranged in the order of the life cycle, we can distinguish a wave-like pattern. It starts with the Page of Pentacles and ends with the Page of Wands, after which the wave-shaped power variation repeats itself from the Page of Cups to the Page of Swords (figure 4.8). As the wave rises, the level of power of the Royal Arcanum increases: the King and Queen are at the top of each wave.

4.6 The Royal Arcana of Cups.

4.7 The Royal Arcana of Swords.

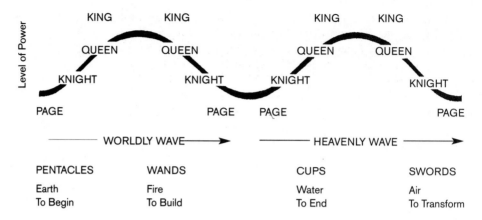

4.8 Wave-shaped power pattern in the Royal Arcana.

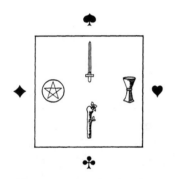

4.9 The geomantic order of the Tarot emblems in the life cycle is the same as those in a deck of ordinary playing cards.

The Royal Arcana related to the other arcana in the Tarot

The Royal Arcana carry the four Tarot emblems as a "coat of arms." The geomantic order of the Tarot emblems in the life cycle is the same as those in the deck of ordinary playing cards (see figure 4.9). We can now combine similarities in card meanings and in this way correlate the arcana to each other. The correlations indicate connections between all the arcana, and reveal the Tarot as a strong, dynamic, psychological, and philosophical matrix.

Correlation of the Royal Arcana with the Major Arcana

The Royal and Major Arcana are connected through psychological similarities. These relationships are:

- Kings are related to the four ruling Major Arcana (figure 4.10);
- Queens are related to the four tending and caring Major Arcana (figure 4.11);
- Knights are related to the four principle-disseminating and offering Major Arcana (figure 4.12);
- Pages are related to the four Major Arcana that deal with learning and emotional growth (figure 4.13).

Using this order of Tarot emblems, the Major and Royal Arcana can be arranged into a mandala (figure 4.14). In this mandala the four Major Arcana Intuition (Juno), The World, Truth (Jupiter), and The Universe have a special function: they are the transitions from one area of work to another, and connect two neighboring royal families. They are the four corners of the moving cross in astrology, and are also called the *axis-arcana*.

4.10 The Kings are correlated with the four leading and ruling Major Arcana.

4.11 The Queens are correlated with the four nurturing and caring Major Arcana.

The Royal Arcana mirrored and juxtaposed

The complete organizational structure of the Tarot is represented by the mandala that shows the relationships between the arcana (figure 4.14).

In this mandala the order of the Royal Arcana of Pentacles and Wands, and those of Swords and Cups, are each other's mirror image—the mirror plane being placed between the arcana The Universe and The World. In the same way the Royal Arcana of Wands and Cups, and of Pentacles and Swords are mirrored with the mirror plane located between the arcana Intuition and Truth.

Because of this double mirroring, all members of the Royal Families are facing each other. The Page of Pentacles is opposite the Page of Cups, the Knight of Pentacles is opposite the Knight of Cups, the King of Swords is opposite the King of Wands, the Queen of Wands opposite the Queen of Swords, and so on.

4.12 The Knights are correlated with the Major Arcana that symbolize sacrifice and the dissemination of principles.

4.13 The Pages are correlated with the Major Arcana symbolizing learning and emotional growth.

It is remarkable that this mirroring also happens in the game of chess: at the start of the game the white and black kings and queens are opposite each other.

The axis-arcana in the Tarot

In the mandala in figure 4.14 the two mirror planes form a right angle. The two mirror planes are the lines (called the axis arcana) that connect four pairs of Major Arcana. Together, the two mirror axes in the Tarot form a sort of "cardan suspension" or "joint," stabilizing the Tarot.

Just as a compass in cardan suspension can move in all directions and stay horizontal in all circumstances, the truth-axis and

THE 16 ROYAL ARCANA AND THEIR FUNCTION IN THE TAROT

world-axis give the Tarot a flexible stability as a philosophical instrument.

Neighbor relations between the Royal Families

In the mandala of Major and Royal Arcana (figure 4.14) the members of the Royal Families encounter each other at the four corners:

Pages meet Pages, Kings meet Kings. These mirror social-psychological situations from real life.

- The Royal Families of Swords and Pentacles have contact with each other through their children, the Pages. This often

4.15 The axis arcana and the cardanic mirror suspension in the restored Tarot.

happens when a family starts living in a new neighborhood: the old and the new inhabitants meet via their children. The Page of Pentacles and the Page of Swords are children who play with each other and discover things. In this way they express the Major Arcana adjacent to them: The Last Judgment and The Fool.

- The Royal Families of Wands and Cups are linked through their young Kings. New, production-oriented enterprises always start with investments. The King of Pentacles and the King of Wands are friends or colleagues who work together harmoniously and intuitively. Thus, they express the meanings of the Major Arcana placed next to them: The Lovers and Intuition.

- The Royal Families of Wands and Cups have contact via their adolescents, the Pages. They discuss, like students on campus, political, social, and philosophical issues and reforms. In this way they express the Major Arcana close to them: Justice and The World.

- The Royal Families of Cups and Swords communicate via their elderly Kings and discuss serious matters of life and death, good and evil, in both an emotional and a rational way. In this way they express the meaning of the Major Arcana Truth and The Devil.

THE 16 ROYAL ARCANA AND THEIR FUNCTION IN THE TAROT

The Royal Arcana placed opposite each other in figure 4.14 have relationships that are intrinsically of a more distant kind. The royal family of Pentacles has a materialistic focus, whereas the royal family of Cups is aimed at more spiritual matters. Similarly, the royal family of Wands deals with production, activity, and career, while, to the royal family of Swords, thinking, contemplation, and resignation are of essential importance.

All arcana in the Tarot organized in one mandala

In figure 4.14 we showed how the Major and Royal Arcana are organized in a mandala. In this figure we can combine these cards with the 40 Minor Arcana as well, because of their relationships with the royal families via the Tarot emblems. The Minor Arcana are correlated in a one-to-one relationship with the other arcana, because there are 40 Minor Arcana and 40 Major and Royal Arcana. The Minor Arcana are placed in a wider band mandala around the already correlated Major and Royal Arcana, until one grand Tarot mandala results, which shows the complete organizational structure of the Tarot (figure 4.16).

The 20 quartets in the Tarot

In the complete mandala the Tarot arcana or cards are arranged in groups of four. One group of four Tarot principles is called a quartet. On the sides we find quartets consisting of one Major Arcanum, one Royal Arcanum and two Minor Arcana. On the corners a group of four consists of two Major and two Minor Arcana. *The four arcana within one quartet form a symbolic unit that refers to the principle or law captured by the Major Arcanum in that quartet.* The Royal Arcanum within a quartet guides the realization of the principle, while the two Minor Arcana illustrate the actualization of that principle in two steps. In figure 4.17a the material field in our archetypal world is represented through the first ten quartets; in figure 4.17b the spiritual field in the second ten quartets.

Studying the 80 arcana in the Tarot, grouped in 20 quartets, substantially deepens the interpretation of a Tarot card in a spread, as the card in question calls to mind, before our "inner eye" the other three cards in that quartet. The structure in the Tarot offered by the Tarot quartets substantially diminishes the difficulty of mastering the meanings of the 80 arcana in the complete Tarot. When divining with the Tarot, the Gestalt of the complete quartet clarifies and gives further depth to the message contained in a card.

Thus, the whole Tarot is before us, as an ordered and structured comprehensible network of archetypes, philosophical principles, and psychological notions, ready to be used to deepen the meaning of our lives.

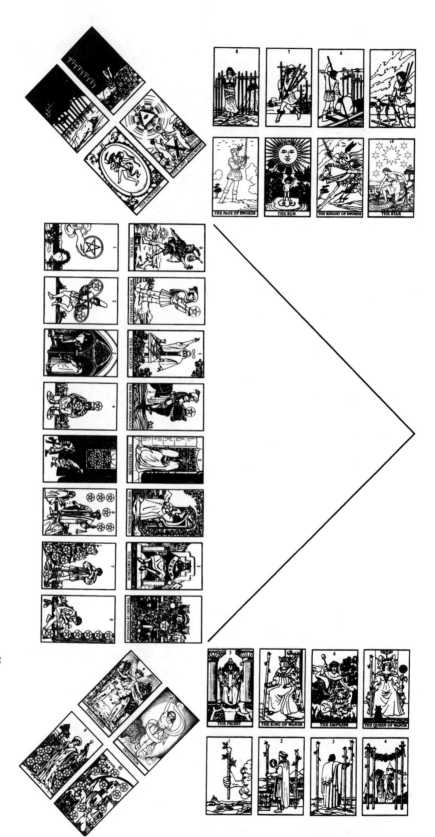

4.16 All 80 arcana of the Tarot geomantically ordered in a mandala of 20 quartets.

THE 16 ROYAL ARCANA AND THEIR FUNCTION IN THE TAROT

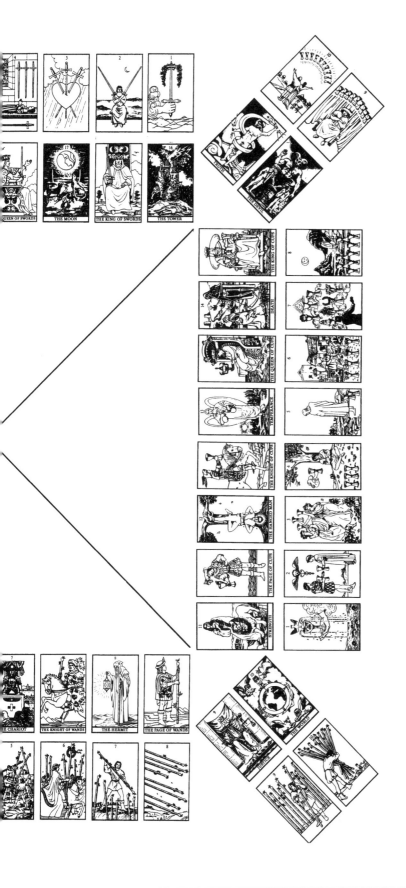

The 20 quartets in the Tarot

4.17 The ten Tarot-quartets
of the material field.

THE QUEEN OF PENTACLES

3 — THE EMPEROR

THE KING OF PENTACLES

6

7

8

4 — THE LOVERS

INTUITION

9

10

THE KNIGHT OF WANDS

6

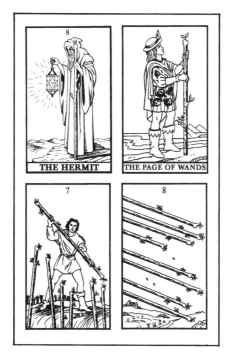

8 — THE HERMIT

THE PAGE OF WANDS

7

8

9 — JUSTICE

10 — THE WORLD

9

10

4.18 The ten Tarot-quartets
of the spiritual field.

THE 16 ROYAL ARCANA AND THEIR FUNCTION IN THE TAROT

THE QUEEN OF CUPS

DEATH

THE KING OF CUPS

6

7

8

THE DEVIL

TRUTH

9

10

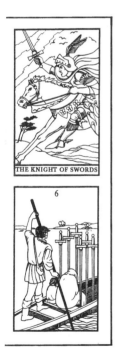

THE KNIGHT OF SWORDS

6

THE SUN

THE PAGE OF SWORDS

7

8

THE LAST JUDGMENT

THE UNIVERSE

9

10

The History of the Tarot

The lips of wisdom are closed
Except to those ears that can hear.
—*The Qabbala*

The Sphinx and the Great Pyramid,
Cairo (2800 B.C.)

CHAPTER 5

The History of the Tarot

The first version . . .

Long ago, there was a first version. Maybe it gradually developed in Egypt more than five millennia back, or maybe, as P. D. Ouspensky put it, Raymond Lullius was the first to record existing knowledge about the Tarot. In any case, those who conceived the Tarot must have had *objective knowledge*—undisputed wisdom that is intuitively sensed by everyone as being true. The concept of objective knowledge is explained at the end of this chapter.

The Tarot was brought into this world and disseminated by adepts who, as time passed, put their own seal on it and partly changed it, being of the opinion that these changes were improvements. In this way different versions emerged such as: the Alchemist Tarot, the Tarot of Marseilles, Wirth's Tarot, Waite's Tarot, Crowley's Tarot, and many others, like the Fat Women Tarot, the Tarot of the Cat People, the 007 Tarot, and so on. We believe that none of these is objective. The table of astrological correlations in Wirth's *Le Tarot des Imagiers du Moyen Age* shows that confusion, especially regarding the order of the Major Arcana in the various Tarots, became very serious in the course of history.

Legendary past

The Tarot and the I Ching are ancient cosmologies that may be linked. Gurdjieff writes in his book *All and Everything: Beelzebub's Tales to his Grandson*, that the Atlanteans compiled their most fundamental 144 laws as engravings on the two well-fitting halves of an ivory globe. One side would have contained the 80 arcana of the Tarot, the other half the 64 hexagrams of the I Ching. Knowing that Atlantis would go under, priest-scientists saved the two half globes. The one with the Tarot laws landed via the Mediterranean in Crete and in Egypt, while the other half globe went via the Atlantic and Indian Oceans to India and China and became the I Ching.

After the end of Atlantis, survivors in Ireland, England, France, and Scandinavia used the 24 fundamental principles in the Tarot when they verbalized the alphabet and time. We find the number 24 in the Futhark, the Nordic runes alphabet, and in megalithic edifices such as Stonehenge. Also, Egyptian hieroglyphic writing distinguishes, apart from the usual pictograms that indicate complete words, an alphabet of 24 symbols that indicate sounds,

5.1a This prehistoric relief, cut in a cave in Capo di Ponte (Italy) may be an attempt to depict the universe.

5.1b The structure of this Buddhist temple in Cambodia represents the World Mountain, the mythical center of the universe.

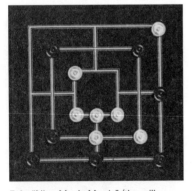

5.1c "Nine Men's Morris" (the mill game) is one of the oldest board games in the world. Artisans scratched it on roof slabs of the Kurna-temple in Egypt. It was also found, carved in stone and bronze, in excavations in Troy, Ireland, England, and Norway. The game is played on the 24 intersecting and corner points.

with which words were formed. This story illustrates the common basis and the resemblance of the Tarot and the I Ching and might indicate that those two systems could be related.

According to James Churchward in his book *The Lost Continent of Mu*, the 24 letters of the Greek alphabet are even older. He states that they are kernel symbols of tribes of the continent Lemuria, flooded 13,000 years ago. These originally Lemurian symbols are the root of the Greek alphabet and the character symbols of the 24 character Cara Maya alphabet.

It is also possible that at different times in different places, through study, the same objective knowledge was acquired in somewhat different forms. Objective truth manifests itself throughout the whole of creation. Humankind carries this objective knowledge within and will, in principle, express it in similar ways (figures 5.1a, 5.1b and 5.1c).

We can only guess at the origins of the Tarot. According to tradition, the beginning of the Tarot was in Egypt. Some symbols in particular arcana are recognizable as ancient Egyptian. The archetypal cycle of life and death that is so clearly reflected in the Tarot was also the cornerstone of the ancient Egyptian and Indian religions and mythologies. The Egyptian Bembine tablet is a pictorial summary of a series of ritual operations and elements that are also found in the Tarot (figure 5.2).

The cradle of western culture is in the Middle East, from Egypt to China and India. Egypt, Sumer, Greece, Palestine, and India especially played major roles. In the old cultures, clerical and scientific activities were not separated. It was in the Greek culture that philosophical and scientific thinking slowly became detached from priestly Knowing-and-Being. This uncoupling remained incomplete, however, which is why we find particular Tarot symbols in some hermetic and alchemist manuscripts.

Priests who passed it on to adepts in initiation rites kept secret the objective-archetypal knowledge structure that is now called the Tarot. In order to prevent improper use, very little of this knowledge was put in writing. For that reason research into the sources of the Tarot is difficult.

The Teraph or Teraphim is another legendary source of the Tarot. Eliphas Levi (pseudonym for Alphonse Louis Constant, 1810–1875), in his book *Le Dogme et Rituel de la Haute Magie*, wrote:

. . . And as the sages would not leave anything to chance, they read the answers of Providence in the oracles of the Tarot, which the Hebrews called the Teraph or Teraphim.

According to Levi, the Teraphim was an alphabet and oracle:

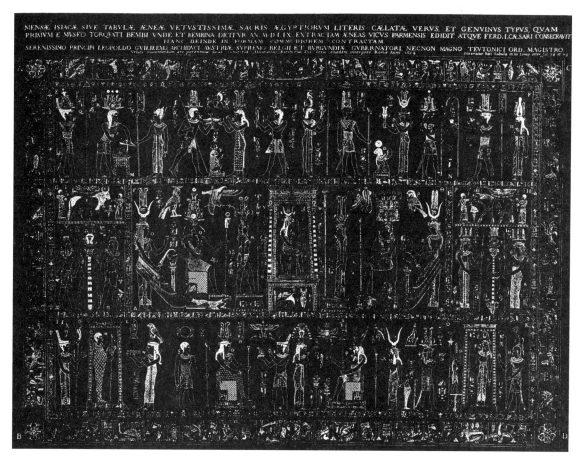

MENSÆ ISIACÆ SIVE TABVLÆ ÆNEÆ VETVSTISSIMÆ SACRIS ÆGYPTIORVM LITERIS CÆLATÆ VERVS ET GENVINVS TYPVS QVAM PRIMVM E MVSEO TORQVATI BEMBI VNDE ET BEMBINA DICITVR AN M D LIX EXTRACTAM ÆNEAS VICVS PARMENSIS EDIDIT ATQVE FERD.I.CÆSARI CONSECRAVIT HANC DEINDE IN FORMAM COMMODIOREM CONTRACTAM SERENISSIMO PRINCIPI LEOPOLDO GVILIELMO ARCHIDVCI AVSTRIÆ SVPERNÆ BELGII ET BVRGVNDIÆ GVBERNATORI NECNON MAGNO TEVTONICI ORD. MAGISTRO

5.2 The Egyptian "Bembine tablet of Isis and Osiris" (depicted in the book *Oedipus Aegyptiacus* [1654] by the Jesuit Athanasius Kircher) is a complete ceremonial cycle. The cycle represented in this tablet is related to the Tarot: for example, in The Magician sacrificing in the upper row on the left, and in the bottom row Death and resurrection portrayed by the divine couple Osiris (Jupiter, Truth) on the left and Isis (Juno, Intuition) at the right.

. . . This admirable book, the inspirer of all sacred books...is the most perfect tool for fortune telling that may be used with complete confidence.

In The Old Testament of the Bible, the Teraphim is mentioned several times as an important and valuable tool for prediction (Hosea 3:4), but also as a detestable oracle (II Kings 23:24 and Ezekiel 21:21).

The Tarot may also have been a book with the laws and wisdom of the Therapeutai, a Jewish sect in the last century B.C. The main objective of the Therapeutai was wisdom and healing. They resemble and may have had contact with the Essenes, an important religious group in Palestine from 2200 B.C. until A.D. 100. The Essenes also focused on study and meditation.

The Tarot is mentioned in an indirect way in the Revelations of St. John, 10:8–11 (The New King James Version, 1982):

Then the voice that I heard from heaven spoke to me again and said, "Go, take the little book, which is open in the hand of the angel who is standing on the sea and on the earth.

So I went to the angel and said to him "Give me the little book."

And he said to me: "Take it and eat it; and it will make your stomach bitter; but it will be as sweet as honey in your mouth."

Then I took the little book out of the angel's hand and ate it, and it was sweet as honey in my mouth. But when I had eaten it, my stomach became bitter.

And he said to me, "You must prophesize again to many people, nations, tongues, and kings."

Here the angel is Raphael, also depicted in the major arcanum Temperance.

James Pryse, in his book, *The Apocalypse Unsealed*, explains that the little book is the Gnosis, which amongst teachings and initiations also contains the Tarot. The revelation of esoteric knowledge is sweet to the mind. However, when the instruction is assimilated by the Self it becomes bitter to our worldly nature, since it means the extirpation of every impure thought and desire, and incessantly urges the initiated to disseminate the esoteric knowledge they have acquired (Gurdjieff and Pryse).

The Tarot in Alexandria

Until about 300 B.C. the cultures in Egypt, Crete, Greece, Sumer, and India developed rather independently, although they traded and warred extensively. Alexander the Great (356–323 B.C.) opened a new phase in the development of mankind. During his rule he conquered Tyros, subdued Egypt, Syria, and powerful Persia, and even entered India. He had in mind the creation of one culture formed from the amalgamation of the Greek, Egyptian, and Asian civilizations. Although after his death his powerful empire soon fell apart into three major states, the opening of new trade routes and the establishment of more than 70 Greek cities in Asia contributed to the emergence of the more homogenous Hellenistic civilization.

Alexandria, the Hellenistic center in Northern Egypt, founded by Alexander the Great, was of enormous importance in the development of the sciences from about 330 B.C. until the Islamic victories around A.D. 700, thus for about a thousand years. After the establishment of Alexandria, its population grew quickly to several hundreds of thousands and consisted of Egyptians, Greeks, Macedonians, Persians, Syrians, Indians, and others.

The Museion, which was the dwelling of the nine muses who looked after the arts, and the adjacent library, the Serapeum, were Alexandria's centers of spiritual life. The library was the greatest of the antique world and comprised 400,000 to 500,000 scrolls. The Ptolemaic rulers, in competition with the library of Pergamon, decreed that every stranger who visited Alexandria had to give to the library a copy of each of the books he possessed. In this way Alexandria became a very important center of cultural exchange.

According to legend, the Tarot was present in the Serapeum, and at that time it seems to have consisted of 80 tablets, each carrying a philosophical picture with a symbolic meaning. Many priest-scientists and visitors from other Mediterranean countries would have viewed the Tarot tablets in the Serapeum. In this way knowledge of the Tarot could commence its journey through the Middle East.

During the wars of Julius Caesar around A.D. 30, a large part of the Serapeum was destroyed by fire. A legend tells that a lunatic who wanted to become immortal through this act set the library on fire. The final blow was dealt by the Islamic forces who conquered Alexandria in A.D. 642. The expression of the caliph of Omar about the Alexandrine library is notorious:

> *"Either the content of the books is contrary to the Koran, in which case they need to be destroyed, or the content is in agreement with the Koran, in which case they are useless and can be destroyed as well."*

Under the direction of Roman Catholic priests, the Spanish occupants of Middle America did the same with almost all the Aztec writings. Hence, up to now we have little insight into the background of the Aztec culture.

Little can be said about the Tarot's tribulations after the destruction of Alexandria. However, by the time of the fire at the Serapeum, the Tarot had already been disseminated via trade contacts and was used by the people as a pictorial-philosophical reference book and oracle.

The Romany tribes traveling from India through Egypt—hence the name Gypsies—kept the Tarot tablets and used them as a philosophical instrument. During the next seven centuries, the tablets wandered throughout Asia as the Tarot of the Gypsies and would surface in Europe through the Crusades.

At this point it is interesting to note that around the sixth or seventh century in India the game of chess came into fashion. Chess is related to the Tarot: in the beginning it seems to have been played by four players at a square chessboard. The positioning of the pieces on the chessboard is reminiscent of the Royal Families in the Tarot. The four main Indian castes are also correlated with the Tarot: the caste of business with Pentacles, the caste of tradesmen and farmers with Wands, the caste of priests with Cups, and the caste of soldiers and rulers with Swords.

The Crusades

The Crusades contributed to the dissemination of information about the Tarot throughout Western Europe. The Crusades resulted from the request for assistance by the Byzantine emperor Alexius to the Roman Catholic Church, in his fight against the invading Turks who had conquered all of Asia Minor and now were at the gates of Constantinople. The first official crusade organized by Pope Urban and the nobility ended in triumph. By the end of 1079, the crusaders took Asia Minor from the Turks. In July 1099, after a bloody five-week siege, the crusaders occupied Jerusalem. On Christmas Day 1100 they founded a new, Latin

5.3a Grand Master of the Templars: Jacques de Molnay.

S	A	T	O	R
A	R	E	P	O
T	E	N	E	T
O	P	E	R	A
R	O	T	A	S

5.3b The words "SATOR" and "ROTAS," carved in the Templars' building at Gisors in France, were very important to them. The words form an anagram and are related to the Tarot invocations (S)ATOR) (Isis, Juno, the "anima Christi") and ROTA (The World, The Wheel of Fortune, the karmic wheel).

When the anagram is interpreted from the bottom word upwards, it reads: "The turning (ROTAS) stage (OPERA) is being held (TENET) with the arrival (AREPO) of the seeding god (SATOR)."

The anagram also contains the words PATER NOSTER. The word TENET forms the cardinal cross with beams of equal length, the symbol of the Templars. The character "T" is present in the middle of each of the four sides of the anagram and at the four ends of the dominant cross.

kingdom. It was called Outremer, had Jerusalem as its center, and was divided into the territories of Edessa, Antiochia, and Tripoli.

Culture transfer from East to West—the Templars

During the period from 1100 to 1250, the Christian bastion Outremer was a center of exchange between eastern and western cultures. A new religious order emerged: the Knights Templar, or Templars, called after the temple of King Solomon in Jerusalem. Nine knights founded the order, among them André van Montbart, Hugo van Payns, and Godfried van Saint-Omaars. The sect was legalized in a special papal council in 1128. The order consisted of knights, chaplains, armed soldiers, and tradesmen.

The Templars were monk-soldiers. Because of their outlandish manners, the Byzantine Christians disliked them. On the other hand, the Templars valued the Arabian culture and assimilated Greek and Arab scientific and philosophic knowledge, esoteric knowledge, and rituals of mystery schools, such as those of the Essenes and the Hermetic congregations in Alexandria. In this knowledge was included the Book of Thoth-Hermes Trismegistus, as well as the Tarot, which at that time combined alchemy, astrology, and hermetic knowledge. Most likely it was the Templars who conveyed the Tarot to Western Europe (figure 5.3a–b).

The Crusaders and the Templars took with them to Western Europe the Asian, Greek, and Arabic cultural treasures they valued. They were successfully introduced into Italy and later, northern parts of Europe, such as France and Germany. The result was a period of enormous cultural growth and change—the Renaissance—meaning *rebirth*. Painting and sculpture techniques transcended the Roman style. The European cathedrals, which were built in the ensuing centuries (of which those in Rheims, Chartres, and the Notre Dame in Paris are the absolute summits), bear objective elements such as the Golden Mean. The Gothic style of building clearly shows Byzantine elements (figure 5.4).

In this way western culture was enriched enormously with Greek, Asian, and Arabic cultural elements such as astrology and astronomy, Arabic mathematics and algebra, the Arabic decimal and the columnar number system, including the positional use of the zero. The natural sciences were gradually liberated from Aristotelian dogmatism, which had controlled scientific thinking for more than a thousand years, and became based on experiment instead of pure, abstract conjecture.

In the meanwhile the Christian dominion Outremer was under continuous pressure from Turkish (Islamic) attacks. In 1187, Saladin, the great leader of the Saracens, recaptured the Crusaders' fortress in Jerusalem. Several other crusades took place but without much success.

The home base of the Templars was France. Around 1070 they

5.3c The Templars' anagram in an idio-syncratic edition by Eliphas Levi, who named this hexagon the *Clés des Grands Mystères (Key to the Great Mysteries)*. The white triangle pointig upward: *Dieu-Père*–Osiris, Jupiter, Yang; and the black triangle pointing downward: *Nature-Mère*–Isis, Juno, Yin, together form the Star of David. The unification of counterparts is expressed by the "Five Names of God" in the square with Truth in the center. *Le ménage cosmique* maintains the rota-tion and consists of the four creatures described in Ezekiel, and which also are the attributes of the four evangelists (see Chapter 2, the Major Arcana The World and The Universe). Remarkably, these four animals also correspond with Hindu and Vedic symbolism.

5.4 The rose window in the cathedral of Rheims is based on the number 12.

conducted an esoteric school in Troyes, capital of Champagne. The order was managed well and grew explosively. In 40 years it founded more than a thousand abbeys, and after 70 years there were more than two thousand. Their wealth was partly the result of importing goods from Asia to Western Europe, but the order also received many donations. These were used for very efficiently exploited land reclamations. In this way the order became incredibly rich, although the Templars' wealth did not filter through to individual monk-soldiers, who abided by their vow of simplicity.

In 1307 the French King Philip IV Le Bel arrested the learned grandmaster Jacques De Molnay, and had the other members of the Order of the Knights Templar, in total about 100,000, murdered. After a seven-year trial, De Molnay was burned to death at the stake together with his faithful follower, Godfrey de Charnay. According to the Inquisition, annihilation of the order was necessary because of the purported worship of heretic idols. For similar reasons, between A.D. 800 and 1300, the Church of Rome conducted a holocaust of about 500,000 Cathari—members of other dualist sects.

To King Philip the vast economic power of the order was much more important. After the destruction of the Templars, their possessions were divided between the Roman Catholic Church and the French Crown. Along with the Templars, the open use of the Tarot also disappeared. However, one group of Templars put the secret teachings of their Order, including the Tarot, into safe-keeping.

The Freemasons

The Freemasons emerged during the period when the Order of the Knights Templar had great cultural and economical influence. It is a spiritual congregation that originated in the twelfth century from the French, English, and German cathedral builders, called masons (stone masons). It was a group of considerable size, which also comprised architects and others in the building trade.

The medieval methods of building were as refined as their resulting edifices. The bricklayers were held in very high regard because of their skills and knowledge, and so could associate freely with each other. They formed groups and societies in which they discussed building problems and techniques. Often, the builders stayed overnight high up in the scaffolding, because that was easier than making the long and dangerous journey down and up again. In this way a closed, productive, spiritual atmosphere developed in which, besides problems of their trade, they discussed philosophical and religious issues.

The Freemasons traveled, because of their standardized building methods, through Western Europe and hence had a cosmopolitan attitude that led to the dissemination of philosophical and scientific ideas. In many churches and cathedrals,

Freemason symbols can still be found (figure 5.5).

5.5 Freemason symbols.

In France, the workshops of the Freemasons were called *loges*, which is the French word for lodge or lodging. At present, the Order of the Freemasons is still divided into lodges. Originally, the Freemasons excluded non-members, not intentionally, but because of their professional terminology, which caused many barriers for laymen, much the way computer jargon does today. Later the Freemasons developed into a philosophical association in which, because of philosophical interests, people with other vocations were also included. In this way the Order of Freemasons was formed.

The Freemasons learned about the original Tarot via the Templars. This Tarot, as indicated, consisted of 24 Major Arcana, 16 Royal Arcana, and 40 Minor Arcana. However, the Freemasons kept this knowledge to themselves. Oswald Wirth in his book *Le Tarot des Imagiers du Moyen Age* (1889) indicates that members of the Freemasons read and used the Tarot.

The historic past of the Tarot

The historic (written) past of the Tarot starts in the second half of the fourteenth century. According to Cavendish, in his book *The Tarot* (1975), it was mentioned first in about 1377 by Brother Johann, a monk from Brefeld in Switzerland. In an article about game cards, he wrote:

> . . . *A particular game, called the card game, has come to us in Anno—Domini 1377. In this game the world's status the way we know it, is described and depicted in an excellent way. But how it was invented, where and by whom, is completely unclear to me* . . .

He continues his description of a card game with 52 or more cards in four card colors.

In 1392 the treasurer of King Charles VI of France noted in his books that he had paid to Jacquemin Gringonneur 56 *Sols de Paris* for three decks of colored game cards for the king. From this Gringonneur deck 17 cards have survived to this day. These cards are not numbered, but for the rest are very much like the Tarot cards we use today, so the Tarot was most likely known by the people before 1392. With Gringonneur the trade of cardmaker, in English *carter* and in French *cartier*, became a reality.

From the fourteenth century onward, many card games existed, all originating from the Tarot. By the end of the fourteenth century, card games were immensely popular, with the result that on January 22, 1397, the *Prevot de Paris* (commissioner of police) issued a decree in which he prohibited working people from playing the card game, tennis, and any other ball games except on holidays. Card games were also regularly prohibited in other countries.

In Germany, during the Synod of Würtzburg in 1329 the Roman Catholic church prohibited certain games, including those with cards.

Although by the fifteenth century activities around the Tarot became quiet as a result of opposition by the Church and various decrees prohibiting its use, the Tarot never disappeared altogether. Card games were not only used for amusement, but from the sixteenth century they were also popular as teaching aids. Tarot games with different numbers of cards and pictures, such as the Visconti deck of 1415, appeared in France and northern Italy.

In the following centuries the Marseilles and Venetian Tarot became the standards. These decks consist of 78 cards, namely 22 trump cards and 56 others, divided into four suits. Each suit had four court cards and ten numbered cards.

5.6 The Royal Arcana of Pentacles (in this case symbolized by disks), and Pentacles Two from the Minor Arcana. In the lemniscate, the name of the Swiss carter Claude Burdel and the year of manufacture.

Ordinary playing cards and the Tarot

Anyone who compares a deck of ordinary playing cards with Tarot cards will conclude that the ordinary cards have been derived from the Tarot. The ordinary cards were, and still are, used for games and gambling, thus for materialistic purposes. The deck of ordinary cards was developed from the Tarot by leaving out the Major Arcana except for The Fool, which became the Joker, and simplifying the remaining cards. Apparently, the derivation of ordinary playing cards from the Tarot took place before 1370.

Various versions of the original Tarot

Since the fifteenth century several versions of the Tarot have survived. These Tarot versions are very important, as they point to a common origin. For example, two versions of the Marseilles Tarot are known. Both versions consist of 22 Major Arcana and two blank cards. The difference is that one version contains the arcana *Juno* and *Jupiter*, and the other instead the arcana *The Female*

Pope (La Papesse) and *The Pope (Le Pape)*.

These two versions have been derived from *one* earlier version that contains the two Major Arcana Juno and Jupiter *as well as* The Pope (The Priest) and The Female Pope (The Priestess). That earlier, original Tarot has been altered: the two arcana Intuition (Juno) and Truth (Jupiter) were veiled and made invisible by super-imposing on them The Female Pope (The Priestess) and The Pope (The Priest). In that way only 22 Major Arcana remained visible. The two blank cards that were added to each deck (and as they remain today) served for initiated people to supplement and complete the set to the original 24 Major Arcana. The two missing Major Arcana were indicated by means of a small – (minus) and + (plus) sign on the blank side.

Intuition (Juno, Yin) and Truth (Jupiter, Yang) have never had a rank number in the Tarot. These two arcana represent the divine polarity principle—the animus and the anima in the macrocosm and the microcosm. In this way they fulfill, in the Tarot as a replica of the universe, the "True Dogma" or "The Key of Two."

The obfuscation of Juno and Jupiter caused other changes, for example, in the order of the other Major Arcana. In some instances, The Female Pope and The Pope were exchanged for Juno and Jupiter. In this way the faulty concept became entrenched that each visible and covered arcanum represented one and the same archetype.

The Tarot underground

The opposition by the Church and the popularity of ordinary playing cards forced Tarot workers to go underground. In the next centuries, until about 1770, intellectual interest in and work with the Tarot was limited to a small initiated group of people. The Tarot remained important in the esoteric life of mystic and secret congregations. The Gypsies also stuck to the Tarot notwith-standing the opposition. The divinatory aspect of the Tarot espe-cially was developed by the Gypsies, who disseminated it through Europe during their wanderings.

From the Middle Ages via the Renaissance to Rationalism

While from 1500 onward the Tarot was used in secret ways, in the western world a process of secularization was simultaneously taking place. It reduced the overbearing power of the Church and started the Reformation, marking the end of the Church's absolute power. Substantial progress was made in the natural sciences and new continents were discovered.

Western culture developed into the Renaissance (1300–1500), the Baroque (1500–1700), and the Classicist period (1750–1850). The attitude towards the dogma of Divine Providence became more liberal, when more and more natural phenomena could be understood through application of the laws discovered by the natural sciences. This development in western thinking led in the

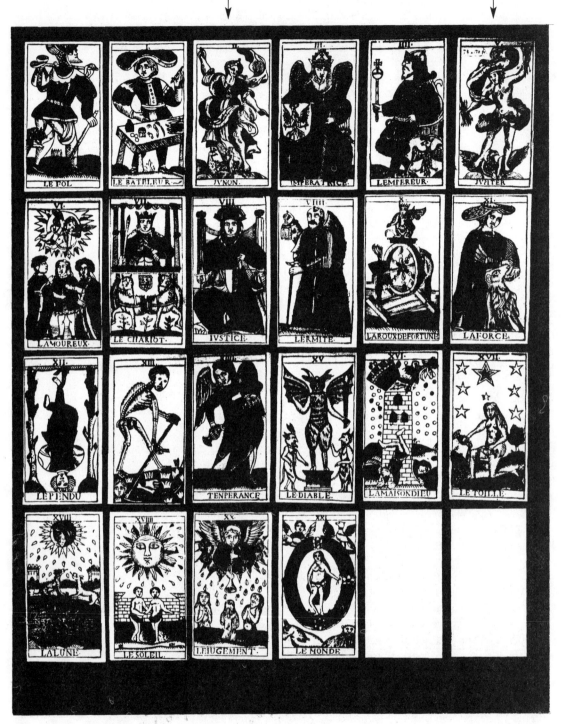

5.7a A version of the Major Arcana of a Marseillan-Swiss Tarot, manufactured in the end of the sixteenth century. Here, Juno and Jupiter have been given the place of The Priestess and The Priest.

THE HISTORY OF THE TAROT

5.7b A version of a Marseillan-Swiss Tarot from the beginning of the seventeenth century, in which The Female Pope and The Pope have taken the place of Juno and Jupiter.

nineteenth century to Rationalism. Figure 5.8 gives an overview of the idealistic developments in the centuries after the Renaissance.

The world of the Middle Ages is directed toward:	Develops via the Renaissance into:	In the seventeenth century, Rationalism is focused on:
THE IDEAL (SPIRIT)	→	REALITY
THE UNIVERSAL	→	THE DISCRETE AND SPECIFIC
SOCIETAL/COMMUNAL	→	THE AUTONOMOUS INDIVIDUAL
NON-REALISTIC ART	→	REALISTIC ART
DOGMATIC SCIENCE	→	EXPERIMENTAL SCIENCE

5.8 Historical development of Rationalism.

The Tarot made public again after centuries

According to Rationalism, everything can be explained in the end through the natural sciences. This trend in thinking led to positivism and lasted till the last quarter of the twentieth century. It has also evoked an emotional reaction that increased the interest in emotional and mystical matters.

Rationalism stimulated renewed interest in ancient Egyptian, Roman, and Jewish cultures. Often, successful extensive excavations, sightseeing trips, and colonization were undertaken. Rationalism's inquisitive propensity helped in the rediscovery of the Tarot. Information about this philosophical system became part of books that described earlier, "primitive" forms of culture and spiritual life.

The work of Count Antoine Court de Gébelin (1773)

Antoine Court de Gébelin, born in 1725 in Nîmes (France) and deceased in 1784 in Paris, studied theology in Lausanne and subsequently became a minister of the Reformed Church. De Gébelin was very interested in old mythologies, occult and secret teachings, and in the languages in which religious teachings were written. He compiled the results of 20 years of extensive research in an enormous work of eight volumes: *Monde Primitif, analysé et comparé avec le monde moderne.* This book, which was very much respected in his time, circulated from 1773 till 1784. In 1776 Court de Gébelin became member of the Freemasons.

In *Monde Primitif,* Volume I, chapter *"Du Jeu des Tarots,"* Court de Gébelin broke the mysterious silence around the Tarot. He tells how, during a visit, he found Duchess "H" and some friends very busy with the game of Tarot:

> . . ."We are playing a game which you surely do not know." "That is possible. What is it?" [asked Court de Gébelin]. "I have seen people play it when I was young, but I do not know anything about it."

After that they showed him the Tarot cards one by one and explained their meanings. Gébelin, knowledgeable because of his research, did not need much time to conclude that the Tarot was of ancient Egyptian heritage. The time was ripe for this thesis, because in the eighteenth century, ancient Egypt, the Rosicrucians, and occultism in general were the center of attention.

Gébelin describes the Tarot in detail. In Volume 9 of *Monde Primitif* he reproduced pictures of the Major Arcana (figure 5.9), and attributed the four "colors" to the four classes in Egyptian society:

The Pentacle	Trades and commerce
The Wand	Farmers, agricultural laborers
The Cup	The clerical class of priests
The Sword	The governors and military nobility

Gébelin also correlated various arcana with Egyptian gods and religious principles. Isis correlated with the Priestess; Osiris with The Chariot; the dogs of death, which guard the Tropics of Capricorn and Cancer with the Moon; and Sirius, the Dog Star, which played a very important role in the ancient Egyptian cosmology, with the Major Arcanum The Star.

According to Gébelin the Tarot is based on the Egyptian classical *Book of Thoth*. The word Tarot itself was a derivation of the Egyptian words "tar," which means "road" and "ro," for "royal." "Taro" would thus have the meaning "royal road" (to knowledge and wisdom).

More recently, some Tarotists have proposed that the word Tarot has been derived from the word "TAO." This word means "The Path," the source, the primordial cause of all things, the physical universe, and the "ten thousand things therein." It was used by the Chinese philosopher Lao Tse to indicate "the right way of living," and "the right way of acting." Qabbalistically-oriented Tarotists correlate the Hebrew character THAU with the Major Arcanum 21 The Universe, as a depiction of perfection in harmonious cooperation between parties (figure 5.10a–b).

At the end of the eighteenth century the French royalty collapsed. Through mismanagement, the economic situation of the country had become critical. As a result, the French Revolution was imminent. Hundreds of thousands would die by the guillotine and the ensuing Napoleonic wars. As humans in times of insecurity have an urgent need for clarity about their situation, the politically insecure climate in France helped in the resurrection of the Tarot.

The contribution of Alliette (Etteila) (1783)

The first to exploit the need for clarity and security in the Tarot at the end of the eighteenth century was Alliette, a wig-maker, "professor of algebra," and a fortune teller and clever opportunist with a great imagination. He published his work under the pseudonym Etteila.

5.9 The Major Arcanum 8 The Hermit (VIII) and the Major Arcanum 13 Death (XIII) in *Monde Primitif* (1787).

5.10a The Major Arcanum 21 The Universe by Jean d'Aigle, with Egyptian, Qabbalistic, astrological, and Biblical symbolisms and correlations.

5.10b Document from *Les XXII Arcanes Symboliques d'Hermes* by Jean d'Aigle, pseudonym for Jean Monchartre (Monti-Trinita, 1921).

In 1783 Etteila's famous work appeared, *Manière de se récréer avec le Jeu de Cartes nommées Tarot*. In this book he fascinated his readers with impressive stories about the source of the Tarot. Etteila designed a deck of Tarot cards, which was adapted to his way of fortune-telling and deviated in a major way from the Tarot of Court de Gébelin. Many Tarot workers are of the opinion that Etteila's cards obscured insight into and understanding of the Tarot. For this reason the Tarot by Etteila has led its own life and claimed little interest. *The Grand Etteila Egyptian Gypsies Tarot Deck*, published by J. M. Simon, contains descriptions in French and English.

The value of Etteila's contributions with regard to the Tarot is not in his symbolism, as this obscures more than it clarifies, but in the increased popularity of philosophical instruments as such, which he realized with his version of the Tarot.

The Tarot by Eliphas Levi (1854)

Eliphas Levi (pseudonym of Alphonse Louis Constant, 1810–1875) contributed substantially to modern occultism through his book *Le Dogme et Ritual de la Haute Magie*, written between 1854 and 1856. This book consists of two parts, each of which is divided into 22 chapters. Each chapter has one arcanum as its theme. In fact, the 22 Major Arcana are each "shelves" through which Levi classifies his secret information. This writing gave the Tarot much depth. Through Eliphas Levi, the Tarot acquired forever an important place in occultism (figure 5.11a).

Eliphas Levi called an arcanum a *key*, by which he meant a key to insight. The word key evokes strong associations with a door that can be opened. From a Tarot point of view this is not entirely correct. An arcanum is *not only* a stage or phase through which one passes, but also the reflection of a synchronistic moment. It is as well a structured conceptual tool that, as a philosophical instrument, can clarify indistinct situations and in this way give an insight into future possibilities.

Because of the above-mentioned presupposition, Levi could not use the Tarot as a philosophical instrument. Therefore, it is no wonder that Levi did not write a manual about the Tarot and got stuck in the occult. However, Levi did intuitively use the archetypal structure of the Tarot to categorize secret teachings and rituals.

Contrary to Court de Gébelin and Etteila, who sought the origins of the Tarot in Egypt, Levi proposed *that the Tarot was a sacred and secret alphabet,* which was given to the Hebrews by Enoch, Cain's eldest son. In his book *Le Dogme et Rituel de la Haute Magie,* Levi systematically described the 22 Major Arcana and correlated them to the 22 letters of the Hebrew alphabet. He also related the Major Arcana with its 22 paths to the Qabbalistic Tree of Life, and was the first to correlate the first four letters of the word TARO with the *Causa Poenae* INRI (figure 5.11b).

Later Tarotists did not deny the link between the Tarot, the Hebrew alphabet, and the Qabbala proposed by Levi. Because of the present day complexities and inaccessibility of Hebrew mysticism, and the superimposition of the Hebrew alphabet onto the already obfuscated order of the Major Arcana, the link between the Qabbala and the Tarot has not yet proved to be of much use for daily Tarot work. Gérard Encausse (Ephesus) continued Levi's Qabbalistic line in the Tarot, which was later abandoned by Edward Arthur Waite.

Levi died in 1875. At that time there was much interest in the Tarot. In the next years, especially in 1888 and 1889, several versions of the Tarot were published. In 1888, Ely Star, pseudonym of Eugène Jacob, a quack, reproduced the Tarot by Court de Gébelin in *Les Mystères de l'Horoscope*. He determined the correlations between the Major Arcana and the zodiacal signs and planets.

5.11a The Chariot by Eliphas Levi. He called the cards keys to insight. Levi related the Tarot to various secret teachings and the Qabbala.

Samuel Liddell MacGregor Mathers and the Order of the Golden Dawn (1888)

In England interest in the Tarot also grew gradually. Kenneth R. H. Mackenzie, a member of the Rosicrucian Society in Anglia (a subsection of the Freemasons) and author of *The Royal Masonic Cyclopedia* (1877), was very impressed by Levi's work and visited the master in Paris in 1861. In the book *Eliphas Levi and the French Occult Revival*, Christopher McIntosh reports that when Mackenzie visited Levi in 1872, Levi showed him a series of 22 Tarot drawings he had prepared himself. It seems that Mackenzie planned to write a book about the Tarot and possibly started, but certainly did not finish it. In those times in occult circles in England, the Tarot was the center of attention.

Samuel Liddell Mathers continued in England the interest in the Tarot that Mackenzie had initiated. A domineering person, he married Moina Bergson, sister of the French philosopher Henri Bergson, who was a member of the Rosicrucian Society, and played an important role in the founding of the London Hermetic Order of the Golden Dawn.

Under the leadership of Mathers the order reached the pinnacle of its prosperity at the end of the nineteenth century. The order had many prominent members, such as the writers Arthur E. Waite; William Butler Yeats; Alistair Crowley, designer of his own Tarot; Arthur Machen, author of thrillers; and Anni Horniman, founder of the Abbey Theatre in Dublin (figure 5.12).

5.11b The four letters of the word TARO written as a monogram and correlated with the four letters of the word INRI, the way this was embroidered on the Templars' banner.

The Tarot had an important place in the teachings of the Order of the Golden Dawn. Mathers and Yeats experimented with mental pictures and visions, which they "transmitted" to others. They recognized the inherent strength of the visual archetypes in the Tarot and were convinced that these could influence the thoughts of a person without that person's being aware of it.

In 1888 Mathers published the book *The Tarot: Its Occult Signification, Use in Fortune-telling, and Method of Play*. In this book

5.12 Initiated members of the Golden Dawn carried on their breast the sign of the Rosicrucians, based on the legend of this secret fraternity, founded in the fifteenth century by Christian Rosycross.

5.13 The Priestess in the Tarot by Wirth. On the book in her lap is the Yin-Yang symbol. In this way Wirth related a very important element in Asian philosophy to the Tarot.

he also describes various anagrams, permutations of the word TARO:

TAOR   Egyptian goddess of the dark. Der Tor–German for *The Fool.*

TOAR   Law, teaching scroll, in Hebrew: Torah: *The Priestess.*

TROA   Throne, thronos (Greek), royal rule, *The Emperor.*

ATOR   Egyptian goddess Hathor of happiness, love, and initiation, *Intuition, Juno.*

ROTA   Wheel—in Latin, *The World.*

RATO   With measure and consideration—Latin, *Temperance.*

ORAT   He speaks—in Latin, *Truth, Jupiter.*

Mathers' anagrams are seven out of a part of a group of 24 possibilities. The four letters in the word "T-A-R-O" can be placed in 4 x 3 x 2 x 1 = 24 different orders. Each of these anagrams is correlated with a major arcanum and is called an "invocation." In Chapter 7 we will discuss the 24 Tarot anagrams extensively.

The Tarot by Oswald Wirth (1889)

On Europe's mainland, work on the Tarot continued. Wirth and Papus especially contributed substantially to the Tarot. Oswald Wirth was a Swiss Freemason, member of the French branch of the Theosophical Society (founded by Madame Blavatsky in New York in 1875), and disciple of the French magician Marquis Stanislas de Guaita. In 1889 Wirth published a hundred sets of 22 hand-painted Tarot cards under the title: *Le Livre de Thoth. Les 22 arcanes du Tarot dessinés à l'usage des initiés sur les indications de Stanislas de Guaita.* Oswald Wirth had a major influence on many contemporary occultists. Wirth's Tarot cards (figure 5.13) are serene and beautiful, and used by many—next to the older Marseilles Tarot and the more recent Tarot by Waite.

Wirth compiled his knowledge and discussions about the Tarot and the 22 Major Arcana plus the two blank cards in his book *Le Tarot des Imagiers du Moyen Age,* which he dedicated to the Marquis de Guaita. In this book, Wirth gives a very readable, matter-of-fact, and extensive overview of the 22 Major Arcana and the many symbolic aspects of the Tarot without lapsing into occultism or grandiloquence.

It is noteworthy that Wirth was the first to mention a relationship between the Tarot and the I Ching and also to suggest correlating these two philosophical systems with each other. In the margin of his book he gives pictures of Jupiter (Truth) and Juno (Intuition).

The contributions of Dr. Papus (Gérard d'Encausse) to the Tarot (1888)

Gérard d'Encausse (1865–1916) was a beloved French doctor with extensive academic training (figure 5.14). He was gifted with psychic powers and extraordinary diagnostic skills. Along with Mesmer, he was very interested in hypnosis, magnetism, and related techniques. He ascribed all healing to *"the force of Christ."* He was a member of the Qabbalistic Order of the Rose Cross, which the Marquis de Guaita had founded and of which Oswald Wirth was also a member. D'Encausse himself took over the leadership of the secret order, which called its members "Martinists."

M. Le D'Encausse (Papus)

5.14 Gérard d'Encausse (Dr. Papus), author of several occult treatises, among them, *Le Tarot Divinatoire* (1909).

Using the pseudonym "Dr. Papus," he was able to popularize occultism, having an overview of this field. In the beginning of the twentieth century, he traveled through Russia and became friends with Czar Nicholas II. He served in the French army during the First World War and died in 1916, having predicted his own death up to the day and hour. When the coffin with the remains of Dr. Papus stood in front of the altar in the Cathedral of Notre Dame in Paris, "coincidentally" an eroded finger of an angel sculpture high up in the church broke off and fell on the lid of the coffin during a silence in the mass. The hundreds of people gathered saw this as a sign from God.

D'Encausse said: *"Materialism has given us everything we can expect from it."* For him this was a rationale to look back to the ancient world for the foundation of a synthesis of all knowledge gained, expressed in a few fundamental laws. Number mysticism plays an important role in his occult philosophy. In 1888 he published his *Traité Elémentaire de la Science Occulte*. This compilation covered the Tarot as well. In the same year Papus included Wirth's Tarot cards in his manual about the Tarot: *Le Tarot des Bohémiens* (1989). In this book he also elaborated on the links between the Tarot, the Qabbala, and the Hebrew alphabet. In addition to these works, Papus also wrote *Traité Méthodique de la Science Occulte* (1891) and *Le Tarot Divinatoire* (1909).

The Tarot by Sir Arthur Edward Waite (1910)

Arthur Edward Waite (1857–1940) was initially interested in spiritism and theosophy. In 1891 he joined the Order of the Golden Dawn, in which he played an important role.

With Levi and Mackenzie as its major leaders, the order had its origins in the Rosicrucian Society, who had passed on their teachings verbally from generation to generation. In 1903 when Waite became the leader of the temple of the Golden Dawn in London, he reformed the order's rituals in a Christian sense. However, he drew little attention and closed his chapter of the Golden Dawn in 1914. Waite died in London during the "Blitzkrieg" of World War II in 1940.

5.15 Arthur Edward Waite, designer of the most used Tarot deck in the world.

Waite was extremely interested in occultism. He studied closely the Qabbala, alchemy, the Rosicrucians, the Freemasons, and the

Grail legends in order to discover secret traditions. In his book about the Grail—the legendary bowl or cup that the knights of the Round Table of King Arthur tried to locate—he proposed that the four sacred objects in those legends (the bowl, the lance, the cup, and the sword) carry back to the four "colors" in the Tarot: Pentacles, Wands, Cups, and Swords.

Based on his very thorough occult knowledge and the Anglo-Saxon Tarot tradition, he designed a new deck of Tarot cards. They were painted under his guidance by his friend Pamela Coleman-Smith, also a member of the Golden Dawn.

5.16 The Lovers and The Devil, by Waite. Notice the matches in symbolism. In the life cycle these two cards form the Principal Arcanum "I COMMIT."

In his book *The Pictorial Key to the Tarot*, which was published in 1910, he describes and discusses his new Tarot designs. The book settles in a very assertive way all sorts of occult intrusions and vagueness in the Tarot and gives an extensive bibliography.

The Tarot by Waite startled many people, and in the beginning encountered much resistance, because not only each Major and Royal Arcanum, but now also each Minor Arcanum, was clarified by means of a symbolic picture. In the ensuing decades Waite's Tarot—the Rider Tarot—turned out to be very important. Although a great number of other versions of the Tarot have been designed since then, of which many have been compiled by Stuart Kaplan in *The Encyclopedia of Tarot*, the Tarot by Waite is still the standard and the most popular modern Tarot deck. In *A New Model of the Universe*, Ouspensky describes in short poetic sketches the Major Arcana of this Tarot and mentions its use for meditative purposes.

Waite's work was, and still is very important. He rectified the archetypal symbolism in the Tarot and detached the Tarot from the Qabbala, with the result that in the twentieth century the Tarot became much more accessible. Given the fact that Waite's cards are exceedingly helpful in representing the life cycle according to the restored order, Waite must have known that the two blank cards had a meaning and, with a picture, could have added them to the Major Arcana, and adjusted the numbering. The reason why he did not disclose these discoveries is not clear. It is likely that Waite was very aware that the spirit of the times did not allow the publication of secret teachings. In those times a philosophical researcher was very dependent on access to various, often closed and secret, mystical societies. Premature publication of this information would certainly have cut him off from, or put him into conflict with, these movements. On this subject, more can be found in the books written by Ravenscroft, *The Lance of Destiny* and *The Mark of the Beast*. Umberto Eco writes about the same issue in *Foucault's Pendulum*.

The Tarot by Aleister Crowley (1875–1947)

One of the last influential Tarot workers was Aleister Crowley (1875–1947). Born in the same year as the psychologist Carl Jung, he was raised in the spirit of the Brothers of Plymouth, which instilled in him a lifelong hatred of Christianity. Crowley was rebellious, full of energy, a mountain climber, womanizer, and member of many secret societies. After a mental crisis he joined the Order of the Golden Dawn in 1898, where he began as a devoted pupil of Mathers. Soon, severe differences of opinion developed, with the result that Crowley was asked to leave the order. Next, he founded the Order of Thelema, and delved into sexual magic.

In the Age of Aries (2000 B.C.E.–A.D. 0) as well as the Age of Pisces (A.D. 0–2000), objective knowledge was the domain of priests. Crowley was convinced that he was the Great Devilish Being 666 mentioned in the Book of Revelations, with the mission to destroy Christianity and replace it with Crowleyanity.

Crowley also claimed that he was an incarnation of Eliphas Levi. He wrote his own guide of 300 pages about the Tarot, *The Book of Thoth: a Short Essay on the Tarot of the Egyptians*, which was published in 1944 in a limited edition of 200 copies. In this book Crowley condemned the Tarots of others as senseless and pitifully grotesque. He produced his own designs, which were painted under the influence of drugs by his friend Frieda Harris (1877–1962). As veneration to Crowley she had the number 666 tattooed on her breast. The end of Crowley's life was very lonely—none of his friends could cope with his grandiose ideas. In 1947 he died, alone, in a pension in London.

Archetypes have a profound spiritual impact, which can be so powerful that we cannot detach ourselves from them. The first impression of Crowley's Tarot is one of richness of color and beauty. However, it does not have the substance necessary to convey objective and liberating information to the Tarot reader. The superfluous use of archetypes in Crowley's Tarot emphasizes this aspect. His Tarot is useless for meditative and divinatory purposes, since the channels that are opened when meditating on his arcana focus mainly on power, sexuality, and brutal archetypes with a hodgepodge of confusing occult information. Thus, the Crowleyanic associations dominate the original, simple, liberating esoteric content of the Tarot arcana. In addition, the names Crowley gave to the Major Arcana cause bewilderment, especially to the developing Tarot student, and give false information about their meanings. For example, Arcanum 11, Strength, is called "Lust" by Crowley, and depicts a naked, sensual woman riding on the back of "The Beast"—this has nothing to do with the real meaning of this arcanum.

Crowley did however make an important contribution to the restoration of the Tarot. In his opinion *two cards had to be added to the Tarot, which he did.* It is likely that Crowley acquired the information about the existence of the two veiled Major Arcana when he was still with the Golden Dawn. He designed the two Major Arcana and called them *Magi,* as amplifications of the Major Arcanum The Magician. However, Crowley was not able to give them the right position in the Tarot. He did not dare to publish them officially—likely for the same reasons that Waite did not do so. In 1972, the two unveiled arcana were shown as drafts in an article in the journal *Man, Myth and Magic.* Fourteen years later the publisher A. G. Muller/C. H. Neuhausen added to the Crowley Thoth Tarot Deck the two extra Major Arcana and in this way expanded the number of Major Arcana in the Crowley deck to 24.

Robert Graves and the Tarot (1895–1985)
An interesting contribution to the Tarot was made by Robert Graves (born July 1895 in London, died December, 1985, Majorca). Graves is best known for his book *I Claudius.* Of the other books from his hand *The White Goddess: A Historical Grammar of Poetic Myth* is famous as well. In this magnificent book, a poet's quest for the meaning of European myths, he describes ancient legends and shows how matriarchal poetry and religions were superseded by patriarchal systems. He discusses the wanderings of the Celts and reveals their tree alphabets.

In the first edition of *The White Goddess* (1948) he indicated at the end of chapter 15 how the tree alphabet could be correlated with the Tarot, but did not pursue this matter.

The period after Waite: growing interest
The efforts of many Tarot workers during the last centuries culminated in Waite's contribution to the Tarot. He liberated the Tarot from the shackles of occultism for good, and consolidated the Tarot's symbolism and knowledge.

After Waite, many others designed Tarot decks. Kaplan in his book *The Encyclopedia of Tarot,* gives a detailed overview of the

5.17 Two Tarot cards from a deck created by Aleister Crowley in collaboration with Lady Frieda Harris. Jupiter is above and Juno below. These were used as test designs in *Man, Myth and Magic*. The monkey at the feet of both symbolizes Thoth, the Egyptian god of wisdom.

many Tarots that are in existence. The new Tarots are all variations on the same theme but do not add anything to the symbolism and structure of the Tarot. Thus, after Waite, the content of the Tarot remained basically the same. In the meanwhile, interest in the spiritual and practical value of the Tarot grew among psychologists. Psychology had developed as an independent science from the second half of the nineteenth century, more or less simultaneously with the development of the Tarot. Carl Jung, especially, developed the concepts of the collective unconscious, archetypes, and synchronicity, concepts that are important for a better psychological insight into the way the Tarot works.

In the 1960s and 1970s, curiosity about esoteric matters grew explosively. Since then there has been increasing interest in various oracles, such as the I Ching, astrology, runes, palmistry, and the Tarot.

Jo Onvlee, Tarotist, Tai Chi master, and I Ching expert from Amsterdam, must be mentioned as a typical exponent of those times. He studied various forms of occultism, made them more accessible and disseminated them. It was this researcher of occult knowledge who in modern times was given the idea that the two blank arcana in the Tarot should bear a picture. At the same time, one of the authors of this book, Onno Docters van Leeuwen, created a series of sculptures, which represented the 22 Major Arcana. Jo Onvlee indicated that to the 22 known Major Arcana two more were to be added. In the ensuing research, valid information was gradually gleaned about the nature of these two arcana. Various Tarots were compared (see Figures 1.12 and 5.7a–b). The 24 Major Arcana were exhibited in the restored order for the first time, in polychrome ceramic, in 1975 in the Kosmos Center for Meditation in Amsterdam (figure 5.18).

After an article in 1976 by Alexandra Gabrielli in the Dutch socio-philosophical magazine *Bres*, Stuart Kaplan included the *Ceramic Tarot* as the *Docters van Leeuwen Porcelain Tarot* in *The Encyclopedia of Tarot*. In the years that followed, the two authors of this book gathered and scrutinized evidence about the original Tarot. They made their findings and new knowledge public in the book and the rectified deck of 80 Tarot cards *De Tarot in de Herstelde Orde (The Tarot in the Restored Order),* which originally saw the light in Dutch in 1995.

Objective knowledge, forces, and creations

At the end of this overview of the history of the Tarot, we want to emphasize that the Tarot has been known to humankind, and has prevailed as a psychological and philosophical tool for millennia. Few other bodies of knowledge have been in use for such a long time. The Tarot generates resonance in deep layers of the soul and gives insight into our personal situations. This is possible because the Tarot is *objective knowledge*, and summons fundamental processes in the same way that objective music—for example, by Bach, Mozart, and Beethoven—heals people and changes everyone's mood in a very similar way. Objective architecture exists as well: objective buildings such as megaliths like Stonehenge, the Great Pyramids, and particular temples and cathedrals call up the same deep emotions and tap inner powers in everyone. The information in the Tarot consists of objective archetypes or primordial human imaginings, brought together in a polar, hierarchical, mathematical, and hermetic structure. When contemplating a Tarot card, these objective archetypes communicate directly with our inner being.

Objective knowledge is the result of being one with Truth, and is independent of time and person. Its essence does not change with time; it is real and, once mastered by us, is forever our cultural heritage. In past millennia objective knowledge was guarded by closed "schools," such as the Essenes, Catharis, Dervishes, Templars, Freemasons, Rosicrucians and the Work (Gurdjieff). They determined when people were mature, pure, and intelligent enough to be initiated into the secret sciences. This is how the Freemasons, Rosicrucians, and the Work kept secret the knowledge of the two hidden Major Arcana, Juno and Jupiter. This information was largely held in the inner circles of the societies, which thought these pearls of wisdom had to be reserved for the appreciative, initiated few who could "carry it in their crown," instead of "feeding it to the swine." Within these esoteric groups the words of the *Kybalion* have always been honored:

When the footsteps of the Master are heard,
The ears of those open who are ready for his teachings.

Objective knowledge—Truth—is very difficult to accept. Only when they exert themselves to the utmost can truly Truth-loving human beings bear it and accept it. This is why objective creations have so much force. Untrue persons will move away or even react aggressively by attacking a piece of objective art that reveals the truth to them. This happened to Michelangelo's sculpture *The Pieta* (1499), for example, and Rembrandt's painting *The Nightwatch* (1664).

For the same reason, objective creations are eagerly used for commercial purposes. Examples are (1) specific music with objective qualities (Gregorian chants, Pachelbel, Bach, Mozart) in the background of radio and TV advertisements, (2) rock arrangements of classical compositions, (3) commercial use of esoteric knowledge in "New Age" religions and publications. This type of commercialization may substantially obstruct the novice in his or her search for Truth. It is very important to offer objective knowledge in as pure a form as possible.

Fortunately, objective knowledge protects itself and, in essence, cannot be adulterated. Objective laws radiate their light so strongly and so directly that only a truth-loving person can accept and embrace them.

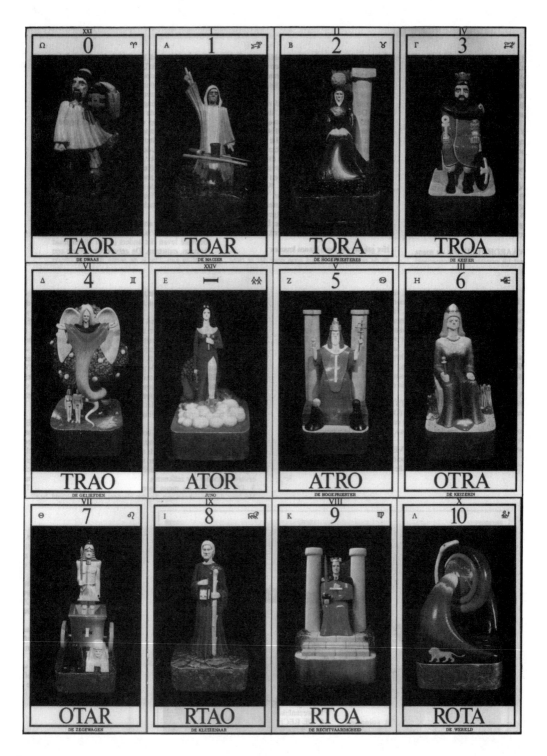

5.18 The porcelain "24 Major Arcana of the Tarot." At the top of each arcanum the Roman numerals indicate the Rider-Waite Order. The Arabic numbers indicate the order that resulted from the re-introduction of the two hidden Major Arcana. The Greek alphabet and the symbols of the zodiac correlate with the restored order, the permutation of the word TARO, and the name of each Major Arcanum. The Tarot in bone china sculpted by Onno Docters van Leeuwen is the property of the city of Amsterdam. It is given in loan to the A.M.C. Collection of the Academic Medical Center, where it is on permanent display.

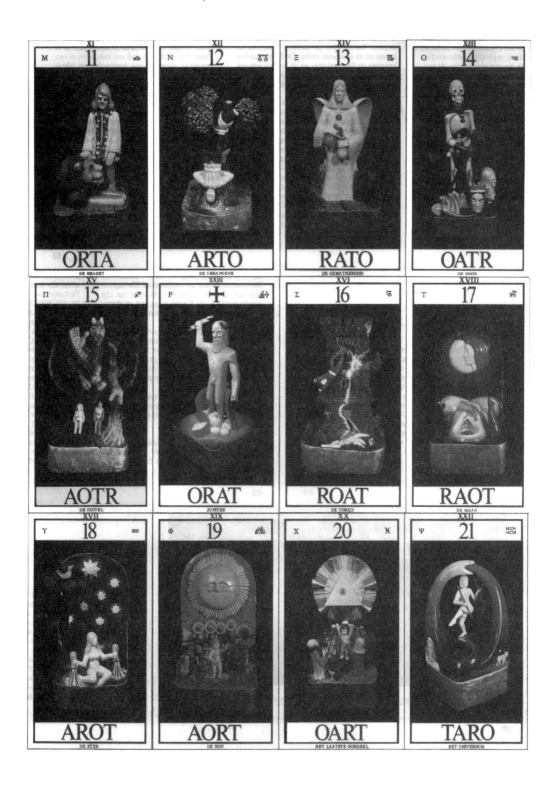

The porcelain 24 Major Arcana of the Tarot

The "New Age"

The history of the Tarot shows us that the accessibility of previously occult and esoteric knowledge has increased explosively. The end of the twentieth century marks the end of the Piscean Age and the beginning of the Aquarian Age. In the new age humankind is being given a new chance to acknowledge Truth, and—based on this acknowledgement—behave lovingly, with virtue, conscientiously, and in contact with the divine.

The sign of Aquarius stands for cooperation in freedom, equality, and fraternity. Aquarius harbors new ideas, artistic opinions, inventions, and humane philosophies. Under the banner of all-inspiring Truth as the life-giving cause of things, in the Age of Aquarius we will actively search for our souls and the essence of all that is, and pour this essence, this water of life, from our vessel over the earth.

As we cannot complete this task in cooperation with others if everyone does not have the same knowledge, we more and more enrich ourselves via information retrieval, processing, and exchange. The turbulent development and application of information broadcasting and processing, through radio, films, television, VCRs, computers, interactive multimedia, as well as information relay systems such as fax machines, mobile phones, satellites, and the Internet, has directly to do with the onset of the new age. The development and use of information processors will continue to grow.

We will also see more associations, encounter groups, transformative training, alternative healing techniques, and publications regarding alternative visions on spiritual and psychological matters. For example, *The Celestine Prophecy* and *The Tenth Insight*, both by James Redfield and published in the first half of the 1990s, point out new, holistic insights into humankind in this world and the spiritual forces and energies that are surrounding us.

Keeping in mind that real and true initiation always liberates, and hence is freeing, separates the wheat from the chaff. Many new age groups ask outrageous amounts of money—far more than a simple reimbursement of costs—for "chaff." These are modern forms of trade in indulgences: they do not liberate us, but instead, put us in a bind.

Nonetheless, objective knowledge, for ages kept secret, is now becoming available to everyone. For example, a new generation of scientists copied and disseminated the Qumran-scrolls from the Dead Sea freely around the world in order to break the secrecy around them and to make their translation, study, and interpretation possible for everyone. Because of this, we understand better how over the centuries the old heritage became integrated into the Tarot. In this new age many possibilities for individual development and the unfurling of the full scope of our talents will become reality.

Once again, we are learning about our own divine descent. Those who are able to accept this will become their own priests and priestesses. The objective knowledge comprised by the Tarot may assist those who embark on that path, provided it is represented well and used for proper purposes.

The Tarot Obscured, Restored, and Completed

Because nothing is hidden that will not be made public
And nothing is covered that will not be revealed.
—*Gospel by Thomas, Logion 6*

This nineteenth century deck of Tarot cards by Grimaud reveals the hidden Major Arcana Juno and Jupiter. Juno traditionally wears a diadem with one pearl, symbolizing the inner truth (Sophia). Jupiter brandishes lightning rays to illuminate and purify dark situations. The numbers assigned to these Major Arcana (2 and 5) are from the obscured Marseillan order.

CHAPTER 6

The Tarot Obscured, Restored, and Completed

Reincarnation

Over time, the Tarot has been changed, chiefly when it was introduced into Western Europe after the Crusades. Christian theology and its perspective on life after death have played a central role in the changes.

A major wisdom of the Tarot reveals the cyclic process of emergence, blooming, decline, death, regeneration, and reincarnation. Throughout the world the belief in life after death is commonplace. It existed in ancient Egypt, where the body was embalmed. It was also commonplace to give various gifts to the deceased. *The Egyptian Book of the Dead* (figure 6.1), *The Tibetan Book of the Dead (Bardo Thödol)*, and the Tarot are evidence of the conviction of countless generations that the soul lives on after physical death.

6.1 A page from the *Egyptian Book of the Dead*. Life after death was a cornerstone of ancient Egyptian religion and philosophy.

The *Bardo Thödol, The Great Liberation Through Hearing*, is an ancient Tibetan teaching which is read aloud to a person who is dying or has just died, in order to assist the soul through the transitions ahead (*bardo* = gap or transition). One of the main verses of the Six Bardos reads:

Now, when the bardo of the moment before death dawns upon me,
I will abandon all grasping, yearning, and attachment,
enter undistracted into clear awareness of the teaching,
and eject my consciousness into the space of unborn mind;
as I leave this compound body of flesh and blood
I will know it to be a transitory illusion.

The *Bardo Thödol* is announced with the appearance of the White Light (equivalent to the Tarot Major Arcanum Temperance):

> *O son of noble family (name), now the time has come for you to seek a path.*
> *As soon as your breath stops, what is called the basic luminosity of the first Bardo, which your guru has already shown you, will appear to you.*
> *This is the dharmata, open and empty like space, luminous void, pure naked mind without center or circumference. Recognize them, and rest in that state, and I too will show you at the same time.*

The *Bardo Thödol* is very rich in wisdom and worth reading. Unfortunately, the framework of this book does not allow a complete analysis. At some point, the soul has to let go of material possessions; in the Tarot this archetypal situation is depicted in The Tower:

> *If you are attached to the possessions you have left behind, or if you feel attached to them through knowing that someone else is owning and enjoying your things, you will get angry with the people you have left behind, and that will certainly cause you to be born as a hell-being or a hungry ghost, even if you were going to reach a higher state. In any case, you cannot get them; it is no use to you, so give up attachment and yearning for your possessions; abandon them, make a firm decision.*
> *Whoever is enjoying your things, do not be possessive but let them go. With one-pointed concentration think that you are offering them to your guru and the Three Jewels, and remain in a state without desires.*

The *Bardo Thödol* describes the transition from arcanum The Moon to arcanum The Star as follows:

> *O son of noble family (name), if you have not understood what has gone before, from now on the body you had in your past life will grow fainter and your future body will become clearer, so you will feel sad and think, "I am suffering like this, so now I shall look for whatever kind of body appears," and you will move about, backwards and forwards, towards anything that appears.*
> *The six lights of the six realms will shine, and the one in which you are going to be born because of your karma will shine most brightly.*

At the end of the *Bardo Thödol* the soul enters the womb; in the Tarot this correlates with the Major Arcanum The Sun:

> *Again, it is very important to concentrate like this: "I will be born as a universal emperor for the good of all sentient beings, or as a brahmana like a great sala tree, or as the son of a siddha,*

THE TAROT OBSCURED, RESTORED, AND COMPLETED

Or in a family of a pure lineage of dharma;

Or in a family where the father and mother have faith; and taking a body with merits which can benefit all sentient beings, I will do good."

Concentrating on this thought, the womb should be entered. At this time you should bless the womb you are entering as a palace of the gods, and supplicate the buddhas and bodhissattvas of the ten directions and the yidams, especially the Lord of Great Compassion, and enter the womb with the longing of a request for transmission.

Life after and before death

Especially in the non-western world, the belief in the cyclic process of life and death is widespread. In prehistoric Western Europe and pre-Columbian America burial goods and mummification indicate a general belief in the life cycle of death and reincarnation.

Most westerners have a different attitude toward death and dying. They do not talk much about death. The Christian Church does not accept the concept of reincarnation; it does endorse an after-life though. Western ethics are geared toward work, (unnecessary) suffering, and survival. Many people are afraid to die. The suppression of thinking about dying as an integrated part of life has contributed to the obfuscation of the Tarot.

Near-death experiences

Progress in the medical sciences has improved the quality of life for countless people and has postponed death for many. Therefore, especially in the western world, people live longer. Also, in clinical situations people who have just died sometimes can be brought back to life and give us a glimpse of life after death.

Although our knowledge about life after death and before birth is very limited, people who have been at the boundary between life and death have reported that after death the human soul goes through a number of stages. A near-death experience seems to be a wonderful learning experience. Reports about entering into a bright light are common (figure 6.2). People who have come back have inwardly changed substantially, are not afraid of death any longer, and consider it simply a transfer to another level of reality. For them, loving and helping their fellow men has become one of the most important goals in life.

Resurrection versus reincarnation

The censure of the Tarot by Church authorities is due to its incompatibility with some aspects of Christian dogma. A first important point is life after death. The Tarot life cycle articulates this concept in the night-arcana:

THE HANGED MAN → TEMPERANCE → DEATH → THE DEVIL → TRUTH → THE TOWER → THE MOON → THE STAR → THE SUN → THE LAST JUDGMENT → THE UNIVERSE

Christian dogma states that we all will resurrect on Judgment Day, and at that time will be judged by God for our acts and achievements on earth. Christianity in general (according to official Roman Catholic doctrine) disputes the principle of reincarnation of the soul in a new body, and thus of the cyclic process of life and death.

From about A.D. 400 to 700 the Roman Catholic Church established its dogmas and the official contents of the Bible in several councils. Earlier, belief in reincarnation was widespread in Western Europe. A core Christian dogma is that a man in his lifetime has to try to actualize Christ in his soul. According to this doctrine we have to achieve that goal in *this* life; it is irrelevant whether or not reincarnation occurs afterward.

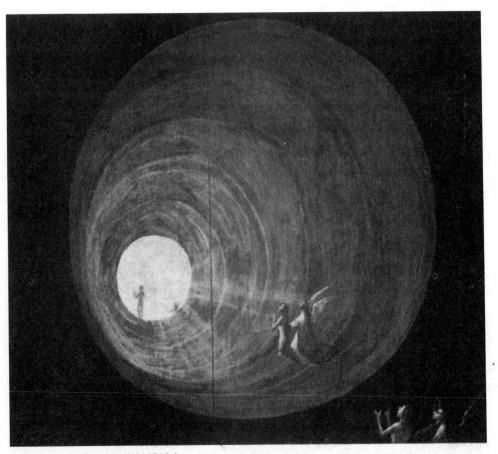

6.2 Hieronymus Bosch, 1450–1516. In the process of dying, angels guide the soul of the deceased through a tunnel to a clear, loving, and understanding Light. For the soul the perception of time, hence, insight into life, changes.

The clergy was of the opinion that reincarnation was a useless and distracting concept. For this reason they decided to keep knowledge about the concept of reincarnation away from ordinary people. In this way, Christianity came to emphasize God's judgment of the deceased and the subsequent sojourn in purgatory until the resurrection from death on Judgment Day.

THE TAROT OBSCURED, RESTORED, AND COMPLETED

Christianity redirected the faith in reincarnation to belief in resurrection. The principle of reincarnation in the Tarot conflicts not only with the dogma of resurrection, but also with the Christian ethos that outlines our tasks in life as singular, to be completed diligently here and now. These incompatibilities were important factors in the decision to ban the Tarot as a philosophical system. Yet, many well-documented near-death experiences reported over the last decades have contributed to a revival of the belief in reincarnation.

Divine providence versus free will

Another reason for the Church's ousting of the Tarot is the incompatibility of the philosophically independent Tarot with the Christian dogma of divine providence. This dogma, which evolved from the personification of God, states that He guides His creation by His divine government. He works in His transcendent and unknowable way. We do not know, cannot know, and are not allowed to know what plans He has for us. Everything that happens is part of His divine plan, which He only can alter. We are incapable of knowing, understanding, or changing it: we have to take life as it comes.

This doctrine, among fundamentalist and/or extreme groups, may lead, for example, to refusing vaccination against illnesses. Such groups may consider this an improper act against God's plan. This attitude has caused, and still causes, much suffering.

The Tarot as philosophical mediator opens the inner eye for the present and the future through the application of the synchronicity principle. This states that things happen along parallel lines. Insight into and knowledge of one set of events gives indications about what is going to happen in another more or less parallel series. The potential for insight into and preparation for future situations in life places the Tarot as a philosophical instrument in direct conflict with the dogma of Christian providence.

The power of the Church of Rome

Banishment of the Tarot was also driven by the doctrine that states that only the servants of God—more precisely, the clergy—can communicate directly with God. According to Roman Catholic belief, the Pope is infallible, in spirit a direct descendant of the apostle Peter, and a representative of God on earth. This doctrine put the clergy into a position of power. Many of them let themselves be paid for their mediation with God by the illiterate masses who simply had to believe without asking questions. By the end of the Middle Ages this led to an excessive trade in indulgences, whereby sinners could redeem their sins through payments to the Church.

In the Middle Ages the Roman Catholic Church copied the Bible only in Latin and granted the privilege of studying the Bible only to monks. Philosophical and scientific texts at those times were available only in Latin and Greek. The Roman Catholic Church held and still holds onto the power of information. In sermons during the Holy Mass and other church services the information in the Bible was scantily provided to the believers by short Bible readings. Scientists who translated the Bible from Latin into French, English, or German were tortured and burned at the stake. Roman Catholic masses were held in Latin until the second half of the twentieth century. The library in the Vatican is still closed to the public.

This behavior stems from the role of guardian of belief that is presumed by the Roman Catholic Church. In this regard, the Church is no different from other religious and esoteric groups. There is, however, a difference in the violence and cruelty exerted on those who dared oppose Church doctrines.

These are the main reasons why the Church dealt firmly with the Tarot, a philosophical instrument without dogma, that provides a direct insight into matters of life and death, and in which knowledge is translated into essential archetypes that can be understood without special interpreters or mediators. The Tarot leaves it to the individual to decide how to use the insights it reveals. Hence, it was no wonder that the Tarot rapidly became popular among the people in medieval times. The use of the Tarot as a pictorial system of philosophical principles was a direct threat to the clerical monopoly on philosophical, psychological, and social understanding of the human environment. This was enough reason for the Church to ban the Tarot.

Thus during the Middle Ages the Church destroyed most of the body of knowledge about the Tarot, depriving it of its vitality and lessening its influence. Hence, in the Middle Ages essential information on the Tarot became concealed. It would take centuries of mental and spiritual growth and scientific liberation before the Tarot could be reassessed on its authentic value as a major cultural heritage and source of inspiration.

Verbal transfer of information and memorization schemas

In order to understand the way in which the Tarot was obscured by the clergy, we first must clarify ways and aids that were used in the past to memorize extensive information such as stories, myths, fairy tales, ceremonies, and rites. In those times philosophical and esoteric information was normally passed on orally. Written transfer of information was the exception.

There are many examples of the astounding capacity of illiterate people to memorize facts and verbally transfer knowledge. In traditionally illiterate aboriginal cultures such as the African, Indian, and Polynesian, during official ceremonies such as salutations of chiefs, initiations, and religious festivities, the complete history of the tribe and other tribal stories were often recited from memory. Not one word was left out. Often, symbolic images and memorization diagrams or schemata—mnemonic devices—were used to assist with the process of information recall.

In early times the Tarot was conveyed verbally in a similar way. The adept was shown the Tarot and the arcana were laid out in the

6.3 Sand drawing of the Navaho Indians. This memorization schema, in use for thousands of years in healing rituals, represents the ever-changing cosmos by means of a swastika.

order of the Tarot life cycle. Then, the student was allowed to lay out the cards in the right order and repeat the citation of card meanings until the structure and meanings were known, so that these meanings could be abstracted and transferred.

In the past the order of the Tarot arcana was not coded by number. Some of these old unnumbered card decks are still in existence, such as the Visconti Sforza Tarocchi from Milan, dated approximately A.D. 1430 (figure 6.4).

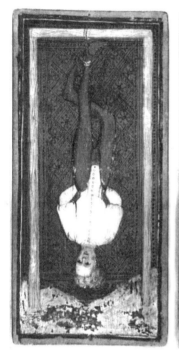

6.4 Tarot cards from the Visconti Sforza Tarocchi. The cards in this Tarot do not bear numbers: the order of the arcana was remembered through memorization schemas. The Visconti Sforza Tarot is based on a much older version that was acquired by Charlemagne (ca. A.D. 774) during his rule of Lombard in Northern Italy. The original was richly illustrated with tempera paint and sheet gold on parchment sheets.

Some memorization schemas for the Tarot were (and still are) the life cycle mandala, which comprises all 80 cards (already discussed) and the Chain (figure 6.5 a–b).

The Tarot memorization schema, the Chain

The Chain was a popular aid used to memorize and recall the order of the Major Arcana (figure 6.5a). According to this schema, the 24 Major Arcana are arranged in a special pattern of eight joined triplets. The top row contains Major Arcana, with highly abstract, spiritual principles. The middle row of Major Arcana indicate situations of choice, rule, or mediation. The Major Arcana in the bottom row comprise the worldly archetypes. The resulting band of three rows of cards read like the teeth of a saw (figure 6.5b).

In the Chain the three horizontal bands of spiritual, mediating, and material arcana, together with a superimposed saw-like structure, completely fix the position of each Major Arcanum, like links in a physical chain. It is very unlikely that during the verbal transfer of Tarot knowledge, any essential or structural knowledge was lost, simply because of the clear structure of the information that had to be memorized.

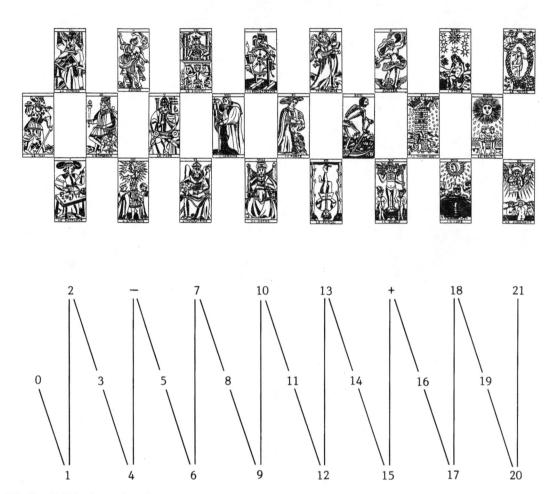

6.5a The 24 Major Arcana from the Tarot of Marseilles, ordered according to the memorization schema, the Chain. The top layer comprises the spiritual arcana, the middle level the archetypal and mediating arcana, the bottom level the material arcana.

6.5b Diagram of the direction of reading in the schema, the Chain.

Through the memorization schema, the Chain, all arcana and their proper order were passed on unchanged for centuries. Some meanings of the Arcana may have been altered, however, through subjective interpretations, such as the arcanum The Priest, which during the Middle Ages when spiritual and worldly power coincided, was named The Pope.

Changes in the original Tarot

The changes in the original structure of the Tarot were not accidental, but made on purpose. In circles of Tarot workers, Rosicrucians, Freemasons, Gnostics, Liberal Catholics, and the Work (Gurdjieff), it is known that the obfuscation of the Tarot was ordered and executed by highly ranked bishops and other leaders in the Roman Catholic Church. In secret meetings the Church leaders decided to undermine the power of these pagan idols and "black magic" rather than issuing a total prohibition of the Tarot.

Quashing the Tarot was not an easy task for the medieval clergy, because the Tarot had become widely known and used. Thus, a ban by the Church would not work. The obfuscation mainly happened through concealment of two essential Major Arcana, followed by changes in the order of the remaining Major Arcana. The unveiling in this chapter breaks open this secret.

Truth (Jupiter) and Intuition (Juno) obscured

As we have seen, two very important and central arcana, the archetypal female wisdom named Intuition and personified in Sophia and Hera (Juno), and the archetypal male wisdom Truth, personified in Zeus (Jupiter), were obscured in this century by hiding them respectively under the arcanum The Priestess and the arcanum The Priest. The clergy wanted to control these two powerful principles and did not want to leave them in the hands of the Templars or ordinary people. From then on, the Tarot comprised only 22 Major Arcana. However, occult societies kept the knowledge of the complete Tarot and the existence of the two hidden arcana to themselves. Using the Tarot became a secret practice.

It was clear to the clergy that the gaps in the Tarot and the Chain that had been caused by the removing the Major Arcana Jupiter and Juno would reveal the obfuscation immediately. More changes to the Tarot were necessary. To emphasize the importance of the Roman Catholic Church, The Priest was renamed The Pope (Le Pape) and The Priestess, The Female Pope (La Papesse). The order of the Major Arcana had to be changed and the three-layered structure of the Chain rebuilt, so that the introduced flaws became inconspicuous (figures 6.6a–d).

As a result of these further changes, the arcanum The Moon pushed the arcanum The Star from its central top position in the life cycle. In the Chain, The Pope was moved up next to The Female Pope. The Chariot moved from the spiritual level down to the material level next to The Emperor. The deeper meaning of this change is that, from then on, material victories were the true ones. In the new order the arcanum Justice is situated next to The Pope. This means that sins acquired the status of diehard facts, which had to be pursued, judged, and punished relentlessly from a spiritual frame of reference, as in the Inquisition. Some arcana moved from worldly into spiritual positions. An example is The Hanged Man: the Church changed pagan, materialistic sacrifices into more spiritual sacrifices, such as penances and prayers.

Death, originally positioned in the Chain at a spiritual/archetypal level, moved down to the material level. Fear of death developed into a very material threat: the end of everything.

While the obfuscation was in progress, occultist circles, which knew that the original Tarot comprised 24 Major Arcana, added the two concealed arcana as white-painted, blank cards to 78-card-decks. In this way the number of Tarot cards in a deck was restored to 80; this is still going on today. The presence of the two blank cards in 78-card Tarot decks made it reasonably easy for initiated users to restore the Tarot to its original 24 Major Arcana. They drew a plus (+) symbol, indicating Jupiter on one blank card, and on the other a minus (–) symbol, indicating Juno.

The Major Arcana Jupiter and Juno did not disappear overnight. In the following centuries 78-card Tarot decks appeared that contained the two blank cards, Jupiter and Juno, such as in the Tarocco Siciliano, but left out The Priest/The Pope and The Priestess/The Female Pope. Examples of such "Juno-Jupiter" decks are those made by the cartiers J. B. Benois, L. Carey, J. Gaudais, R. C. Heitmann, F. Heri, J. K. Jerger, S. Ioia, J. P. Mayer, J. G. Rauch, Renault, and B. Schaer. Stuart Kaplan gives examples of the cards in these decks in his *Encyclopedia of Tarot* (1983).

Notwithstanding this temporary survival, gradually, the decks containing Juno and Jupiter lost ground. The changes in the Tarot were carried out according to a particular method or algorithm. This on the one hand allowed the initiated to retrieve the old, 24-card Tarot in its original order without great difficulty, and on the other it gave rise to a new version of the Chain that propagated the mutilated and obfuscated Tarot, causing confusion everywhere. Below, the original Tarot Chain is shown, along with the step-by-step changes in the order that resulted in the new, obfuscated version of the Chain.

Changes in the order of the remaining Major Arcana

Having concealed Juno and Jupiter by placing them under The Priestess and The Priest respectively, the next step was the filling of the spaces. The clergy wanted to change other things in the Tarot as well through alteration of the order of the remaining 22 Major Arcana:

- The Tarot began to point less clearly at the relationship between clerical and worldly power.
- Justice became more strongly related to the clerical powers (with the establishment of the Inquisition as a result).
- Death started to acquire a more important position than Temperance, because of the dogma of resurrection, which rejects reincarnation.

As the order of the Major Arcana was well known through the common systems of verbal transfer of knowledge, these changes had to be carried out in such a way that they could be introduced covertly into the domain of Tarot knowledge.

The concealment algorithm

The order of the Major Arcana in the Chain had to be changed in such a way that (1) the disappearance of Juno and Jupiter became inconspicuous, and (2) the original position of these two cards could be retrieved. To thoroughly understand the meaning of the steps and card positions, we suggest that you re-enact the following obfuscation algorithm with a deck of Tarot cards.

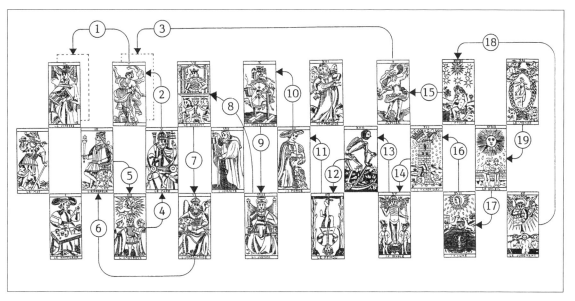

6.6a The 24 Major Arcana of the Tarot in the memorization schema, the Chain, showing all the steps used to change the rank order.

Step 0   The Fool and The Magician retain their position. Everyone knew the start of the Chain, so the beginning could not be changed.

Step 1   Juno is hidden under The Priestess who, from now on, guards the female principle of Truth.

Step 2   The Priest is placed in the original position of Juno and masks it with its power (pointing out that the clergy is responsible for these changes in the Tarot). The Priest and The Priestess are now positioned at the same level and next to each other.

Step 3   Jupiter is hidden under The Priest. The Priest represents and guards the male principle of Truth. Juno and Jupiter are—though hidden—now positioned at the same level as well.

6.6b Diagram of the changes in the original order of the Major Arcana after step 4.

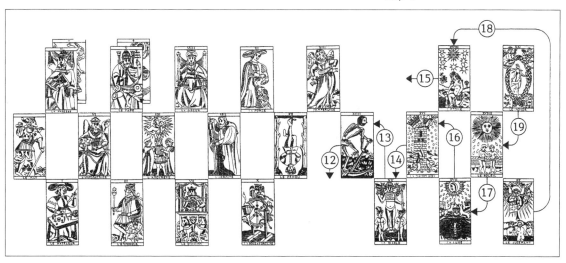

Step 4 The Lovers move to the position of The Priest. From now on marriages take place in the Church and sexuality becomes a problem for the Church fathers.

Step 5 The Emperor moves to the position of The Lovers. It becomes difficult to distinguish between sexuality and oppression.

Step 6 The Empress is placed in the position of The Emperor. The Empress and The Emperor are next to each other: this suggests a marital bond and symbolizes the importance the Christian Church attaches to marriage.

Step 7 The Chariot moves to the place of The Empress. Rule in the world is now based on power and weapons instead of spiritual richness and inspiration; The Chariot is now placed at the same level as The Emperor and assumes a more materialistic nature.

The Hermit stays where it is: a hermit does not move, as he has already reached his goals.

Step 8 Justice is placed in The Chariot's original position. Justice is now next to The Priest, indicating the link between justice and the clergy—leading to the Inquisition.

Step 9 The World (Wheel of Fortune) moves to the position of Justice. Justice becomes worldly; fortune, money, and justice begin to influence each other.

Step 10 Strength moves to the position of The Wheel of Fortune. More and more emphasis is placed on the power of money in the world.

Step 11 The Hanged Man moves to the position of Strength. Martyrs for free belief and thinking stand up.

Step 12 Death moves to the position of The Hanged Man. Death now precedes Temperance and is emphasized as the indomitable end of the body.

6.6c The changes in the original order of the Major Arcana after step 11.

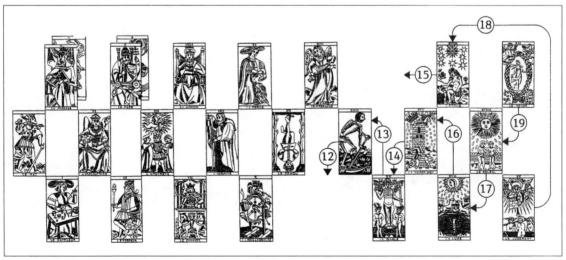

6.6d After step 19, the original order of the Major Arcana has changed into the order of the Tarot of Marseilles.

Step 13 The Devil occupies the position of Death. Death is now preached as hell, and as such is intended to scare people, which it often does.

Step 14 The Tower moves to the position of The Devil. The Tower in the position formerly occupied by The Devil is stagnating to the spiritual liberation of mankind.

Step 15 The Star takes the position of Jupiter. The human spirit is being poured out into matter and becomes the absolute Truth. The consequence is the emergence and prevailing power of science and rationalism.

Step 16 The Moon is placed in the position of The Tower. Spiritual liberation becomes illusory. The Moon is now at the top of the life cycle instead of The Star. This means that pretense and error will dominate.

Step 17 The Sun moves to the position of The Moon. Solitary, integrated thinking is obscured by lunar-fragmented knowledge and scientific materialism.

Step 18 The Last Judgment is put in the empty place earlier occupied by The Star. In the end, the Tarot will be resurrected and The Star and other arcana will reclaim their positions.

Step 19 The Universe moves into the position of The Sun. The Universe keeps its overarching position, connecting the current cycle with the next.

The above structural changes led to the Tarot of Marseilles, which contains 22 Major Arcana.

As mentioned previously, in spite of this initially successful operation, maintaining the obfuscation of Juno and Jupiter became difficult. A clear indication of this can be found in early and later versions of the Tarot of Marseilles (figure 6.7a–b). In one version Juno and Jupiter are absent, as they are hidden by The Priestess (The Female Pope) and The Priest (The Pope). In another version

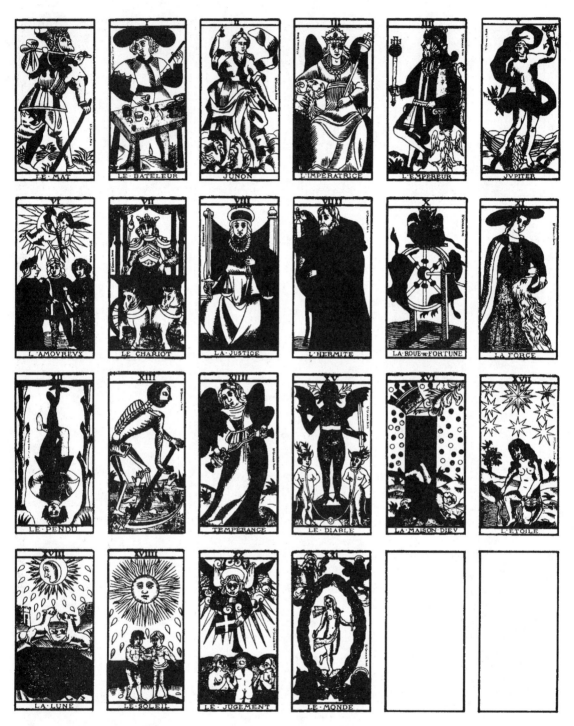

6.7a A version of the Tarot of Marseilles in which La Papesse (The Priestess) is covered by Junon, and Le Pape (The Priest) is covered by Jupiter (Truth). By B. P. Grimaud, Paris, 1748.

Juno and Jupiter are present, covering The Priestess and The Priest respectively. Both versions contain the two blank cards as well.

The formation of the 52 ordinary playing cards from the Tarot
The obfuscation of the Tarot has had another important effect,

THE TAROT OBSCURED, RESTORED, AND COMPLETED

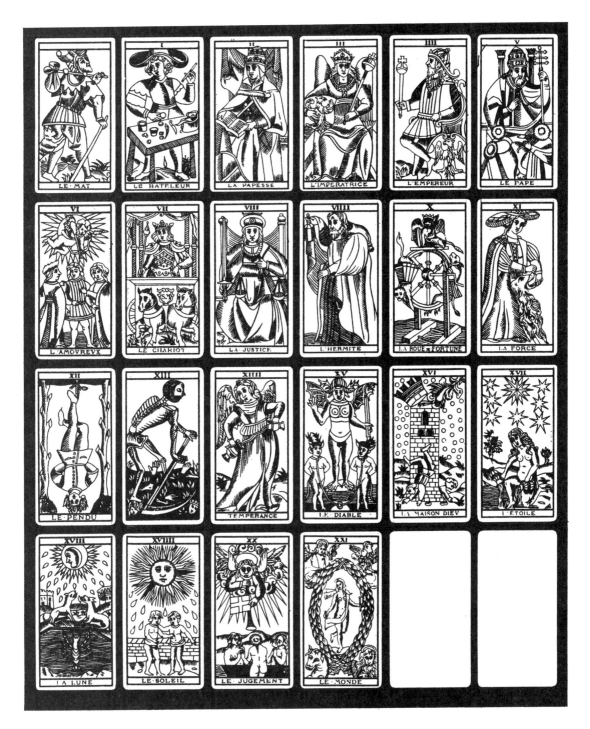

namely the formation of the "ordinary playing cards." It is remarkable that these cards are called "ordinary" because this implies that there was another (extraordinary) game of cards: a card game that became less and less known over time.

6.7b A version of the Tarot of Marseilles in which Junon (Intuition) is covered by La Papesse (The Priestess), and Jupiter (Truth) is covered by Le Pape (The Priest). B. P. Grimaud, Paris, 1830.

The formation of the ordinary playing cards from the Tarot went as follows:

- The Major Arcana, with exception of The Fool (in the ordinary game of cards called the Joker) were separated from the other cards in the Tarot, officially forbidden by the Church, and removed. From then on, the Major Arcana could only be used in particular closed fraternities and passed on only to the initiated.
- In the Royal Arcana the four Pages were removed from the Royal Families, as The Fool (the Joker) represented these young people.

In the Minor Arcana the symbols gradually lost their spiritual depth. This happened as follows:

- In the case of *Pentacles*, the outer five triangular points were taken from the encircled pentagram, leaving a pentagon. Later, the circle was removed, and the remaining pentagon was simplified into a diamond shape, which was easier to draw.
- *Wands* lost the living stem; only the leaf remained. In English the symbol continued to be named clubs.
- The spiritual and religious meaning of the emblem *Cups* was diminished by changing it into hearts, a symbol for the soul but also of (earthly) love and emotions.
- *Swords* lost much of the spiritual-religious meaning— conscience, reason, and justice—because it was replaced by the more oppressive halberd symbol, and called spades.
- The difference between an upright and a reversed card was done away with by mirroring the picture, which made it easier to play the cards.
- The four kernel colors (black, red, yellow, and blue) as we know them in the Tarot of Marseilles, were reduced to two colors—black for clubs and spades and red for diamonds and hearts.

The abovementioned transformations did not happen everywhere. Ordinary playing cards in Mediterranean countries such as Spain, Italy, Greece, Turkey, and Morocco still use disks, wands, cups, and swords as emblems.

The gender of the Major Arcana

Each of the Major Arcana is linked to a gender. When you study different versions of old Tarot decks, it becomes clear that substantial confusion exists about the gender of some of the Major Arcana, for example:

6.8 Playing cards with old Tarot emblems; the back of the cards shows a pattern of luck-bringing horseshoes.

The Fool—Although all newborn children have a gender, they cannot and do not express it as such in their behavior. For this reason the gender of The Fool is undetermined.

The Magician—Male, without question.

The Priestess—She is the traditionally female, nurturing teacher. She is situated close to the black (Yin) pillar.

The Emperor—Male.

The Lovers—Both male and female. It also called *The Choice*. In this phase the person must make a fundamental decision with regard to the way he or she wants to develop sexual relationships. The archetypal choice also has a place in Greek mythology. At some point in his life Hercules is at a crossroads where two women approach him: Virtue and Vice. After having heard both women defend their case, Hercules chooses Virtue. The Lovers also points at the fundamental choice between a male- or a female-oriented way of life.

Intuition—Intuition is clearly of the female gender. In a Greek deck, in which Intuition is named *Hera*, she points at a pole that bears a symbolized vulva. Intuition wears a diadem with one pearl of Wisdom.

The Priest—Male.

The Empress— Female.

The Chariot—Male. The person in The Chariot expresses himself and metaphorically spreads his semen. The Chariot is not only a cart; it is also a cradle that protects the victorious person. There are two sphinxes—a black female and a white male: the person in The Chariot is able to control both complementary forces. The Chariot has an archetypal link with The Star.

The Hermit—Male, with a balanced animus and anima. The Hermit retreats; hence his sexuality is subdued. He wears a simple cloak that hides his sexual features. The light in the lamp carried by The Hermit is the Star of David *with a point in the center*. This star consists of two triangles—the male and female principle connected via the central point of Love and Compassion: "Love is the Lord of heaven and earth." From here all actions should start. A Star of David without this central point of Love leads to an endless chain of haphazardly chosen eye-for-an-eye actions.

Justice—Male, also with a balanced animus and anima, and wearing a toga that hides sexual features. The archetypal figure in Justice has open eyes. In this way he can see both sides of any conflict that he has to resolve. Often Justice is depicted as female to emphasize the compassion that is necessary in proper judgment.

The World—At first sight this arcanum does not seem to have a gender. The World as archetype, though, is clearly female; we never talk about "father earth." The Major Arcanum The World summarizes and expands a person's fate. The Roman goddess of fate is *Fortuna*. In Greek mythology the lot is spun by three female *Fates*: Clotho (the spinner), Lachesis (the apportioner) and Atropos (the inevitable). Thus, although invisible, The World is related to the female gender.

Strength—Male. Though Strength is often depicted as female, this confusion has its ground in the Biblical story in which an angel came down to Daniel in the lions' pit to close the lions' mouths. However, angels are above human gender.

The Hanged Man—Male.

Temperance—Undetermined gender. The angel Raphael is depicted, who preserves the soul that is passing away.

Death—Undetermined gender. A skull can be of either sex. In language the gender is undetermined also. The word "death" in French—*Mort*—is of female gender; in German the word—*Tod*—is male; in Irish the word—*Bás*—is male as well.

Truth—This fundamental archetype is of the male gender.

The Tower—Undetermined gender. There are two twin-like figures in this arcanum, one alive, the other dead.

The Moon—Female.

The Star—Male, with a balanced animus and anima. In The Star the soul formulates and commits to an encompassing, new plan of life. This has male as well as female aspects—such as the toga and an effeminate expression. The Star and The Chariot as a complementary pair both find their ground in the Principal Arcanum *I Manifest*. To prove oneself in life is thought of as a male activity.

The person in the constellation Aquarius is traditionally portrayed as a male water bearer.

The Sun—Both male and female. Either gender is chosen. Some old decks show two children.

The Last Judgment—Male: the central figure is Jesus Christ (as he exists in each of us).

The Universe—Both male and female. In the Hindu religion it is the dual god-pair Shiva-Kali.

The resistance of the Church to the Tarot and to ordinary playing cards

The Church was for centuries—until about 1950—very apprehensive about "ordinary card games" as well as the Tarot, and saw playing them as a sin. From about 1400 the clergy stated that the game of cards was invented by the devil. In 1423 the Franciscan priest St. Bernardino of Siena declared cards to be a creation of Satan. The Church and the Inquisition called them the book of the devil, and the devil's dolls. They were also linked with pagan knowledge of the Old World.

The initial opposition of the Church to ordinary playing cards was their connection with the Tarot. When the Tarot disappeared from the "ordinary man's sight," the Church remained opposed to ordinary playing cards because they strongly promoted materialism (caused by the absence of the Major Arcana!); cards were, and still are, played for money. The spiritual system, the wheel of life represented by the Tarot, changed into a money-collecting and redistributing device—a roulette wheel.

Gypsy Tarot versions

In countries and ethnic groups where the Church could not influence cultural heritage, such as in Asia Minor, and among the Gypsies, the Tarot was preserved rather unscathed. Gypsies have long been associated with fortune telling. Skills at fortune telling are a great asset for a Gypsy woman. A very diverse society of people scattered all over the world, Gypsies have always lived within another society that considers them "strange" and is often hostile to them. Gypsies thus developed methods of self-protection. They spoke *Romanes,* an old Sanskrit-based language, which for centuries has remained unwritten.

The Hungarian Tarotist Emil Kazanlar, born in the Middle East from Persian and Iraqi parents, has developed an ecumenical Tarot deck based on the concept that different religions lead equally to God. Kazanlar has openly stated: *"It is incorrect that the Tarot would have only 78 cards, the number has to be 80. The Female and Male principle have to be added."* In his beautifully rendered, multilingual Gypsy Tarot, Kazanlar has included the archetypal male and female principles as two extra, unnumbered cards. For the female principle he chose Empress Maria Theresa from Austria (crowned by the moon), and for the male archetype Akbar the Great from India (crowned by the sun). In this Middle Eastern Tarot version, the order of the Major Arcana has not been changed.

King Arthur, the Knights of the Round Table, and the Tarot

Over the centuries much has been written about King Arthur. The continuing interest in the Arthurian legend indicates the presence of archetypal content. The first Arthur biography by the British historian Geoffrey of Monmouth, *Historia Regum Brittanniae* (1135), is a Latin chronicle that tells in brief of the emergence and downfall of Arthur. Henry II of England commissioned Wace, an Anglo-Norman writer who lived from about 1100 to 1174 in Jersey, to write a history of Britain called *Roman the Brut* (1155), about the reputed founder of the Britons. Wace worked up Geoffrey of Monmouth's chronicle in verses, added King Arthur's Round Table and mentioned many adventures that took place around King Arthur. His contribution helped to increase the popularity of the Arthurian legends. In the period between 1170 and 1190, Chrétien de Troyes wrote a number of Arthurian novels covering episodes of King Arthur's rule. Most ensuing Arthurian novels are based on Chrétien de Troyes' beginnings.

According to legend, Arthur was a son of King Uther Pendragon and Lady Ygraine of Cornwallis, widow of Duke Gorlois of Cornwallis. As a result of a promise, Uther surrendered his son to the wise wizard Merlin, who brought him to the farm of Hector and Iloide to have him grow up together with their own son, Kay. Merlin educated Arthur and taught him everything he would need to know as the future king. Following the death of his father, the young Arthur successfully passed a test with the sword Excalibur and was crowned king. He won many battles and conquered Ireland, Iceland, and Norway. Finally he returned to his court at Carleon-on-Usk. Here, surrounded by many faithful companions in arms he founded the Order of the Knights of the Round Table as a fraternity that would strive to maintain high and courtly ideals. The most important assignment was the quest for the Grail, which esoterically may be interpreted as an introspective, spiritual exercise.

The idea of an all-sustaining and all-inspiring "greal" or brew is rooted in Celtic myth. Legends tell of Celtic cauldrons of rebirth into which slain warriors were dipped to become reborn; such cauldrons have been found in England dating from around 100 B.C. The Grail was thought to be the cup that contained the blood of Jesus Christ and was kept and brought to England by Joseph of Arimathea.

There are many legends about the quest for the Grail. They are very appealing, because they contain many archetypes. In the context of this book, the Grail legends are important for three reasons. First of all, the archetype of the Grail is present in the Royal and Minor Arcana of Cups. Hence, through the Grail legends our insights into the meanings of the cards may become more profound. Second, the typology and characters of King Arthur's knights are archetypal as well. Some of these archetypes have a clear resemblance to the Major Arcana of the Tarot. Third, it is important to mention that a Round Table may well have existed. The Round Table is said to be a gift from King Leodegrance on the occasion of the wedding of King Arthur to his daughter Guinevere.

In the Guildhall of Winchester Castle, a round table is displayed that was commissioned and made around 1340 by King Edward III (figure 6.9). On this table the 24 names of the Arthurian knights are mentioned. Most names on the table are also often mentioned in the Grail legends about King Arthur and his knights. These names and their order on the Round Table of Winchester served as a starting point for our correlation of the knights with the Major Arcana of the Tarot.

6.9 The 24 Knights of the Round Table of Winchester correlated with the 24 Major Arcana. King Arthur's throne is placed in the center.

The 24 Knights of the Round Table correlated to the 24 Major Arcana in the Tarot

The 24 seats at King Arthur's Round Table are an invitation to correlate Arthur's knights with philosophical and cosmological concepts. As the rank of the knights at the Round Table of Winchester is fixed—as well as that of the Major Arcana and the zodiacal signs—the question is to which knight we have to assign The Fool (Aries).

We have carried out the correlation by starting with six "key knights" who appear in many of the Grail legends and bear a

6.10 Primary correlation of six Knights of the Round Table of Winchester with six Major Arcana.

KNIGHT	MAJOR ARCANUM
Kay	*The Magician*
Kay is the archetypal temperamental hero, like Hercules and Cuchulain. Bestowed with magical powers, he could make himself as tall as the tallest tree. On the coldest day he was like glowing fuel to his comrades. At Arthur's court he is the passionate and brutal cook.	There is only one type of magic, and that is *doing* with full consciousness. The Magician offers his skills and talents and thus changes the world around him.
Tristram de Lyons	*Strength*
Tristram is alone in his great love for Isolde, and is therefore persecuted. "De Lyons" is part of his name because he appeared with a lion that he controlled through spiritual strength.	Is alone in strong convictions and is hence persecuted, as Daniel is. The lions in the pit leave Daniel untouched.
Parcival	*Temperance*
Finder, custodian, and bearer of the Grail.	The angel collects the blood of humankind in its Grail.
Lancelot	*The Devil*
Strong, sexually fascinating knight bound in adultery with Arthur's wife Guinevere in a drama full of frustration at Arthur's court, filled with jealousy, depression, and self-punishment.	Sexual fascination binds. Adulterous love is bound to lies. The lie is half the truth. Dark destiny.
Galahad	*Truth*
The most pure knight. It is said that he healed the Fisher King with a salve of Christ's blood.	Is pure and incorruptible.
Mordred	*The Tower*
Arthur did not accept his bastard son Mordred. The resulting tensions led to both Arthur's and Mordred's downfall.	Symbolizes the downfall of the untrue.

THE TAROT OBSCURED, RESTORED, AND COMPLETED

pronounced symbolism. Then, the remaining 18 knights were correlated with the Major Arcana, as set forth in this book.

Ector de Maris

Sir Ector was the loving foster-father of the young Arthur (son of Uther Pendragon and Ygraine, spouse of his enemy Gorlois, Duke of Cornwall). Merlin entrusted Arthur to Ector without divulging Arthur's real identity. Ector fulfilled his task with honor, and cooperated with higher forces represented by Merlin and the Lady of the Lake. Later, Ector was included in the circle of Knights of the Round Table. Because Ector is ignorant of the identity of Arthur, at least at the beginning of the storyline in the Arthurian legends, he is related to the arcanum *The Fool*.

Kay

Kay, King Arthur's cook, learned as a young child from practical experience—just as Arthur did. He developed a great, creative spirit and acquired legendary magical powers. The Celtic *Romance of Kilwych and Olwen* says about him:

> He could hold his breath under water for nine days and nights and sleep for the same period. No physician could heal a wound inflicted by his sword. His natural heat was so great that in a deluge of rain whatever he carried in his hand remained dry a hand-breath above and below.

These characteristics correlate Kay with *The Magician*, who uses his capacities and talents to gain and use knowledge. Kay was temperamental and sometimes cruel, which made him less popular with many. Nevertheless, Arthur had great affection for him.

Pellens

According to Gareth Knight in his book, *The Secret Tradition in Arthurian Legend* (1983), the Lord of Annwn, the underworld, named Pwyll, later is called Pellas, Pellens, or Pellam—the keeper of the Castle of the Holy Grail in Corbenic. Pellens admitted the use of magic to lure Lancelot into marrying his daughter Elaine of Corbenic. Homes and castles are ruled by female intelligence and practicality. Therefore, Pellens correlates to *The Priestess*.

Saser

Saser, also called Safer (Sapher) had ten brothers, among them the Saracen knight Sir Palomides (correlated with The Priest). Saser assisted Palomides in protecting four of their brothers who suffered under the oppression of Karados. Saser correlates with *The Emperor*. It is remarkable that The Emperor and The Priest are also interpreted as brothers, the first active at a material level, the other at a spiritual level.

Bors de Ganys

Bors was a nephew of Sir Lancelot. Bors' father was King Bors de Gaul, brother of King Ban of Benwick. Bors de Ganys was one of the strongest knights and third in the trio of successful Grail knights. Stability and reliability were his predominant characteristics. He was the one who found the Grail, together with Parcival and Galahad. After the great quest he returned on his own to inform King Arthur about the developments. At first he refused to defend Queen Guinevere when she was accused of infidelity, but later changed his mind. According to legend Bors died in Palestine where he participated in the Crusades. Bors de Ganys is correlated to *The Lovers (The Choice)*.

Lamorak

Lamorak was the eldest son of Pellinore and a great, heroic figure with enormous power and primordial vitality. He fell in love with and slept with Morgause, a very strong, intuitive, paradoxical, Medusa-like woman (likened to the dark side of Isis). The love between Lamorak and Morgause was overpowering and passionate. Lamorak is correlated with the arcanum *Intuition*.

Palomides

Palomides was a Saracen knight who, after his baptism, became a Knight of the Round Table. He fell in love with Isolde of Cornwall. After the death of Pellinore, he pursued the Questing Beast, the archetypal symbol of immorality mentioned in the Revelation to John. Palomides is correlated with the arcanum *The Priest*.

Lucan

Lucan was one of the old and strong knights around King Arthur and was called "the Butler," which means "the bearer of arms." He carried Arthur's spear (Bedivere carried Arthur's swords). Lucan and Bedivere stayed with Arthur from the beginning till the end. The knight Lucan is correlated with the arcanum *The Empress*.

La Côte Mal Taillée (Bruin le Noire)

Kay gave Bruin Le Noire the nickname *La Côte Mal Taillée*, because he arrived at Arthur's court in a rich but badly fitting and torn coat. The coat had belonged to his father, who was killed in it. Bruin wore the coat until he had avenged the death of his father. La Côte Mal Taillée was a very successful and fierce fighter. He is correlated with the arcanum *The Chariot*.

Bleoberis de Ganis (Blubrys)

Bleoberis was a noble knight with a strong social sense. Graciously, he accepted the victory of King Anguish when Tristram defeated his brother. During the last days of the Round Table, he departed with Bors and Ector as knights of the cross to the Holy Land. Bleoberis is correlated with *The Hermit*.

THE TAROT OBSCURED, RESTORED, AND COMPLETED

Bedivere

Bedivere was one of the first Knights of the Round Table and Arthur's bearer of arms together with Lucan. He carried the wounded Arthur on his back to the beach where the barque with the three mourning queens met them. This story assigns to Bedivere the attribute of guide. Bedivere is the one who, in the end, threw Arthur's sword back in the lake from whence it had appeared. Bedivere is correlated with the arcanum *Justice*.

Gareth of Orkney

Gareth simply walked into Arthur's court. Kay placed him in the kitchens to work; in this way he was given the nickname *Beaumains*, which means "beautiful hands." Gareth showed himself to be a good fighter and was knighted by Lancelot, of whom he became a devoted adept. Later, he was tragically killed by his master during a battle staged to prevent Guinevere from ending her life at the stake. Destiny, with its upward and downward movement, had a strong effect on Gareth's life. He is correlated with the arcanum *The World*.

Tristram de Lyons

Tristram, also named Tristan, is one of the great lovers of medieval mythology. Nephew of King Mark of Cornwall, and son of King Melodias of Lyonesse and Queen Elizabeth, he is the Cornish connection in the Round Table. He was named "de Lyons" for several reasons. Tristram's father seems to have been born in the Scottish province Lyonesse, also named Lothian, and later moved to Cornwall. Secondly, according to legend, Tristram appeared with a powerful lion as a companion, which is the archetype of supreme spiritual strength.

Of Breton origin, the story of Tristram and Isolde was popular in Cornwall. King Mark sent his nephew Tristram out to bring his bride Isolde home. While Tristram was escorting her to Cornwall, he fell in love with Isolde after accidentally drinking a love potion prepared by Isolde's mother. Tristram and Isolde went through difficult times in which they often had to go undercover to stay out of reach of King Mark, who pursued them. Finally, separated from Isolde, Tristram married another Isolde (namely, Isolde with the White Hands), but they were not happy. Later, Tristram went to Britannia, was gravely wounded and sent for help from Isolde, who had once before cured him of a serious wound caused by a poisoned arrow. Isolde sailed to Britannia with a magic cure. Her ship carried a white sail to indicate that she was aboard. However, an incorrect report of a black sail caused Tristram to lose the will to live and he died of his wound without having seen his real love, Isolde of Cornwall, again. Tristram, symbol of spiritual power, is correlated with the arcanum *Strength*.

Lyonell

Nephew of Lancelot and descendant of King Ban of Benwick. Lyonell was the brother of Bors de Ganis. He was given this name because of a birthmark on his chest that resembled a lion. Shortly after Lyonell was knighted he fought a lion, which he killed. During his life Lyonell assisted Lancelot on many occasions. As a sign of gratitude Lancelot made him King of Gaunes. Lyonell was killed in the battle of Winchester, fought between the armies of Lancelot and the sons of Mordred. Lyonell is correlated with the arcanum *The Hanged Man*.

Parcival

Parcival was brought up by his mother in a forest far from Arthur's court at Camelot, completely ignorant of courtly manners and the meaning of knighthood. The mysterious Queen of the Wastelands, one of the three ladies who took Arthur to Avalon after he had been wounded in the battle with Mordred, was Sir Parcival's aunt. A calling made him travel to Arthur's court where he was duly made a knight and set off in quest of the Grail. Later he persecuted a knight who had offended Guinevere. In the end Parcival met the Fisher King, of whom he failed to ask the Grail question. The purity of Parcival may have permitted him to see the Grail, but only Sir Galahad, Lancelot's son, was allowed to touch it. In the end he became the custodian of the Grail. Parcival's uncomplicated mind did not offend. He matured to have great insights and wisdom. Parcival is correlated with the arcanum *Temperance*.

Gawain (in Welsh Gwalchmai, Latinized, Walwanus)

Nephew of King Arthur and one of the most courteous and important knights at Arthur's court, Gawain was a strict upholder of chivalry and the enemy of Sir Lancelot. Gawain was involved in many adventures and had various identities. Although most of Arthur's knights did not fear fighting that might end in death, Gawain was a violent killer. He was challenged to a beheading contest by the giant Green Knight, which he accepted. Another story tells that when one of the knights at Arthur's court killed his dog, Gawain beheaded that knight, and when the knight's wife wanted to intervene, he chopped off her head as well! Gawain showed remorse and accepted the humiliating punishment of apologizing to Queen Guinevere while sitting backwards on a horse with the decapitated head of the lady he killed in his hands. Gawain's anger because of the death of his two brothers at Lancelot's hands caused many fights that gave Mordred the opportunity to stage a rebellion against King Arthur. On his death bed, mortally wounded by Lancelot, Gawain had bitter remorse about his actions that caused the fragmentation of this fraternity of knights. Gawain is correlated to the arcanum *Death*.

Lancelot

Lancelot is a very important person in the Arthurian Grail legends. He, his kindred, and colleagues are of French origin. Gareth Knight in *The Arthurian Legend* mentions that Lancelot was the son of the King of Banwick (situated in present-day Belgium), who lost his kingdom and died when Lancelot was still a baby. At the age of 18, Lancelot, son of a widow, was taken by the Lady of the Lake and presented at court, his arms provided by her. He was renowned as the best knight in the world and became Queen Guinevere's favorite; they fell deeply in love with each other. The triangular relationship Arthur-Guinevere-Lancelot made Arthur's life continually difficult. Arthur was not interested enough in Guinevere, while in Lancelot, Guinevere found her soul mate and sexual fulfillment. Lancelot's liaison with Guinevere was diametrically opposed to the then young Christian morality. At a joust Lancelot met Elaine of Corbenic, with whom he fell in love and begot his son Galahad. Guinevere became very jealous and banned Lancelot from Arthur's court. Lancelot, torn between two loves, wandered like a madman for years through the forests. After being cured at the court of King Pelles, he lived with Elaine until their son Galahad reached 15 years of age. Guinevere was disconsolate during Lancelot's absence. Later, Lancelot returned to King Arthur's court and took part in the search for the Grail. Because of his adultery with Guinevere, and even more because of his fundamental ambiguity, he could not find the Grail. Lancelot is correlated with the arcanum *The Devil*.

Galahad

Galahad was the son of Lancelot. According to legend, Galahad also was a descendant of Joseph of Arimathea, who sailed as a tin merchant to Britain with the Holy Grail. As soon as Sir Gahalad had taken his place at the Round Table, the presence of the Grail was felt in Camelot. A mysterious lady announced how the sacred vessel would come and feed all knights.

In the beginning of Arthur's reign Sir Galahad fought his father, but he gave in when he saw how chivalrously Lancelot behaved and became his devoted supporter. He exceeded his father in purity. According to legend, Galahad healed the Fisher King of the Wasteland, who had been wounded between his thighs, with a salve of Christ's blood from the Holy Grail.

He, Parcival, and Bors received a sacrament from the long-dead Joseph of Arimathea and saw the Grail in a vision. According to legend he took "Our Lord's body (the Grail) between his hands" and then died. Another story tells that he refused to eat and starved himself to death when he believed that Lancelot had died. He was buried with honors close to his father's castle. Sir Galahad is correlated with the arcanum *Truth*.

In figure 6.12, King Arthur's throne points between Galahad and Mordred in the direction northeast. This area represents the realm of death and birth, the self-radiating pure light, *"the Celtic Heaven, which was the Sun itself—a blaze of light caused by the shining together of myriad pure souls"* (Robert Graves in *The White Goddess*). Buddha is also traditionally placed in this northeast corner, outside the wheel of life, in Nirvana. Through this esoteric opening a soul may be liberated from the cycle of life and death, by becoming one in All.

6.11 Woodcut from 1587 of the wheel of birth and death indicated by the houses 1 (childbed) and 8 (death). In this picture the 12 houses are correlated with the 12 signs of the zodiac and the corresponding planets.

Galahad flashes Truth's lightning across the opening in the direction of Mordred, who is aiming to destroy him.

Mordred

Mordred was the bastard son of King Arthur. After Arthur realized that he had begotten a child with his half-sister Morgana, in an attempt to kill Mordred, he proclaimed that all children that were born at the same time as Morgana's child had to be openly displayed. However, Arthur's attempt to kill Mordred did not succeed. According to M. Z. Bradley-Zimmer, in her book *Mists of Avalon*, Mordred was raised by King Lot at Orkney's court, and later sent to his father. King Arthur included him in the Knights of the Round Table, but did not accept him as his son. This decision would turn out to be fatal to both.

When King Arthur had to go to war in Britannia, he appointed Mordred as his regent, but his scheming son tried instead to take the throne and force Guinevere to marry him. On the king's return a terrible battle was fought near Salisbury—south of Stonehenge—in which most of the Knights of the Round Table were killed, including Mordred. Three mysterious women, Morgana, the Queen of Northgales, and the Queen of the Wastelands, took Arthur, who had been mortally wounded by Mordred during the battle, to Avalon in a black boat. While keeping in mind that all Arthurian archetypes are double-faced, showing their good and their evil potentialities, Mordred is correlated with the arcanum *The Tower*.

Alynore

Little is known about Alynore. Alyn is an area in northeastern Wales that has been an important gateway between England and Wales since the Roman occupation. Alynore was the son of a niece of Urien, brother of Açon. He was the major domus of Clarence. Alynore took part in the battle against the Saxons at Clarence and Karadigan. He assisted Agloval to defend the home of his mother against the army of Agrippe. Alynore is correlated with the arcanum *The Moon*.

Lybyus Discophorus

About this knight all we know is that he would have been "the white knight" and that his second name means bearer of a (light-radiating) disk. For this reason Lybyus Discophorus is correlated with the arcanum *The Star*.

6.12 The 24 Major Arcana of the restored Tarot correlated with the 24 Knights of the Round Table of Winchester Castle. King Arthur's throne is projected in the northeast direction. There is a moral story hidden the Table of Winchester Castle: Galahad, Arthur's purest and most virtuous knight, casts a lightning bolt of truth to Mordred over the head of king Arthur, killing both Mordred and Arthur.

Brumeur

Little is known about Sir Brumeur. Gareth names him in a beauty contest, which is held when Brumeur and Tristram and their wives meet each other. The knight Brumeur is correlated with the arcanum *The Sun*.

Degore

Degore, also called Thor, was the son of Pellinore and half-brother of Agloval, Drian, Lamorak, Parcival, and all their sisters. Degore took an active part in the search for Merlin and was involved in various adventures during his mission—for example, the return of the white hunting dog that was stolen by Sir Abalin from Lady Cacheresse. Degore is correlated with the arcanum *The Last Judgment*.

Dagonet

Dagonet, the jester at King Arthur's court, also became a Knight of the Round Table. His witty, philosophical ridicule made him one of the most popular members. He was closely befriended by Tristram, whom he freed more than once from the hands of King Mark. Dagonet is correlated with the arcanum *The Universe*.

The Round Table of Winchester as anchor for the Tarot

The Round Table of Winchester was manufactured at the end of the Crusades and the beginning of the Renaissance. At that time the flow of esoteric knowledge from the East was well underway and the Tarot had become well-known in Western Europe. Gothic cathedrals emerged and the Freemason and Rosicrucian orders were formed. Freemason symbols in old English churches, and the Rose Cross of the Rosicrucians in the middle of the Round Table of Winchester, indicate that these esoteric fraternities influenced the naming and order of the Knights of the Round Table. Conceivably, the naming arrangement of the 24 knights in the Round Table of Winchester had the same purpose as the laying down of the structure and number of Major Arcana in the original Tarot (figure 6.13). The archetypal elements represented by the 24 Knights of the Round Table and the archetypes in the 24 Major Arcana are based on the same objective, psychological structures in the collective unconscious.

The Tarot and the 24 moon phases

The moon passes through several phases. Well known are New Moon (0°), First Quarter (90°), Full Moon (180°), and Last Quarter (270°). Moon phase psychology, a branch of astrology developed in the first half of the twentieth century by Else Parker and J. van Slooten, distinguishes 24 moon phases. A person's moon phase expresses his/her *persona*, the attitudes of the soul towards fellow humans and society, the roles the person plays, and his mission (but not talents or actual behavior). Moon phases within 0° to 180° represent a period of development up to complete maturity (the first 12 Major Arcana), and those within 180° to 360°, the decline and end of life (the second 12 Major Arcana). For example, people born around the New Moon ($345°$ to $5°$) are analytically inclined, somewhat aloof, and sober. Full Moon people ($175°$ to $195°$) are romantic, warm-hearted, and gregarious. People born around the First Quarter manifest themselves by doing something special; those born around the Last Quarter ($255°$ to $285°$) determine what others have to do. We have correlated the 24 moon phases with the 24 Major Arcana in the restored Tarot (figure 6.13).

The Tarot and other sources of esoteric wisdom
The archetypal and mythical foundations of the restored Tarot warrant further links with other sources of wisdom. First of all, the Bible—especially the New Testament and the Apocryphal Books—contain many wise messages that are also found in the Tarot.

Esoteric knowledge explicit in the restored Tarot also wells up in Mozart's Masonic opera *The Magic Flute*. In Act II, Scene 3, Sarastro, the high priest of Isis and Osiris, sings:

In diesen heil'gen Hallen	*In these holy halls,*
Kennt man die Rache nicht,	*One does not know revenge.*
Und ist ein Mensch gefallen,	*And when one has fallen,*
Führt Liebe ihn zu Pflicht.	*Love will guide one to do his duty.*
Dann wandelt er an Freundes Hand	*Then at one's Friend's hand one changes*
Vergnügt und froh in's bess're Land.	*Contented and joyful in a better land.*

The friend's hand is God's loving guidance to humankind. In Act II, Scene 8, two men in armor sing from two esoteric mountains:

Der, welcher wandert diese Strasse voll Beschwerden,	*He who roams along these difficult paths,*
Wird rein durch Feuer, Wasser, Luft und Erden;	*Is purified through Fire, Water, Air and Earth;*
Wenn er des Todes Schrecken überwinden kann,	*If he can conquer his Fear of Death,*
Schwinngt er sich aus Erde himmelan.	*He'll swing himself from Earth towards heaven.*
Erleuchtet wird er dann im Stande sein,	*Enlightened he will then be in the position,*
Sich den Mysterien der Isis ganz zu weih'n.	*To fully dedicate himself to Isis' mysteries.*

6.13 The 24 Major Arcana of the Tarot correlated with the 24 moon phases as formulated in the book *Moon Phase Psychology* (1950), by Else Parker and Dr. J. van Slooten.

In this duet the elements are named in the right order, the same as the emblems in the restored Tarot. "Purification through Fire, Water, Air, and Earth" is shorthand for "becoming a better person by passing through the Tarot life cycle fields of Wands (Summer), Cups (Autumn), Swords (Winter), and Pentacles (Spring)." In this sequence Fire is mentioned first, as the field of Wands follows after the commitment to love in The Lovers and Intuition and the abandonment of all thoughts of revenge—as indicated in Sarastro's aria. Earth is named last to indicate that one has to go through at least one reincarnation to achieve enlightenment.

In Chapter 7 esoteric, mathematical, and musical structures in the Tarot are revealed and linked with the colors of the rainbow. Chapter 8 expounds divination and compares the Tarot with other cosmologies and metaphysical considerations of humankind and its place in the universe.

Mathematical and Esoteric Structures in the Tarot

Pointers to Infinity

Mathematical and Esoteric Structures in the Tarot

Eternal loops

The author Douglas Hofstadter, in his book *Gödel, Escher, Bach: an Eternal Golden Braid*, discusses extensively infinite loops, which he calls "strange loops." According to him:

> The "Strange Loop" phenomenon occurs whenever, by moving upwards (or downwards) through the levels of some hierarchical system, we unexpectedly find ourselves right back where we started.

Strange loops are not pure repetitions. In the process of one loop cycle something changes. Still, at the end we do find ourselves back where we started. Strange loops are mind structures that return to themselves and thus are dynamic depictions of eternity. For this reason they are also called *eternal loops*.

A work of art can bring an eternal loop to life in the mind of the observer and give it a wonderful beauty. The graphic artist M. C. Escher dedicated many of his lithographs to eternal loops, and Douglas Hofstadter points out that J. S. Bach built strange loops in his *Musical Offering*.

Computer programs may also contain eternal loops; they are called recursions. A recursive program contains a procedure that repeats itself. Unless precautions are taken, such programs continue endlessly (see figure 7.8). An example of an artistic recursion is the well-known Quaker Oats box, with a picture of a man holding a box with a label depicting a man holding a box with a label depicting a man holding a box, and so on to infinity.

Esoteric-eternal loops

Eternal loops are depicted in early esoteric literature as Ouroboros, the snake that eats its tail. Waite drew the Ouroboros as a lizard that eats its tail—a symbol of eternal life—on the clothing of the Page, Knight, and King of Wands (figure 7.1).

Eternal loops appeal to us because they are at the root of our consciousness and creative thinking. When considering or experiencing an eternal loop—for instance, by listening to particular music—interactions occur between different levels of consciousness. Mental activities at very "high" levels of consciousness connect with "low" perceptive consciousness and influence these perceptions, while at the same time these low-level perceptions determine thinking processes at very high levels of consciousness. The Self becomes conscious the moment it can reflect upon itself.

THE WORLD

KNIGHT OF WANDS

THE UNIVERSE

7.1 Esoteric-eternal loops.
a Ourobouros, the self-devouring snake, on a medieval manuscript.
b The Major Arcanum in the Tarot called The World (The Wheel of Fortune).
c Ourobouros loops are depicted on several of Waite's Tarot cards.
d Ourobouros in the Major Arcanum The Universe.

Eternal loops in the Tarot

The Tarot is an eternal loop. This is evident when we lay out the cards in the life cycle mandala. The life cycle keeps repeating itself. When one Tarot cycle is over, the next starts. In Chapter 2, figure 2.12, the life cycle is depicted as a spiral. During its progression through life cycles, our soul improves its expression and comes closer to its divine destiny. This process is called *individuation*.

In the preceding chapters we showed that the Tarot was not a loose assembly of pictures with symbols, but a hermetically closed system of abstract laws. The Russian philosopher Gurdjieff spoke about 24 objective laws that are valid for humans. These laws have a mathematical background in common that turns them into a strange, eternal loop.

When all the arcana of the Tarot are ordered in the life cycle mandala, an eternal loop appears. This loop is even more strongly visible if we use only the Major Arcana. When a life cycle has been completed the next one starts (at a higher level), and this process goes on and on. The word T-A-R-O written in a circle is also an eternal loop.

The word TAROT as an eternal loop

The origin of the word TAROT is disputed. According to Court de Gébelin the word is derived from two Egyptian words: TAR, meaning way or road, and RO, meaning royal. He is almost right; the words are not from the Egyptian. The first syllable of the word TAROT is the primordial sound TA, TAU or TAO, meaning way or path. The second syllable is the primordial sound RO, meaning king or royal. So, TARO means Royal Path. This concept is also present in karma yoga from the Vedas in India, in the Tao of

MATHEMATICAL AND ESOTERIC STRUCTURES IN THE TAROT

Taoism, in the THAU from the Hebrew Qabbala, and in "I am the way, the truth, and the life" from the Bible (John 14:6).

Originally, the word TARO was written with four letters. The closing letter T was added later so as to connect with the beginning of the word. The correct pronunciation is TARO with a long O. In English and French, correctly, the closing letter is silent.

The word TARO consists of two vowels—the spirit, life of a language—and two consonants, the structural part of a language. The vowels are the skeleton of the word and give it character, the consonants are the muscles and give the word volume. If we leave the vowels out of a word, it is still more understandable than when we leave out the consonants. Some languages—for example, the Semitic languages—only notate the consonants.

The A and O are the vowels that indicate the beginning and the end: the A (alpha) and O (omega). As spoken, the consonant T has a halting effect. The T (Tau) was and still is a universal symbol; it symbolizes sacrifice, resurrection, and support. Among others, we find the T symbol in the texts of the Incas, Quiches (Mayan tribe), Egyptians, Chaldeans, Chinese, and Hindus.

7.2 Tau depicted as supporter (table or altar) of the universe (circle/globe containing the Yin-Yang principle). This Chinese ideogram is akin to the Egyptian Ankh symbol.

7.3a The Tau cross and The Hanged Man.
b Tau as Tree of Life in The Hanged Man.
c Tau as an unfolded cube.
d Tau in a Mayan manuscript.

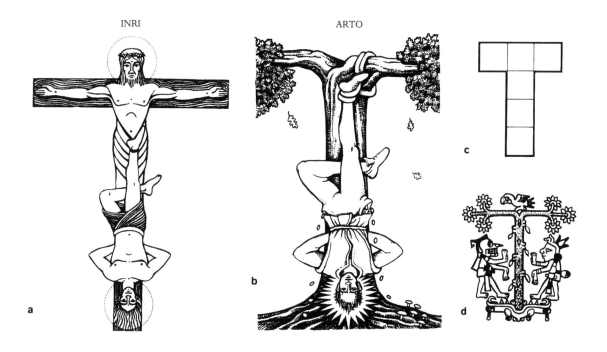

INRI

ARTO

a

b

c

d

The origin of the very old T symbol, according to Churchward, is to be found in the motherland, the legendary continent of Mu or Lemuria, which sank in the Pacific Ocean. The T is the sacrificial table, alTar, on which all things are dedicated to heaven. The consonant R in TARO has a rolling action that indicates movement or progress. For this reason the R is in the middle of the word TARO. The word TARO is a primordial word and a very powerful invocation that can be repeated without end:

$$\rightarrow\text{TAROTAROTAROTARO}\rightarrow$$

This series of sounds is part of an eternal invocation of an eternal loop. This simple loop, the word T-A-R-O written in a circle, returns to itself without end. The Tarot also contains a much more complex eternal loop.

Tarot names—Tarot invocations

In the word TARO the position of each of the four letters T, A, R, O can change by swapping the position of two letters. This is called permutation. If the letter T remains stationary as the first letter, there are six possible letter combinations:

TARO   TAOR   TOAR   TORA   TROA   TRAO

With the T in second position, again there are six permutations possible, and so on. The permutation of the letters in the word TARO gives in total 4 x 3 x 2 x 1 = 24 different words. Each of these words is a primordial sound structure, which represents the essence of a Major Arcanum. Hence, the 24 permutations of the word TARO are called the *Tarot invocations* or *Tarot names*.

Samuel L. Mathers' Tarot names correlated with Major Arcana

Tarot worker Samuel L. Mathers, in his book *The Tarot* (1888), was the first to include several permutations of the word TARO, each of which correlates with the essence of a major Arcanum. He also pointed to etymological connections with particular languages (figure 7.4).

MATHERS' TAROT INVOCATIONS

Invocation	Meaning of the word	Name of Arcanum	Meaning of Arcanum
TARO	The whole Tarot	The Universe	All arcana in one
TAOR	Egyptian goddess of birth and darkness (Taoret)	The Fool	Comes from the dark
TORA	Law (Hebrew)	The Priestess	Teaches laws of life
TROA	Throne (Greek: Thronos)	The Emperor	Rules over life
ATOR	Egyptian sky goddess of joy and love	Intuition (Juno)	Foundation of true, joyful life
ROTA	Wheel (Latin)	The World (Wheel of Fortune)	Rotates
RATO	Relationship between two magnitudes	Temperance	Connects two ways of existence
ORAT	Speaks (Latin)	Truth	Speaks for itself

7.4 The eight permutations of the word TARO by S. L. Mathers (1888) and their meaning in relation to the Major Arcana. Linguists are invited to study the correlations between the other Tarot invocations and languages.

Correlation of the 24 Tarot invocations with the Major Arcana

In this book we complete the correlation of the Tarot invocations, commenced by Mathers. The first step is to arrange the 24 Major Arcana in the cycle of life mandala and correlate them with Mathers' eight Tarot names (figure 7.5a).

7.5a The eight Tarot names by Mathers correlated with the Major Arcana in the life cycle.

The Universe		The Last Judgment	The Sun	The Star	The Moon	The Tower	Truth (Jupiter)
	TARO		....	....	....	....	ORAT
The Fool	TAOR						..... The Devil
The Magician							..... Death
The Priestess							RATO Temperance
The Emperor							..... The Hanged Man
The Lovers							..... Strength
	ATOR		....	....	....	....	ROTA
	Intuition (Juno)	The Priest	The Empress	The Chariot	The Hermit	Justice	The World

The mathematical structure in the TARO invocations is striking. In the Tarot names of an opposite and complementary pair of Major Arcana, the second and fourth letters swap places. By applying this principle we find, for example, the Tarot names for Strength, ORTA, and Death, OATR (figure 7.5b).

The Universe		The Last Judgment	The Sun	The Star	The Moon	The Tower	Truth (Jupiter)
	TARO	. . . .	. . . .	. . . .	. . . .	. . . .	ORAT
The Fool	TAOR						. . . . . The Devil
The Magician	. . . .						OATR Death
The Priestess	TORA						RATO Temperance
The Emperor	TROA						. . . . . The Hanged Man
The Lovers	. . . .						ORTA Strength
	ATOR	. . . .	. . . .	. . . .	. . . .	. . . .	ROTA
Intuition (Juno)		The Priest	The Empress	The Chariot	The Hermit	Justice	The World

7.5b Ten Tarot names correlated.

In the diagrams here, it is obvious that, in the first and third quadrants, the letter T in the two series of invocations remains unchanged and that, in each permutation, two other letters change position.

Assuming that the permutations start with the word TARO, we may conclude that in each sixth permutation the letter T changes position. It is possible to use an algorithm for the permutations in which the letters swing around the T as a fixed point; the letter T determines which of the two other letters permutate. In this way the missing permutations (invocations) in the first and third quadrants can be determined (figure 7.5c).

The Universe		The Last Judgment	The Sun	The Star	The Moon	The Tower	Truth (Jupiter)
	TARO	. . . .	. . . .	. . . .	. . . .	. . . .	ORAT
The Fool	TAOR						AOTR The Devil
The Magician	TOAR						OATR Death
The Priestess	TORA						RATO Temperance
The Emperor	TROA						ARTO The Hanged Man
The Lovers	TRAO						ORTA Strength
	ATOR	. . . .	. . . .	. . . .	. . . .	. . . .	ROTA
Intuition (Juno)		The Priest	The Empress	The Chariot	The Hermit	Justice	The World

7.5c Fourteen Tarot names correlated.

MATHEMATICAL AND ESOTERIC STRUCTURES IN THE TAROT

Through application of this swing, or pendulum-algorithm, the permutations in the second and fourth quadrant can be executed, and the appropriate Tarot names found (figure 7.5d). The appendix to this book contains a table that shows all the permutations (and the application of the pendulum-algorithm) in an endless loop.

		The Last Judgment	The Sun	The Star	The Moon	The Tower	Truth (Jupiter)	
The Universe								
	TARO	OART	AORT	AROT	RAOT	ROAT	ORAT	
The Fool	TAOR						AOTR	The Devil
The Magician	TOAR						OATR	Death
The Priestess	TORA						RATO	Temperance
The Emperor	TROA						ARTO	The Hanged Man
The Lovers	TRAO						ORTA	Strength
	ATOR	ATRO	ATRO	OTRA	OTAR	RTOA	ROTA	
Intuition (Juno)		The Priest	The Empress	The Chariot	The Hermit	Justice	The World	

7.5d All Tarot names correlated.

The six Tarot anagrams: the hermetic seal on the Tarot

The 24 permutations of the word TARO can be combined in a unique series of six magic squares or anagrams, by placing the Tarot names in the order of the life cycle in four rows—one row for each Tarot emblem (quadrant). The resulting six anagrams together hermetically seal the order of the Major Arcana and their invocations. Therefore, the order of the Major Arcana as presented in this book simply *is* the correct one.

7.6 The 24 permutations of the word Tarot form six magic squares or anagrams that each contain four Major Arcana. When the invocations in the six squares are read from left to right, their order is the same as in the Tarot life cycle.

The first magic square contains the four Major Arcana of the fixed cross, and the fourth square, the four Major Arcana of the cardinal cross.

T A R O	T A O R	T O A R	T O R A	T R O A	T R A O
A T O R	A T R O	O T R A	O T A R	R T A O	R T O A
R O T A	O R T A	A R T O	R A T O	O A T R	A O T R
O R A T	R O A T	R A O T	A R O T	A O R T	O A R T

The Universe	The Fool	The Magician	The Priestess	The Emperor	The Lovers
Intuition	The Priest	The Empress	The Chariot	The Hermit	Justice
The World	Force	The Hanged Man	Temperance	Death	The Devil
Truth	The Tower	The Moon	The Star	The Sun	The Last Judgment

Summarizing, the pendulum-algorithm for the 24 permutations of the word TARO complies with the following conditions:

- The Tarot is an eternal loop in 24 stages: after 24 steps the permutation starts again.
- The Tarot name TARO indicates the beginning and the end of a cycle of permutations.
- In each step of the cycle, each stage logically follows from the preceding one.
- The letter T is the letter upon which the permutations are founded. The Greek letter Tau is a universal, archetypal symbol that symbolizes a cross where the horizontal beam rests at the top of the vertical beam. It also symbolizes an altar (see figures 7.3a–d). It is found, for example, in the Major Arcanum The Hanged Man.
- The permutation-algorithm generates Mathers' invocations in the right place (at the proper Major Arcanum).

The Tarot invocations are part of objective language

Objective language is a universal means of communication. Words in this language consist of sound structures that are archetypal. Objective words are very powerful: they are immediately understood by everyone at a spiritual level, and connect with higher levels of existence.

In our world, an objective, universal, mystical language called Zenzar is spoken by illuminated and holy persons. The 24 Tarot invocations are part of Zenzar. As now all 24 permutations and correlations to Tarot arcana are known, additional Tarot invocations—Zenzar words—can be discovered in our everyday languages (figure 7.7).

Outside theosophical circles, the language Zenzar is not well known. Readers who know more words in Zenzar that correlate with any of the 24 Tarot invocations are invited to share their knowledge with the authors.

Specific links exist between objective forces, Tarot divination, and the use of Tarot-Zenzar incantations as objective language in magical expressions. These links and possibly invoked forces and effects are discussed in Chapter 8.

The Tarot crown of thorns

By connecting the same letters in subsequent Tarot invocations, four "musical lines" are formed, one for the letter T, one for the letter A, and so on. The four musical lines together form a braided ribbon (figure 7.8a). The musical lines in the ribbon of Tarot invocations form a remarkable pattern. In 22 of the 24 permutations, two letters remain static. In the passage from The Lovers to Intuition and from The Devil to The Universe, all letters change. At those moments we are involved in important changes that will influence our perception of life (figure 7.8b).

The musical ribbon has a point of symmetry located between The Hermit and Justice. When converted into a musical piece, at this point, a mirror fugue results; with exchanged voices, the melody moves back to the start.

Tarot & Zenzar Invocation	Tarot Arcanum	Corresponding "everyday word" and its meaning	Meanings of the Arcanum
TAOR	The Fool	Egypt: "Taoret," goddess of birth and darkness	*The new comes (per definition) from obscurity*
TOAR	The Magician	Dutch: "Tovenaar," wizard	*Influencing matter*
TORA	The Priestess	Hebrew: "Torah," the law	*Being taught and learning (the laws of life)*
TROA	The Emperor	Greek: "Thronos," throne	*Regal government*
TRAO	The Lovers	German: "Treue;" Dutch: "trouw," loyalty, fidelity	*Unification through commitment*
ATOR	Intuition (Juno)	Egypt: "Hathor," goddess of love	*Knowing and Being*
ATRO	The Priest	Gaelic: "Treo," guidance, leadership	*Guides humans to live a virtuous life*
OTRA	The Empress	Spanish: "Otra," other; Latin: "Ultra," over	*Striving for wealth*
OTAR	The Chariot	French: "Haute Arrivé," arrived at a high place	*Controlling the situation*
RTAO	The Hermit	English: "Retire," stepping back	*Contemplating*
RTOA	Justice	English: "Toga," gown; Dutch: "Toga"	*Administering Justice*
ROTA	The World	Latin: "Rotare," turning	*Life has me in its hands*
ORTA	Strength	Latin: "Orta," being taken up with	*Detachment, inner belief*
ARTO	The Hanged Man	Tibetan: "Bardo," being suspended in between	*The ultimate sacrifice uplifts*
RATO	Temperance	Latin: "Rato," with measure	*Mediation between the material and spiritual*
OATR	Death	English: "Lost his wild oats"	*Disintegration*
AOTR	The Devil	Latin: "Aorist," eternal repetition	*Without thought of completion*
ORAT	Truth (Jupiter)	Latin: "Orare," to speak	*Total insight in the Self and everything in All*
ROAT	The Tower	English: "Roaring"	*The ego detached in a tumultuous downfall*
RAOT	The Moon	French: "Raout," grave, solemn evening party	*The soul renews itself during the night*
AROT	The Star	English: "Arise," "arose"	*The renewed soul—chosen goal—is actualized*
AORT	The Sun	Latin: "Aorta," main artery from the heart	*Connected with everlasting light/energy*
OART	The Last Judgment	English and French: (O)art	*Art surpasses a human's life*
TARO	The Universe	Egypt: "Tar," way; "Ro," king, royal; Chinese: "Tao," the universe's path that we have to follow	*The royal way of virtuous life, consonant with the universe's path requires cosmic consciousness*

7.7 Taro (Zenzar) invocations, their correlations with words in our everyday languages, and their meanings. Samuel L. Mathers, 1888. Art van Remundt, 1999.

Order #	Major Arcanum	Invocation	TARO letter Musical Cincture
			T A R O
21	The Universe	TARO	
0	The Fool	TAOR	
1	The Magician	TOAR	
2	The Priestess	TORA	
3	The Emperor	TROA	
4	The Lovers	TRAO	
–	Intuition (Juno)	ATOR	
5	The Priest	ATRO	
6	The Empress	OTRA	
7	The Chariot	OTAR	
8	The Hermit	RTAO	
9	Justice	RTOA	
10	The World	ROTA	
11	Strength	ORTA	
12	The Hanged Man	ARTO	
13	Temperance	RATO	
14	Death	OATR	
15	The Devil	AOTR	
+	Truth (Jupiter)	ORAT	
16	The Tower	ROAT	
17	The Moon	RAOT	
18	The Star	AROT	
19	The Sun	AORT	
20	The Last Judgment	OART	
21	The Universe	TARO	T A R O

7.8a List of all Tarot invocations and braided band of four musical lines, formed by connecting similar letters in the Tarot names. The arcanum The Universe is placed at the beginning and the end of the table to indicate the closure of this strange loop, and the infinity of this ribbon of invocations.

MATHEMATICAL AND ESOTERIC STRUCTURES IN THE TAROT

The Tarot ribbon is symbolic of Christ's crown of thorns. In an esoteric sense, Christ is crowned with the endless cycle of life (figure 7.9).

Tarot four-fold sounds

The four musical lines in the crown of thorns can be expressed by means of the human voice and/or musical instruments. In general, as the archetypes in the Tarot are strong spiritual powers, we have to be careful if we want to control them and not be controlled by them. Distortions, such as psychedelic versions of the Tarot and Zenzar, increase this risk. So it is very important that Tarot invocations and incantations be done properly.

7.8b Major transitions in the Tarot mandala, and the point of rotational symmetry in the band of four braided musical lines.

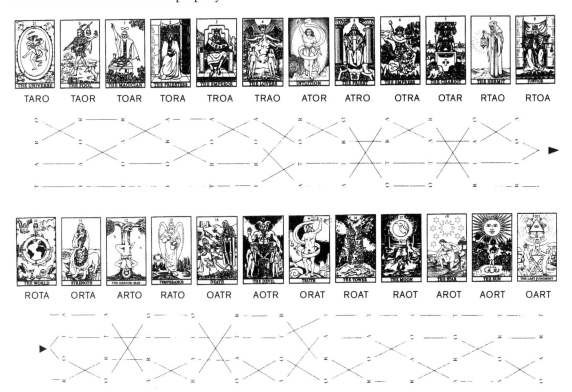

| TARO | TAOR | TOAR | TORA | TROA | TRAO | ATOR | ATRO | OTRA | OTAR | RTAO | RTOA |

| ROTA | ORTA | ARTO | RATO | OATR | AOTR | ORAT | ROAT | RAOT | AROT | AORT | OART |

Invocations work according to the principle that if we think of somebody or something, in our mind we call the name of that person or object. Thinking without speaking is almost impossible. This applies even more to deep thinking; it is common to assist meditative thinking, for instance, through the voice. For these reasons, in all religions much care is taken to execute incantations and invocations properly, such as Gregorian chants, Vedantic mantras, and Indian incantations.

The four musical lines naturally bring to mind a musical piece with four voices: bass, tenor, contralto, and soprano. *Each TAROT invocation can be represented by a chord of four tones.* The question is which tone to assign to each of the letters in each of the TAROT invocations. We approached the problem of the correlation of

7.9 The Tarot crown of thorns. Interpreted esoterically, Christ is crowned by the eternal life cycle, as represented by the Tarot itself.

tones with the Tarot names as follows. Each of the four letters T-A-R-O in a Tarot name is correlated with a particular tone, and each Tarot name results in a harmony comprised of four tones. The position of a card—upright or reversed—is important, too. In a reversed invocation, the four tones are used half a tone lower.

With regard to tuning prior to playing or singing Tarot incantations: ideally, all musical Tarot invocations should be based on Just Temperament. In this way of tempering, all intervals are pure and the frequencies of the tones are in simple proportion to one another. Today's commonly used Equal Temperament does not have pure intervals apart from the octaves. Music in Just Temperament is very expressive, and strikingly clear and pure in tonality.

We determined the separate tones for each of the letters by starting with the invocation "TARO." This incantation consists of four rising octaves of the tone "a." The letter A in the word TARO is represented by the "a" of 420 Hz. In Just Temperament an "a" of 420 Hz is numerologically more appropriate than the standard "a" of 440 Hz (420 can be divided by the numbers 1 through 7). In the invocation of the word TARO reversed, the letter A is represented by the tone "g" (figure 7.10).

THE TWO STANDARD TAROT CHORDS

Tarot name	Position	Taro standard accord			
T⁺A⁺R⁺O⁺	upright	a	a^I	a^{II}	a^{III}
T⁻A⁻R⁻O⁻	reversed	g	g^I	g^{II}	g^{III}

7.10 The two standard chords and incantations based on the word "TARO."

The remaining 46 chords for the 23 upright cards and the 23 reversed cards can be determined by the position of the letters T, A, R, O in the invocation and the position of the Tarot name (upright or reversed).

There are four letters, namely T-A-R-O, in each invocation. Each letter can take one of four positions. Thus, in total, 4 x 4 x 2 = 32 different tones have to be assigned to the letters and their possible positions. These tones have to be selected from the tonal range between "g" and "a≈≈" inclusive. As this range comprises more whole and half tones than necessary, a key has to be chosen—that is, a particular selection of whole and half tones has to be made. For music based on upright Major Arcana only, we selected the key D-major. For music based on reversed cards only, we assigned the key D-minor. Other selections of keys are also possible; the reader is free to experiment with these. Figure 7.11 lists the resulting set of 32 tones. The frequencies in this table are based on Just Temperament as published by H. Mersenne in his book *Harmonie Universelle*. From this table, a Just Tempered chord of four tones can be composed for each Tarot invocation.

Letter	Position In Invocation	Tone	Frequency (Hz)	Letter	Position In Invocation	Tone	Frequency (Hz)
0 +	4	a^{III}	1680	A +	4	$c\#^{II}$	525
0 –	4	g^{III}	1512	A –	4	c^{II}	504
0 +	3	$f\#^{III}$	1400	A +	3	b^{I}	572 ¹/₂
0 –	3	f^{III}	1344	A –	3	bb^{I}	448
0 +	2	e^{III}	1260	A +	2	a^{I}	420
0 –	2	d^{III}	1120	A –	2	g^{I}	378
0 +	1	$c\#^{III}$	1050	A +	1	$f\#^{I}$	350
0 –	1	c^{III}	1008	A –	1	f^{I}	336
R +	4	b^{II}	945	T +	4	e^{I}	315
R –	4	bb^{II}	896	T –	4	d^{I}	280
R +	3	a^{II}	840	T +	3	$c\#^{I}$	262 ¹/₂
R –	3	g^{II}	756	T –	3	c	252
R +	2	$f\#^{II}$	700	T +	2	b	236 ¹/₂
R –	2	f^{II}	672	T –	2	bb	224
R +	1	e^{II}	630	T +	1	a	210
R –	1	d^{II}	560	T –	1	g	189

7.11 Table of tonal values of Tarot letters in Tarot invocations, upright (+) and reversed (–), in order of decreasing pitch.

Tarot music

The table in figure 7.12 can be used to compose Tarot music. Every series of Tarot invocations can be converted to a musical piece in four voices. Each voice sings the course of one of the letters T, A, R, or O, and uses the four tones assigned to this letter (depending on their position in the Tarot name).

As an example, the table in figure 7.12 contains the series of chords that would result if the 24 Major Arcana were sung in the order of the life cycle, in upright position. Using this table the 24 Tarot incantations can be converted into ordinary musical notation.

THE MAJOR ARCANA AS MUSIC IN FOUR VOICES

Major Arcanum	Invocation	Incantative Chord			
The Universe	TARO				
The Fool	TAOR	a	a^{I}	a^{II}	a^{III}
The Magician	TOAR	a	a^{I}	$f\#^{II}$	b^{II}
The Priestess	TORA	a	e^{III}	b^{I}	b^{II}
The Emperor	TROA	a	e^{III}	a^{II}	$c\#^{II}$
The Lovers	TRAO	a	$f\#^{III}$	$f\#^{III}$	$c\#^{II}$
Intuition (Juno)	ATOR	a	$f\#^{II}$	b^{I}	a^{III}
The Priest	ATRO	$f\#^{I}$	b	$f\#^{III}$	b^{II}
The Empress	OTRA	$f\#^{I}$	b	a^{II}	a^{III}
The Chariot	OTAR	$c\#^{III}$	b	a^{II}	$c\#^{II}$
The Hermit	RTAO	$c\#^{III}$	b	b^{I}	b^{II}

7.12 The 24 Major Arcana as a cycle of 24 Tarot chords.

MATHEMATICAL AND ESOTERIC STRUCTURES IN THE TAROT

Justice	RTOA	e^{II}	b	b^{I}	a^{III}
The World	ROTA	e^{II}	b	$f\#^{II}$	$c\#^{II}$
Strength	ORTA	e^{II}	e^{III}	$c\#^{I}$	$c\#^{II}$
The Hanged Man	ARTO	$c\#^{III}$	$f\#^{II}$	$c\#^{I}$	$c\#^{II}$
Temperance	RATO	$f\#^{I}$	$f\#^{II}$	$c\#^{I}$	a^{III}
Death	OATR	e^{II}	a^{I}	$c\#^{I}$	a^{III}
The Devil	AOTR	$c\#^{III}$	a^{I}	$c\#^{I}$	b^{II}
Truth (Jupiter)	ORAT	$f\#^{I}$	e^{III}	$c\#^{I}$	b^{II}
The Tower	ROAT	$c\#^{III}$	$f\#^{II}$	b^{I}	e^{I}
The Moon	RAOT	e^{II}	e^{III}	b^{I}	e^{I}
The Star	AROT	e^{II}	a^{I}	$f\#^{II}$	e^{I}
The Sun	AORT	$f\#^{I}$	$f\#^{II}$	$f\#^{II}$	e^{I}
The Last Judgment	OART	$f\#^{I}$	e^{III}	a^{II}	e^{I}
The Universe	TARO	$c\#^{III}$	a^{I}	a^{II}	e^{I}
		a	a^{I}	a^{II}	a^{III}

In Figure 7.13a–b the Tarot incantations of the 24 Major Arcana are given in musical notation and combined into one ribbon.

The beginning and the end of this musical composition should be connected to turn it into an eternally continuing loop. The Tarot incantations in figure 7.13a–b are all transposed one octave down to make them easier to sing.

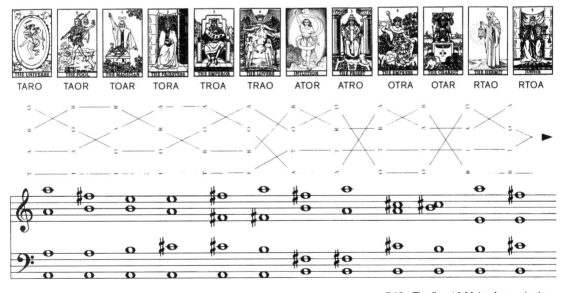

7.13a The first 12 Major Arcana in the mantra TARO-ROTA-ROTA.

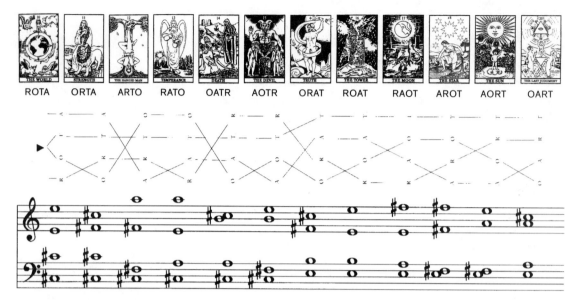

| ROTA | ORTA | ARTO | RATO | OATR | AOTR | ORAT | ROAT | RAOT | AROT | AORT | OART |

7.13b The second 12 Major Arcana in the mantra TARO-ROTA-ROTA.

In figure 7.14 the mantra TARO-TORA-ROTA in four voices is given in normal musical notation; all tones have been transposed one octave.

The musical piece in figure 7.14 evokes a peaceful, meditative, and unearthly atmosphere, especially when played on instruments tuned in Just temperament. As it does not have a clear beat, it is an ever-continuing play of sounds. We have called this mantra TARO-TORA-ROTA: the Tarot is an eternal, cyclic, and changing law.

There are many other possibilities. A Celtic Cross spread may be converted into a brief musical piece and sung or played. Figure 7.15 represents the Celtic Cross from figure 9.21 in musical form. Also, Tarot canons may be composed; figure 7.16 shows a Tarot-canon for four voices in which the same "O" melody begins four times, one beat after another. A change to another key will convey a different atmosphere.

The three musical incantations in figures 7.14–7.16 are in counterpoint. In all three the vertical structure is completely specified and fixed—apart from the selection of the key. Yet the horizontal structure of the musical pieces is elementary. Composers may enrich Tarot invocation-based musical pieces by developing their horizontal aspects, thus giving each of the four voices melodic richness. An example is the *TARO-TORA-ROTA Variations* in figure 7.17. Readers are free to use sets of four-tone Tarot incantations for musical compositions, providing that in such compositions *The Complete New Tarot* is acknowledged as the source.

Incantation of the 24 Major Arcana as Life Cycle
TARO-TORA-ROTA

Rob and Onno Docters van Leeuwen

7.14 The 24 Major Arcana as a musical piece for four voices. The cycle of 24 chords can be repeated as an endless mantra.

Celtic Cross Incantation for the Restored Tarot

Rob and Onno Docters van Leeuwen

7.15 This incantation is based on the spread for the restored Tarot, discussed in Chapter 9 and shown in figure 9.22. The sequence of invocations is:
TARO→ ATRO → OATR → ARTO → OART → ORAT → AORT → AROT → RATO → ROTA.

MATHEMATICAL AND ESOTERIC STRUCTURES IN THE TAROT

Canon on the "O" in the Restored Tarot Life Cycle

Rob and Onno Docters van Leeuwen

7.16 Tarot-canon in four voices on the musical "O" line in the Life Cycle.

7.17 The first 38 bars of the sonata *"TARO - TORA - ROTA, Laws of the Changing Universe,"* for flute and guitars. The subjects in these variations are the two incantations in figure 7.14 and 7.15.

MATHEMATICAL AND ESOTERIC STRUCTURES IN THE TAROT

2

The Tarot color cycle

Tarot invocations evoke energies. Smells, sounds, and colors are physical, as well as spiritual energies. Both energies are expressions at our level of the supernal Light of the Cosmos, the Self-radiating Light. Its Freemasons symbol, the one-eyed pyramid, is incorporated in the Great Seal of the United States of America (figure 7.18).

The archetypal color *white* is composed of a mix of electromagnetic energy waves. The archetypal color *black* is the absence of light. A third archetypal color is *Mother-Earth brown,* a mixture of the colors red, yellow, and blue in a ratio of about 3:2:1.

Each of the 24 Major Arcana is linked to a color and has a particular main color theme in the background. The gradual color change through the arcana, when arranged in the life cycle mandala, resembles the change of colors throughout a day. The day side arcana have light and sunny colors, the night side, dark blue and purple.

The colors assigned to the arcana are based on Goethe's color circle. He divided the three primary colors red, yellow, and blue into 6, 12, and 24 colors, and arranged them in a circular gradation. The color of the clear sky during sunrise, and the soft yellow-green of new leaves in Spring, have been assigned to the first Tarot-quartet: The Fool, the Page of Pentacles, and the One and Two of Pentacles. The colors of all subsequent arcana follow logically. As the zodiacal signs are coupled with the Major Arcana, the zodiac is linked to the color circle as well (figure 7.19).

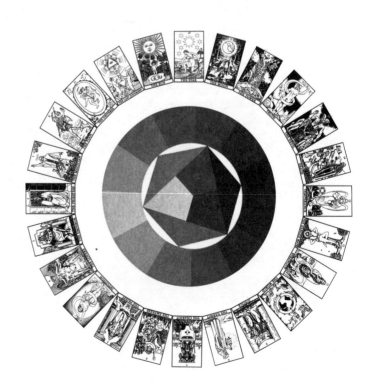

The authenticity of the restored Tarot

The Roman Catholic Church, the Vatican, and Islam don't give full access to their secret archives and libraries. Without access to these sources it is difficult to further investigate in a historical and scientific sense the obfuscation of Juno (–) and Jupiter (+) in the Tarot. Nonetheless, the authenticity of the 24 Major Arcana Tarot is supported by at least ten facts:

1. In very early versions of the Tarot, Juno and Jupiter are included as female and male archetypes.
2. From the word TARO 24 permutations can be derived, each of which can be assigned to one Major Arcanum. The meanings assigned to the TARO permutations, their Zenzar meanings, and their etymological links with other languages are striking.
3. The 24 TARO permutations, when placed in the order of the Tarot life cycle grouped in four, form six magic squares—a structure that seals the correct order of the 24 Major Arcana hermetically.
4. The order of 24 Major Arcana is logical as a human life cycle. It correlates with the zodiac, the 12 astrological houses, the 12 nidanas in Buddhism, the 24 moon phases, and the 24 hours in the day.
5. The 24 Major Arcana correlate well with the position, name, and character of the 24 Knights of the Round Table, as displayed on the table in the Great Hall of Winchester Castle.
6. The 24 Major Arcana correlate well with the colors in Goethe's color circle.
7. Numerologically, the restored Tarot comprises the structure of the New Jerusalem (figure 7.20).
8. It unites the cosmological-philosophical principles 2: Yin-Yang; 3: the trinity; 4: quadruplicity; 5: pentacles governing nature; 6: the Star of David and seal of Solomon; 7: the Divine octave; 8: the eight-spoked Vedic Sun wheel and the lemniscate as eternity symbol; 9: the enneagram (Gurdjieff); 10: the binary zero and one; 12: the zodiac; 24: the hours in the day and the 24 prophets (Gospel of Thomas Logion 52).
9. The 24 Major Arcana correlate in order and meaning with the 24 symbols in the Nordic rune alphabet (figure 8.1).
10. The restored Tarot consists of 81 philosophical principles (80 arcana and Tao as the common back of the cards). *The Tao Te Ching* by Lao Tse consists of 81 chapters.

The greatest strengths of the completed, restored Tarot are the inclusion of the male and female archetypes, its hermetic geomantic structure, as represented in the pictorial content of its Major and Minor Arcana.

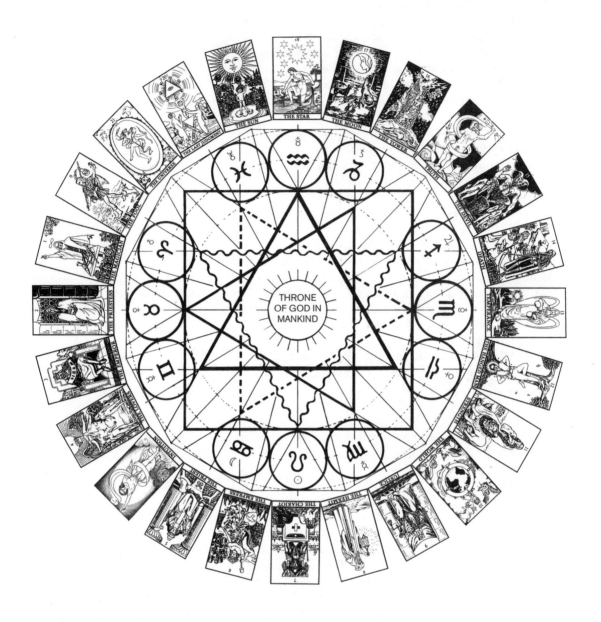

7.20 Mandala of the 24 Major Arcana of the restored Tarot correlated with The New Jerusalem (the Diamond Town of consciousness, Truth, and Love) in the Revelations of John 21:9–27.

The structure of The New Jerusalem is based on the geometry and cycles of the earth and moon. This diagram, from *City of Revelation*, by John Mitchell (1972) shows the 12 gates linked with the 12 signs of the zodiac.

The obscured and the completed Tarot as a world spread

The Tarot has been obscured via an algorithm that in itself contains symbolic information on how to restore the Tarot to its original order. Application of the obfuscation algorithm not only served to mutilate the Tarot; at the same time, it is also the key to its restoration.

The Tarot is not only a game of cards, but also a mirror image of our unconscious. Its obfuscation, as discussed above, changed the symbolic order of the Akashic chronicles, stored in the universal consciousness of humankind from time immemorial. The obfuscation of the Tarot, used as a spread for humankind and the world during the second millennium A.D., revealed what was in store for humankind during that period and which principles would become important in forthcoming centuries.

The Star, symbol of heavenly guidance, hope, and cosmic energy, has a central position at the top of the life cycle (Figure 7.21).

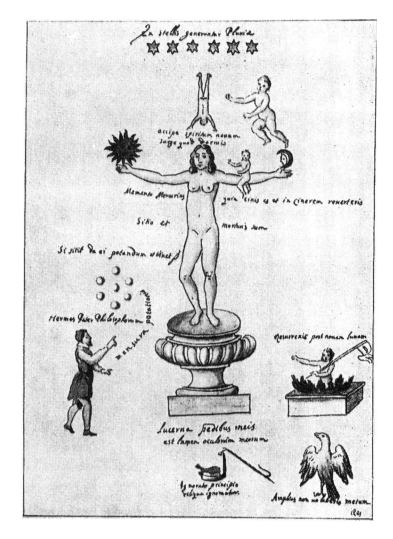

7.21 The traditional alchemistic order of the Three Celestial Bodies. At the top of this diagram, from right to left, the celestial bodies are ordered counter-clockwise: moon, stars, sun. The inverted human at the position of The Star is descending from the stars and in the process of reincarnating. The text under the person summarizes the arcanum The Star; it reads: *Receive new spirit. Arise, for you are asleep.* (From *The hermetic and alchemistic figures of Claudius De Domenico Celentano Vallis Novi*, manuscript, written and illuminated at Naples A.D. 1606).

One of the most serious consequences of the obfuscation of the arcana Truth (Jupiter) and Intuition (Juno) was the shift of a number of cards that changed this order. The Moon, principle of pretense, sleep, corruption, suffering, etc., pushed The Star from its proper position at the top and became more influential than The Star.

Another major consequence of the obfuscation of the male and female archetypes, Truth (Yang) and Intuition (Yin), was that the existence of the animus and anima, present in the psyche of every human being, was denied. This obfuscation veiled the words:

So God created human beings, making them to be like himself. He created them male and female. (Genesis 1:27)

Suppression of women and the sexual struggle of men (with celibacy, for example), hypocrisy, and cruelty (as in the Inquisition, among other historical occurrences) were for centuries clearly visible manifestations of these changes.

The obfuscated world spread was synchronous with the spirit of those times and took place during the age of Pisces. This period is now at an end and we are moving into the Age of Aquarius. This is thought to be a herald of better times. That the restoration of the order of the Tarot is happening *now* is no coincidence.

In the restored Tarot the two essential arcana, Truth and Intuition, have returned. The Star and all other arcana have been returned to their proper positions (figure 7.22 a–b).

STAR

SUN

MOON

MOON

SUN

STAR

a

b

7.22 Positioning of The Star:
a The original and correct position of the Major Arcanum The Star at the top of the Tarot life cycle.

b The Major Arcanum The Moon, *incorrectly* placed at the top of the life cycle as result of the obfuscation of Jupiter (Truth) and Juno (Intuition). In both cases the numbering of the cards is incorrect—this is caused by the absence of Juno and Jupiter in the deck.

Other 80-card Tarot versions may now join ranks, and in this way undo the damage that was done during the Middle Ages. Gradually the 80-card Tarot decks will become the norm again.

The complete Tarot, as presented it in this book, is synchronous with the principles of Aquarius—an age in which truth, freedom, the equality of men and women, hope, vision, harmony between people, and consciousness will prevail.

7.23 Diagram of the hermetic and alchemistic order in the "Law of Three." The Peacock in the center is the alchemistic symbol of Hermes (Mercury).

THE UNIVERSAL LAW OF THREE-FOLDEDNESS

RIGHT	MIDDLE	LEFT
Sun	*Star*	*Moon*
Gold	Mercury	Silver
Yang	Tao	Yin
Positive	Neutral	Negative
Male	Neuter	Female
Rajas	Sattva	Tamas
Active	Neutralizing	Passive
Birth	Life	Death
Father	Child	Mother
Right eye	Third eye	Left eye
Day	Morning	Night
Thesis	Synthesis	Antithesis
Future	Present	Past

7.24 In this figure, the 24 Major Arcana and the four "aces" of the Tarot of Marseilles—numbered according to and placed in the restored order—form the swastika mandala.

MATHEMATICAL AND ESOTERIC STRUCTURES IN THE TAROT

Theory of Divination

Everything that happens in this world
happens at the time God chooses.
— *Ecclesiastes 3:1*

Eternity cannot be named.
—*Art van Remundt*

CHAPTER 8

Theory of Divination

Predicting

Predicting literally means foretelling something that people can't see as yet by themselves. It is the disclosure of knowledge about things that still have to occur. Predicting is also called *divining*, as it is believed that it may divulge the will of the gods. A subcategory of divining is *oracling*.

Predictions normally are not made in plain language. Often they are given in symbols that are cryptic for the questioner, but intelligible for the diviner. The means by which these messages are conveyed may be cracks in a bone that has been burned for some time, shapes formed by the tea leaves that remain in a cup, positions of planets, lines in hands, selected Tarot cards, or many others.

Divining

Divining is a phenomenon common in all civilizations. The word comes from Latin and means "discovering the will of the gods" (divine = godly). This meaning is based on the belief that the gods determine the fate of humankind. These days, divining has a wider meaning. It is an interactive process with two aspects:

1. Using a particular method, information is acquired about a question.
2. The questioner is assisted in the interpretation of the acquired information.

The first aspect of divination is generally known, but the second is often left out of the discussion, even though divination particularly involves the counseling of others. Both sides of divination must be integrated in the consultation.

Divination has been common throughout the world for many centuries, among primitive tribes as well as in the eastern and western cultures of today: it simply belongs to us. In all cultures people regularly seek help in predicting the future. They do not necessarily see this as uncovering the will of the gods, but more as acquiring an insight into developments that are about to happen as a result of their present state in the world.

Foretelling—Oracles

The word "oracle" is derived from the Latin verb *orare*, which means "to speak." Hence, it is a verbal way of predicting. In an oracle, either a synchronistic choice is made from a limited, predetermined set of expressions, such as in the I Ching, or a person who is in trance makes particular statements. Prediction with Tarot cards cannot be called oracling, as the Tarot cards do not bear verbal expressions.

Methods of divination

There are many methods of divination. The simplest are binary methods such as picking up stones. It is decided beforehand what outcome will show a positive answer. For example, let's say odd numbers bring luck and even numbers mean doubt and discouragement. The question is asked, for example, "Does she love me?" Next, an unknown number of stones or marbles is picked from a pile, and the stones are counted: one = yes, two = no, three = yes, four = no, etc. The last stone gives the answer. Divining by plucking a flower and pulling out the petals one by one, or blowing away in stages the seeds from a dandelion, works according to the same principle. The great variety of divinatory methods can be classified into three main groups:

1. The interpretation of natural phenomena as the will of a god (intuitive divination).
2. The interpretation of the way chance operates upon an object provided by a person (inductive divination).
3. The interpretation of the way god's will (or chance) acts upon meanings (interpretative divination).

Combinations are possible as well.

Intuitive divination

The prototype of the intuitive diviner is the medium, a priest or priestess, shaman, witch doctor, etc., who enters a state of trance to generate oracles. The required state of trance can develop spontaneously or be induced by drugs or by autokinetic techniques, such as prolonged dancing. In the western world intuitive divination often is induced by autohypnotic techniques, such as staring into a glass sphere, a white wall, a red lamp, or a swinging pendulum.

Often the "possession of the medium by a god or spirit" is accompanied by an impressive ceremony culminating in a speech by the god or spirit through the medium. This is common in many religious traditions. In ancient Egypt, sleeping in the temple was employed with the purpose of becoming inspired by the god to whom that temple was dedicated. Diviners of nomadic tribes can, even today, still go into trance in front of their tribe members and speak as if their own spirit is silenced and replaced by another. Intuitive divination can also be a totally private matter. Someone can go into a meditation after which that person is spoken to by a god, a ghost, or angel. The Bible gives many examples of such events.

Inductive divination

Inductive divination uses inductive reasoning to discover the *causes* of different kinds of events. Inductive divination phenomena in nature are determined by chance. Since it is impossible for such chance phenomena to be influenced by humans, this increases the validity of the reading. Examples are the reading of celestial events; changes in the weather or shapes of clouds; the flight of birds; the positions of the sun, moon, stars, and planets (astrology); and the shape of intestines (haroscopy). Reading the cracks in a shoulder blade (scapulimancy) is practiced in North America and Asia, and the reading of lines in palms (chiromancy) or feet, or patterns in the iris (iridology) is also known in western culture.

Another form of inductive divination interprets phenomena in nature that results from the ritual manipulation of objects. Examples are the reading of smoke rising from a sacrifice, the way a spear falls (to indicate the direction of a search or conquest), the plucking of petals from a many-petaled flower while uttering a sentence, and the ritual throwing of stones or particular objects. In all these cases, the purpose is to acquire information by interpreting the way objects move when they are "controlled" by nature alone. Other examples of inductive divination are the reading of tea leaves in a cup and the Aloha oracle, a ritual in which seven colored beads are grasped from a pot and thrown; the answer is determined by interpreting the colors and position in which the beads fall.

Interpretive divination

Interpretative divination is based on reading a collection of pictures, symbols, or patterns that has been determined by divine laws, or by chance. This includes prediction via *astrology,* a system that interprets the meanings of the positions of planets and star constellations; *numerology,* a system that reduces words and names to numbers that have a particular meaning; and *Tarot cards, Rune stones,* and *I Ching hexagrams.* In an I Ching oracle, thrown coins or selected stalks mathematically form patterns of six lines, whole or broken, called hexagrams. Each hexagram is a highly stylized image with a specific meaning. All these systems have in common the notion that synchroncity is omnipresent, and therefore the future course of one series of events may be clarified by interpreting another series of events.

The Runes oracle

The Runes oracle and the Tarot are related divinatory systems. The Runes oracle is an old Scandinavian-German method, which uses 24 stones, each bearing a letter of the old rune alphabet, the Futhark. Each rune symbol has a divinatory meaning. Figure 8.1 lists the runes and their meanings, correlated with the Major Arcana of the Tarot. The similarity in the meanings of the two systems is remarkable and indicates that they may have emerged from the same source of objective knowledge.

The importance of divination to the western world

Although humankind has always had a strong desire to know what the future holds, in the western world fortune telling has questionable connotations. There are several reasons for this. Western culture is largely based on Christianity, a religion opposed to any form of gaining knowledge about what God has in store. A committed Christian sees no use in foretelling the future and may actually consider it to be blasphemous. Such a person does not need to know what tomorrow will look like, and will solve problematic situations with an eye to personal goals and Christian norms.

Another reason for skepticism about fortune telling is the western, rational attitude toward life, which is difficult to combine with situations that cannot be explained scientifically. Rationalism states that each tangible event has a physical cause that we know or don't yet know, and that everything outside this chain of cause and effect does not exist. This manner of thinking excludes divination, prophetic dreams, telekinesis, telepathic communication, clairvoyance, and any other such system.

8.1 Meanings of the Runes in the Runes-oracle correlated with the Major Arcana of the restored Tarot.

THE 24 RUNES CORRELATED WITH THE 24 MAJOR ARCANA OF THE TAROT

Rune	Name	Meaning	Major Arcanum	Number
	URUZ	Wild life energy, new beginning, unexpected visit	The Fool	0
	OTHALA	Place of birth, property, inheritance, being yourself	The Magician	1
	BERKANA	Gentle growth, guided development, care	The Priestess	2
	TIWAZ	Male energy, ruthless dedication, invincible warrior	The Emperor	3
	ANSUZ	Protection, a safe place, new events, challenges	The Lovers	4
	FEHU	The god Freyr, plenitude, love, mysticism, and philosophy	Intuition (Juno)	-
	GEBO	Unity (also with the divine), partnership, presents	The Priest	5
	INGWAZ	Fertility, offspring, energies needed for a new life	The Empress	6
	RAIDHO	Wheel, sun-chariot, travels, cycle of seasons, career	The Chariot	7
	KENAZ	Transforming powers, torch, change in life	The Hermit	8
	JERA	Collecting the harvest after a year of labor, reward	Justice	9
	WUNJO	Happiness, luck, light, finding balance in your life	The World	10
	NAUDHIZ	Test, the necessity of doing what is right, endurance	Strength	11
	EIHWAZ	Evergreen, eternal life (as death of moments), sacrifice	The Hanged Man	12
	LAGUZ	Water, the unconscious, seeing deeper, changes	Temperance	13
	ISA	Ice, stagnation, patience, without passion	Death	14
	THURISAZ	Thorn, test, bad times, exploitation by others, patience	The Devil	15
	OTHALA	The god Odin, mouth, communication, relationships	Truth (Jupiter)	+
	PERDHRO	Limited vision, enclosed space, secret	The Tower	16
	HAGALAZ	Winter, hail, unexpected events and dangers	The Moon	17
	SOWILO	Sun, energy, health, victory, success	The Star	18
	ALGIZ	Horse, travel, change	The Sun	19
	DAGAZ	New day, darkness replaced by light, breakthrough	The Last Judgment	20
	MANNAZ	Mankind, relationships, cooperation	The Universe	21
		Blank Rune, unknown, own development	TAO, common back of II Arcana	

However, in the 1950s, a branch of psychology developed called parapsychology, which aims to scientifically describe and investigate these phenomena.

Notwithstanding the reservations mentioned above, divination is widespread in the western world, astrology being the most popular divinatory method. There are many kings, queens, presidents, politicians, and tycoons who at regular times and in secret ask for advice from astrologers, clairvoyants, shamans, etc. With the dawn of the Age of Aquarius, interest and belief in the value of other forms of divination such as I Ching, the Tarot, runes, and western and Chinese astrology is on the increase. The western mind is opening up to other aspects of existence.

The material world and the psychological world, or why divination works

Many of us have experienced how well predictions sometimes turn out. How is this possible? The simple answer "pure coincidence" is not satisfactory, because so many different predictions are possible that the probability of a prediction turning out right by chance is negligible: something else is going on.

The explanation is not easy and cannot be given in a comprehensive way. In divination, matter participates in a mysterious and unexplainable way. Every successful divination is proof of an interaction between matter and spirit. Matter and spirit are intertwined. C. G. Jung says about this issue:

Psyche is a quality of matter because we exist as matter. . . Just as in Chinese philosophy the male (Yang) carries the seed of the female (Yin) and vice versa, in matter the seed of psyche may be discovered and in psyche the seed of matter.

Psyche and matter exist in the same world and influence each other. This was generally accepted until deep in the Middle Ages. It was expressed in alchemy, a combination of physics and metaphysics.

In the seventeenth century, physics liberated itself from ties with religion, philosophy, alchemy, and the unconscious through acceptance of a mechanistic world concept. René Descartes (1596–1650) discriminated radically between mind and matter. His disciples found support in Newton's theory of gravity, in which physical processes are controlled by mechanical, causal laws. When the starting point of a system is known with absolute certainty, the end-point can be predicted. In Newton's opinion the formulation of his laws was only one aspect of matter. He was, as an alchemist, searching for laws that would apply to the whole universe, materially and spiritually. A consequence of the work of scholars such as Descartes and Newton was that the universal interpretation of phenomena and life in western thinking lost more and more ground.

Over the next four centuries, classical physics and chemistry assumed the world to be a machine of which absolute causality and laws governed all movements and processes. In the centuries after Newton, through systematic research, many of those laws were discovered. The quick maturation of the natural sciences "robbed" matter of its soul. Matter was considered inanimate. Observable phenomena were combined through causal relationships only. If an idea or thesis could not be tested in a causal and physical way, that idea was philosophical or religious and not scientific, and thus not suitable for inclusion in the already existing body of natural scientific knowledge. In the same way, from a rationalistic viewpoint, a picture on a Tarot card and the position of that card in a spread could not possibly have anything to do with our character, soul, past, or future. The western world's scientific conditioning has a very strong tendency to inhibit the idea that spirit and matter may interact in an acausal way.

8.2 "It is true, without fabrication, certain, and very believable: what is below is the same as what is above, and what is above is the same as what is below, to bind the wonders of all things in one principle" (Mutus Liber, 1702).

The matter-spirit dualism in western thinking is the most important reason why divination is addressed with so much skepticism. Non-western cultures do not take this duality for granted; in those cultures, divination is considered a normal process of information gathering.

In the second half of the twentieth century, a bridging process started over the chasm between the material and psychological worlds. On the one hand, connections were made from the side of nuclear physics, thermodynamics, quantum mechanics, and information theory, as these disciplines now accept acausality under certain conditions. On the other hand, bridges were beginning to be built from the sides of parapsychology, the media, literature, and science fiction movies, which accumulated and disseminated "factual proof" of the existence of acausal processes and events.

Acausal thinking in the natural sciences

Since the 1950s, nuclear physics has not been exclusively causal in its ways of thinking. Some physical processes are now viewed as illogical: for instance, the position and velocity of an object cannot both be measured exactly at the same time, *even in theory*. The very concepts of *exact position* and *exact velocity* together have no meaning in nature. The uncertainty principle states that the product of uncertainties in position and velocity is equal to or greater than a tiny physical constant (about 10^{-34} joule-second). Only for extremely small masses does this product of uncertainties become significant. Hence, the position or speed of a molecule, atom, or nuclear particle cannot be predicted with absolute certainty. Only the chance of finding a particle at a particular point in space can be calculated.

The implication of this development in philosophical thinking is that what was thought to be part of the absolute, concrete causality laws in physics has been shown to be flawed. Thus, at the very foundation of matter, some of the universal, causal laws do not apply. Instead, matter behaves in some ways at this level in an acausal manner, just as the spirit does.

Werner K. Heisenberg (1901–1976), a German physicist and philosopher discovered a way in 1925 to formulate quantum mechanics in terms of matrices for which he was awarded the Nobel Prize in 1932. In 1927 he published the *uncertainty principle* for which he is best known. He sacrificed the existing, mechanistic model of discrete particles moving in prescribed paths (for example, electrons around an atomic nucleus) for an approach in which, through matrix algebra, he could specify sets of possible values for physical variables at the particle level (possible positions of a particle in space). Heisenberg's work on quantum theory profoundly influenced the development of atomic and nuclear physics.

In quantum mechanics two atoms are not always independent, but sometimes relate to and influence each other on a very fundamental level. In such a situation, interdependence between atoms creates a bond between them and one object determines the other. Here profound coherence is more important than independence. Just as it is accepted in quantum mechanics that one particle does not exist separate from the other, in psychology object and subject do not exist independently either. In both cases there is mutuality.

The Nobel Prize-winning physicist Wolfgang Pauli (1900–1958) stated that with Newton and Descartes, physics had gone the wrong way. He fought a heavy inner battle to create a synthesis between the psychological and the material. Pauli corresponded extensively with Jung about this matter. Thirty years after his death, his letters became public. They caused a shock in the world of physicists, who, through advances in physics, had become more sensitive to Pauli's ideas by then than they had been during his life.

According to Pauli, a researcher is part of, and a codetermining factor in, experiments. The alchemists assumed this too. Pauli stated that quantum theory cannot completely describe reality, as it denies the existence of the unconscious. Matter comprises an extra element, which is the psyche. The physical sciences will remain fragmentary if their scientists do not heal their split mentality by relinquishing this matter-spirit dualism. As the psychological and material exist in the same world, they must find common ground in each other, and at some level there must be a connection or common foundation of physical and psychological concepts.

Parapsychology investigates the boundary between the two and has—despite its scientific yoke of matter-spirit dualism and a laborious battle for recognition—carried forward much valuable material.

The search for parallels and analogies between physics and psychology will not and cannot lead to the unification of these two sciences, because we then jump intellectually from one field to the other. It is impossible to find one formula that covers both psychology and physics. We have to jump off both islands, "forget" what was learned, and concentrate on what emerges from one's own inner world. Pauli says:

> Background physics remains unnoticed. To the three dimensions space, time, and causality, a fourth dimension must be added: the emotional significance of the researcher. The total psychological state of the observer plays a complementary role in a quantum-physical experiment.

There are various situations in which man sojourns in the borderland between the psychological and the material. In dreams, for example, we explore the really unified human. It is therefore expedient to listen to the myths of the soul.

Creating art is becoming aware of spiritual forms or structures and making them tangible. Enjoying art goes the other way around, that is, observing the tangible in order to become aware of spiritual, abstract structures. How otherwise could a musical piece (in fact, just a series of air vibrations) be able to evoke such deep emotions? Each artist brings together in his or her creations the psychological and the material, and everyone who enjoys a piece of art does the same. In a state of spiritual mutuality, we can experience and recognize the unity of spirit and matter. Divination explores the realm where psyche and matter overlap each other. Although life goes the way it is meant to go anyway, divination may help us to understand our path better and walk that path more fittingly.

The meaningful combination of circumstances, or how divination works

Predictions are based on meaningful coincidences of circumstances. Jung did not ask for the cause of an event, but for its sense. He defined time as a continuum filled with conditions, which, simultaneously in different places, can create coherent events. Divination doesn't have to do with cause and effect, according to Jung, but with *synchronicity:* a meaningful coincidence of circumstances that are not causally connected. The book that Jung and Pauli wrote about this matter, *Explanation of Nature and Psyche, Synchronicity as a Principle of Acausal Relationships (Natur-erklärung und Psyche: Synchronicität als ein Prinzip akausaler Zusammanhänge),* was published in 1952.

Synchronicity is perceptible if, at the same moment, different events happen that turn out to be meaningful to each other, but that also could have taken place independently of each other at different times. According to Jung, mutually meaningful events are related through a network of time, and happen concurrently.

Later in his life, Jung always studied the horoscope of his patient. He did not believe that the personality was formed through the powers of the stars and planets, but through the characteristics of the moment of birth. The planetary positions in astrology could then be considered as measurable variables from which the quality of time can be read or deduced. Just as with wines, a person is to some extent determined by the qualities of the year and season (the astrological constellation) and place in which he or she is born. Everything always happens at the right time.

According to the philosopher, essayist, and writer Aldous Huxley (1894–1963) and many others, there is *always* synchronicity, because everything from the first moment of creation, the Big Bang, is in tune. This coherence of the ten-thousand things (Lao Tse) can only be noticed in a state of raised consciousness. Through commitment, emotional involvement, and love, our psyche can tune in to a particular situation, and synchronicity may be observed.

During divination, a broadening of consciousness occurs, the duality between matter and spirit becomes vague, and psychological and material structures are brought closer together. In this way, we can obtain a direct insight into our situation. We can improve our understanding of synchronicity and tune into it by means of special exercises and experiments, discussions, study, and meditation. The Tarot offers exercise and study material for this purpose.

Tarot divination and synchronicity

A Tarot spread may be envisioned as a series of archetypal snapshots of a segment of eternity-space that has the questioner's interest. In a divination, the shuffling and parting of the cards opens the way for them to synchronistically arrange themselves in an order that reflects the questioner's situation. This is why a Tarot spread is normally full of meaning to the diviner.

When the cards have been laid out, the Tarot consultant reads the cards in the spread and translates their symbols into the questioner's context, in everyday language. In this way, the questioner may gain a better understanding of the situation and become more aware of potential developments. The insights thus gained may help in choosing the right path. We can change the final outcome of a predicted situation by deviating from our normal patterns of behavior, but this requires great willpower, continuous consciousness, and truthful judgment of our own actions.

The worldwide use of the concept of synchronicity is an important acknowledgment that meaningful coincidences *do* occur without causal relationships. Nonetheless, synchronicity itself is nothing more than a name for a phenomenon. The issue at hand is that in a Tarot divination the cards that pass through the shuffler's hands *do* connect with some invisible superstructure! There must be a mechanism through which the cards in a spread reflect part of some deeper order that contains our past, present, and possible future.

The contemporary physicists David Bohm, David Peat, and Michael Talbot believe that synchronicities offer evidence of an implicit order behind the ordinary day-to-day order of all things. Peat believes that synchronicities are flaws in the fabric of everyday reality—momentary fissures that allow us a brief glimpse of the immense and unitary order that underlies all of nature. The question is *how* and with *what* are we synchronous when we divine with the Tarot? For answers to these questions we need a proper cosmological model of our universe.

Cosmologies

Cosmology brings together astronomy, physics, philosophy, and metaphysics in a joint effort to understand not only the stars one sees in the sky, but the whole universe, its origin, its structure and order, its space-time relationships, its processes, and ourselves in that universe. Cosmologies try to give answers to questions about ourselves, our lives, and our universe. In ancient societies, cosmology and religion were inseparable and constituted the main body of mythology. The Tarot is an archetypal, and process-oriented cosmology that is very ancient.

In the early years of the twentieth century, Albert Einstein developed a *relativistic space-time cosmology*, based on his theories of special and general relativity, and developments in astronomy. According to his theories, mathematically, time and space are the same thing. The three space coordinates, together with the fourth time coordinate, form four-dimensional space-time. Einstein's relativity theory suggests that gravity warps four-dimensional space-time. Sir Arthur Stanley Eddington proved this to be correct in 1919, using a total eclipse of the sun to measure the predicted deflection of light from a star by the gravitational field of the sun.

In the second half of the twentieth century, Einstein's relativistic space-time cosmology was developed further by integrating chemical, nuclear-physical, and astronomical research findings, newly developed mathematical techniques, quantum mechanics, computers, and space technology. Stephen Hawking explained, through the integration of relativity theory and quantum mechanics, the existence of black holes and, ultimately, the beginning and evolution of the universe from the Big Bang. At this point in time there is not yet enough evidence to conclude whether the expansion of the universe will go on forever, or slow down, stop, reverse, and implode in a Big Crunch.

Ouspensky's concept of points in eternity-space, and fate lines consisting of strings of actualized eternity points, seems to be based on relativistic space-time cosmology. However, if we combine the concept of eternity lines running through space-time with the widely accepted Big Bang theory, new questions arise. Do all eternity lines emerge from the Big Bang? Do they all end in the Big Crunch? What is our purpose in life if everything started the same way and possibly will finish the same way?

Tarot meditation

Ken Wilber writes in *Sacred Mirrors, The Visionary Art of Alex Grey* (1990):

> *Men and women possess at least three different modes of knowing: the eye of the flesh, which discloses the material, concrete, and sensual world; the eye of the mind, which discloses the symbolic, conceptual, and linguistic world; and the eye of contemplation, which discloses the spiritual, transcendental, and transpersonal (ego-less) world. These are not different worlds, but three different aspects of our one world, disclosed by different modes of knowing and perceiving.*

The Tarot offers a way to explore the spiritual aspects of our world. Tarot meditation is closely connected with divination and therefore a proper preparation for it. The members of The Golden Dawn used Tarot meditation regularly. The notion that the phenomena in this world are a coherent pattern of which the Tarot is a pictorial reflection is a good starting point. During Tarot meditation and study, the Tarot worker tries to achieve a state of rest, stillness, depth, and awareness in the transcendental or astral world. At the astral level one meets the spirit in its totality, including the unconscious. Provided that this process is executed well through Tarot meditation and under guidance, a new and independent plane of existence can be attained.

Tarot meditation begins with the selection of a Major Arcanum. Saturate yourself with the picture like a painting. Next, close your eyes and visualize the selected arcanum. Take time to fill in the details and make the visualization as lively as possible. Next, concentrate on the arcanum on an astral level—enlarge the picture, walk into the Arcanum, and keep walking. The arcanum will come to life. In the Major Arcanum Strength, for example, you will witness the taming of the lion; in The Emperor, the control of matter; in The Hanged Man, the ultimate sacrifice. The arcanum is the point of entry and exit. The first journeys should be kept brief. Determine a time—for example, 15 minutes, not more. Longer journeys have the danger of loss of physical consciousness.

Through Tarot meditation we become much more familiar with the Tarot cards, their deeper meanings, and the relationships between those meanings. Transcendental wisdom will illuminate the arcana that we live through. Similarly, through meditation on a Tarot spread and its question, a total picture of the situation may emerge before our eyes.

Objective forces and tasks

Objective forces change the face of humankind, the world, and the universe. They drive entities along evolutionary lines toward true being-and-knowing. They unfold new parts of the cosmic holograph. In our world, neutral objective energies and forces always unfold positively and negatively with positive and negative effects on our lives. The objective 12 Principal Arcana unfold themselves as 12 complementary pairs of Major Arcana.

As we live predominantly in a physical and mental world, we can see the world in a *neutral* way only with great difficulty. Every thought we have brings peace or war, love or fear. True neutral thinking requires us to move into the transcendental world. Only in mystical experiences or through regular meditation will objective presence and thinking arise. The mystical writer Jakob Böhme (1575—1624) calls it *Experiencing the Unearth. The Tibetan Book of the Dead* says:

> *The essence of reality is open, empty and naked like the sky,*
> *Luminous emptiness without center or circumference,*
> *Unobstructed, sparkling, pure and vibrant, pristine awareness.*
> *Your intelligent, cognizant, radiant mind*
> *Is the pure Buddha of Immortal Light.*
> *To recognize this is all that is necessary.*

Truthful and intense involvement in an objective task, for example, creating a piece of art, working on an important scientific discovery, or working with the Tarot or other esoteric systems, requires objective perception and thought. Carrying out an objective task requires and calls up objective forces. These forces are not only positive; by necessity they work out in negative ways as well.

There are many examples of strong negative forces that have made life very difficult for many people who sought to or had to accomplish great tasks. Mozart called up strong negative forces when he used secret masonic knowledge about the proper order of the four tarot elements (earth, fire water, air) in his objective opera *Die Zauberflöte*. He died early. J. S. Bach became blind and Beethoven became totally deaf in his later life. The now-famous painters Vincent van Gogh and Rembrandt van Rijn died in poverty. Charles Babbage, the inventor of the first mechanical, true computer could not complete his analytical engine because of mechanical imperfections. Marie Curie, discoverer of radioactivity and double Nobel Prize winner, died of radiation illness after a long life of dedication to science and humanity. Her beloved husband, Pierre Curie, with whom she worked on the isolation of radioactive elements, died early in a strange traffic accident. Objective art, such as Michelangelo's *Pieta* and Rembrandt's *Nightwatch,* have called up enormous aggressive, negative forces that caused those with deviant minds to severely damage these pieces of art.

Because of the uni-directionality of time, during the unfolding (explication) of an important structure, *negative forces attain the upper hand first.* They impinge severely on the unfolder and on weak structures in or around him or her. Suddenly an engine block may split, a knife may shatter, a hard disk may crash, a series of accidents may happen in quick succession, behavior may abruptly and inexplicably become irresponsible, relationships may break down, moods may become deeply morose, or perhaps health may suddenly and severely deteriorate.

Generally, these unwanted and unavoidable negative forces become stronger as the objective task comes to a close. In some circumstances, they make it impossible for the person to complete the work (as in the case of Mozart's *Requiem*). The negative effects may also spread to close relatives. In such a situation we have to be aware that negative forces *are* at work.

Notwithstanding the severe difficulties caused by the negative complements of invoked Objective forces, normally we *will not stop working on the task.* Strong, moral commitment makes it psychologically impossible to get off-track. The deeper reason for this is that working on the important task means progress along a *self-chosen* karmic fate-line.

The archetypal depiction of the unfolder of an objective task is the Major Arcanum The Hanged Man. The awareness of the sacrifice lightens the burden and makes it possible to continue. The task *will* be completed and positive forces *will* commence their lasting effects after the negative forces have run their course. Negative forces can be coped with by living consciously and cautiously, working slowly, and understanding what is *really* happening. The incessant drops of water will hollow the stone.

We might ask why objective forces do not manifest themselves in a way where positive and negative effects emerge simultaneously. The consecutive appearance of negative and positive forces is an objective law. This law has a uni-directional outcome, which becomes visible when the effects of negative forces cease over time, while the effects of the positive forces remain permanent. In this way, objective progress is anchored in time, developments become irreversible, and completed explications are fixed into evolution.

The Tarot, Zenzar, and magic

The Tarot and magic are related. A major difference between the two is that the Tarot *itself* does not go further than *depicting* events in the future via symbols, while magic tries to *change* events in the future. The advice a Tarot reading gives us enhances our knowing-and-being, making it easier for us to carry on with our life in a constructive way.

When we follow up on advice given via a spread, we enforce magic. Gurdjieff does not distinguish between white, purple, or black magic. There is only one way of magic, and that is *to do and be with full consciousness.*

Tarot invocations can be used effectively as magical incantations. As the Tarot comprises the essence of all aspects of life and death in 24 Major Arcana, its 24 invocations do the same. The Tarot invocations are a syntactical and grammatical backbone of the mystical, holy, objective language Zenzar.

Tarot invocations can be combined to form powerful sentences with magical power. By speaking a Tarot invocation regarding a situation, the speaker, through his or her consciousness, connects that situation with a higher level of existence. By doing this, he or she calls up the related Major Arcanum (or, more precisely, the Principal Arcanum), and lays it over the situation. Thus the situation is changed: it is given new archetypal characteristics, a new holographic structure, and a new entry in the Akasha chronicles. In space-time terminology, the situation is pushed to a new position on the evolutionary line in time-space, like a bead on a string.

For example, the magical Tarot expression to cleanse a room in which unethical things have happened is:

TAOR–AOTR– ORAT–ATRO–AROT

Or translated:

The fool followed the devil instead of the truth. Now I establish morality in this room and manifest in the arising light.

It is self-evident that magical sentences built from Tarot invocations may be used only for purposes that bring Truth to the world. Incorrect use of magical sentences in Zenzar may have grave karmic consequences for the person who utters a magical Tarot sentence and the persons involved in the situation at hand. As the karma of the diviner and the pertaining person(s) are connected, a magical Tarot invocation will move the situation along an evolutionary line in time-space.

A final word before turning to practice

This chapter lifted only the edge of the veil over the higher levels of our consciousness and existence and the position of the Tarot in it. The Tarot is a divine instrument, linked to the universal synchronicity present in every entity. Working with the Tarot can be learned partly from books and writings, but above all it needs to be developed and understood from within ourselves. In this regard Chuang Tzu's story "Duke Hwan and the coachbuilder" is illustrative.

Duke Hwan and the coachbuilder

The world thinks that the best explanation of Tao can be found in books. But books are only a collection of words. Words carry something valuable: the thoughts that they convey. Those thoughts, however, are the result of something else, and that "else" cannot be expressed in words. If the world attaches value to words or to books, it may value what does not deserve to be valued; what it values is not what is really valuable. What we see and discuss are only external form and color; what we listen to, only name and sound. Unfortunately, people think that form, color, name, and sound are sufficient to represent the real Tao. Therefore, those who know don't speak, and those who speak don't know. How would the world be able to know its real being! The story of Duke Hwan and the coachbuilder goes as follows:

Duke Hwan was reading a book in his lounge. Outside, in the court, coachbuilder P'hien was constructing a wheel. Putting down his hammer and chisel, P'hien went upstairs and said: "I request to ask His Highness what words you are reading." The duke said: "The words of the Sages." "Are they still alive?" asked P'hien. "They are dead," was the answer. "Then, my Ruler," P'hien resumed, "the words Your Highness reads are only the dregs and residue of the old Savants." The duke said: "How can you, coachbuilder, make comments about a book I am reading? Can you explain this? If not, you'll have to pay with your life." The coachbuilder spoke: "Your servant will discuss this from his own trade. When I make a wheel and I am careful, it looks all right, but the result is weak; if I hit hard, it is tiring and the joints don't fit. If the movements of my hand are not too gentle and not too wild, the image in my mind is realized. But I cannot put that into words: there is a knack in doing it. I cannot teach my son that knack and he cannot learn it from me. Therefore, although I am 70 years old, I am still making wheels. As the old Sages have departed together with what they could not say, then what Your Highness is reading cannot be but the dregs of the Old Wise ones."

Divination with the Tarot

The future casts its shadows forward
Judge not that ye be judged.
—*Matthew 7:1*

CHAPTER 9

Divination with the Tarot

Preparing for divination with the Tarot

Those who want to work with the Tarot have to know the pictures, names, structure, invocations, and all quartets of the Tarot arcana. In the beginning it is not essential to know all card meanings, but thorough insight into the Tarot's structure is imperative.

The order of the Tarot in the life cycle and the grouping of the arcana in quartets are of great assistance when memorizing and meditating on the Tarot arcana. The Tarot as described in this book is most suitable, because this deck consists of 24 Major Arcana. If the Rider deck by Arthur E. Waite is used, the two Major Arcana Truth (Jupiter) and Intuition (Juno) must be added by fixing their images onto the two blank cards in the Rider deck, and the Major Arcana must be renumbered according to the numbering given here.

Over time, the cards become acquaintances. A relationship develops that becomes more and more profound, until the 80 arcana call up a treasure house of ideas and associations when they show their faces.

Tarot readings are always done with the same deck. When learning to do Tarot readings for others, it is advisable to begin doing it for relatives, using only the 24 Major Arcana in the upright position. Put the 16 Royal Arcana and 40 Minor Arcana aside.

When you have gained enough experience divining with the Major Arcana, gradually familiarize yourself with the meanings of the remaining arcana. The best way to do this is by regularly arranging all 80 arcana in a mandala of Tarot quartets (figure 4.16). When you have had sufficient experience with all the cards, start interpreting reversed cards in spreads. Five to ten minutes of meditation is recommended prior to a serious Tarot consultation, so that you are completely available and ready for the event. As you prefer, your meditation can be separate from the reading or seamlessly attached to the reading through the ritual shuffling of the cards.

After the Tarot consultation you don't have to sort the cards, but be sure to put them back in the box, or wrap them in silk cloth to prevent the deck from becoming incomplete.

Tarot cards must be treated with respect. In this way you show reverence to the creator and the questioner concerning this valuable loose-leaf book of wisdom. It is recommended that you don't allow others to use your deck, except when the questioner shuffles and parts the deck of cards.

As diviners, we must be aware of the profundity of each arcanum by considering its meaning upright and reversed. Light has to be brought where it is needed. Fear of illuminating the darkness and the negative aspects is limiting. A reversed card gives us the opportunity to give the interpretation of a spread more depth.

Divination *for others* is possible when you know all the Tarot arcana and their meanings by heart. In general, it is wise not to read the Tarot cards too often for yourself or anybody else, because at some stage an overabundance of information will make proper interpretation impossible.

Although it is possible to divine *for ourselves*, the results often will be of limited value. This is so for two reasons. First, the Tarot cannot solve the basic problem that we can often see someone else's dilemmas very well; in fact, far better than we can see our own. Second, repeated divinations for ourselves may cause confusion, because it may be unclear what is manifesting itself in the cards: is it the change that has been resisted, or is it the correction that in the meanwhile has already been made?

To keep the deck of cards *in tune*, it is a good idea to use them for divination only. For purposes of study (for example, arranging the cards in quartets or mandalas), you can use a second, possibly smaller sized deck. For meditation, it is desirable to use Tarot cards with a large format, so that all the details are clearly visible and it is easier to enter the arcanum.

Karmic cleansing of a deck of Tarot cards

A deck of Tarot cards may be checked for completeness and cleansed of previous karmic influences at any time. This is done as follows:

1. Place all 24 Major Arcana upright in one top row, from zero at the left to 22 at the right.
2. Place all 16 Royal Arcana in one middle row: from Page to King, for each of the emblems, Pentacles, Wands, Cups, and Swords.
3. Place all 40 Minor Arcana in one bottom row, from one to ten, for Pentacles, Wands, Cups, and Swords.
4. Check to make sure that all the cards are present. If there is one missing, there is no solution other than buying another deck.
5. Shuffle all cards seven times.

All the cards will have changed position and are ordered in a synchronistically correct way. The Tarot divination may now begin.

Comprehensive interpretation of a spread

When reading a spread, we not only have to look at the separate cards, but also relate them to the meaning of the place each takes in the spread, and to the other cards in that spread. The occurrence of more than one card of the same suit (Pentacles, for example) or with the same number has a special meaning. Specifically, we need to consider:

- The specific meaning and purpose of the chosen spread.
- The specific meaning of each arcanum in each position in the chosen spread.
- The cohesion between an arcanum with its surrounding arcana, and the general impression of the total picture.
- The Tarot quartet to which each arcanum in the spread belongs, the general idea behind that quartet, and the place of that quartet in the life cycle.
- That Major Arcana increase the strength of a spread.
- That Minor Arcana indicate practical life and working conditions.
- That Royal Arcana point at relationships and managerial matters.
- The way in which particular emblems are emphasized; for example, a spread with:

> Many Pentacle cards points at talents and money.
> Many Wands cards indicates production and conflict.
> Many Cups cards stresses emotional situations and news.
> Many Swords cards indicates heavenly justice, mental processes, and renewal.

When the interpretation of a spread has been completed, the cards are joined again into one stack. As shuffling and parting must precede every reading, the information in a particular spread can be kept for later, by copying the cards onto one of the Tarot Divination Worksheets at the end of this book. If you stay in touch with the questioner, you can check the extent to which the reading has made sense and predictions have come true.

A Tarot consultation is a karmic event

A Tarot divination is an interactive karmic happening in which two people meet in one eternity-moment. During this shared event one person uses the experience of the other to gain insight into the course of his or her eternity-line through life (figure 9.1). During the Tarot consultation, somewhere in time-space, two fate-lines touch or cross each other. Without the connection between the evolutionary lines of the questioner and the diviner, it would be impossible for one to predict the future of the other because they would be doing different things in different places.

During the consultation the karma of the diviner and the questioner are connected. For this reason, it is important that during the consultation nothing be mentioned that would bind the diviner to the questioner in a lasting way. Therefore, physical death must never be predicted.

Although Tarot consultations over the telephone and via the Internet have become fashionable, we disapprove of the use of telephone, fax, or computer for Tarot consultations. First of all, they cannot replace the effects that live interaction and the physical

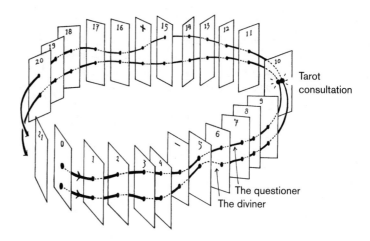

9.1 Evolutionary lines touch during a Tarot consultation: the karmas of the questioner and the diviner are temporarily linked.

nearness of the questioner and diviner have on the profundity of the event. Second, unknown and uncontrollable distortions may happen by unknown forces, which unsolicited can join into divination via electronic channels.

Because of the inevitability of karmic unification during a consultation, divination may only happen between two persons. A spectator interferes with a reading, makes it impure, and gives rise to confusing influences, because a third time-line is crossing the other two. Spreads evolving from situations in which more than two persons are present are difficult to interpret: the arcana in the spread may become disjointed—whose evolutionary line (or lines) are being read? For this reason pregnant women usually are discouraged from engaging in a Tarot divination. Children should not be part of a Tarot reading either, since children are so open-minded that they may experience the revealed arcana as traumatic—not knowing the underlying values.

The Tarot as a psychological instrument

Tarot divination gives insight into the ways in which people try to attain goals in life. As such, it is an important aid in psychological counseling and problem solving. Divination in its broad sense is an interactive process in which a diviner assists a questioner in Self-knowledge. The diviner can, through his or her interpretation of the cards, limit the behavioral alternatives available to the questioner. A diviner must never judge. The diviner's wisdom and insight, acquired in synchronicity with the All and the grace of God, has to be loving. Tarot consultations are sessions of insight, never sessions of judgment.

The questioner comes to the Tarot because he or she has a problem that may not be solved using the usual methods. Uncertainty and fear may indicate that somewhere along the line a mistake was made. Frequently, the problem pertains to decisions made in the past, which led to outcomes over which the questioner does not have control. The questioner needs insight into the situation, so that he or she can correct errors, and undo decisions and judgments.

Often, questioners face an existential or essential discrepancy between ideals and goals on the one hand, and the reality of life on the other, but unknowingly they have created this situation themselves. A questioner may already have tried to solve the problem or reduce the burning feeling of insecurity before presenting the question to the diviner. Some questions have their source in the unconscious, in which case a character spread such as the Mirror or the Horoscope would be indicated. The diviner may assist the questioner in formulating the question—this can often happen while the cards are being shuffled.

A diviner uses the Tarot to suggest a solution to the questioner's problem. In this regard, Gurdjieff's Law of Three is worth mentioning. This law, when applied to problem solving, states that any proper solution to a problem should comprise three alternatives: the first and the second normally are each other's antithesis and therefore reasonably easy to find. The third alternative reconciles or integrates the other two solutions and stimulates progress; often that third alternative turns out be the best.

Tarot consultation in practice

The best environment for a Tarot consultation is a quiet, sparsely furnished room, with a completely clean and empty table, preferably covered with a billiard-green cloth. The green has a calming effect and shows up each card well. The consultation may be recorded by means of a cassette recorder, so that the questioner may listen to the conversation again at home. It is very important that the diviner keep the discussion professional and to the point. In practice, it sometimes happens that the diviner acquires factual information about the problem in a discussion prior to the divination. This has to be prevented, as information beforehand may influence the reading.

The introductory discussion should make the questioner feel at ease so that he or she opens up for the forthcoming Tarot consultation. The date of birth is significant for the diviner to determine the zodiacal sign. In this way the diviner can adjust the discussion of the problem: with an Aries, he or she would talk in a different way than with a Libra; with a Cancer, differently than with a Capricorn. The diviner may also first read the questioner's palms, to become familiar with his or her character, to break the ice, and to build up the karmic connection.

It is also important for the diviner to know the nature of the problem, in order to determine which spread to use: the Bow spread, the Mirror, the Celtic Cross, the Ouroboros, the Horoscope, the Chakra, or some other.

Finally, in the preparatory stage of Tarot consultations that focus on changing situations, it is essential to establish a valid time span for the divination—for example, three months, half a year, or a whole year; periods longer than two years are not recommended. If a questioner requests that a character or personality be clarified (for instance, through a Mirror or Horoscope spread), a time span is often unnecessary, as such situations change very slowly.

When these preparations have been completed, the diviner gently takes the deck of Tarot cards and starts shuffling, while discussing and (re)formulating the question together with the questioner. The cards have to be held and handled with the image side invisible (turned down, toward the table). The diviner first shuffles the cards, taking as much time as needed for the cards to feel right. Next, the questioner shuffles. The cards only show the common back. The questioner determines intuitively when the cards have been shuffled enough and places the pile of cards face down, on the table, between the questioner and the diviner.

The diviner invites the questioner, "Part this deck of cards with one hand." The pile that is taken from the top of the stack is not used; it is returned to the box in which the Tarot cards are kept. The topmost card of those remaining from the parted deck is the entry point and the first card of the spread and the reading. Each card is picked up, turned over like a page of a book (figure 9.2), and put on the table in front of the diviner.

9.2 Turning over the Tarot cards.

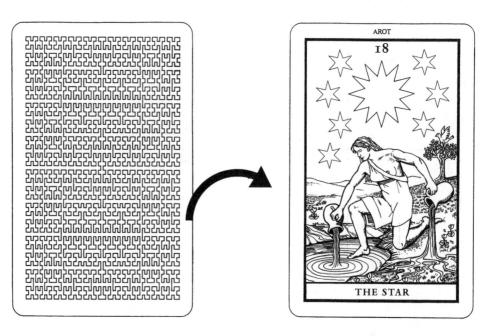

The diviner places the cards one by one in the positions of the spread, naming each card and stating the meaning of that card and the position in which it is placed in the spread. This procedure is repeated until the spread is complete. Thus, having summarized the whole spread briefly, the diviner absorbs the spread in its entirety, looks at the cards and their relationships, and meditates on it for a while, to deepen insight.

Then the diviner starts to explain what is seen. In principle, first the meanings of the cards are explained to the questioner, and then the diviner starts to speak less formally and more freely, finally arriving at a vision of the Gestalt and characteristics of the spread. Often, the questioner sees it too, since he or she already knows the answer in an unconscious way.

The most important rule in a Tarot consultation is to *interpret with compassion and gentleness without becoming involved*. Predictions sometimes hit hard and may cause psychosomatic complaints. The truth may be unpleasant, but must never be cruel.

The archetypal and psychological clarity of Tarot arcana gives them great pervading power. The questioner sees the pictures on the Tarot cards, too. The truth in the cards may be overtly clear and very difficult. For these reasons, during the interpretation, sincere gentleness is imperative.

When a very serious Major Arcanum appears—like the Moon, Death, the Devil, or the Tower—the diviner's best choice is to discuss it in a metaphorical way. A Tarot consultation may stir up the questioner and cause an emotional release, which may continue after the consultation. In such a case the two fate-lines may start running parallel, a possible consequence being that the diviner loses his or her independent judgment or becomes emotionally attached to the questioner. This is a mistake, as the purpose of Tarot consultations is to liberate the questioner.

The best thing for the diviner to do in such a case is to keep a cool head and not enter into a binding relationship with the questioner. *"Let him who can (and will) be himself not belong to someone else"* (Paracelsus).

Sometimes it should be recommended that another divination not take place within too short a time because the situation will not have changed much. Tarot consultations at short intervals put the cart before the horse and may cause confusion and uncertainty.

When the diviner is finished, the cassette recorder is stopped and the last sentences can be replayed; often they are the most important ones. *The final advice given to the questioner has to be positive, liberating, freeing, healing, and problem solving.*

Tarot spreads: geomancy

In each Tarot spread the cards are arranged in a specific pattern in which each position has a special meaning: this is called geomancy. In the many books about the Tarot many ways of spreading and reading the cards are discussed (figure 9.3). Some methods use only three, others, all 80 Tarot cards. Methods with a few cards are fast, but lack detail in depiction and prediction. Methods with many cards are more explicit, but time-consuming. The framework of this book does not allow discussing all the ways of spreading the Tarot cards, but it will deal with the synchronicity test and seven often-used spreads that give the most satisfactory results.

It is always good to keep notes of the spreads done, for reference later. This book contains six divination worksheets for recording spreads. These sheets may be copied freely. In this way you can build up a journal of readings.

It makes sense to begin with the use of simple spreads. When after a period of training and experience, you master these, you can go on to more complex spreads.

TAROT SPREADS

Method	Number of Cards
One Card Spread	1
Basic Spread	3
Synchronicity Test	4
Question Spread	5
Five Cards Spread	5
Bow Spread	7
Celtic Cross	10
Ten Cards Spread	10
Mirror Spread	10
Ouroboros Spread	10
Clock Spread	12
Horoscope Spread	12
Chakra Spread	13
21 Cards Spread	21
Seventh Card Spread	22
Italian Method	22 followed by 48
Wheel of Fortune	27
Gypsy Spread	42
42 Cards Spread	42
Royal Spread	54
54 Cards Spread	54
The Grand Play	67
The Tree of Life	70
Name Spread	One card per letter
The Inner Order	All cards

9.3 A few of the methods of divining with Tarot cards.

The synchronicity test

Divination with the Tarot is based on synchronicity. Shuffling the cards is a ritual necessary to open the psyches of the two humans involved. When the diviner and the questioner shuffle the cards, they try to achieve synchronicity between the situation and the order of the cards. The justification for this is doubt that the cards are in tune. When we feel that the cards are right, we intuitively know that synchronicity has been achieved and that the eternity-lines of those who are present are touching. If the diviner totally believes in the synchronicity of his or her cards, the cards do not need to be shuffled and can be picked up from a pile by the diviner.

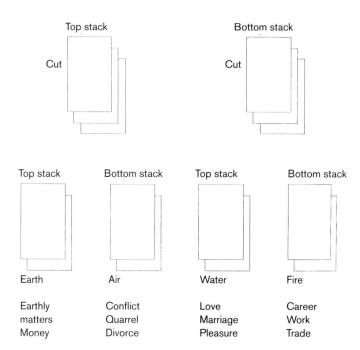

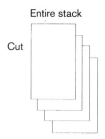

Entire stack

Cut

Top stack   Bottom stack

Cut   Cut

Top stack   Bottom stack   Top stack   Bottom stack

Earth   Air   Water   Fire

Earthly   Conflict   Love   Career
matters   Quarrel   Marriage   Work
Money   Divorce   Pleasure   Trade

9.4 Synchronicity test according to the Inner Order.

With the synchronicity test, you can easily determine if a questioner and diviner are in tune (figure 9.4). You can skip this test if you want, but for the sake of completeness it is mentioned here.

The synchronicity test is, in fact, the first step of the spread called the Inner Order, named after an occult society with the same name, to which W. B. Yeats, Oscar Wilde, and MacGregor Mathers belonged. A Tarot divination may start as follows:

1. Select from the complete deck of Tarot cards the Significator. This is the card that best reflects the situation and the questioner's problem. Then put the card back in the deck. The diviner shuffles the cards first; then the questioner shuffles.
2. When the cards have been shuffled enough, the questioner divides the deck in two piles of about equal size, after which the two piles are parted again. This gives four piles of Tarot cards, which divide the questioner's situation into the four

phases of the life cycle and the Aristotelian elements. From left to right these are:

Earth—material matters, money, and growth
Fire—work, career, business
Water—emotional matters, love, marriage, pleasure
Air—conflict, separation, and regeneration

3. The questioner is asked to which of the four categories the problem most belongs: Earth, Fire, Water, or Air. Then the diviner checks to see if that pile contains the Significator. If it is not in the chosen pile, this indicates that the questioner and/or diviner are not in tune with the situation. In this case, the session should be recommenced at least two hours—but not more than 12 hours—later. The Significator remains the same, but the cards are shuffled and parted again. This is repeated until the Significator is in the right pile.

If the Significator is in the right pile, questioner and diviner are in tune, the order of the cards reflect the questioner's situation, and the divination can start. The Significator is put back into the pile of cards in the same place it came from, and the four piles are reunited into one deck in exactly the same order as before the separation. The cassette recorder is started, the deck is parted, and the bottom part is laid out in the spread selected by the diviner.

The Base spread
Before a Tarot reading is carried out, for example a Celtic Cross, you can do a Base spread. The questioner shuffles the cards, having the question in mind. Then, the diviner asks the questioner to divide the cards into three piles, next to each other. The first pile represents the past, the middle one the present, and the third one the future.

The diviner turns each pile over and names it: "This is the past, this is the present, this is the future." Next, the diviner names the cards on top of each pile and will include the three of them in the interpretation after the real reading. Then the questioner is asked to reunite the deck. The diviner watches which pile is taken up first, second, and third. The order indicates the questioner's unconscious approach. If the pile of the future is picked up first, the questioner (and the question) is strongly oriented towards the future. If the pile representing the past is next, the indication is that the questioner's past is most important. Since in this case, the pile of the present would remain as the last one, this would mean that the questioner has few ties with, or is not much worried, about the present. This method offers six possible orders of picking up the piles and of orientating the problem.

The Bow spread

The Bow spread is suited for beginners and gives an expeditious answer to specific, clearly delineated problems (figure 9.5a–b). The Bow represents a situation of tension between two extremes: the past (card 1) and the result (card 7). Only action can release the tension. The questioner draws the bowstring, and thus is the person who does the work and makes sure that the arrow hits the target (card 4) by releasing the bowstring. Paradoxically, the goal is at the same time, the obstacle, because without resistance there is no tension. Next to the goal or obstacle are the hidden factors (card 3) and the attitudes of others (card 5). Further, this spread contains the present (card 2) and the action to be taken (card 6). The Bow gives a compact and concrete answer about the way the problem might be solved.

THE BOW SPREAD

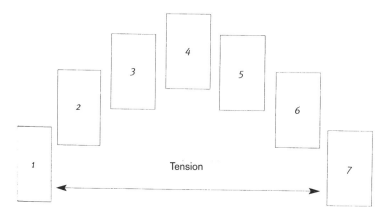

9.5a The Bow spread.

Card Position	Meaning of the Position
1	Symbolizes the past.
2	Symbolizes the present.
3	Symbolizes the hidden factors.
4	Symbolizes the goal or obstacle.
5	Symbolizes the attitudes of others.
6	Symbolizes what the questioner should do.
7	Symbolizes the final result to be expected.

9.5b The meanings of the fields in the Bow Tarot spread.

The spread and interpretation
After shuffling and parting the cards, the diviner takes the first seven cards of the bottom pile and lays them out in the Bow.

Another way to choose the cards is to present the questioner with all 80 cards in a fan and have him or her select the seven cards, one after another.

The diviner puts the cards in the Bow face down. When the seven cards have been selected and arranged, the diviner turns over each card and names the meaning of the card position and card. Next, the spread is discussed with the questioner, in the light of the action advised by card 6.

Example 1: A Bow spread

The situation

A married, male academic has a temporary appointment as researcher at a university. His contract finishes soon and it is uncertain if it will be renewed. He has been informed that in Hong Kong, Singapore, and Jakarta there are substantial shortages of academics and that in those places more can be earned than at home.

The question

The questioner asks if it makes sense to try and find work in the Far East. The diviner decides to do a Bow spread as the question is clearly defined.

Card 1 **The Past: The Magician**
The questioner has been a pioneer in his profession and has been able to combine his various talents in projects. Being diplomatic, he has developed a good track record.

Card 2 **The Present: The Priest**
The questioner is in a phase in which he develops new norms and values. The questioner has to choose between happiness in the family and a safe environment and uncertain financial future, or an uncertain situation with many possibilities for his career and material well-being.

Card 3 **The Hidden Factors: The Emperor**
There is a dominant father figure, institutionalized power and/or established morality in the life of the questioner. In a hidden way, this influences the questioner in his decision. The questioner has to take this power into account.

Card 4 **The Obstacles/Goal: The Page of Swords**
The inner development of his consciousness and alertness make it very difficult for the questioner to remain resigned and wait to find out if he has a job or not. The questioner keeps his thoughts to himself in a discreet way, likely because of the implications and dangers of working in Asia. Diplomacy is necessary. In fact, the Page of Swords (growth and alertness) stands for the questioner himself.

Card 5 **The Attitudes of Others: Three of Wands**
Others around the questioner stimulate him toward the realization of new enterprises and projects. The

questioner feels like a fish out of water. It is clear that he has to be very careful in the execution of the plans that are the subject of the question. The questioner may be drawn into competition or his plans may be thwarted.

Card 6   **The Recommended Action: Knight of Pentacles**
This card, which correlates to Spring and the zodiacal sign Aries, very clearly indicates the new action. Through internal structuring and a practical and materialistic attitude, the questioner will achieve most goals. Old matters can be completed and the new enterprise started in a patient, methodical, and proactive way.

Card 7   **The Final Result: The King of Pentacles**
The questioner will start the overseas enterprise and succeed. He will develop his talents further, stay active in his professional field, and have financial and material success. He will become a man who has made it.

The Mirror or Lightning spread

The Mirror spread symbolizes a hand mirror, set in a cross-frame, that reflects the questioner's character (figure 9.6a–b). The spread is also named the Lightning or the Bolt, indicating a flash of sudden insight. Lightning is the White Light, an attribute of Nepalese priests and of Jupiter, and a symbol of truth. Tibetan priests manipulate a symbolic bolt of lightning as a ritual object to remember the greatness of God, to be conscious of mortality, and to live and act humbly. In ancient Greece it was a double axe.

The positions of the cards in this spread are similar to the ten centers in the Qabbalistic mandala known as the "Tree of Life." Therefore, some Tarotists call this spread the Tree of Life spread or Arbor Vitae spread.

The Mirror spread tells the truth about the questioner. It is used if the questioner wants to acquire a better insight into his or her character and being. The Mirror spread is a method of gaining insights into character and existential structures, and fills a gap in the range of Tarot divination methods that are available. Being an introspective spread, it illustrates the general psychological structure of the questioner. In a lightning flash, it may give a person clear insight into him- or herself. The ten-card Mirror spread reflects the state of the soul and clarifies character features that have a certain stability in a person's life. Therefore, it cannot be followed up by a second Mirror spread. In this regard it differs from a Celtic Cross, which may be followed up by another Celtic Cross reading, and other Tarot spreads that are more future-oriented and may elucidate the development of a particular situation.

THE MIRROR SPREAD

9.6a The Mirror spread.

9.6b The meanings of the fields in the Mirror Tarot spread.

Card Position	Meaning of the Position
1	This is your ego, this is what you are in your actions.
2	This is your personal past and source, your father.
3	This is your love, your mother, your future.
4	This is what you have learned, the base of your actions.
5	This is your crown, your ideals, moral power.
6	This is your handle, your material position in the world.
7	This is your karma, as result of your choices.
8	This is your manifestation, also in the future.
9	This is your understanding, and the value of your problem the way it is now, the assignment to your soul.
10	This is the judgment, what will ultimately happen to you.

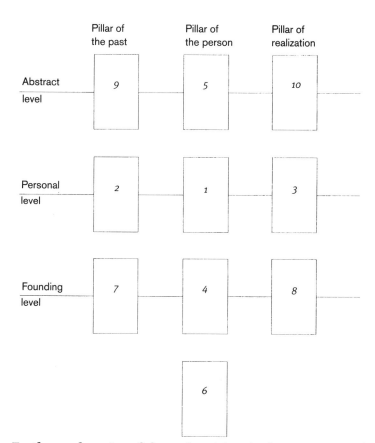

	Pillar of the past	Pillar of the person	Pillar of realization
Abstract level	9	5	10
Personal level	2	1	3
Founding level	7	4	8
		6	

Further explanation of the card positions in the Mirror spread

The Mirror has the same expressiveness as a horoscope. It shows a person's character with various crosscuts (figure 9.7). *Vertical:* the person (cards 5, 1, 4, 6); the past (cards 9, 2, 7); and the actualization in the future (cards 10, 3, 8). *Horizontal:* the person's abstract being (cards 9, 5, 10); the personal determinants of the existence (cards 2, 1, 3); and the foundation (cards 7, 4, 8).

Cards 1, 2, 3, 4, and 5 together form the Mirror or Lightning Bolt.

Card 6 is the point where the Lighting hits the earth, or where the mirror is attached to the earth via the mirror's handle.

Cards 7, 8, 9, and 10 depict the emanation of the person. This is the flash that radiates in all directions—the moment of truth when the questioner sees him or herself in the mirror, or in the eyes of someone else.

Card 1 The questioner's vital life force and actions. This card in essence indicates the interface between the Self (Essence) of the questioner, which is invisible, and his or her visible and tangible personality, in harmonic and ordered interaction with the environment.

Card 2 The questioner's personal background and past, sources of power, father, and origin.

Card 3 The compassionate, loving, caring, motherly aspects as well as the questioner's future. The questioner (card 1) is positioned between the father and the mother and fulfills the past in establishing what is hidden in the future.

Card 4 The foundation represents what the questioner has learned. It is his or her foundation, personal laws, practical learning experiences.

Card 5 This crowns the questioner and indicates where he or she wants to go, the spiritual power.

Card 6 The handle the questioner holds rules his or her life. It is the person's material position in this world and the physical laws to which he or she is subjected.

Card 7 The past as a chain of causes and effects in which the questioner is/was the actor. It is the questioner's karma, sins, guilt, as well as collaborative groups he or she founded.

Card 8 The manifestation of the questioner's positive force of attraction, victorious fulfillment in the future (also in battle), and the way this is experienced by the questioner and others.

Card 9 The value of the questioner's essence, his or her task in life and understanding of it—often also the problem or the "cross to bear" in life.

Card 10 The future that the questioner deserves and which will come. This judgment is called up because of the way the person lives his or her life. It is the result of the karma in card 7, which is diagonally opposite this card—part of a (very slowly changing) character spread pointing in the direction the questioner's life ultimately will lead.

Example 2: A Mirror spread

The situation

The questioner is a male metalworker who loves his work and is dedicated to it. He has great interest in spiritual matters.

The question

The questioner wants to know what is the structure of his life; what is he up to?

The spread and interpretation

After shuffling and parting the cards, the diviner puts all ten cards in Mirror arrangement face down. After a moment of silence, the diviner turns the cards over one by one, names the meaning of the position and the name of the arcanum in that position, and discusses the spread with the questioner.

Card 1   **Your ego and actions: The Universe**
The questioner is a Taoist, philosophical and broad-minded.

Card 2   **Your past, your source, your father: Ten of Pentacles**
The past and parental background and home is rather fortunate and cozy.

Card 3   **Your future, your mother: Five of Swords**
The mother—thinking of the future—is more dispassionate than the father and says: "Don't get overwhelmed." The questioner confirms this; his mother worries about him.

Card 4   **Your feet, what you have learned, your support base: King of Swords**
The Ego, the "bad I" who causes damage to others, has collapsed by the questioner's own volition. Judging himself, the questioner has turned away from his ego. The questioner reports that by his own choice he has started to work in volunteer service. Power struggles pass him by and do not harm him; he knows his place and silently laughs about what is happening around him.

Card 5   **Your crown, your ideals and moral power: Knight of Pentacles**
This card is related to the Magician. The questioner's mastership is in his work—the construction of parts based on assignment and drafts—he has mastered this completely.

Card 6   **Your handle and material position in the world: The Fool**
The questioner's affirmation of life on earth, and the way others see him, corresponds with the archetype The Fool. In this position, The Fool may also indicate that the questioner is a joker or entertainer. Knowing the questioner, this is true. At his workplace, funny situations often arise.

Card 7   **Your karma as a result of your choices: Death**
The Death card in this position is difficult to explain. It deals with the questioner's past as a chain of cause and effect, in which the questioner himself was the actor. Death at this point of karma says in a special way that the past and prior lives are not important for the questioner any more. At this statement the questioner then remarked, "So, really, I might not have a karmic past any more." The diviner confirmed this: "Your karma is finished, gone to ashes, dead. Something has happened making this new start possible for you. The Universe in card position #1 supports this. You do not have to do anything; you may choose for yourself. You have positive

vibrations, anyway." The questioner answers that he may need to learn to feel the deep emotions of others.

Card 8   **Your manifestation, also the future: The Star**
This card means incarnation, a new beginning for a pure soul, and is the extension of card 7.

Card 9   **The value of the problem, the assignment of your soul: Three of Wands**
The questioner has to work on himself and be careful so that he will not run into problems.

Card 10   **The judgment, outcome: Six of Swords**
The questioner "crosses the great water." He makes a grand leap and in this way "becomes another being." The questioner confirms this; he has gone through a number of big changes in his life. This process is ongoing: the questioner's soul is proceeding into an unknown domain. Now, two years later, the questioner is very active in gathering Gnostic knowledge.

The Celts and the Celtic Cross

Arthur E. Waite referred to the Celtic Cross as a very old spread. It is the one that is used most in the western world. For this reason, at this point, we will elaborate to some extent on the Celts and their culture.

The Celts descended from very old Indo-Germanic tribes who lived in the region between the Ural, the Caucasus, and Persia. They had their own language and, likely, had early eastern spiritual knowledge. The Celts' great cosmological knowledge and practical magic skills are legendary. At midwinter the sun rises exactly behind Stonehenge's Heel Stone, casting a long shadow right into the center of the structure.

The Celts were the first to domesticate the horse (4000–3000 B.C.), which allowed them much greater mobility and fighting power than the tribes that surrounded them. From around 2000 B.C., they invaded east Mediterranean countries in Europe. The Doric invasion in Greece moved them westward along the two sides of the Mediterranean Sea, where, around 400 B.C., they attacked the Roman Empire with Hannibal from Carthage. They lived in France, the northern part of Spain, and England. After the invasions of the Saxons and Vikings, they settled in the north of Scotland, Wales, and Ireland.

As discussed in chapter 6 of this book, Druids upheld the Celtic culture—preserving it in memorized rituals, legends, ballads—and sun worship. From the priests a king was elected who ruled for one year and then was ritually killed. Beginning in A.D. 600, the Celts were christened. This change took place smoothly since Druid priests in their philosophy had long expected the Sun-Man-God to arrive. Miraculous sacrificial cauldrons are a recurrent motif in Celtic myths. Some overflow with plenty; others restore the dead to life, while still others contain a special brew of wisdom. Ultimately, the early Celtic cauldrons found their expression in the Arthurian Grail legends.

The Celtic Cross is of Druid, pre-Christian origin, and is not linked to Jesus' death on the cross. The Celtic cross has equal beams and is almost always positioned in front of, or surrounded by, a circle representing the sun (figure 9.8a–b). Celtic crosses have a psyche-clarifying and calming emanation, making it a very appropriate mandala for meditation. Many Irish people still attribute great magical powers to the old Celtic crosses in their country.

The early Celtic Church had male and female priests who were allowed to marry. Celtic priests paid great attention to vibrations and natural forces and were chosen for their gifts of radiance. They concentrated on healing by means of herbs, the laying on of hands, and personal emanation.

9.8a An early Celtic cross. The circle symbolizes the sun's daily path.

The Christian cross was used little by the Celts, as a Celtic curse rested on the crucifix. This was logical, as the Celtic religion rejected the Roman Catholic dogma of deliverance; it was incompatible with their idea of reincarnation. Christ was not considered the Son of God, but *the New Man*, a special being dwelling in a special body. The first Celtic Christians did not believe that Christ died to repent for their sins. They considered Christ's death as a continuation of the pagan tradition that a king sometimes had to die in order to save his people.

The Celtic Cross spread

The Celtic Cross spread with Tarot cards is used as divinatory method when the questioner is searching for insight, clarification, and an image of the future. After shuffling and parting the cards, the diviner lays out the Celtic Cross spread (figure 9.9). While positioning the cards, the diviner mentions the meaning of the position and the name of the card.

Step 1   Card 1 is laid down, face up, and card 2 is positioned horizontally, on top of card 1: this cross symbolizes the questioner. The empty place underneath the first card represents the invisible, inner structure, the essence of the questioner.

Card 1 is the questioner's personality and card 2 is the problem that is currently blocking or impinging on the questioner.

Step 2   The cards 3, 4, 5, and 6 are laid down clockwise in a circle around the cross. The circle symbolizes the sun's orbit and daily sequence. Card 3 is positioned under the cross, at the earth. Humankind rises together with the sun clockwise: cards 4 and 5 are laid down. Then the sun descends and card 6 is laid down. The Celtic Cross is now complete.

Step 3   Cards 7 to 10 form the base on which the cross is placed. In step 3, the base is built up: the cards 7, 8, 9, and 10 are

9.8b The 16.5 foot (5m) tall cross of Monaster-boice (County Lough) combines Celtic and Christian symbolism. It bears the Celtic circle and cross with equal beams, and has a church on top of the vertical beam. The figure in the center is probably Jesus Christ, the 12 figures at the base his apostles.

laid down in an upward direction; normally, this base is placed to the right of the cross that was formed by the cards 1 to 6. The arrangement of both figures together is called the Celtic Cross.

Expansion of a Celtic Cross spread

In most instances, the Celtic Cross spread will be quite clear in its message. However, if the last card—the outcome—is very special or very serious, the questioner may be eager to know how the

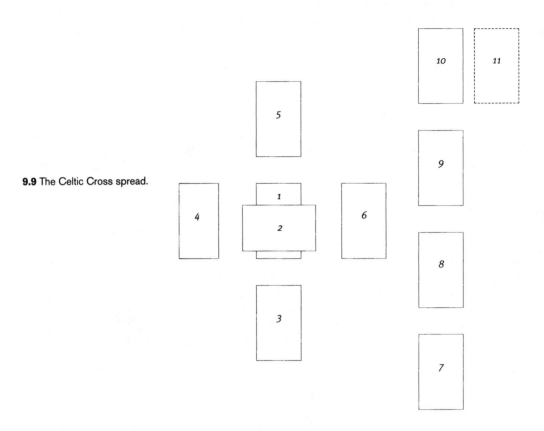

9.9 The Celtic Cross spread.

Card Position	Meaning of the Position
1	This covers the questioner.
2	This crosses the questioner.
3	This represents the questioner's foundation.
4	This is behind the questioner and has a diminishing influence.
5	This crowns the questioner.
6	This is in front of the questioner and will happen soon.
7	This is the questioner in relation to the question.
8	This shows the interaction of the questioner with his or her environment (outer life).
9	These are the questioner's hopes and fears (inner life).
10	This is the outcome, the result to be expected.
11	The parallel card may clarify the final outcome, the result to be expected.

course of events may continue after card 10, the last span of time, has lapsed. In this case, the message may be expanded by a further Celtic Cross spread, by placing card 10 in position 1, and then, shuffling and parting all the remaining cards and the nine cards of the first Celtic Cross. The second Celtic Cross gives a comprehensive overview of the situation that may develop after card 10.

The parallel card

A parallel card can be drawn from a second, identical deck of Tarot cards after it has been shuffled. The parallel card may be taken from the deck or selected from a fan. This card may clarify the final outcome in case the interpretation of card 10 presents questions.

Further explanation of the card positions in the Celtic Cross spread

Card 1   **This covers the questioner.**
This card stands for the questioner's personality and the way he expresses it in relation to the question. Hence, this card shows how the questioner presents himself to the outside world and what masks his essence. This card also indicates the atmosphere or environment in which the questioner works and lives. It describes the situation of the moment around the question and what is important in it.

Card 2   **This crosses the questioner.**
This card points out the nature of the problems and obstacles with regard to the question and the immediate influences that confront the questioner. It symbolizes the questioner's cross. If card 2 is favorable and not in conflict with card 1— if it is positioned close to card 1 in the life cycle mandala (see figure 4.16 on pages 148–149)—it supports the questioner's personality. If, for example, The Fool were card 1 and card 2 were the Three of Pentacles, card 2 would not be positioned crosswise, but upward left against card 1.

Card 3   **This card represents the questioner's foundation.**
This card shows the practical basis, formed by backgrounds and experiences in the distant past, which gives rise to current events that influence the questioner's attitudes. It also gives information about the unconscious of the questioner and his or her temperament with respect to the question.

Card 4   **This is behind the questioner and has less and less influence.**
This card indicates the recent past. It deals with influences and occurrences that have happened recently, but are now fading away. They may also be circumstances or situations from long ago, which are still exerting pressure on the questioner.

Card 5   **This crowns the questioner.**
This card shows the questioner's conscious and unconscious ideals, possibilities, and goals. It is the best the questioner has in store and what can be achieved.

Card 6   **This is in front of the questioner; it becomes more important and will become reality soon.**
This card shows the sphere of influence that gains in strength with regard to the question. It is the future that casts its shadow forward, revealing influences, relationships, interactions, and outcomes that will soon become reality.

Card 7   **This is the questioner in relation to the question.**
This card shows the questioner in the current situation and the surrounding circumstances with regard to the question. Card 7 therefore is of great importance in the interpretation of the outcome depicted in card 10.

Card 8   **This shows the interaction of the questioner with the environment.**
This card sketches the questioner's environment, home, work, and friends and reflects the opinions of those in that environment, as well as the questioner's reactions to these influences.

Card 9   **This is what the questioner hopes and fears.**
This card sheds light on inner emotions, hopes, fears, hidden thoughts, and wishes the questioner has about the future and keeps hidden. This card shows the questioner's inner life but does not indicate what will happen. A negative card often indicates a flaw in the questioner's attitude pertaining to the question.

Card 10   **This is the outcome, the result to be expected.**
This card summarizes all the influences of the other cards in the spread, which culminate in the result to be expected. That endpoint at the same time is the beginning of the next development. The life cycle makes very clear that there is never total stagnation, but always change, always movement. This card gives the final answer to the question. The diviner can look at card 5, the crown, for confirmation or cancellation of the statement in card 10.

Card 11   **The parallel card.**
This card does not need to be drawn if the final outcome is clear. In case of doubt it can clarify the questioner's situation further.

Example 3: A Celtic Cross spread

The situation

The questioner is an advertising designer and artist, and divorced.

The question

The questioner would like to know what he may expect in the next half year.

The spread and interpretation

Card 1   **This covers you: The Fool**

The questioner wants to start anew, has the knowledge, but does not know how to use it, or in which direction to go.

Card 2   **This crosses you: The Priestess**

It is a matter of acquiring knowledge. Apparently there is a woman who teaches the questioner. The questioner then immediately identifies his friend, a clever lawyer. The card crosses the questioner and this means that it is often difficult for him to accept the friend's assistance, because these lessons are projected squarely onto the questioner's way of existence. The knowledge acquired is used in card 7 in this spread: The Magician.

Card 3   **This forms your foundation: Six of Swords**

The questioner is underway, trying to escape, which is a very deep aspect of his psyche. On a shaky base, he has a tendency to keep shifting his boundaries.

Card 4   **This is behind you and has less and less influence: Five of Wands**

In the past the questioner has fought intensely, and endured chaotic situations for the sake of his personal growth or development. He adds that these matters are now in the past and not of much interest any more.

Card 5   **This crowns you: The World**

The questioner wants a revolutionary change in his life. He wants to aim only at spiritual work and painting. The inner strength for this is acquired by the inner calm that comes after the battle. This card, in combination with card 3, the six of Swords (crossing the great water), means that the big change indeed will take place. The questioner says that he has plans to make an overseas journey to organize important matters.

Card 6   **This is in front of you: Eight of Wands**

The questioner finishes fighting and throws the weapons down. He mentions that at the moment he is fighting over taxes, but he does not have to fight himself; this is now done for him by card 2, The Priestess.

Card 7	**This is you in relation to your question: The Magician**
	The summary of the questioner and his question: he knows what he wants and can do.

Card 8	**These are influences between you and your environment: The Queen of Wands**
	The environment sees the questioner as a sunny, inspiring, and entrepreneurial person.

Card 9	**These are your inner emotions: Two of Cups**
	This is the honest sharing of the soul. The questioner really tries to do this.

Card 10	**This is the outcome: The Lovers**
	The outcome is marriage or a similar committed relationship. The questioner says that he has been single for quite some time, ever since his divorce. According to this spread, a woman will arrive, a great love. In this case The Lovers does not mean making a choice, as the questioner is uncommitted. The questioner reveals that he has a platonic relationship with a girlfriend. The questioner may expect that this love will now also become physical, or that there will be a physical relationship with another woman. The World, in combination with the Two of Cups and The Lovers clearly indicates that, in this case, the resolution will be the development of a mature relationship.

Card 11	**In this divination a parallel card has been drawn: The Page of Pentacles**
	The diviner comments, "A woman with money, younger than the questioner." "That might well be possible," says the questioner, because his existing platonic love satisfies this characteristic. The questioner does not require further clarification, finds it a nice spread, and is content with it. He summarizes it by saying, "Love is coming up."

The jumping card

Finally, it must be mentioned that during the questioner's shuffling a particular card jumped (or fell) out of the deck. This card is called the jumping card because it jumped forward before the spread could "show its face." During the shuffling, various cards may step forward. These cards are remembered by the diviner and when the spread is completed, taken into account in the spread.

In the example given above, the jumping card was Ten of Cups. This card means love, liberation, and unity of the male and female principle. Thus, this jumping card emphasizes the outcome of the spread.

The Ouroboros spread

The Ouroboros spread involves ten cards. It can be done as an independent spread after having shuffled and parted the cards according to the rules. It is indicated when insight is necessary into human problems that have a paradoxical or circular logical nature, so-called "catch-22" situations. However, more commonly the Ouroboros spread is used to analyze a Celtic Cross spread laid out earlier and to clarify the relationships between the cards.

In the Ouroboros spread ten cards are arranged in a circle that returns to itself. In fact, it is the projection of a spiral: the last card meets the first one, but at a higher level. At the top of the Ouroboros is the point of augmentation: the beginning meets the end, the first card meets the tenth card. At the bottom are cards 5 and 6: these form the point of change, the division between the past and present on the one side and the future on the other (figure 9.9a–b).

In the Ouroboros several parallel and oppositional relationships between cards deepen the insight into the questioner's problem. For instance, the cards in positions 3 and 8 indicate the questioner's horizon: psychological foundation (3) and environment (8) as a reflection of their psychological state (see figure 9.11). These two cards are in opposition, as well as extensions of each other; there is a natural field of tension between them.

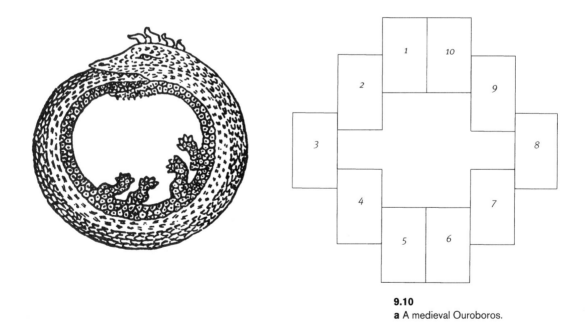

9.10
a A medieval Ouroboros.

b The Ouroboros spread.

Horizontal connections in an Ouroboros spread

Horizontal connections indicate extremes at the same plane of existence.

9.11 Horizontal relationships in the Ouroboros spread.

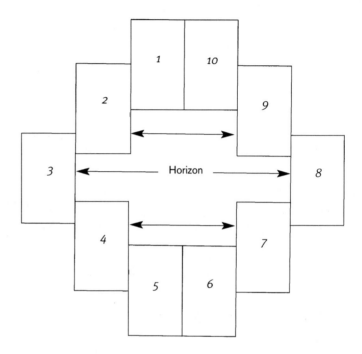

Card 2 and Card 9	That which crosses the path of the questioner, leads to hope, fear, and other emotions.
Card 3 and Card 8	The questioner's psychological foundation and environment as a reflection of a psychological state are two extremes at the questioner's horizon. These two points and a third point, the questioner, together determine his or her current plane of existence.
Card 4 and Card 7	What is behind the questioner forms the basis of the situation and the problem.
Card 5 and Card 6	The highest goals, ideals. and commitments determine the point of change. This is the immediate future—as in tomorrow.

Vertical connections in an Ouroboros spread

Vertical connections are crosslinks on the horizontal connections (figure 9.12).

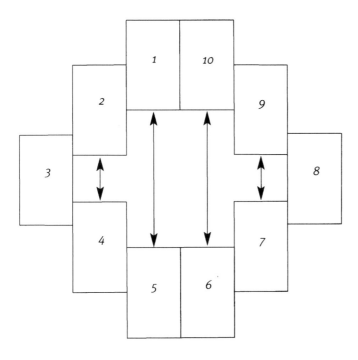

9.12 Vertical relationships in the Ouroboros spread.

Card 4 and Card 2   The past crosses the questioner's plane of existence and leads to the problem now confronted.

Card 5 and Card 1   The abstract ideals, highest goals, and commitments direct the person's actions. In this way they determine personality and the way the questioner acts in his or her plane of existence.

Card 6 and Card 10 The things are gaining influence, will happen soon, and are crossing the questioner's plane of existence. This indicates to what extent the final result coincides with the original objective.

Card 7 and Card 9   The questioner in relation to his or her emotions.

The personal square in an Ouroboros spread

The cards 4 + 2 + 7 + 9 contain four important elements: decreasing influences (card 4), the problem (card 2), the inner emotions (card 9) and the questioner in relation to the issue (card 7) (figure 9.13).

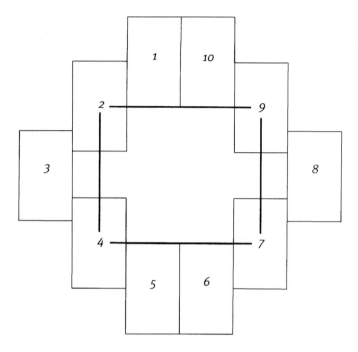

9.13 The personal square in the Ouroboros spread.

Oppositions in an Ouroboros spread

Opposing cards in the Ouroboros spread create a tension that leads to action (figure 9.14).

Card 1 and Card 6   The person, opposed to his or her future, wants to know what is in store.

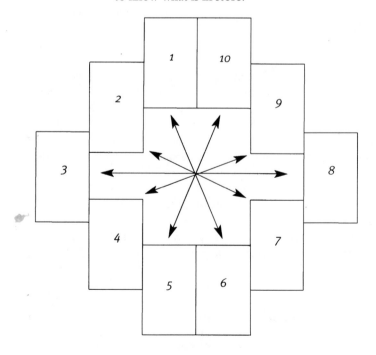

9.14 Oppositions in the Ouroboros spread.

Card 2 and Card 7	The issue that crosses the questioner's path opposes the questioner and forms the problem.
Card 3 and Card 8	This is the questioner's horizon.
Card 4 and Card 9	That which is in the past is the source of what the questioner hopes and fears; at a higher level it gives shape to inner motives.
Card 5 and Card 10	The questioner's ideals and highest goals confront the actual situation and inspire him or her to achieve outcomes that are in line with those ideals and goals.

The Horoscope spread

The Horoscope spread offers insight into a person's character and situation in life. Character is defined as the questioner's disposition in terms of emotions and determination, his or her reactions to stimuli from the outside world.

In a Horoscope spread, 12 Tarot cards are laid out counterclockwise, each in the position of an astrological house, starting with the First House (figure 9.15).

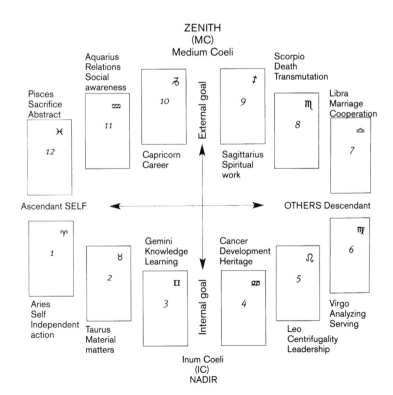

9.15 The positions of the Tarot cards and houses in a Horoscope spread.

SECTORS IN A HOROSCOPE AND FIELDS IN A HOROSCOPE SPREAD

House and card position:	This field indicates the questioner's:	Related Sign:		Related Planet:	
First	Personality, temperament, demeanor as an independent and free individual	Aries	♈	Pluto	♇
Second	Attitude toward possessions of all kinds, gains and losses, feelings related to the card placed in this house	Taurus	♉	Venus	♀
Third	Learning, mental capacities, school life, education	Gemini	♊	Mercury	☿
Fourth	Development as a child, taking in impressions from the environment	Cancer	♋	Moon	☽
Fifth	Leadership, offspring, love, instinctive affection, joy, creativity	Leo	♌	Sun	☉
Sixth	Work, analysis, putting things in order, serving, health/illness	Virgo	♍	Mercury	⊕
Seventh	Cooperation, business, balance, marriage, conflict	Libra	♎	Venus	♀
Eighth	Transformation, inheritance, reorganization, death, regeneration	Scorpio	♏	Mars	♂
Ninth	Spiritual thinking and leadership, (mass) communication, long distance travel, languages	Sagittarius	♐	Jupiter	♃
Tenth	Aspirations and ambitions, career, calling, status, and reputation	Capricorn	♑	Saturn	♄
Eleventh	Social conscience, friends and acquaintances, clubs, and societies	Aquarius	♒	Uranus	♅
Twelfth	Abstraction, sacrifice, becoming conscious of limitations, seclusion, service to others, tests	Pisces	♓	Neptune	♆

9.16 The meanings of the 12 houses in a Horoscope and a Horoscope spread.

In this spread, the Tarot cards function as points of power, like planets in the houses in a horoscope. The use of the Horoscope spread requires the diviner to be knowledgeable about astrology, especially the meanings of the Twelve Houses (figure 9.16).

A horoscope is a symbolic representation of the position of the sun, the moon, and the planets in the zodiac at birth. Birth is defined as the moment at which a soul determines its existence in the world by choosing the place and the time of the start of that existence. The newborn's character and course of life runs synchronously with the position and movement of the planets.

The horoscope is a tool that translates the symbolism in the celestial constellations into psychological terms.

The zodiac is a loop of 12 star constellations and cosmic signs in the heavens: in a horoscope, these 12 signs are projected on a circle. The horoscope itself is divided into 12 sectors, called "the houses of the horoscope." Each house symbolizes a fundamental aspect of the character and life of the person concerned. Each planet imparts principles held by the star sign and the house in which the planet is located. For example, Venus brings in aspects of love and relationships; Jupiter, aspects of fortune; Saturn, those of fate.

In a Horoscope spread, one Tarot card is placed on each of the 12 houses, so instead of celestial bodies, Tarot cards work in each sector. In this way the diviner acquires a snapshot of the questioner's character and present situation.

The first step in the interpretation of a Horoscope spread is to consider the individual cards in the 12 houses. For instance, someone who has The Priestess in the First House will have a substantial inclination to become a teacher; someone with the One of Wands in the First House is a pioneer who might invent or build things, for the benefit of society. The Chariot in the Eleventh House would reveal charismatic leadership of groups, and make many people assemble for productive, social goals.

A questioner who has The Moon in the Eleventh House would have many problems with social relationships, not necessarily all of them his or her fault. He or she may well be able to build relationships with other people, for example, through a favorable card such as Two of Cups in the Seventh House, but for a variety of causes will lose them again and again and will be on their own a great deal.

In astrology, and in the Horoscope spread, apart from the houses, signs, planets, and elements, we need to look at the aspects between the planets. An aspect is the angle between two planets or Tarot cards in a Horoscope spread. Celestial bodies or Tarot cards in a horoscope at angles that are 30 degrees or multiples of 30 degrees (the major beneficial aspects being 60 and 120 degrees), affect each other in a harmonious way. They help the questioner be in situations at the right time and in the right way. Angles of 45 degrees or multiples (the major stressful aspects being 90 and 180 degrees) between planets or Tarot cards hinder each other's influence. They reveal problems and difficult situations.

Since in a Horoscope spread all the houses are occupied by energy-producing Tarot cards, there are many (46) aspects and influences between them (figure 9.17). This makes analyzing an aspect of a Horoscope spread somewhat complicated. It is outside

The 46 aspects between houses in a Horoscope Spread			
(Double aspects have been greyed)			
Angle (in degrees) of aspect between houses			
60 positive	**90 negative**	**120 positive**	**180 negative**
1+3	1+4	1+5	1+7
1+11	1+10	1+9	1+7
2+4	2+5	2+6	2+8
2+12	2+11	2+10	2+8
3+5	3+6	3+7	3+9
3+1	3+12	3+11	3+9
4+6	4+7	4+8	4+10
4+2	4+1	4+12	4+10
5+7	5+8	5+9	5+11
5+3	5+2	5+1	5+11
6+8	6+9	6+10	6+12
6+4	6+3	6+2	6+12
7+9	7+10	7+11	7+1
7+5	7+4	7+3	7+1
8+10	8+11	8+12	8+2
8+6	8+5	8+4	8+2
9+11	9+12	9+1	9+3
9+7	9+6	9+5	9+3
10+12	10+1	10+2	10+4
10+8	10+7	10+6	10+4
11+1	11+2	11+3	11+5
11+9	11+8	11+7	11+5
12+2	12+3	12+4	12+6
12+10	12+9	12+8	12+6

(Left axis label: **House combinations**)

9.17 Overview of all aspects between cards in a Horoscope spread. In this table all permutations are given; the second time an aspect appears in this table (e.g., after 2 + 5 appears 5 + 2), it is shaded. In total there are 46 different aspects between the cards in a Horoscope spread. Two cards in positive aspect bring out the positive aspects in both. A negative aspect between two cards weakens them both.

the framework of this book to discuss the astrological meanings of aspects. Those who want to apply them to Horoscope spreads are advised to get them from astrological manuals.

The Horoscope spread is easy for diviners who have an astrological background, because they already know the meanings of the 12 houses and the aspects between planets. Other diviners can train in the Horoscope spread by using this spread for someone well known to them. Interpretation of the influences of the cards on the houses is then easier, since the character and situation of the person are known.

Example 4: A Horoscope spread
The situation

A male teacher has experienced relationship problems with various people for a long time, but he thinks that he is a friendly, open person. Obviously, the cause is in his character, but how? Now in his second marriage, serious problems are emerging. He wants to know what is behind these relationship problems—what causes them and what he can do about them. The diviner decides on a Horoscope spread, as this is a character problem. The diviner's strategy is to look especially at the cards in the Eleventh and Seventh Houses and their aspects with the cards in the other houses.

The spread and interpretation

The resulting spread is given in figure 9.18. The position of The Moon in the Eleventh House is remarkable!

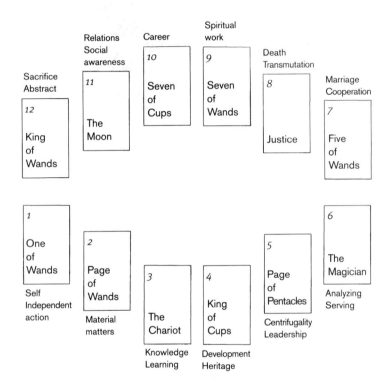

9.18 Example of a Horoscope spread and the aspects between the card in the Eleventh House and other cards.

Card 1   **The Self: One of Wands**
The questioner is at heart an industrious pioneer who has done a great deal of epoch-making work from which many sectors of society are benefiting.

Card 2   **Material matters: Page of Wands**
The questioner is a steady wage earner, enjoying jobs that require a lot of speaking and writing and making judgments; the Page of Wands is part of the same quartet as the Major Arcanum Justice.

Card 3   **Knowledge and learning: The Chariot**
The questioner can learn very well and master new knowledge. It is no wonder that he is an academic.

Card 4 **Descent and social setting: King of Cups**
The questioner is from an artistic family that encourages study and scientific/academic careers. Friendly, broad-minded, sensitive, and conscious, the questioner is also interested in the supernatural.

Card 5 **Leadership, love: Page of Pentacles**
The questioner is able to manage his growing wealth. In demeanor and relationships he is inventive but also childish and absent-minded. He is certainly not a charismatic leader.

Card 6 **Work, analytical skills, and service: The Magician**
The questioner has substantial analytical skills, which he likes to use, display, and/or help people with. Loving to perform by giving lectures, he may be a teacher in a subject that requires much analysis, such as psychology or computer science.

Card 7 **Marriage and cooperation: Five of Wands**
This card suggests that in situations where cooperation is needed, many conflicts are inescapable. The questioner hurts himself and the social groups of which he is a part. The heart of the matter is that the way the questioner wants to manifest himself—as a pioneer—puts him in conflict with others. This card and the pioneer's card in the First House are in opposition to each other! It is clear that the urge to pioneer at the forefront may create conflict with others—a tragic situation. A commitment to fight at a professional front and a commitment to protect and be present at home are difficult to combine. Further aspect analysis may reveal more causes of the relationship conflicts in which the questioner involves himself time after time.

Card 8 **Ambitions and transitions: Justice**
This card in this position indicates that the questioner faces judgments with an open heart, does not have a problem with change in general and has no (substantial) fear of death and dying.

Card 9 **Spiritual work and communication: Seven of Wands**
The questioner's metaphysical work is in many cases a spiritual battle. Rather than creating completely new things, the questioner will find himself in situations where he has to conquer obstacles, such as complacency or old, rigid structures, and implement new technological or psychological findings.

Card 10 **Career, ambitions, status: Six of Cups**
The questioner recognizes the joys of childhood in his

own career. This card, too, is an indication that the questioner's career is in teaching or lecturing. In these fields the questioner experiences a joyful karma, makes many right decisions naturally, connects with many new friends, and has nice memories.

Card 11   **Relationships and social conscience: The Moon**
Notwithstanding the good relationships in the field of education, the questioner will suffer a lot in other relationship areas. He is also subjected to undermining activities such as slander and manipulation, probably because he does not recognize these activities in others. Childish innocence and openness is a feature of the Page of Pentacles, which in this spread is located in the Fifth House, in direct opposition to the Major Arcanum The Moon in the Eleventh House. This means that the questioner's naïve, open, and trusting way of dealing with people, which works well for him in educational settings, leaves him wide open to the schemes and plots of others who attempt to destroy the relationships dear to him. In this way the questioner engages in one life cycle after another of building new relationships, rather than enjoying the same relationships for a long time, until he learns to listen to his gut feelings about who deserves his trust and who does not, and which relationships are innately good—notwithstanding their ups and downs. The Moon is a Major Arcanum in which the soul is cleansed; this arcanum in this position has an important karmic meaning. Working on relationships is likely to be a karmic assignment for this questioner.

Card 12   **Sacrifice and abstraction: King of Wands**
The questioner is reliable, sympathetic, of high moral standards (this card is part of the quartet in which The Priest is the Major Arcanum) and wealthy—in principle. However, this card in this house indicates that time and again, the person will have to forego mental, physical, financial, and social achievements, and will not really be able to enjoy them.

Synopsis: The questioner has to look at his position in life from a different point of view. The real solution cannot be pure "Wands" or productivity based, because that is where his problems are coming from. He cannot expect a mental or analytically based "Swords"-like solution to the problems either, because The Moon in the Eleventh House is the second major relationship problem generator and karmic assignment. The solution for the questioner's interpersonal problems must be sought in changing emotional "Cups" behavior. The person will have to express his emotions and transfer them to loved ones. We may deduce that this person's emotional expression so far has been rather childish, maybe even foolish (Page of Pentacles in the Fifth House). In one way or another the questioner will have to "grow up" psychologically, so that his behavior and emotional expression toward others will become less erratic and more firm. He may need guidance to achieve this (King of Cups in the Fourth House). He may need to redirect his interests and persevere to achieve spiritual liberation through systematic assistance to others. He also will have to take up some form of creative work to express his emotions and re-establish his artistic footing. Third, the questioner will have to find a better balance between working on and advocating progress, maybe through strict work rules. He will have to "live through" the effects of his actions in an objective way and develop systematic empathy for those around him at home and at work, based on love.

The Chakra spread

The Chakra spread portrays an image of humankind as a psychosomatic unity and shows the internal and external operation and condition of the seven chakras (figure 9.19). A key to investigation of internal and external life, character, and health (figure 9.20b), it is also called the Alchemists Pyramid spread.

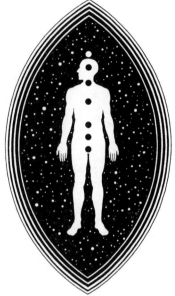

9.19 The seven chakras portrayed as macro/microcosmos.

The word *chakra* consists of two parts: "cha" = energy and "kra" = to act or behave. Chakra thus means energetic conduct. The Indian Vedanta philosophy considers the human body and soul a psychosomatic unity, divided into seven energy and activity centers, the seven chakras. The spirit descends into matter and combines with it via the seven chakras. If all chakras function well, the basal energy transmutes, when moving up from one chakra to the next higher, to a finer vibration and different quality. An overview of the names of the chakras, their meanings, influences, related illnesses, and pertaining parts of the human body is given in figure 9.21.

James M. Pryse, in his book *The Apocalypse Unsealed*, explains in a stunning way the Biblical revelation of Jesus Christ—also called the Revelation of St. John—as the Initiation of John to perfect functioning of the energetic centers or chakras.

Tantrism speaks of the kundalini snake, which uncoils and erects itself along the spinal cord, prompting each chakra to intense activity.

In summary, the Chakra spread sheds light on the questioner's various levels of internal and external energies and conduct. It is a synergetic combination of the Vedanta and Tantric partition of the body that links with the various levels of functioning of the psyche and the archetypal-psychological symbolism in the Tarot. In the Chakra spread (figure 9.20a–b), the Tarot cards are used to acquire information about the way the chakras are functioning and their stage of development. In fact, a developmental snapshot is taken of each chakra and depicted by a Tarot card.

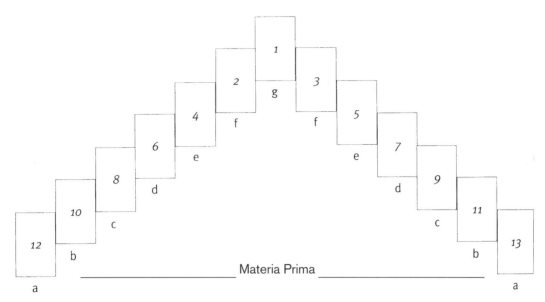

9.20a The Chakra spread.

a: Card 31 and 12 symbolize the Root Chakra
b: Card 11 and 10 symbolize the Spleen Chakra
c: Card 9 and 8 symbolize the Solar Plexus Chakra } Physical
d: Card 7 and 6 symbolize the Heart Chakra
e: Card 5 and 4 symbolize the Throat Chakra
f: Card 3 and 2 symbolize the Forehead Chakra}
g: Card 1 symbolizes the Crown Chakra } Ethereal

9.20b The meanings of the seven chakras in the Chakra spread.

The Chakra spread and its interpretation

After shuffling and parting of the cards, the diviner arranges 13 cards, face down, in the Chakra spread according to the numbering in figure 9.20a. The seven chakras are divided into internal cards 13, 11, 9, 7, 3, external cards 12, 10, 8, 6, 4, 2, and the manifestation, card 1.

The seven chakras are divided into physical and ethereal polarities. The top of the pyramid (card 1) is the keystone and summary of the questioner's energy centers and their energy states.

Example 5: A Chakra spread

The situation

The questioner is an artist. She is divorced and lives and works on her own. She has problems with her love-relationships, work, and health. She works with reiki, a holistic healing method.

The question

The questioner is interested in a mind-body picture of herself. To this effect, she would like to do a Chakra spread.

THE CHAKRAS AND THE FIELDS OF ENERGY AND ACTIVITY TO WHICH THEY RELATE

	FIRST CHAKRA	SECOND CHAKRA	THIRD CHAKRA	FOURTH CHAKRA	FIFTH CHAKRA	SIXTH CHAKRA	SEVENTH CHAKRA
SANSKRIT NAME	Muladhara	Svadhistana	Manipura	Anahata	Vishudda	Ajna	Shasrara
MEANING	Root/Base	Lovable	Sparkling Jewel	To disentangle	To purify	To observe	Thousand forms
COMMON NAME	Tail-bone chakra	Spleen chakra	Solar plexus chakra	Heart chakra	Throat chakra	Forehead chakra	Crown chakra
PLACE	Perineum	Lower belly	Just above the navel				
ELEMENT	Fire	Water	Fire	Air	Ether/sound	Light	Thoughts
APPEARANCE	Solid	Liquid	Plasma	Gas	Vibration	Image	Information
FUNCTION	To survive	Lust	Willpower	Love	Communication	Intuition	Insight
EXPRESSION	Founding	Sexuality	Power	Equilibrium	Creativity	Imagination	Knowledge
COLOR	Red	Orange	Yellow	Green	Blue	Indigo	Violet
BODY PARTS	Legs Bones Intestines	Ovaries Testicles Womb Kidneys Bladder Genitals	Pancreas Muscles Digestive system	Thymus Lungs Heart Arms Hands	Hypothalamus Thyroid Throat Ears	Pineal gland	Hypophysis Central nervous system Cortex
IN CASE OF BAD FUNCTIONING	Obesity Constipation Frequent illness	Impotence Frigidity Problems with bladder, womb, genitals	Stomach Ulcer Diabetes Hypoglycemia	High blood pressure Asthma Angina pectoris Heart infarction	Neck pain Throat pain Flu	Headache Nightmares Blindness	Alienation Confusion Depression
EXOTERIC MEANING	Physical body	Life principle	Astral body	Passions	Thinking, intelligence	Spiritual soul	The spirit
SANSKRIT TERM	Rupa	Prana	Linga Sharira	Kama Rupa	Manas	Buddi	Atma

9.21 Overview of the chakra fields, their meanings, influences, parts of the human body, and related illnesses.

The spread and interpretation
FIRST CHAKRA
Card 13 **The Root Chakra (internal): Three of Wands**
This card shows an awaiting and alert attitude. The pirate ships in the distance in this chakra field indicate parasites, bacteria, or viruses lying in wait (parasites and such can also be interpreted in a metaphorical way). The questioner will have to watch out for them.

Card 12 **The Root Chakra (external): Page of Cups**
This card shows trusting, loving others, and giving (sexual) energy.

Synopsis: These two cards portray an inner contradiction in the way the questioner's Root Chakra currently operates. To the outside world, she likes to give and believe in her (love) communication, but internally she wants to stay in control, so she sits on the fence because of the possible dangers. This results in a passive attitude. The questioner will easily feel chilled, because her basal energy is given away on the outside, but internally it is needed to support the alertness of her psyche.

The questioner says that she is very susceptible to parasites and viruses and easily feels chilled.

SECOND CHAKRA
Card 11   **The Spleen Chakra (internal): The Empress**
A tenacious Cancer card in this "intestinal" position may indicate too much holding on—and therefore, constipation. The luscious growth, also represented by The Empress, possibly indicates profuse intestinal flora.

Card 10   **The Spleen Chakra (external): The Tower**
Shows a severe infection or disturbance in the intestines.

Synopsis: These two cards show poor bowel movements and possible stomach infection, which may cause fatigue and depression. The questioner says that she indeed has problems with her bowels and has had an intestinal infection. Also, she says that she is more or less constantly tired and depressed. Being troubled about others, she has amassed many worries. In her case, energy is burned by prolonged digestion and hanging on to excretions that should have been discarded long ago.

THIRD CHAKRA
Card 9   **The Solar Plexus (internal): The Sun**
This sound card on the solar plexus cannot be better and indicates an abundance of inner will power and growth.

Card 8   **The Solar Plexus (external): The Magician**
Shows an inquisitive, warm, extroverted will. The Magician in this position indicates creativity.

Synopsis: These two cards show much inner growth, will power, and creativity. There is absolutely no limitation here. The solar plexus is in good health. The solution to the problems in the Spleen Chakra may be found here. As the solar plexus internally and externally is very sound and strong, it is probable that those close to the questioner have no idea of her health problems, and may think that she can do anything.

FOURTH CHAKRA
Card 7   **The Heart Chakra (internal): The Chariot**
This card of manifestation and victory in the heart position is very good in itself. But because The Chariot also often indicates conflict, it is possible that the questioner sometimes may suffer from heart palpitations or pains due to intense inner turmoil, from such causes as indignation, agitation, love worries, and sorrow.

Card 6   **The Heart Chakra (external): The Universe**
This is also a good card in a good position. The questioner gives space to others and herself, is independent and, in principle, open to others and to everything The Universe offers.

Synopsis: These two cards show an open and creative Heart Chakra. There is certainly no narrow-mindedness. The occasional great inner agitation (The Chariot) can be transformed and channeled into creative activities (The Universe). This has a great chance of success, because The Magician in the extroverted solar plexus will support it.

FIFTH CHAKRA

Card 5   **The Throat Chakra (internal): Six of Pentacles**
This card indicates that internally the questioner is well able to accept her destiny. The questioner is humble and has the capacity to receive and to share. She can listen well.

Card 4   **The Throat Chakra (external): Five of Pentacles**
Indicates that the questioner feels different from others, and possibly even shut out. It is also probable that the questioner denigrates herself again and again and has a feeling of being undervalued, so that she is insecure and lonely. This card on her Throat Chakra indicates physical problems with her throat. The questioner confirms that her throat feels squeezed and sometimes even painful. She has difficulty swallowing and feels congested; speaking is sometimes painful.

Synopsis: These two cards in the Throat Chakra fields depict the problems well. Isolation and humility lie at the root of the questioner's choked feelings. It would seem that this blockage is connected to the problems with her Spleen Chakra. There is a saying, "Gut clean, throat clean." Spiritually, the questioner takes things in easily, but has trouble letting go.

SIXTH CHAKRA

Card 3   **The Forehead Chakra (internal): Six of Cups**
The questioner's third eye is the stage for the most tender and blissful memories and fantasies. The pineal gland works well. She extends loving service to others. This may sometimes cause difficulties in dealing with the emotions of others. The questioner may want to give too much. As the Six of Cups in itself is a card of dreaming and fantasies, its affect on the third eye may be very strong. The questioner may become stuck in a world of dreams and dwell in blissful past experiences.

Card 2   **The Forehead Chakra (external): Four of Cups**
This card indicates that the questioner is offered opportunities, gifts, and possibilities for her to create a piece of art. As this card also implies meditation, voluntary solitude, introversion, and deferment, the opportunities offered her by the outside world remain vague, which hampers the questioner in acting or striking at the right

moment. This card also points to the possibility of depression, fatigue, and headaches.

Synopsis: The meditative aspects of these two cards on the Forehead Chakra show a rich and pure inner emotional life. The contemplative side of the Four of Cups and the dreaming in the Six of Cups strengthen each other and intermingle easily. The result may well be alienation and distance, requiring frequent emotional and spiritual reorientation. The feeling remains that something is going to happen soon, that a mild fantasy will unexpectedly become reality (Six of Cups). There is also a great yearning for a new friendship, a new encounter, a new environment, a new sacrifice (Four and Six of Cups).

SEVENTH CHAKRA

Card 1   **The Crown Chakra: Five of Cups**
This card shows Neaniskos mourning the death of his friend Jesus Christ. It is a somber card in a position that should be occupied by a radiant card. The toppled cups that have the questioner's attention cannot possibly be put right. The contents are lost, the sacrifice spilled, and everything looks fleeting and hopeless. In this chakra, feelings of mourning and depression will emerge, with dull headaches as the possible bodily effect. However, there are two upright cups left. The figure in the card does not see them, because he has turned his back to them: the questioner has to accept that salvation will come from unexpected sources. Five of Cups on the Crown Chakra suggests to the questioner that the feelings of mourning may be warranted, but that she should give up identifying with them and direct her attention to the side with the two well-filled cups. The cards in the positions of the third and fourth chakra suggest how the questioner can digest the deprivations that are causing her mourning.

The One Card spread

This method is the most direct and true form of Tarot divination, however also the most difficult and confrontational one. A diviner needs to be experienced in the Tarot as well as in meditation to use the One Card spread. The method can be applied to any problem that requires direct, objective analysis. When the problem is formulated, a meditation follows. Then, intuitively one card is pulled out. The meditation is then continued on the card. When the relationships of the card with the quartet to which it belongs, and the opposing card and quartet in the life cycle mandala are included in the meditation, the ensuing interpretation, the root of the problem, and the solution become clear.

The advantage of this method is that it gives the questioner an objective representation of the overall situation. The difficulty is that this objective picture is not split up into positive and negative aspects, as there are no other cards in this spread to give extra

9.22 Celtic Cross reading done in December, 1991, by the members of the Abraxas group to clarify the nature, purpose, and future of this book. In a series of ten Tarot meditations on the question, the arcana in this spread were revealed one by one.

information. The diviner has to work them out personally through further meditation. This method of divination fails or succeeds depending on absolute honesty and self-reflectivity, the willingness to consider the pertaining situation in all its aspects, and the trust and willpower to implement the solution.

The spread for the restored Tarot

The Celtic Cross reading below was done by a group of Tarot workers practicing the Tarot as described in this book. The question was addressed to the Tarot itself: "What are the thoughts of the Tarot with regard to the restoration of its order and the book being written about it?" The resulting spread is shown in figure 9.22.

Card 1   **The Universe** points at the complete Tarot itself in its proper cyclical order.

Card 2   **The Priest** crosses The Universe. This points to the fact that the power of the church, for ages and through

DIVINATION WITH THE TAROT

ingrained habit, still does cross the Tarot through censorship and obfuscation. The Priest however, can be interpreted positively as well. From the latter point of view, the real priest or priestly knowledge supports the Universe and is custodian of the Tarot.

Card 3   **Death** at the foundation tells that right now the Tarot has disintegrated.

Card 4   **The Hanged Man** in the past symbolizes the Tarot's suffering and martyrdom; this is a decreasing influence.

Card 5   **The Last Judgment** as crown above The Universe attests that the Tarot will be resurrected from death and accepted in its new, completed form.

Card 6   **Truth (Jupiter)**—the truth about the Tarot will manifest itself in the near future.

Card 7   **The Sun** as a summary of this Celtic Cross spread means that the cross deals with a becoming, a new birth of the Tarot.

Card 8   **The Star** appears in the firmament. In interaction with its environment, the restored Tarot is connected with new forces of life and confirms that a new incarnation of the Tarot is happening.

Card 9   **Temperance** in the position of the inner emotions indicates that the Tarot is in a process of transition internally, as well as in the way people feel about it. Its body of knowledge and the opinion of people about the Tarot is in a process of transformation.

Card 10   **The World**—the final result is that the restored Tarot will be delivered to the world and that this will cause important karmic changes for humankind, and for the world itself.

The restored Tarot as a spread for humankind

Lastly, the restored Tarot, the 80 cards in the order presented in this book, is a spread for humankind that reflects our status and future in this world. In the earlier 78-card Tarot decks, two Tarot arcana were missing and could not express their meaning and powers. The other arcana occupied incorrect positions in the life cycle: this frustrated these arcana in the manifestation of their underlying principles. The completion and restoration of the Tarot has placed each of the 80 arcana in their proper position. Thus, the spread for humankind in this world is restored as well.

The revelation of the Major Arcanum Truth (Jupiter) and its presence in the spread for humankind implies that striving for and

9.23 "The Royal or Priestly Art." In this allegorical image, the moon, star, and sun are placed in the same order as in the *Tarot Restored*. The two figures in the foreground are Juno and Jupiter, silver and gold. (From *Philosophia Reformata* by Mulius, Frankfurt, 1622).

disseminating truth will have an increasing influence on the events to happen in this world. Similarly, the revelation of the Major Arcanum Intuition (Juno) indicates that women will face the world in a liberated and high-spirited way.

It is very important that the Major Arcanum The Star has returned to its proper position at the center, high up in the life cycle, with The Sun to the right and The Moon to the left. It is now similar again to the hermetic and alchemistic order of the three heavenly bodies: the male to the right, the female to the left, and the child—the hope, promise, and expectation, the third eye of supernal vision—in the middle (figure 9.23).

The Star in its right position announces a new era in which—after a long period of pretense and decline without prospects—vision, clear insight, and hope will prevail. As the four Tarot emblems—Pentacles, Wands, Cups, and Swords—are now in the correct order, fundamental understanding and application of the life cycle in physical and psychological processes will gradually expand and improve.

We may expect that The Star will remain in its restored position at the top of the life cycle. After the Tarot's restoration and completion, the next developmental step will be further abstraction of the Tarot (as an organized body of knowledge and principles).

J. J. Hurtak, author of the book, *The Keys of Enoch*, predicts that there will be a tremendous acceleration of the physical sciences into the spiritual sciences—truly transmuting the world of material form into the Kingdom of Light. When, in about 2,000 years' time, the age of Aquarius passes into the age of Capricorn, the Tarot may be completely integrated into a totally abstract, objective, and holistic system of knowledge and skills, in which human, spiritual, physical, and scientific laws are integrated.

For those searching for wisdom, guidance, and learning, the Tarot may be of great value. It may enable us to understand better our origin and availability for the tasks that are given us in life.

The Meanings of the Tarot Cards

Sincere words do not stand out;
Words that stand out are not sincere.
Those who know are not "learned."
Those who are learned do not know.
The righteous do not possess much.
Those who possess much are not righteous.

The Wise does not gather
By using for others what he had.
He has more
By giving to others what he owned
He owns even more.
Therefore, the Way of Heaven is to do good and not to cause harm;
The Way of Man is to act for others and not compete with them.

—*Lao Tse*, Tao Te Ching

CHAPTER 10

The Meanings
of the Tarot Cards

Introduction

When we do a Tarot card reading for someone, we get a feeling for
the cards. We create a mental image of the meanings of the cards
on the table as well as an image of the Gestalt of the message

10.1 A quartet lies at the foundation of
quick and effective interpretation of a
Tarot card.

embodied in the cards. When recalling the meaning of an arcanum from memory, it helps to summon before the inner eye the quartet of which that arcanum forms a part (figure 10.1), and the Major Arcanum that is complementary to the Major Arcanum in that quartet. It is our task to phrase these meanings in such a way that the questioner will understand their message.

This chapter gives an overview of the meanings of each card. The question and the context of the Tarot consultation will determine which meanings are most appropriate. Only after the meaning of each card in the spread has been articulated can the diviner consider relationships between the cards in that spread and, via the completed image, pass on to the questioner the message embodied by the spread.

The meanings of upright and reversed cards

In a Tarot spread the pictures of the arcana are either upright or reversed. This chapter gives the upright and reversed meanings of each arcanum. The issue of reversed cards needs to be discussed prior to the overview of the meanings of all Tarot cards. "Upright" and "reversed" together reflect the duality intrinsic to our existence on earth. Hence, in a spread a Tarot card is not either upright or reversed; in a way it is always both, but one aspect is more pervasive than the other. Even though one normally sees only one side of the coin, the other side exists, too.

Example: An upright Swords One card indicates sharpness and purity of abstraction and power of thinking. By means of reasoning it is possible to discover very powerful laws and use them in technology and society. It is also possible, through reasoning, to affect someone's attitude in a positive way.

A reversed One of Swords card traditionally points to the abuse of reasoning with the purpose to destroy. It is possible to use the power of light to give life or to kill. Psychologically, the One of Swords reversed indicates that through reasoning, someone's identity or valuable idea is shattered or driven into the ground (figure 10.2).

Reversed Tarot cards traditionally have a negative connotation. For this reason reversed cards in a spread are experienced as unpleasant. Still, avoiding reversed cards is not possible. Each arcanum does not really convey two different meanings, one upright and one reversed. In fact, they comprise only one, encompassing both positive and negative aspects of the basic archetype.

The message in a reversed Tarot card is profound and penetrating. It clarifies the negative aspects of situations. A reversed card in a spread clarifies a psychological object in the questioner's dark, unconscious attic that is revealed because a torch (the spread) is shining on it. Only by lighting up the darkness are the objects and structures that it hides revealed. Sometimes a reversed card represents a more favorable situation then it does when upright.

For example, in The Devil reversed, the archetypal message is that he falls from his pedestal and is longer supported by his lies.

THULE SOCIETY

10.2 Swords One upright, compared with the emblem of the powerful and ultra-secret fraternity, Thule, which paved the way for Hitler and National Socialism. The sword and the three pentacles are positioned upside-down and are quite clear about the nature and purpose of this group. In the crest of the KGB (right), the sword is also placed upside down.

Therefore, The Devil reversed is less negative than The Devil upright (figure 10.3).

Reversed cards may be misunderstood; therefore, their meanings have to be studied carefully. For example, The Hanged Man reversed seems more positive, because he is not hanging, but standing on one leg, bound to a tree. The negative connotation in this case is that the ultimate sacrifice that *has to be undergone now*

THE DEVIL

10.3 The Major Arcanum The Devil, upright and reversed. When the arcanum The Devil is reversed, he drops from his half truth. He loses the support of his lies. The pentacle on his forehead is turned upright. These effects give The Devil a more positive and humane inclination and appearance.

cannot be delivered for some reason, so useless, wrong, or hypocritical sacrifices, boredom, or a situation of passivity and stagnation may result.

When considering an arcanum in general, always read the meanings of the card in both its upright and reversed position. When the card is upright in a spread, reading the upright meaning alone may be sufficient, but *if a card is reversed, it is important to study both its upright and reversed meanings.*

Apart from the fact of whether a card is upright or reversed, the Tarot life cycle is a powerful frame of reference that always indicates development. The question in a Tarot consultation clarifies the questioner's stage of development in this cycle and the direction in which further development will take place within the laws of karma. Over the centuries, the meanings of the cards, especially the Minor Arcana, have been changed through misunderstandings, copying of wrong texts, exchanges of pieces of text, and so on. In this chapter we will relate the meanings and images of the Tarot arcana to the structure of the restored Tarot and its life cycle. In the Tarot life cycle, the Ten of Swords means the absolute end of the full-grown fetus's stay in the womb through its birth into the world; therefore it also means the definitive start of the new life. In a metaphorical way, the Ten of Swords means the absolute end of a period, a life, a plan, or structure and its direct link to a new beginning (figure 10.4c).

Over the ages, the Ten of Swords has gradually acquired a negative connotation that is way out of proportion. The Ten of Swords in figure 10.4a symbolizes a heavenly fence—this symbol is correct.

10.4 Variations in the meanings and interpretations of Tarot cards in different decks.

a Ten of Swords in Arthur Edward Waite's Tarot.

b Ten of Swords in the Tarot by Aleister Crowley.

c Ten of Swords in the restored Tarot.

a

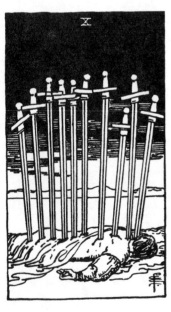

b

10

Ruin

c

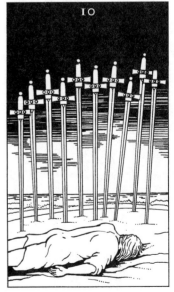

Birth into this world splits the time-space continuum into the separate dimensions of time and space upon which physical reality is based. This demarcation of space and time makes it impossible for a new incarnation to go back into the cycle that has just been completed. The Ten of Swords does *not* indicate violent death as depicted in figure 10.4a. Neither does it mean the ruin of that violent ending as in figure 10.4b; the archetypal images in these cards fall short of the quintessential meaning of the Ten of Swords archetype as given in figure 10.4c.

The meanings of the Major Arcana

In a spread the Major Arcana indicate key influences of archetypal principles that play an important directing or regulating role in the questioner's life. They point to ideals, attitudes, psychological achievements, shortcomings, goals, and principles, as well as the general color of a situation.

For instance, Justice in a spread means that there will be, or has been, a judgment about a worldly situation in which the questioner is directly involved. This judgment may be carried out in an appropriate (upright card) or an inappropriate way (reversed card). Justice does not say anything about the outcome of the judgment. However, the content of the judgment may shine through in the cards that surround the Justice card.

The meanings of the Royal Arcana

Tarot cards with members of the royal families represent powers or persons within the questioner's environment who can influence matters in his or her life from the outside. These influences may be positive (upright) or negative (reversed).

For example, the King may be the father, friend, husband, or lover of the questioner, or a male member of the family—in any case, an influential person or power. Similarly, the Queen represents a mother, girlfriend, female member of the family, spouse, or mistress. Sometimes, if the questioner is incorruptible, powerful, noble, and kind hearted, the questioner may be the King or Queen. Nonetheless, these cards are more likely to indicate an external influence on the questioner's life than that the questioner is himself such an influence.

The Knight and The Page also indicate others who have an impact on the questioner, but with less distance. Sometimes, they do represent the questioner. A Knight symbolizes the propagation of a concept, idea, or plan, or the battle to secure its place. A Page symbolizes a message about a concept, idea, or plan, or the study of that concept, idea, or plan. In both cases, the concept is related to the emblem on the card and the questioner's situation.

A superior or a friend may surface in a spread as a Knight; a brother, sister, assistant, or colleague as a Page. The Knight acts, carrying the emblem of the family (Pentacles, Wands, Cups, Swords) and bringing it into the world. A Page is an investigator who becomes engrossed in the family's emblem in order to give it new perspectives.

The cards in the Royal Arcana also convey a whole different level of meaning:

- The Page symbolizes the body.
- The Knight symbolizes the ego.
- The Queen symbolizes the soul.
- The King symbolizes the spirit.

The King and The Queen point to the foundation of the questioner's consciousness related to the Tarot emblem showing. The Knight and The Page point to the questioner's active use of the emblem.

The four categories of Royal Arcana listed above together embody the Tarot life cycle and their four emblems.

The meanings of the Minor Arcana

The Minor Arcana relate to the life and psyche of the questioner, and directly to the practicalities of daily life. The four emblems on the Minor Arcana are all old archetypes. They categorize life's events, situations, and problems into four major clusters: material and psychological growth; production; emotional issues; and purification-planning-regeneration.

The insight into a life situation depicted by a Minor Arcanum in a spread can be augmented by combining that Minor Arcanum with the other three arcana in the Tarot quartet to which it belongs. The Major Arcanum in that quartet symbolizes the principles that are at stake in this situation.

The questioner's slant in matters of leadership, planning, and organization are symbolized by the Royal Arcanum in a quartet and the development or close history in life by the other Minor Arcana in that quartet.

Pentacles

Pentacles symbolize earth, money, property, trade, labor, business, talents, as well as gained goods, services, and money. Since earliest times, the pentacle also symbolized humankind, the five major body parts (head, trunk, two arms, two legs), the five senses, the five human races, and the five elements (earth, fire, water, air, and the ether). Since 2000 B.C., magical powers have been ascribed to the pentacle, which protects humans and animals against demons that cause illness. For these reasons, from the Renaissance until the late nineteenth century, the pentacle was an important medical emblem.

Cards with Pentacles pertain to working with the material world and the body in a practical way as a means to creativity and self-expression. Pentacles relate to work, craftsmanship, career, art, and material possessions. They emphasize material affairs more than spiritual matters. Another attribute of Pentacles is Spring—the process of personality formation—as a form of growth and learning in children, and (adult) students who take courses. Intuitive thinking, observing, and understanding belong to Pentacles as well. Pentacles stand for money and coins; they also express creativity, the fulfillment of matter by somehow manipulating it, and the refinement of matter by the spirit. We find the highest degree of self-fulfillment in matter through love, sexuality, and the creation of new life.

Wands

Wands symbolize fire, energy, growth, creativity, and the phallus. Now the production and development of ideas—not growth—is important. They are a social symbol of solidarity in a productive society where not only matters of leadership are brought into play, but also conflict, competition, the struggle for life, affective preferences, age, health, and sexuality. In general, Wands symbolize action. Wands store energy, such as is the case with firewood, but also transform energy, and symbolize tools. Sticks have many purposes: canes, magic wands, crankshafts.

Wands can also serve as building material for houses, bridges, carts, vessels, etc. Last but not least, Wands are also potential offensive and defensive weapons.

In the life cycle mandala the earthly arcana are to the left, the watery arcana to the right. Water makes the earth fertile, so that trees can grow in it. Above Wands is the sky, in which the sun provides Wands with energy.

Cups

Cups symbolize water, emotions, feelings, the unconscious, and the inner being. In Cups arcana, spiritual entities take form. Cards with Cups are about emotions, about the self and sharing your heart with others. Cups also pertain to relationships, communication, and religion.

The cup as a sacrificial implement is very old and is found in all religions. As a religious symbol and archetype, it is amplified when the cup contains a fish. The cup also symbolizes the Grail with the blood of Christ.

Just as with Pentacles, Cups relate to observation and insight, in contrast to Wands and Swords, which are action and judgment-directed. Cups highlight inner growth and the search for integrity, emotional expression, secret, occult matters, Autumn, and the process of dying.

Strictly speaking, Cups symbolize the spirit in the body (the contents of the cup and the cup itself) and what happens with it, also in relation to others (communication). Cards with Cups indicate how the power, the energy, the consciousness, and the spirit express themselves and how the spirit, through the heart, finds its way to the outside world. In the series of Cups arcana, humankind becomes whole. It becomes obvious to us that real fulfillment requires communication via an interdependent dialogue in which individual feelings are exchanged and enriched.

Swords

Swords symbolize air. Though intangible, air is present and essential for life on earth. Swords include the concepts of thought, reason, logic, and ambition. Swords also suggests electricity and electromagnetic radiation, both of which propagate with very clearly perceptible consequences through an intangible medium called "ether." Swords arcana illuminate the power of The Word. Excalibur, the legendary sword that gave King Arthur such power in Irish legend, is called "Caladbolg" ("Caliburn" in old English), meaning "cut-steel."

Swords are about the application of consciousness and reason. Hence, they also imply judgments, prejudices, dissemination, and the execution of judgments, information transfer, global communication of ideas, and in a negative sense, demagogy. After the judgment, Swords cut off the old and mark the new beginning in Winter.

We are not alone in experiencing the effects of our thoughts. All thoughts tend to assume material form. The word that was expressed in Wands by means of production, conflict, and competition is evaluated and transformed in Swords into a new thought. Later, in Wands that new word will manifest itself again in tangible form.

TARO

THE UNIVERSE

TAOR

THE FOOL

0 The Fool : *I want.*

Meaning:
The "pure fool." No blame.
Cosmic consciousness.
Spiritual innocence in which cosmic wisdom is contained.
Start. Foolishness.
Childish openness. Spontaneity.
Airiness. Pleasure. Optimism.
The beginning of an adventure.
Various unknown and new possibilities emerge.
Initiative. Autonomy.

Discovers possibilities within himself and in the world.
Positive attitude in life.
Enthusiasm. Ease of manner.
Unconstrained. Candor.
Unattached.
Sees life as a game.

Rashness. Spiritual freedom.
Extravagance.
Ridiculous actions.
Infatuation.
Frivolity.
Is not held responsible.

Uncertainty.
Love of travel.
Alleviation.
Unintended revelation.
"Children and drunks tell the truth."
Irrationality.
Does not take others into account.

Watch out, danger!

Meaning reversed:
Silliness.
Stupidity. Ridiculous behavior.
Superficiality. Negligence.
Absentmindedness.
Lack of perseverance.
Naivety and vanity.
Irresolution. Childish arrogance.
The questioner misses opportunities, causing danger and insecurity.
Irresponsible behavior.
Rudeness. Being uncontrolled.
Apathy.

Silly optimism.
Thoughtlessness. Obsession.
Idiocy. Unrealistic. Instability.
Maniacal behavior.
Chooses the easiest way out.
Impulsiveness. Indiscretion.
Exhibitionism.

Careless in promises.
Exaggerated happiness.
Does not know any form of discipline. Carelessness.
Fear for the future.
Wrong choices. Lunacy.
Absentmindedness.
Averse to listening to advice from others.

Delirium.
Hesitation, instead of going forward with firm strides.
Danger of falling.

The person who draws this card should be careful not to be seduced by what seems to be better than it is in reality. There is also a tendency to start a project without thinking through all details, which may lead to danger.

1 The Magician: *I sacrifice.*

Meaning:
Consciousness through doing.
Life, durability, and power.
Thought and emotions are one.
Creative acts by a free will.
The chaos at the beginning is converted into a creation by working in an orderly way.
Attentive behavior.
Self-realization through willpower and presentation.
Self-control. Being skilled.
Wishes are becoming reality through engagement.
Rich imagination.
Self-reliance.
Self-confidence. Originality.
Dexterity.
Deployment of skills, trade.
Wishes become reality through actions.
Realization of set goals through competency, intelligence, and pleasant demeanor.
Masterpiece. Professional skill.
Originality. Creative willpower.
The will to complete a task from beginning to end.
Ingenuity.
Responsibility.

Capable of influencing others.
Positive attitude in life.
Uses his talents.
Is diplomatic. Also, fooling others.
Flexibility. Spontaneity.
Imagination.
Is offered a new job or given a new assignment.
Organizing. Talents.
Giving meaning.
Mediation.
Synthesizing and analytical skills are in harmony with will power.
Thoughts are made concrete.

Meaning reversed:
Not being able to do anything.
Mental illnesses.
Nervousness.
Weak will power.
The chaos at the beginning stays that way because the work is not really started.
Inattentiveness. Relapse.
Pose, affectation.

Indecisiveness. Disquiet.
Destructive on purpose.

Falling into disgrace.

Blocked circuits.
Manipulation.
Talents are used the wrong way.
Blocked by a "chip on the shoulder."
Wishes and set goals stagnate.
Sense of inferiority.

Incapability.
Pig-headedness.
Procrastination.

Carelessness.
Lack of responsibility.

Fraud.
Fretting, drudgery.
Talents are not used.
Swindling.

Posing, insincerity.
Lack of imagination.
Being unfit for work or a job.

Lack of commitment.
Lack of insight.
Lack of overview and synthesis.
Will power, intuition, and reason are not going together properly.
Refusal to share power with others.

TOAR

I

THE MAGICIAN

This card is also a symbol of unification. The four emblems: Pentacles, Wands, Cups, and Swords are explicit and together in one place. The Magician is the channel through which the new creation becomes reality.

TORA

THE PRIESTESS

2 The Priestess: *I transcend.*

Meaning:
Wisdom. Being learned.
Discernment.
Perceptiveness.
The future is veiled.

Hidden powers are active.
Learning via karma.
Hidden knowledge.
Balance between conscious
and unconscious, positive and
negative.
Capable of teaching others.
Tendency to avoid emotional
commitments.
Objectivity.
Laws are learned or conveyed.
Development, education,
upbringing.
Knowledge and science are
conveyed unadulterated and
pure.

Virtue, humility, and purity lead
to the receiving of wisdom.
Virginity. Fastidiousness.
Apparently without emotions.
Perception, pervasiveness.
Silence and mystery. Gnosis.
Fathoming of concealed desires.
Predictions are being made.
Platonic relationships.
Avoidance of complications.
Practicing teacher or counselor
(male and female).
A spiritual and/or material inher-
itance is received through karma.
Observing and futuristic abilities.
Matriarch. The anima (Jung).
Problems are solved because of
a penetrating attitude.
Patience.
The veiled future.
Experiments aimed at the future.
Recognition. Comprehension.
Tenacity.
Sensible acts.

Meaning reversed:
Frustrated knowledge.
Lack of understanding.

Ignorance.
Impossibility of learning through
conceit or short-sightedness.
Improper judgment.
Negative powers are used for
improper purposes, witchcraft.
Dualistic thinking. Superficiality.
Narrow-mindedness.

Accepts superficial knowledge.

Subjectivity.
Scientism.
Cannot share spiritually.

Superficial knowledge.
Illiteracy. Dumbness.
Inexperience.
Setbacks force to submissiveness
and insight.

Prudence. Hypocrisy.
Sensual delectations. Passion.
Trust in own rational knowledge.
Rationalistic arrogance.
Shortsightedness. Slyness. Deceit.
Self-pity.
Talkative.
Forced disinheritance.

Lack of insight.
"Old spinster."
Moral or physical zeal.
Lack of patience.
Egotism.
Shallow and/or superficial
experiments.

Shortsighted activities.

The woman in whom the questioner is interested. The Priestess
symbolizes the Mater Domina and Sophia, the Divine Wisdom.

3 The Emperor: *I rule.*

THE EMPEROR

Meaning:

Leadership. Fatherhood.
Worldly values and power.
Stability.
Living in a mature way.
Material and spiritual mastery.
An impressive person, authority.
Assistance. Protection.
Emotions and passions are
dominated by reasoning.
A reasonable person.
Male influence.
Control and power over
emotions and "the masses."
Self-confidence.
Well-considered actions.
Material and spiritual wealth.
Talents are fulfilled through
involvement and steady work.
Ambition.
Worthy to execute authority.
Regal attitude in life.
Control over an empire, family,
and business.
Direction. Ruling. Government.
An absolute, patriarchal figure.
Married life. Physical sexuality.
Unyielding spirit. Indomitable
force.
Takes initiative.
Industriousness. Potency. Virility.
Likes to strengthen dominance.
Tenacity.
A strong and capable person
who knows his business and is
competent.
Skillfulness. Thoroughness.
Wealth, well-being, health.
Stability.
The powers of darkness have
to give way or are not given a
chance.
Ready to meet and discuss.
The spirit controls matter.
Strives for truth.
Refinement of matter.

Meaning reversed:

Compassion. Wants to do good.
Lends money.
Unimportance. Anarchy.
Weak character.
Potentate.

Exploiter. Dictator.
Negative emotions are getting
the upper hand.
Loss of control. Confusion.
Impotence. Not being effective.
Fanaticism.
Defeat.
Acts without thinking.
Wallows in opulence.
Plays through life.

Is not taken seriously.
Dominant attitude in life.
Incapability, oppressive
government.
Lack of direction.
Threats of bloodshed.
A bad, argumentative marriage.
Sense of defeat.

Spinelessness.
Weakness.
A bellicose person.
Possibility of injuries.
An amateur. A charlatan, quack.

Obstructiveness.
Fruitlessness through instability.
Indecision. Weak-heartedness.
Succumbs to authority.

Enemies are getting confused.
Paranoia.
Immature demeanor.

This card symbolizes a fatherly person, brother, or spouse, but also
institutionalized power, hierarchy, and "the long arm of the law."

TRAO

4

THE LOVERS

4 The Lovers: *I commit.*
Meaning:
Earthly love and choice.

A time of choosing.
Having to make an important decision.
Freedom of emotions.

Sexual expression. The right creations.
Confidentialities. Confidence and honor.
Enchantment. Sexual attraction.
Strong desires.
Possibilities for the beginning of a romance.
Seduction for positive purposes.
Deep feelings. Harmony.
Optimism and development.
Human love between the sexes.

A meaningful love relationship.

Engagement. Marriage. Love.
Being elected. Evaluation.
Meeting the life partner.
Positive opportunities to form relationships.
Good prospects in materialistic, interpersonal and spiritual perspectives, including children and old age.
Relational perfection.
Being in love.
Paradisiacal state of being with the other, and the environment.

Knowing good, bad, and life.

Animus and anima have developed in equilibrium and harmony.
Being tested. Exam. The need to go through ordeals.
An affair of great importance.
Possible sexual activity outside the established relationship.

Meaning reversed:
Stagnation in earthly love.
Wrong choices.
Ordeal.
The wrong creations.
Cracked plans.
Chance of failure when making a choice.
No trust and belief.

Inner battle between heavenly and earthly love.
Unrequited love.
Speculation.
Inclination to forget about consequences. Chasing the other for the sake of the chase.
Jealousy.
Hopeless love. Ill-fated choice.
Illicit relationship.
Chance of a broken relationship.
External blockages to love relationships.
Being passed over. Obstruction.

Quarrels, about "the children," for example.
Whimsy. Volatility. Parental meddling in a relationship.

Hopeless love. Puppy love.
Unsatisfying love experiences.
Relationship malformations.
Indigence.
Inability to make choices. Wrong choices in emotional relationships.
Not being able to pass a test.

Letting things come "to a head."
Perverted sexuality.

Infidelity.
Frustrations in love and marriage.

A person who is deeply involved in emotions and problems related to a friend. Choice between holy and ordinary love.

(−) **Intuition**: *I see the truth.*

Meaning:
Inner truth. Anima Christi.
Intuition. Hunches.
Femininity. Gentleness.
Spiritual certitude.
Trusting to intuition.
Completion of work and
thoughts.
Renewal of life.
Prophecies are coming true.
Reasoning follows instinct.
Feeling.
Taking an important and proper
decision.
Intuitive observations.
Providence guards you.

Inner peace and assurance.
Prosperity in material, relation-
ship, and emotional perspective.
Practical truth from "within."
Intuition guides the ego to
pursue the right thing.

Intuitively right designs and
creations, according to own
insights.
Own insights can be pursued
without objections.

Love and marriage.
Follow the way of your heart.
Decisiveness.
The female principle (yin).
Growth and evolution of nature.
"Holy" sexuality.
Improved moods through
inspiration.
Being positive again.
Determination.

Meaning reversed:
The inner voice, intuition is
not listened to, not "heard."
Hysteria, erotic tension.
Decisions are procrastinated.
Dejection.
Unfinished business piles up.
Will power without love.
Not being "in tune."
Pure instinctive behavior.
Egoism.
An important decision is not
being made.
Uncertainty.
The ego does not give
Providence a chance.
Inner unrest.
Debts, material and interper-
sonal, now have to be faced.
Veiled intuition.
Interpersonal ways.
Evil-spirited efforts full of
self-pity.

Well-meant suggestions from
others don't address the core of
the matter, or are not listened to.
Depression.
Insincerity.

Feministic self-hatred.

Being content with a superficial
friendship.

INTUITION

The ubiquitously loved mother, counselor, and teacher. The mother-
goddess: Astarte—Babylonia; Hathor and Isis—Egypt; Hera—classical
Greece; Juno—classical Rome; Freya—Scandinavia and Germany;
Mary Magdalene—Christianity.

THE PRIEST

5 The Priest: *I establish virtue.*
Meaning:
Ordination. Absolution.
Inspiration.
Religious service. Moral.
Being religious. Obeisance.
Striving to be devout.
Embodies the communal moral.
A member of the clergy.
Carries out the traditional belief
for the masses. Leader in matters
of belief.
Traditional education.
Particular ceremonies will
happen.
A marriage or other union will
be affirmed.
A virtuous, decent, and god-
fearing life.
Is subservient, true, and serious.
Love for history and cultures.
Norms are determined.
Conformism.
"Holy fire" in work and worldly
matters.
Fertility and productivity.
Cooperation.
Belief in (own) perfection.
Religious and spiritual leadership.
Conventionality. Protocol.

Friendliness. Humanity.
Goodness.
Compassion. Empathy.
Divine inspiration.

The power of the conventional.

Knowledgeable, enlightened
person.
The holy truth is revealed.
Forgiveness.
Generosity.
The Kingdom of Heaven is
within you.
Knowing and being.

Meaning reversed:
Novice. Profanity. Disavowal.
Pharisee.

Godlessness.
Repeated errors.
Bound to communal morals.
Being a "voice in the desert."
Silly expressions of gentleness,
generosity, and magnanimity.

Laid-up probity. Intolerance.
Easily influenced.
Servility.
Religious and worldly matters
are mixed and manipulated.
Narrow-mindedness.
Orthodoxy, fundamentalism.

Trapped in one's own notions.
Sluggishness, unemployment.
Inquisition.

Lame conviction. Impotence.

Resists conventions. Non-
conformism.

Vulnerability.
Frailty—weakness.
Dogmatism.
The church as institution.
Ritualism.
Victim of own ideas.

Being too kind.
Sometimes this person is not able
to tune in to new circumstances
and conditions, or to accept them,
and has the tendency to stay
attached to out-of-date principles.

A person who is able to assist the questioner by word and deed.

6 The Empress: *I collect.*
Meaning:
Symbol of productive, spiritual values and power. Fertility. Love and creative forces. Action, initiative productivity. Physical and sensual energies. Development. Material wealth. Talent.
Expansion. Broadening. Aggregation in a female fashion. Evolution. Natural energy. Growth and development in the material world.
Flowering. Matter aggregates around the spirit that shapes it. Well-off. Status-consciousness. Female way of influencing. Leadership.
Decisions are based on sound judgment and/or intuition. Concentrated on society.

Material wealth. Luxury.

Broad-minded about sex. Sensuality. Loves life and love. Enjoys nature's horn of plenty. In the prime of life. An achievement is made. Rich in relationships, love, and work. Good physical health. Interest in the details of everyday life. Artist's inspiration. The motivating force behind a successful partner, spouse, or group. Mother, sister, spouse, children. Businesswoman, practical and decisive. The custodian of the seed of freedom. The abundance of nature. Possible pregnancy.

Meaning reversed:
Stagnation, turning away from life sources. Vanity. Possible loss of physical capacity.

Procrastination. Fickleness.

Loss of energies. Infertility. Squandering. Wastefulness. Loss of material facilities.

Careless use of resources.

Seduction.

Sheer materialistic interests.

Hedonism. Excessive luxury. Eagerness to spend money. Polygamy. Nymphomania. Vamp.

Yearning for more. Despondent woman. Passivity. Delays in reaching goals in life. Unreliability.

Lack of interest. Laziness. Inertia. Lack of concentration. No creative thoughts. Worries and fear.

Whining, nagging, badgering. Deceit. Infidelity. Secret dealings. Temporary loss of creative powers. Whimsy. Materialism.

OTRA

THE EMPRESS

The Empress represents Urania. She is the Babylonian goddess Ishtar, and the Greek goddesses of beauty, agriculture, and fertility, Korè and Aphrodite.

Reversed she is Lilith: the vamp of the night and the lost seed. She is also the destructive Indian goddess Kali, and Hecabe: the vengeful mother. (As wife of the Trojan king Priam, Hecabe blinded King Polymestor of Thrace and killed his two sons after Polymestor murdered her son.)

THE CHARIOT

7 The Chariot: *I manifest.*
Meaning:
Dominance and victory.
Accomplishment of splendor
through maintaining the balance
between physical and spiritual
forces.
Presence and awareness.
Determination. Will power.
Mastery over physical and
emotional aspect of the
personality.
Self-discipline.
The Self is in harmony.
Conscious existence.
Struggle and success.
War and triumph (over
difficulties and adversaries).
Conquest. Pinnacle. Triumphant
entry with compassion and justice.
Conflicts terminate.
A personality, a star. Manifestation.
Invention. Vision.
Happiness because of success.

Prosperity in financial affairs.
Profit and promotion. Good
health.
Inspections are carried out.
Possible express order. Sudden
question.
Comfortable travels, holidays.
Conquering illnesses.
Surpassing of sexual dualism
through unification of opposites.
Conception.
Physical and psychological control
over opposite forces and sexes.
Excites and enthuses others.
Rush, haste, sudden urge.
Personal exertions create good
luck and fortune.
Continuing at the pinnacle of
success and popularity.
Need to lead.
Control over own emotions and
those of others.
Disciplining of own weaknesses.
Has seen the evil in it and turned
away from it.
Hard work in productive
solitude.

Meaning reversed:
Battle and failure. No success,
because of mesmerization by
polar forces.

Puts oneself into trouble.
Rash actions. Quarrels.

Animal passions prevail.
Decadent desires. Sensation.
Defeat or Pyrrhic victory.
Fails an exam. Haste.
The war is lost. Defeat. Hazard.

Failing usury.

Has a conflicting influence.

Stardom—playboy. Indulgence.

Squandering of personal energy
sources.

Ostentation. Arrogance. Egoism.

Supervision is necessary.

A business collapses. Bankruptcy.
Plans fail or cannot be executed.
Losing grip of something that
was under control.
Not being able to face, or escape
from reality. Rigid ideas.

One is overwhelmed. Disputes.
Mutiny.
Headlong decisions.
Switches easily to an overbearing,
imperious attitude.

Tyranny.
Control over emotions becomes
urgent. Need for advice.
No self-discipline.
Poor self-knowledge.
Opposing influences.

This question may indicate a conflict between two dominant forces
in the questioner's life. Details are important.

8 The Hermit: *I illuminate.*

Meaning:
Wisdom gained through experience.
Knowledge, spiritual ripeness.
Vigilance. Meditation.
Contemplation.
Solitary study. Patience.
Self-enlightenment.
Being or having a guide.
A generation gap develops.
Searching one's Self. First think, then act.
Returning to the Self.
Lonely seeker of spiritual enlightenment.
Self-renunciation.
Self-devolvement.
Silent advice given and received.
Discretion. Understands others.
Inner strength. Carefulness.
Scrutinizing something from all sides.

The elderly teacher (R)TAO.
Meeting someone who will lead the questioner to the path toward his or her spiritual or material goals.
Deliberation.
Possible depression or recession.
Experience in life and secrets are communicated.
Spiritual training. Initiation.
Retiring from work or daily life.
Emotions are kept inside.
Asceticism of the psyche.
Does not need to be understood.
Seeking isolation to expand one's own spirituality.
Detachment or desertion.
The talented and the erudite are crowned.

Control over physical and emotional longings.
Chicanery.
Pretending to have no feelings.
Knows secrets that may or may not be revealed.
Retains spiritual energy.
Taciturn.

Meaning reversed:

Disguise. Vizard. Politics.
Immaturity. Wisdom is declined.

Extraordinary isolation.
Loneliness. Fear.
Wrong guide.

Rigidity. Generation gap.
Escape in debauchery.

Being a loner.

Cannot deal with others.
Silly mischief. Bad timing.
Dementia.
Trusting one's own insufficient knowledge when somebody else gives advice.

Wrong guide. Stupid actions.
Gives or receives wrong advice.

Illiteracy.
Untimeliness.
Refuses and is afraid of becoming older, fancies cosmetic surgery.
Immaturity.
Superficial knowledge.
Retirement is an escape from reality. Fear of facing facts.

Not using knowledge.
Fear of opening up.
Shallowness, amateurism, fuss.
Dishonesty.
Bankruptcy through neglect.
Failure caused by shabbiness.
Carelessness with unnecessary delays as a result.
Old, weird fool.

Fear of disclosure.
Passive rigidity.

THE HERMIT

There is a tendency to enjoy our own wealth of knowledge without trying to pass on the information or to use it in some application.

RTOA

9

JUSTICE

9 Justice: *I do justice.*
Meaning:
The power that restores equilibrium.
Justice. Equality.
Administering the law.
Reforming judgments.
Earthly justice.
Court matters. Honor.
Reasonable.
A proper and impartial judgment is laid down. Honesty.
Balanced consideration.
Getting or giving advice.
Moral conscience.
Integrity in social affairs.
Rectitude. Tidiness.
Precision.
Steadfast character.
Worn-out and superfluous norms are replaced by adequate ones.
Responds to the noble nature of others.
Money matters are legal and are finalized in a favorable way.
Through observation and perception, being able to avoid seduction and vice.
Proper development.
A balanced "set of brains."
Intellect. Correct observations.
Science. (Chemical) equilibrium.
Being content with oneself.
Receiving a fair reward.
Honorable promotion.
Harmony.
An amiable person.

Friendly wishes. Honest aspiration.
The final result, whether favorable or unfavorable will do justice to the person.

Meaning reversed:
Injustice.

False testimony.

Dishonesty. Imbalance. Bigotry.

Merciless judgment. Intolerance.
Abuse.
Complications in lawsuits.

Prejudices are making the case difficult.
Fanaticism.
Overbearing seriousness and heaviness. Superfluous forms hinder insight.
Sanctimoniousness.

Money matters are crooked or illegal and end in an unpleasant way.
Fraud.

Incorrect observations.
Inequality.
Lack of inner equilibrium.

Delays in court cases.
Bureaucracy.

Juridical difficulties.
Inclemency in judgments.
Being prejudiced.

This card suggests a scrupulous, conscientious person with good intentions, who reacts well to others, takes them into account, and does not take dishonest advantage of situations.

10 The World

(Wheel of Fortune): *I am All.*

THE WORLD

Meaning:
The wheel of fortune. The world as the wheel of karma (dharmata). Revolution.
The capricious nature of luck on this earth.
Circle, environment.
The result of karma in this life. Laws of karma. Good times followed by inescapable bad times.
Ownership, spiritual and material. Inevitable destiny. Prosperity. Godsend. Great enjoyment.

No immediate trouble.
Unexpectedly chances turn for the better.
A new cycle starts in daily life. Richness, success, prosperity. Blessing.
Material capital and spiritual potency.
Progress.
Money has to go round. Active business.
Profit.
The laws of cause and effect are at work. The outcome.
Getting what one deserves.
The materialistic aspect of life.

Life, health, capacities, and property are in continuous motion.
Evolution and culmination.
The solution of a problem is near.
Influences to solve the problem are active.
Unexpected possibilities.
Harvesting what one has sown.
"Many who now are first will be last, and many who now are last will be first"(Matthew 19:30).

Meaning reversed:
The wheel of karma.

Revolution.
Egoism. Failure.

Someone's "small world."

Challenges fate.
"Who sows a wind will harvest a gale."
Failure. Miscarriage.

The negative aspects of wealth.

Success and prosperity are on the decrease.
Unexpected external influences are slowing things down.

Loss.
May indicate gambling.
Unexpected bad luck. Trouble.
"Work" does not help any more.
Going broke. Standstill (until a new approach has been conceived).
Continuous interruptions.

Relapses.
External influences have not been taken into consideration.

Too much abundance.

Good or bad luck depends on the arcana positioned around The World. Things continue and will become either better or worse. Unless the questioner takes up the unexpected possibilities that present themselves, everything will remain the same. Apart from the reversed card being somewhat less favorable, there are no dramatic differences between upright and reversed cards, because of the innate cyclical nature of this arcanum.

ORTA

II

STRENGTH

11 Strength: *I want.*
Meaning:
Spiritual conviction. Energy.
Strength.
Spiritual power.
Steadfastness.
Confidence in a good ending.
The power of belief.
Firm decision. Action.
Fortitude. The driving force.
Physical strength. Concentration.
Triumph of love over hatred.
Higher overpowers Lower.
The power to persevere despite all hurdles.
The holy fire.

Consciousness of the divine does not know of any impediments.
Heroic acts.
Own convictions are giving the power to persevere. Inner certainty.
Making an inspired stand—religious, political, artistic.
Innate skillfulness.
Completion of a presentation.
The questioner is tested.
Confidence.
Showing character.
Inspiring power.
Spiritual and physical strength.
Having a "backbone." Controlled tenderness.
Harmonious powers and healing energies.
Illnesses are cured.
Control over the situation.
Defiance.
Being aware of the temptations and possessing the spiritual and physical means to resist them.
Challenge.
The mind controls matter.
Your convictions are increasing in strength.
Love for animals.

Meaning reversed:
Lack of conviction and belief.

Cowardice. Spiritual weakness.
Materialism dominates.
Abuse of power.
Instability.
Not enough confidence.
Indifference.
No self-confidence. Weakness.

Fanaticism.

Giving in to temptation.

The power, energy, and capabilities are lacking.
Discord.

Drift.
Spiritual freedom is suppressed.

Censorship.

Impotence.

Acting out of character.
Making a fatuous impression.
Petty-mindedness.

Going through life depressed.

Illness.

Distrust.
Does not "connect" with nature.
Is not interested in important spiritual matters.

Cruelty to animals.

12 The Hanged Man: *I sacrifice.*
Meaning:
Brings a sacrifice.
Total change in life.
Inversion. Transition.
Submission.
Clear observations while lacking
power.
Exaltation, great inspiration.
Giving up the ego.
Prophesizing. Predicting.
This is the time to prepare for
new experiences or events.
Religious conversion. Better
oneself.
Repentance.
Life as it presents itself.
Change-over.
Meaningful growing pains.
The start of the way to
regeneration.
Self-sacrifice. The holy sacrifice.
Dedication to the spiritual: the
arts, sciences, religion.
Mediation in a sacrificing way.

One's vision of the world is
reversed. Submission to higher
wisdom.
Revolution.
Sacrificing money, property,
everything, in favor of the
pursued goal.
Trance. Regeneration.
Conscious suffering. Martyrdom.
Wisdom.
A person who dies for his or her
conviction.
Execution. Extradition.
A happening of doubtful nature.
A misunderstood genius.
Floating existence.
Conscious denouncing of the
world.
Period of rest between important
events.
Prepared to surrender to the
voice of the higher Self.
The ego is relinquished to the
higher wisdom.
Initiation.

Meaning reversed:
Lack of, or futile sacrifices.
Being without power.
Unwilling to put in the essential
effort.

The masses, the electorate.
Being attached.
False prophecies.
Life seems senseless. Incarnation-
trauma.
Failure to give up.

Boredom. Arrogance.
Failure in giving oneself up.

Useless self-sacrifice.
Materialistically inclined artistic,
scientific or spiritual efforts.
Egocentric mediation.

Resistance to thinking and to
spiritual influences.

Passivity. Apathy.
Unnecessary suffering, resistance
to medical help.
Sanctimony.

Helplessness. Arrogance. Apathy.

A break in someone's life.

Negative acquiescence.
Passive sacrifice.
The torture is becoming less
severe (The Hanged Man is
standing upright).

ARTO

THE HANGED MAN

To achieve objective sacrifices is necessary, which may not yet lead
to a result. Sacrifices may remain unnoticed.

RATO

13

TEMPERANCE

13 Temperance: *I transcend.*
Meaning:
Transition. Integration.
Mediation (between life and death).
Deadline. Measure. Patience.
Economic use of time and energy.
Adaptation and atonement.
Arrival of a comrade, a friend, or mate.
Association. Associative skills.
Joins a club, organization, union, or other group.
Life energies are mixed.
Associative capabilities.
Exchangeability.
A period of adaptation.
From the past, time influences the present and the future.
Finds harmony with oneself and with the earth.
Being seen by many people.
Good networking.

Successful business and management.
The essence of life (the soul) is guided to another level of existence.
Finding the hallowed measure.

Balance between inward reflection and outward activity.
Radiates confidence, contentment, and peace.
A combination that is successful in material, intellectual, and interpersonal matters.
Makes a good impression. Good influences. Spiritual influences on earth.
Good omen.
There will be more space.

Meaning reversed:
A difficult transition.
Frustration and obstruction.

Impatience.
Fragmentation.
Cannot cooperate with others.

Being hostile.
Has difficulty understanding others.
Conflicting interests.

Discord. Quarrels.

The cup is full.
Waste.
Influence by a non-person.

Infertility. Unproductiveness.

Immoderate religious practices.
Charismatic religious leaders, priests, witch-masters, quacks, sects.

Bad combination.
Unhappy combination.
Competing interests in money matters and personal affairs.
Use of earthly commodities and energy sources without limits.

Bad omen.

A person with moderate tendencies. Someone who is valued, liked, and held in high regard. The father figure, mother figure. The questioner may be too moderate and humble to achieve a goal that is within reach.

14 Death: *I rule.* (Physical)
Meaning:
End, final destruction, death.
Passing away.
Making way for new efforts.
Spring cleaning.
Unexpected, total change.
The end of something, possibly
a personal opinion.
Transformation.
Sudden end.
Earthly desires and family ties
cease to exist.
Loss of personality.
Loss of well-known elements
from life, such as family, friends,
business.
The sun sets, life becomes chilly.
The old is cleansed, makes way
for the new.
The end of a love relationship.
Mourning and moving on, on
your own.
Danger. Failure.

Losing track.
Verbal combat with fatal
consequences.
A flash of bad luck.
Neither life nor rank restrain
death from doing its work.
Illness, possibly with a fatal
outcome.
Loss of income or financial
security.
A debt cannot be paid off.
Start of a new era in life.

Purification.

Meaning reversed:
Coma. Dying off.
It has not really finished.
Immobility.

Stalemate.
Decline.

Growing boredom.
Lethargy. Immobility.
Petrifaction.

Partial change. Renewals are in
danger.

Inertia. Sluggishness. Not being
able to move.
Narrow escape from a serious
accident.
Somnambulism.

Extensive delays during an
innovation.

DEATH

In general people are afraid to die. This fear follows from ignorance and a longing for physical existence, which is wrongly identified with life.

This card does not necessarily mean physical death. It may be
the forerunner of a great change, such as the birth of new ideas or
the development of new expectations.

AOTR

THE DEVIL

15 The Devil: *I commit.*
Meaning:
Fear for the truth.
Darkness. Sinking deeply.
Evil. Lies. Imposture. Deception.
Dissimulation. Slavery. Violence.
Destruction, ravaging, plunder.
Demonic influences are doing
their work.
Negative astral influences.
Depression.
Dishonesty. Repression.
Censorship.
Fatal experience. Stoppage.
A threatening wall blocks
progress.
In binds, one has no choice.
Matter dominates the spirit.
Bound to earth. Slavery.
Conditioning. Addiction.
Senses detached from insight.
Merciless materialism. Evil will.
Hidden, sinister, and vile forces.
Counterfeits.
Not being able to make progress.
Lack of perspective.
Depression. Self-destruction.
Self-punishment.
No success.
Excesses. Torture. Illness.
"Crawling" for others.
The temptation of evil.
Entanglements in a disastrous plot.
Having to deal with vileness.
Negative influences and advice
from outside. Slander.
Scary experiences. Poltergeist.
Lack of principles. Hardened
person.
Lack of humor, except at the
expense of others.
Subservience to another makes
for unhappiness.
Unexpected failure.
A dark destiny.
Analyzing someone's personality
to bits so that he no longer exists.
Cunning propaganda.
Sexuality below dignity.

Meaning reversed:
Knowing oneself is knowing God.

No one can enter the Kingdom
of Heaven without having been
tempted.
Recognition of slavery.
Beginning of the liberation of
slavery.
Secret enemies are obstructing
in sneaky ways.
Divorce. Delay.
Tendency to laziness.
Start of spiritual insight,
illumination.
Tendency to unfaithfulness.

Immorality. Excesses.
Stripping of the shackles.

An illness is finally cured.
Breakthrough of genuine insight
into what has been done wrong
and the detrimental effects it had.

Deceitfulness.
The temptation of pernicious
activities is recognized.
Being wrongfully accused.

Conquering the fear for one's
own essence.
Recognizing the needs of the
other. Possible breakthrough in
sexual experience.
Victory over almost invincible
handicaps.

Propaganda.

This card symbolizes "God upside down." and therefore has a
strong relationship to the arcanum Truth. The Devil reversed falls
from his pedestal, which means the beginning of insight and illumination. Seeing The Devil in oneself may mean the breakthrough
of the good and true.

TRUTH

(+) Truth (Jupiter): *I see the truth.*
Meaning:
Truth is spoken.
The Word, God, Light.
The soul's heavenly judgment.
Belief. Mercy.
Male principle (yang).
Actuality. Presence.
Certainty.
The truth is seen.
Saved from a life-threatening situation.
A shocking experience leads to seeing the truth "in a flash."
Undergoing a fair judgment.
Experiencing recognition.
"God makes things right with a crooked stick."
Acute liberation/illumination.
Sudden insight.
Good beats evil.
The right way reveals itself in all its glory.
Miraculous cure.
The heart of the infection is cut out.
Scientific discovery.
Genuineness, sincerity, and goodness.
Authenticity. Correctness.
Indestructibility.
Objective knowledge is active.
Teaching. Teacher.
Consciousness. Insight.

Meaning reversed:
Not being able to accept the clear light of truth.
To escape in superficialities.
Lack of faith.

Wavering.
Truth is not recognized.
Tendency to renegotiate.

Disavowal of the truth.

Punishment by harsh words.
Denial of own mistakes.
A destructive mind.
Kicking over wayside shrines.
Stagnating illumination.
The bad is renounced.

Delayed healing.

Bad manners.

A bad teacher.

The universal, ever wise, loving, and punishing father. The father-god: Baal—Babylonia; Osiris—Egypt; Zeus—Greece; Jupiter—classical Rome; Wodan/Wer—Germany/Scandinavia; God the Father—Christianity.

ROAT

THE TOWER

16 The Tower: *I establish virtue.*
Meaning:
The consequences of human
ambition and conceit.
Shock. Bankruptcy. Misery.
Heavenly punishment.
Spiritual truth makes ignorance
and perfidy disappear.
Disaster resulting in liberation.
Dismantling of the ego.
The old collapses to make way
for the new.
The materialistic attitude
dissolves.
Liberation from a harness.
Life energy pervades matter
from above.
Egocentric ambitions are
shattered.
Loss of an influential position.
Relinquishing love relationships.
Changes in religious conviction.
Misery may cause the beginning
of a new insight.
Unexpected catastrophe, disaster.
Fall, bad luck.
Sudden deliverance from
imprisonment.
Removal from home or work.
Destruction with positive result.
Life is purified from superfluous
and out-of-date structures.
Possible dismissal.
Becoming injured, as in a traffic
accident, or ruined by bad luck.
Moved by understanding.
Loss of money, safety, love.
Spiritual affliction through
adversity.
Do not turn your home into a
bastion.
A sudden event destroys
confidence.
Purification of the soul.

Meaning reversed:

Enduring tyranny.
One perceives one's own pride
as a blockade.
The imprisonment continues.
Being exposed to tyranny.
Continued suppression.
Not being able to make
significant changes.
Sticking with old ideas despite
ill fortune.

Loneliness.

Being ravaged by bad luck.
A friendship is broken.
Imprisoned by materialistic ideas
having to do with job, home,
relationship.

Living in a rut.
Walking into a premeditated trap
and ending up in an unfortunate
situation.
The removal is postponed again.
Uprooting removal.
Change is blocked.
Remaining caught in a sad
situation.
No chance of change.

Rigid dogmatism.

Bad fights. False accusations.

Chance of a burglary.

Petrifaction.

The meanings of this card reversed are the same as upright, but the indicated events have a less sudden and more gradual character.

The questioner is the builder-owner of his or her own tower. This card indicates the start of a breakthrough into new areas. The soul is liberated from old patterns such as memories, emotions, relationships, and so on.

17 The Moon: *I collect.*
Meaning:
Twilight. Mourning. Sadness.
Sleep. Coma. The unconscious.
Darkness. Disillusion.
Obscurities. Deceitfulness.
Silence after the storm.
Recovery from illness.
Fragmented actions.
The soul is cleansed. Waiting.
Imagination develops.
The core of the individual
recovers.
Clearing the ruins (of The Tower).
The gap of the worlds.
Intoxication.
Drugs, imagination, fantasies,
suffering from nerves.
Unknown enemies. Hidden facts.
Disappointment. Wrong friends.
Deception. Walking into a trap.
Secret plan. Slyness. Defamation.
Secrets and riddles.
Illusions, tricks, dishonesty.
Shame. The name is discredited.
Tricky relationship.
Unforeseen changes in plans.
Unforeseen danger.
Responsibility.
Possible accident involving a
loved one.
Pessimism. Fears. Weariness.
Confusion.
Accidents may easily happen.
Danger.
Not able to avoid danger.
Many dissociating influences are
impinging.
Wily double-dealing.
Clearing out something hostile,
at a worldly or spiritual level.
Warning. Bail.
Making use of the opportunity.
Possessions are missing or lost.
Stealing. Questionable motives.
Fake friends, phony relationships.
Selfishness. Pretence.
Intuition manifests itself in dreams.
Sexual fantasies. Hidden desires.

Meaning reversed:

The storms will abate.
Carefulness. Peace is
re-established.

Assembling of essences.
Sorting out things or thoughts.
Advantage or profit without
having to pay a price.
Temptations are resisted.

Fear for the unknown.
Need for inner growth.
Deceit is recognized before
the damage occurs.
Daily life shackles fantasy.
Sexual frustrations.
Using someone.

A disappointment, but not too
serious.

Instability.

Recognizing the love of God.

Errors are made but the effects
are not too serious.

Clumsiness.

Wrongful inclinations are being
conquered.

Being less demanding of oneself.

Secrets and riddles are resolved.

THE MOON

There is a substantial chance of making mistakes. Various influences are combining to pressure the questioner in a particular
direction.

The meanings of this card reversed are similar to those of the
card upright, but the indicated events have a more positive character.

18

THE STAR

18 The Star: *I manifest.*
Meaning:
Heavenly guidance, descent, outpouring.
Originality and vision.
Incarnation. Being awake.
Inspiration. Prudence.
The pain is over. Hope is dawning.
Incarnation. Presiding in a promising way.
Benevolence. Belief. Trust.
Illuminating prospects.
Life-giving water.
A new perspective or new concept.
An abstract idea is expressed as a new understanding.
Cosmic energy. Being open to all life-giving forces.
The devastation is not final.
Renewal in life presents itself.
Past and present are blending together.
An invention is made.
Meditation.
Fulfillment. Satisfaction.
Enjoyment.
A positive prediction comes true.
Charity.
Altruistic assistance. Subsidy.
Help is offered.
Promising insights.
Spiritual love.
Rising star. Promotion.
Healing.
Increasing vitality, physically as well as mentally. Virility.
Good prospects.
Widening horizon. New life and new energy.
Enthusiastic start of a new path in life. A new perspective.
Freedom and brotherhood.
Hope, incarnation, alertness.
Promotion.
The right balance between wishes and work.
Energy put in affairs will soon pay off.

Meaning reversed:
Lack of modesty.

Hesitation. Bad luck.
Disappointment. Pessimism.
Mistaken hope.

Impotent presidency.

An unsatisfactory affair or business is terminated.

Hope is not fulfilled.
Indifference.
Rashness.

Stubbornness.
Alternation between hesitation and enthusiasm.

Distrust and skepticism.
Instability.

Not being in tune.

Bad health.

Not listening to the inner voice.

Doubting oneself.

Tension. Energies do not find a way out. Stress.
It may be necessary to guard against an enemy.
Alienation of plans or insights.

This is a positive card, which indicates that aspiration and energy are essential factors for success. The card also points at a cosmic constellation during conception.

19 The Sun: *I illuminate.*

Meaning:

The plan is becoming concrete and sees "the light."
Materially happy and satisfied life.
Beneficial developments.
Merry growth. Optimism. Finale.
Creativity and vitality. Action.
Contentment. Liberation.
Warmth.
Satisfaction. Plenty of happiness.
Health. Vitality. Feeling of well-being.
The playfulness of a child.
Artistic transformation.
New forms of artistic and intel-lectual expression emerge.
Impulse to successful change.
Designs are carried out. Talents.
Success. Confidence.
Emotional, material, creative, and social good fortune.
Something new and important in your life develops and is at the doorstep. Reincarnation.
Preparation for "becoming reborn."
Possible pregnancy.
Renewal of all aspects of life.
Saying Yes to life, commitment.
Enjoying a simple life.
Pleasure in daily life.
Good social relationships.
The reward of a new friendship.
Happy marriage and excellent friendships.
Love and devotion.
Contentedness resulting from being open to the other.
Studies are completed.
The sciences and arts are developing.
Achievements in the arts.
Spiritual and material expansion.

Meaning reversed:

Clouds are obscuring the sun.

Loss of optimism.

Unhappy feeling. Being dissatisfied.

Plans are rejected.
Artistic projects stagnate.

Unbridled increase with the danger of burn-out.
Clouded future.

Unrealistic feeling of senselessness.

Sadness notwithstanding sunshine.
Postponed incarnation.
Inertia.

Lack of friendships.

Self-pity.
Postponed triumph does not mean a total defeat.

Love of ostentation.

THE SUN

Higher spirits are bringing about the questioner's future; this card is a good omen.

The questioner takes life as it comes and is happy with that.

OART

THE LAST JUDGMENT

20 The Last Judgment: *I do justice.*

Meaning:

Resurrection. (Re)birth.
Outcome.
Reconciliation. Awakening.
The end of self-punishment and self-hatred.
The mystery of birth and death.
Deliverance from limitations.
Resurrecting from death.
Resurrection of nature.
Regeneration.
A perfectly healthy body and mind.
Rising and progress.
Ecstatic event.
Hard work is concluded with the right reward.
Heavenly and legitimate judgment.

The change in personal consciousness now seeks to be conjoined with the universe.
The necessity for repentance and forgiveness.
Waking up. Aspirations start to develop.
The angel Gabriel trumpets the invincible melody of life.
Change and improvement of position with a lot of hullabaloo.
Presence of angels.
The last, serious meditation that precedes liberation.

Chance of a pregnancy (also metaphorically).
Progress in all its respects.
Development. Promotion.
Exposition.
Success comes easier if one is honest with oneself.
The wish to be immortal.
A positive judicial ruling.
The positive result of a lawsuit or personal conflict.
The moment of reckoning for using someone's facilities.

Meaning reversed:

Delayed birth. Postponement.
Disappointment.
Continuing with judging (others).

Not being able to create/have a happy old age.
Possible loss of opportunities.

Indecisiveness. Procrastination.
Mishap.
Cannot face facts. Being forced to give up the old.
Negative judgment or self-criticism.
Stealing.
Loss of affection.
Tendency to hold on/be attached.

Feelings of guilt.

Waking up slowly.
Fear of death.
Searching for happiness in vain.

Good advice costs a lot.
Deep sorrows.
Difficult labor.

Self-complacency.

The questioner is judged in a negative way.
Cowardice.

Anger.

The way things go determine where the new entity will be born, developed, and used (heavenly justice).

This card also means initiation in new levels of consciousness. We have to be aware of our own actions and how they influence others.

"Stand then, as free people, and do not allow yourselves to become slaves again" (Galatians 5:1).

21 The Universe: *I am all.*

Meaning:
Cosmic consciousness.
Positive attitude in life.
The cycle is joined and
completed.
In concurrence with the times.
Revelation. Synthesis.
Fulfillment.
Satisfying completion of a
particular cycle.
The ending of the old and the
beginning of the new.
Concluding celebrations. Happy
ending.
Recognition. Honor.
Compensation.
All arcana in one. Everything fits
together and is complete.
Definite change.
Being sure of success.
Admiration of others.
Endeavors will succeed.
Assurance. Skillfulness.
Perfection.
Finding the way out. A new
world opens up. Travel.
A range of possibilities presents
itself. Firmness.
Possible migration.
The first steps on the path to
freedom.
Change of location.
The end result of all efforts.
The reward for hard work.
Being capable.
The finale to which all other
arcana pointed.
Eternal life. All-in-One.

Meaning reversed:
Frustrated cosmic consciousness.
Stoppage. Being blocked.
A delayed finish that is not in
tune.
Fear of change.

Unsatisfactory end of a particular
cycle.
Sticking to old habits.

Stubbornness and resistance.

There is no vision.

Possible failure at the end of a
task that was started a long time
ago.

Disappointment.

Imperfection.

Incapacity to round off a
particular task.
Uncertainty with regard to the
completion of a task or study.
Lack of vision is an impediment
to success.

The work of a misunderstood
genius.

THE UNIVERSE

This is a very favorable card, especially when it is surrounded by other good cards. It is the eternal source from which everything stems and to which everything returns.

The mandala (circle or ouroboros) lends the aura of sanctimony and points at the holy mystery of the eternal receiving and giving of life.

The angel (Aquarius) is the symbol of Matthew and represents love.

The bull (Taurus) symbolizes Lucas and represents fertility.

The lion (Leo) is the symbol of Mark and represents power.

The eagle (Scorpio) symbolizes John and represents the world.

King of Pentacles

An important, mature man with dark hair and dark eyes, usually married, intelligent, full of character and sensual power. A successful businessman.

KING OF PENTACLES

Meaning:
Fulfillment of talents.

Skillful and successful leader in business, industry, or investments. Financial and material power and success. Reliable, is not corrupt. Perseveres to accomplish set goals. Has the wisdom and discipline to consolidate achievements. Providence, charity. Owner of substantial property. Wise investments, power, and matter for general benefit.

Businessman, teacher, professor. Mathematical aptitude. Sharp insights. A loyal friend.

Meaning reversed:
Talents have been developed and/or used insufficiently. Lack of personality in money matters. Wants to be rich. Avarice. Uses any means (also corruption, prostitution, trade in drugs) to become financially successful. Incapability of being thrifty. Can be bribed easily. Ignorance and impotence in handling economic and financial affairs. A squandering gambler A failed speculator. Does not want to deal with money matters. An old, mean man or woman. Advice not to gamble or speculate.

Queen of Pentacles

A dark, attractive, beautiful, and well-to-do woman. Intelligent and quiet. A good spouse, homemaker and mother, with grace, dignity and responsibility. Good at raising children.

QUEEN OF PENTACLES

Meaning:
Prosperity, security, safety, and freedom.
Coziness, bountifulness, abundance, luxury.
A rich and generous person with a great sense of responsibility for her possessions and for humanity. A noble soul.
Life in prosperity and good health.

Wisdom, possibly visionary talents.

This card brings love, fertility, and physical ease.
Prosperity, bounty, and charity. Trust.
Sensual enjoyment and creative potential.
The body is used positively as a foundation of talents.
Loyal friend, mother, teacher.

Meaning reversed:
False prosperity via compulsive spending of borrowed money. Fear for failure.

Attempts to realize ideals are in vain.
Is quick and hence often wrong in her judgment.
Fastens suspicion on persons. Illness or impairment. Tiredness.
A person who is mean and cannot be trusted.
Is independent from others.

A rapacious person full of rude materialism.

Physical tenseness and difficulties in sexual relationships.
Is distrusted by others.

Frumpiness.

KNIGHT OF PENTACLES

Knight of Pentacles

A young rider with almost black hair and dark eyes. A thoughtful, functional, and traditional materialist with an industrious and responsible attitude.

Meaning:
A practical materialist and worker, capable of reaching most of the set goals.
A reliable, methodical, and persistent laborer.
A patient, thoughtful worker in a permanent position.
A dependable person with a sense of responsibility.
Sincere, useful, and ungrudging.
Effective in business and service.

Acts are linked to merit.
Internally organized.
Old business is finalized in a conscientious way and new business emerges.
Traditional values from family or upbringing are kept high.

Meaning reversed:
Lack of will power or direction.
Lack of tenacity.

Limited by a dogmatic attitude.

Small-mindedness.
Inertia, sluggishness. Apathy.
A happy-go-lucky, good-for-nothing.

Vanity and undeserved comfort.
The "boss's son" in an enterprise.
A loafer. Self-willed.
Sloppiness in business and services.
Confusion. Stagnation.
Lack of responsibility.

Progressive ideas are counteracted through out-of-date attitudes.

PAGE OF PENTACLES

Page of Pentacles

A young person with brown-black hair and brown eyes. A resourceful child with a careful and dedicated character.

Meaning:
A studious, reflective, and attentive person.
Respect for knowledge and science.
Discovery and development of intellectual, creative, and psychological capabilities.
New impulses.
The wish to learn and acquire new ideas.
Sometimes a dreamer.
Deep concentration and dedication
Preciseness, diligence, and personal discipline. Pure will power leads to results.
Ingeniousness. Thoughtfulness.
A bringer of messages, material and spiritual.
A philanthropist.
Responsible management of growing powers, talents, and/or money.
Good financial news.

Meaning reversed:
Not being able to think logically.

No respect for wisdom.
Not being able to accept apparent facts.
Cannot apply theory in daily life.

Rebelliousness at school or work.

Daydreaming.
Fragmentation of ideas, finicky.

An unrealistic young person.
Being surrounded by people with opposite opinions and convictions.
Loss and squandering.
The person is frightened of developing received talents.
Bad news, or the holding back of important information.

Pentacles One: *Power of the earth*

Meaning:
Vitality. Health. Gold.

Richness. Beginner's luck.
A new start.
The beginning of a new period of development or financial success.
Talent. Creativity. Perfection.
Contentment. Safety.
Worldly prosperity, achieving "it."
Material or artistic success.
Ecstasy.
Productive energy.

A substantial chance to become rich.
Unexpected profit.

Open and swift intelligence.
Development of new plans or goals.
Living here and now.
Every opportunity offered has to be used.

Meaning reversed:
Negative sides of wealth.
Adulterated gold. Riches that corrupt.
Crooked use of prosperity.
Slow starter.
Moodiness, touchiness, slyness.
Refuses to apply productive forces.
Greed. Rigidity.

Prosperity without achievement.
Corruption and squandering.
Materialistic attitude.
No respect for the earth and the environment.
Fake profit.
No desire for financial or creative profit.
Unformed intelligence.
Insecure with regard to opportunities offered.
Has difficulty establishing pure friendships.
Lack of insight into his or her prosperity makes it temporary and without luck.

Pentacles Two: *Playful discovery*

Meaning:
Harmony in the midst of changes.
Manipulating the laws of existence.
New projects are starting up and have some growing pains.
The person concerned may be discredited.
Pleasure, youth, recreation.
Business talent.
Travel, purchases, trade.
Social events.
Person in business.
Uncertainty about the conclusion of affairs.
A charming person with commercial and/or creative talents.

Correspondence.
Playing is learning. Sees life as a game.
Literary giftedness.

Meaning reversed:
Bad luck through lack of balance.
Lack of fantasy.
Disappointing setback through external influences.
Does not know the way out of antagonistic situations.
Pretended luck. Pretended activities.
Worries.
Instability. Wavering. Drifting about without purpose.
Proposals for bartering.
Inconsistent actions endanger success.
Falling through.
Forced happiness and humor.
Simulated pleasure.
Official message.
Has other people work without giving guidance.
Forces and pressures are limiting growth.

Pentacles Three: *First assignment*

Meaning:
The first official assignment.
Valued by the established order.

Competence.
Technical, artistic, and/or
intellectual education or training.
Positive critical evaluation of an
important piece of work.

Capability and master
craftsmanship.
Increasing material prosperity.
Investment of energy or money
in a new project.
Earns a first, small profit.
Encouragement and praise.
Success, power, and some fame.

Inventiveness.
Starting a masterpiece or thesis.

Meaning reversed:
Insufficient ability to earn money.
There is fear of success, criticism,
and responsibility.
Mediocrity. Sloppiness.
Superficiality. Platitudes.
Arrogance.

Apprenticeship.
Not listening to criticism of
others who have more
experience.
Self-pity and weakness.
Possible criticism of one's work
from professional jealousy.
Doing business with a criminal.

Not being able to carry out
accepted tasks satisfactorily.
Possibly a poor work atmosphere
or work environment.

Pentacles Four: *Pride*

Meaning:
Incapable of transfering knowl-
edge, or sharing it with others.
Social indifference.

Wants safety and security.
Hoarding.
Narrow-minded attitude.
Greed. Egoism. Rigidity.
Sticks to material wealth, posses-
sions, circumstances. Is stingy.
Striving for power by means of
possessions.
Has money but stagnates the
economy—money has to
circulate.
Talents are kept under cover.
Possibility of an inheritance.
Keep to oneself what should be
passed on.
Cannot share.
Fear for poverty and insecurity.
Sitting on one's money.

Meaning reversed:
Decline in profits.
Material losses.
Deferrals, procrastination,
resistance.
Business is not dealt with.
Wrong use of money, such as not
using it at all or throwing it away.
Buying respect and status.
Showing off with power and
possessions to impress others.
Extravagance.

Losses and setbacks in material
affairs.
Emotional cramps.

Someone who has a lot of money but lives in spiritual and material
poverty, like Scrooge in Dickens' *A Christmas Carol*.

Pentacles Five: *Isolation*

Meaning:
Identification with pain in life.
Material difficulties.
Severe poverty, spiritually and materially.
Invalidity.
Lack of spiritual insight.
Physical and/or material hardship.
The experience of poverty changes the outlook on life.
Unemployment.
Severe material setbacks.
Exclusion through own negative social and religious attitudes.
The questioner needs to learn gratitude and acceptance.
Lost love or fear of it.
Errors. Loneliness.
Being "out in the cold."

Meaning reversed:
Voluntary hardship.

Money earned the hard way.

Live and learn.

Physical, material, and spiritual hardship changes the outlook on life completely.

Renewed interest in spiritual affairs.
Increasing consciousness that the environment is a reflection of one's own values, being, and living.
Material and spiritual ruin is conquered.
Indigence comes to an end.
Possible marital problems about money matters.

This card may also mean love, especially real love that sees through (external) form. It may also mean a love that costs so much that one is "stripped to the bone" and remains totally penniless.

Pentacles Six: *Mercy*

Meaning:
Submission. Charity. Gifts.
Friendliness. Qualifications.
Wealth is distributed in a fair and honest way.
Everyone gets what he or she deserves.
Surrender of spiritual and material possessions.
Now is the time.

Business gets "off the ground" again.
Material gain.
A job is offered, a subsidy granted.
Sharing of energy, knowledge, skills.
Solidarity. Good-heartedness.
Receiving assistance.
A subsidy is granted.
Humility.
Learning to give and receive.
The development of spiritual resilience.
Carefully looking after financial means.

Meaning reversed:
Dishonesty in business.
Bad debts.
Greediness and egoism.

Possibility of envy.
One cannot succumb.

Difficulty discussing one's problems in a humble way.
Does not dare to be dependent.
Abuse of money and power.
Being proud of money and achievements.
Giving things away out of self-interest.
Puppy love.
God breaks pride.
Discontent. Egoism.
Envy. Having illusions.
Intolerance.

Fear of being robbed.

Pentacles Seven: *Working with love*

Meaning:
Working with love, care, and patience. A period of growth. Innocence and ingeniousness. The business, own enterprise grows. Thriftiness and productive exertions start to pay off.

Money starts to come in; first profit.

Working with care and patience. Results are not tangible, yet. Striving for results in the future through long-term work. One looks after oneself.

The harvest seems to be good. Sense of the product that is being made/delivered. Investments with positive results. How to improve the product further? Care for nature.

Meaning reversed:
Impatient worries about money. Fright. Loss of money. Useless speculations. The growth of the new enterprise stagnates. The attitude toward the work is not very practical. Possibility of shortsighted actions.

Possibility of delays.

It may be necessary to take out loans.

No sense for the product that is being made/delivered. Money worries. Lack of timing. Being (too) early on the market (with a product).

Pentacles Eight: *Work with perspiration*

Meaning:
Skillfulness. Great productivity. Technical progress. Concentrates on the development of a trade or work. Learning quickly. Acting with decision. Modesty towards the work. Skilled in business. Positive ambitions. Talents are put to profitable use. Control. Material affairs prosper. Magnificent plans become reality through own determination. Master craftsmanship. Work pays off. Love for technology. The questioner is the architect of his or her own fortune.

Meaning reversed:
Incorrect use of skills. Ambitions do not find a way out. Impatience. A lack of motivation to commence the work. Too much or not enough ambition.

Being disillusioned.

Useless work. Alienation of own talents. Covetousness. Possibility of overproduction. Magnificent plans are never realized.

Laziness.

An exacting attitude to others. Slyness.

Pentacles Nine: *Profit*

Meaning:
Money now works by itself.
Abundance in all directions.
Material prosperity. Certainty.
Adequate speculations.
Effectiveness.
Interest, living off one's private
means.
No compulsory work.
Success and adaptability in
material aspects.
Perfection of the business.
Consolidation of the production
process.
The enjoyment of rest after
work.
Safety.
A privileged and lonely position
is achieved.
Independence.
Love for nature and spirit.

Creative faculties are cultivated.
Discretion and chastity.

Meaning reversed:
Projects are cancelled.
Squandering of money and goods.
Chance to lose house and friends.
False hope. Disappointment.
Restlessness, doubt.
Living from interest only is
expensive.
Not believing in it, anymore.
Futile projects.
Warning that the current mate-
rial prosperity could turn around.
Possibility of crop failure.

Use it or lose it.

Being dissatisfied with
achievements.
Disappointed expectations.
Possible loss of a valued
friendship or possession.
Vagrancy.

Prudishness.

Pentacles Ten: *Prosperity*

Meaning:
Wealth. Prosperity. Safety.
Inheritances, family matters,
archives, deeds.
Family—ancestors and lineage.
The safety of the family, the
house, and its comforts.
A rewarding marriage.
The power of the conservative—
class and money.
Happiness—luck in love and
material affairs.
Lobbying.
Family matters, emotional and
spiritual.
Dowry, gift, pension.
Trade in property and real estate.
Managing money well.
Good prospects.
Engagement or marriage.
International trade contacts.
Involvement with a multinational.
The power of money.
There is enough knowledge,
money, and power to do what
one wants.
Hospitality.

Meaning reversed:
Bad luck in financial matters.
Chance of losing an inheritance.

Chance of losing family and friends.
Problems with family elders.

Chance of losing "a good family
name."

Chance of a forced marriage.

Upper-class nepotism.
Family scandals and debacles.

Robbery.
Market collapse.
Chance of fatal losses.
The negative effects of
conservatism.
Dangerous risks. Gambling.
Losing money.

Distrust.

King of Wands

A honest, reliable, affable man, married, with red-brown hair and green eyes. Conscientious, energetic, and enterprising, with a noble character.

KING OF WANDS

Meaning:
Fulfillment in the family or enterprise.

Paternal consideration.

Common sense, dedication, and tolerance.
Maintains traditions.
A careful revolutionary.

A trustworthy, friendly man.
Living in the country in a socially integrated way.
A happy and long-lasting marriage.
Possibly an unexpected inheritance.

Meaning reversed:
Deficient social life.

A parental figure who needs support.
A serious, sober man, severe but honest in his judgment.
Possibly exaggerated piety.
Working with a dogmatic, preconceived purpose.
Somebody with excessive, overwrought ideas.
Someone who cannot be trusted.
The lonely life in the country.

Conflicts and quarrels are likely.
Particular advice must be followed through.

Queen of Wands

An attractive, influential woman with chestnut-brown hair and green eyes. An inspiring, magnetic personality. She is sensual, practical, intelligent, honorable, independent.

QUEEN OF WANDS

Meaning:
A woman with fruitful energies.
Success in business.
The inspiring ability of a woman.
Positive use of power.
An influential woman.
Female charm and grace.
Friendliness and virtue.
Dedication to home and garden.
Success in business and other enterprises.

Love and money.
A loving woman with sincere interest in the other.
A gracious hostess.
Peferential treatment by an energetic, broad-minded woman.
A loving spouse.

Meaning reversed:
A matter-of-fact and materialistic woman.
Switches between subservience and imperiousness.

Resistance, obstacles, and opposition in business and other enterprises.
Jealousy and possibly infidelity.

Volatility.

Unstable emotions with regard to the person concerned.
Sickening jealousy.

KNIGHT OF WANDS

Knight of Wands

An attractive, energetic, red-haired young person with green eyes. An impetuous, compulsive individualist with charisma and charm.

Meaning:
A person who manifests him or herself through acts.

Confidence.
Rivalry.
A conflict is battled out.
Fight or flight.
Departure or removal.
Initiative.
Looks events in the future right in the eye without fear.
Settlement of an affair.
Revolutionary vigor.
Progress into the unknown.

Confronts events without fear.

Meaning reversed:
Fights against windmills (Don Quixote).

Lack of energy and confidence.
Incendiary.
Vandalism.
Divorce or break (in a relationship).
Demolishing of teamwork or a personal relationship.
Quarrel.
Disharmony in circumstances.
Interruption and discord.
Discontinuity. Lack of energy.

Hesitation. Letting the right moment pass.

PAGE OF WANDS

Page of Wands

A very intelligent young person with red-brown hair and pale-green eyes, with a remarkable wisdom and verbal powers.

Meaning:
Herald with a message full of promise.
Good news. Important news.
Positive advice.
Letters and messages.
Beneficial testimony.
Defense in a lawsuit.
Verbal and analytical expression.

A brilliant person.
A dedicated friend who can be trusted.
A missionary.
A wise person who assists in spiritual matters.

Verbal and analytical expression.
Loyal friend.
A stranger with good intentions.
A consistent personality.

Meaning reversed:
Gossip.

Bad news. Unpleasant news.
Misleading information.
Anecdotes without value.
Indecisiveness in business and related instability.
Loss of verbal and analytical expression.
Struggling with a language.

Wands One: *Fire-power*

Meaning:
Creation, imagination, fortune.
Start of a collective enterprise.
Creation or invention.
Possible birth of a child.
Start of new work relationships.
A significant experience: travel,
adventure, or escapade.
Sexual potency and fertility.
Starting a family.
Initiatives are taken.
Surging up of personal growth
and development.
Chance of fortune or inheritance.
Promise of fulfillment in the
harvest.
Renewal.
Positive, life-giving dominance.
Realization.

Meaning reversed:
False start. Things go wrong.
The new enterprise does not
become reality.
Foggy outlook on life.
Dawdling over the new venture.
Cancellation of plans.
Fooling oneself.

Sexual impotence and infertility.
Matters are dealt with in the
wrong way.
Bleakness. Empty existence.

A wrong start.

Decadence. Decline.
Bantering and offense.

Wands Two: *Balanced command*

Meaning:
An adult, dominant person.

Growing knowledge and skills.
The courageous entrepreneur is
rewarded with results.
Professional and commercial
success.
Mastery, having a say in the
matter.
Power based on position and
skills.
Is interested in the sciences.
Things go well.
A brilliant personality.
Success.
Commercial success.
A plan of action is drawn up.

Receives a power stream.
Swift recovery.

Meaning reversed:
A prosperous start is followed by
stagnation.
Difficulties.
Unexpected, unpleasant
"surprises," reaching a goal that
turns out to be without value.
Pyrrhic victory.
Sadness and depression.
Sense of emptiness after success.
Apprehension toward
knowledge.
Bodily suffering.
Dominated and held back by
others.
Disavowal of intellect.
Terror of the intellect
(rationalism).
Sorrow amid the splendor of
worldly wealth.
Empty success.

Wands Three: *Alertness*

Meaning:
Entrepreneurial attitude.
Trade and commerce.
The enterprise becomes reality.
Progress, initiatives.
Successful, forward-looking
businessman.
Practical assistance of colleagues.
Partnership. Cooperation works
out well for the enterprise.
Practical knowledge and trust.
In this phase, the questioner
must be alert.
Jealousy and backbiting are
noticed immediately.
The questioner may well be
pulled into competition.
Active, passive, and neutralizing
powers are working
harmoniously.
Exchange of goods and ideas.
Actual assistance.

Meaning reversed:
Difficulties in trade and commerce.

The enterprise, or a substantial
business, fails.
Dishonesty and stagnation.

Being assisted by someone with a
hidden agenda.

Disappointment.

Jealousy and backbiting are
prevalent.
Disturbance of communication.
Grandiose plans fail.
Being swamped by the
competition.
The competition is too clever (for
the questioner).
Be careful with assistance offered.
Clear insight is obscured by the
dark domination of others.

Wands Four: *Completed work*

Meaning:
Newly acquired prosperity.
Work that gives pleasure.
Festivals prior to the harvest.
Solidarity celebrations. Romances.
Company outings, fiestas.
The typical festivities that
precede a contest, fight, or battle,
because of the sense of unity that
has to be built or reaffirmed.
Rest and enjoyment after work.
Profit is ensured.
The harvest can be brought in.
Summer carnival. Merriment, fun.
Love, harmony, merriment. Peace.
The consolidation of a
relationship.
Taking temporary distance from
work after a complete success.
The work is rounded off.
Worldly, entertaining arts.
An atmosphere of mildness.
Contracts are signed.
An exam is passed.
Everything that has been achieved
must be maintained well.

Meaning reversed:
Moderate prosperity.

Looking back to a failed harvest.
A faltering romance.
Being surrounded by dishonest
people.

An annoying, excessively noisy
environment.

Loss of peace.
Insecurity.
Wilted beauty.

Incomplete happiness.

The questioner is not happy in
his or her environment and
wants to desert.
Dissension.

Wands Five: *Combat*

Meaning:
The contest that is invoked when one manifests oneself.
Productive business.
A battle cannot be avoided.
Working together with other groups toward a common purpose.
Bringing in the harvest.
Nature resists.
Lots of effort and conflict to become successful.
Inescapable conflicts have to be fought now.
Violent, formidable problems.
Redoubtable rivalry.
Unabating opposition.
Coalitions may form.

Altercations may work out beneficially.
Conflicts and obstacles.
Unsatisfied desires.
Dualism, inner conflict.
Black-and-white thinking.

Meaning reversed:
Disorderly application.
Entanglements.
Ineffective collective labor.

Business could be better.

Crop failure.
Many debates and complexities.
The questioner is manipulated with the purpose of bringing him or her down.
The contradistinctions become apparent only at the end.
Evading a conflict.

Provisional silence.
Being "very busy," squabbling, disorder.

Beware of an indecisive attitude.

Ructions.
Temporary silence.

Wands Six: *Victory*

Meaning:
Good news! The harvest is in.
Victory after the battle.
Triumphant entry.
A leader emerges and takes responsibility.
Results and success after hard work.
Progress in arts and sciences.
Extrasensory perception.
Important news (from "the king").
Open manifest.
Culmination. Ecstasy.
Conquest.
Fame and popularity; the hero.
Profit, wishes are fulfilled.
Being in harmony with oneself and the environment.
Service and obedience (from a superior position).

Meaning reversed:
The battle goes on. Nobody wins.
Superficial advantage.
Fear of the successful enemy.
There is no leader.

The tyranny of lack of structure.
Waiting "ages" for important news.
False propaganda. Censorship.
Propaganda manifests.
Treason.
Suppression of own talents and potentialities.
Fear.
Being disloyal.
Unclear profit.
Materialistic ecstasy.
Delays and tardiness.

This card means not only victory, but also combat. In the end the decision emerges as to who is the winner. The question is: who actually does win? Winning has advantages, but so has losing. "The first will be the last."

Wands Seven: *Contemplation*

Meaning:
Final battle. Success.
The battle is already won.
An unnecessary fight.

Lonely struggle.
Spiritual, inner battle.
The individual is alone and
opposed to the group.
Having to take a position.
One is holding one's own coura-
geously in the face of the group.
Severe competition in business
and commerce.
Fighting for oneself.
A proper retreat.

Meaning reversed:
Fear of losing the battle.
Opposition.
Being overpowered.
Consternation. Losing "it."
Worries. Secret battle.
One feels defeated.
Be careful not to become
indecisive.
Uncertainty in group situations.
The group is afraid of the
individual, and the individual is
afraid of the group.
Possibility of espionage and
conspiracy. Being astounded,
bewildered. Doubts. Hesitance
with regard to the opposition
leads to failure.

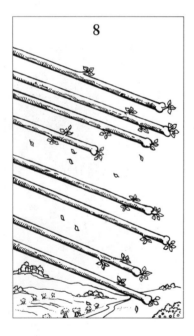

Wands Eight: *Capitulation*

Meaning:
"Hold fire!"

End of the battle.

Contacts are renewed.
Reflective discussions.
Business is drawing to a close.
Time for other, new activities,
possibly work as a consultant.
Sudden inspiration.
The right time to travel or to take
new initiatives to go abroad.
A journey.
Liveliness, love, hope.
Flashes of intuition, spontaneous
representations, or ideas.
The right decisions are taken.
Adequate and swift
communication.
Friends are dropping in.
Positive and strong energies.

Meaning reversed:
Capitulation with negative
consequences for oneself.
Self-judgment. Self-repudiation.
Self-destruction.
Unnecessary quarrels about the
termination of the battle.
Stagnation in business and in
taking other, new initiatives.

Split energies.
Delayed and postponed decision-
making. Impediments.
Domestic fights (are continuing).
Obstruction.
Jealousy of the loser.

Energies are sapped quickly at
the beginning of a project.

Miscarriage, inadequacy.
The holiday festivities fall
by the wayside (due to
mismanagement).

Wands Nine: *Recovery and result*

Meaning:
End of a battle, or a pause.
Protective forces are in place.
Being prepared in case the fighting commences again.
The urge to pull out or withdraw.
Lessons of life have been learned.
Getting through disappointments.
Physical and mental aging.
Looking after oneself and others.
Possibly a handicap acquired during the life.
Over sensitivity to injuries and traumas, physically and psychologically.
Being alert for hidden enemies is essential.
Being prepared for tribulations and adversity.
Quality control and assessment.

Meaning reversed:
Being shell-shocked, exhausted.
Weakness.
"There is no rest for the wicked."
Hindrances and obstructions.
Dangerous fatigue.
Harassment.
Some obstacles have still not been conquered.
Pessimistic outlook on the future.
Lack of sense of damage done to others and self.
Disregarding a handicap.
Not looking after oneself.
Self-neglect. Masochism.
Going downhill physically.
Need for care, physical and mental.
Insensitivity and harshness caused by taking many blows.

Wands Ten: *Stockpiling*

Meaning:
Preparation for a sacrifice for the common interest.
Assembling all forces for the finale.
Carrying off a load or encumbrance.

Autumn of life.
A lawsuit is announced.
Judicial problems are countered and solved.

The success becomes too big.
Circumstances necessitate taking on too many things.
Problems have to be solved soon.

Being overloaded.
Exceptional (taxation) pressure.
There are burdens to be carried.

Meaning reversed:
Insufficient preparation for the finale.

A chaotic collection of forces, entities, and possibilities, which may come to nothing.
Do not waste energy and time.
A lawsuit is probably lost.
Some loss cannot be avoided.
Swindle, intrigue, high-handedness.
Success causes downfall.
Being swamped by one's own collection of forces.
One has to learn to delegate and give others the chance to make mistakes and manifest themselves.
Divorce and departure.

In general, this is a positive card, provided the questioner possesses all the forces that have been assembled, and is able to manage and utilize them.

King of Cups

A man of arts, sciences, religion, and psychological matters, with light-brown hair and light-blue eyes. Influential, sensitive, responsible, creative. Is acquainted with the tides of life and death.

KING OF CUPS

Meaning:
Fulfillment of creative intelligence.
Artistry. Professionalism.
A psychologist, lawyer, artist, clergy person, scientist.
A person with a great sense of responsibility.
Idealism and liberal opinions about behavior.
A friendly, broad-minded, reliable, sensitive, and self-conscious man.
Someone who is full of ideas.
Self-discovery. Considerate of others.
An able psychologist or friend is calling in.
Natural protection and care.
The power that is achieved when spirit and emotions are combined.

Meaning reversed:
An artistic man, full of temperament with an almost violent nature.
Violence behind an unmoved appearance.
Irresponsibility.
Prevarication in business.
Suppression of the emotional self.

Possible rejection of the father (figure).

Possible gift or talent for which the time is not yet ripe.
A sly person without discretion.
May indicate an important loss, death, a scandal,
or miscarriage of justice.
Dishonesty and meanness.
Possibly duplicity and injustice.

Queen of Cups

A very sensitive, loving, intelligent woman with light-brown hair and blue eyes. She is the self-sacrificing, loved spouse or mother.

QUEEN OF CUPS

Meaning:
A dedicated and adored, very sensitive spouse.
Love and a happy marriage.

A woman or friend with a poetic nature and rich imagination.
A good friend and mate, ready to help.
Hidden, tacit wisdom. Goodness.
A dreamer who acts according to her dreams.
Psychic powers.

An intuitive woman.
Reliability.

A wise woman with self-knowledge, virtue, and composure.
Loving intelligence and care.

Meaning reversed:
An intelligent but sly woman.

A marriage frustrated by mood-swings and irrational arguments.
Selfish exploitation of someone else's goodness.
Possibly a mean, immoral, perverse woman.
A daydreamer who fantasizes and cannot be trusted.

Moral corruption. Immoderate behavior.
Inconsistent character.
Hysteria. Shadiness.
Manipulation through moral blackmail.
A disloyal friend or mate.
Loss of a friendship.
Subtle tricks, swindles, fraud.

KNIGHT OF CUPS

Knight of Cups

A romantic person, creative and intelligent, with light-brown hair and blue eyes. Bearer of love, ideas, talents, gifts, and possibilities; disseminates his or her sacrifice.

Meaning:
A love, opportunity, or proposal comes closer.
Arrival, approach, attraction.
Spiritual reward.
A nice visitor. Messages.
Having a calling. The call of duty.
Being asked. Social action.
Being initiated. Self-discovery.
A spiritual gift is disseminated or received.
Transference of feelings.
Romance, attraction.
An artistic or scientific sacrifice.
Love for the other.
A challenge to fulfill one's Self to the benefit of humankind.
The gift to share and carry out imagination and emotions.
Announcement of a new way of life.

Meaning reversed:
Proposals and possibilities have to be studied in detail in order to detect possible deceit, deception, and rivalry.
A hard guest. Unfortunate messages.
Failure. Playing absent.
Half-heartiness.
Unwillingness to listen to "the inner voice."
Craftiness and treason.
Sentimentality.
Subtle artificiality.
Being capable of fraud.
A talent is approaching but its time "has not yet come."
Chance of depressive thoughts, including suicide.

PAGE OF CUPS

Page of Cups

A rather feminine young person with artistic and sensitive inclination, light-brown hair, and blue eyes. Imaginative thinker with a vivid imagination and a loyal and helpful character.

Meaning:
A studious young person brings important news about a birth, for example, or a marriage.
Someone who wants to help and serve.
Loyalty is carried out and experienced.
A reliable collaborator.

A considerate and devoted person.
Fantasy, reflection, and meditation.
Being included in a secret.
A message from the unconscious via an insight or dream provides new information to think about.
Success in working with the unconscious.
New business is done.
Trying to eradicate all the blemishes of a person.
Help and strength are received through unwavering belief.

Meaning reversed:
Spiritual images remain vague.

Influence or being influenced.

Temporary distraction or temptation.
Being attached in a negative way.
Membership in a sect.
Artificiality, being unspontaneous.
Disappointment. Isolation.
A flatterer depicts a situation in a phony way.

Obstructions and disappointments are to happen soon.
Getting on a slippery slope.

Cups One: *The power of water*

Meaning:
Spiritual and/or material sacrifice.
Fulfillment of the Self.
Love is placed above will power.
Love for oneself and the other, happiness, benevolence.
Good feelings. Beauty.
One who forgives and is forgiven.
Purity in thoughts and acts.
An intense and deep love relationship may begin.
Emotionality and sensuality.
Revitalizing oneself at spiritual wellsprings.
Spiritual abundance. Contact with the unconscious.
Giving oneself to God or an esoteric idea.
A good view of things.
Being inspired, creativity.
Physical and spiritual health.
Social conscience. Good interpersonal skills.

Meaning reversed:
Temporary alienation or blockage of contact with the Self.
Oriented towards external matters.
Denial of the voice of the Self.

Muffled joy.
A false heart.
An unanswered love.

False love.
The cup topples.

The source of inspiration dries up.

A sad end to a love relationship or friendship.
Change.

Spiritual collapse.
Spiritual erosion.

Cups Two: *Loving exchange*

Meaning:
Exchanging the sacrifice.
Friendship and harmony.
Love.
Deep communication. Romance.
Spiritual unification. Friendship.
Interpersonal growth.

Intense devoted love between two people.
Two being one.
Cooperation. Partnership.
New or renewed friendship.
Mutual understanding.
Inner harmony between animus and anima (one's male and female natures).
Possibility of engagement or marriage.
In love or business matters, the questioner is in or may expect a positive, dedicated environment.
Forgiveness. Pardon. Grace.
Healing (healing powers).
Considerate to others.

Meaning reversed:
False sacrifice or love.
Possibility of emotional and relational deceit.
Communicative deadlock.
Conflicting wishes between partners.
Spiritual and physical desire.
The partner refuses to work toward an equal relationship.
Alienation develops in a friendship.
Having the wrong friends.
Lack of inner equilibrium, hence too much passion for the other.
Neurosis.

Manipulation of the other.

A love that does not satisfy spiritual and physical needs.
Emotional conflicts that cannot be resolved. Dishonest battle without a solution.
Disturbed destiny.
Considerate of oneself.

Cups Three: *Spiritual prosperity*

Meaning:
The sacrifice is celebrated.
A problem is solved.

A congenial meeting in which a
joint decision is celebrated.
Both parties are happy with the
compromise.
Recognition of mutual reliance.
The three graces.
Healing is near.
Engagement.
Joyful result of an enterprise.
Victory and freedom.
Success, abundance, and freedom.
Optimism and merriment.
Something new that has been
started takes off well.
Artistic inspiration.
Love and solidarity.
Joint happiness with oneness in
thoughts.
The installation of a new
member is celebrated in a
pleasant way.
Healing and comfort.

Meaning reversed:
The sacrifice is squandered.
Extravagance, indulgence.
Excessive pleasures.
Loss of prestige.

Fear for community and
communication.

Withdrawal or exclusion of a
group or club of friends.

The wrong inspirations.
Sabotage.
Debate. Dissidents.

The questioner becomes disliked.

The group falls apart.

Dissolution.

Cups Four: *Doubt*

Meaning:
Procrastination. Indecision.
Reflection. Introversion.
A stationary time in someone's life.
Contemplation in voluntary
emotional isolation.
Opposition. Obstruction.
Internal division.
Emotional reorientation.
Discontent with material and
emotional successes.
A bitter experience. Sadness.
A love relationship lost its "zing."
Alienation and distance.
Doubting everything that has
happened in the past.
Tiredness and depression.
Addicted to sacrificing oneself.
Not being able to say no.
Searching for new values.
Disappointment because, in a
relationship, communication is
no longer possible.
Facing up to a very unpleasant
sacrifice that cannot be avoided.

"Let this cup pass."

Meaning reversed:
After a period of solitude, new
inclinations to participate in life.

Extroversion. Esthetic sense.

New relations.
New interests.
New sacrifices.
New perspectives.

A new approach to old problems.
Too many new impressions.
Gentleness and idealism.

Sometimes there is the fear of
losing contact with those who
are close.

Cups Five: *Emotional bankruptcy*

Meaning:
Suffering, sadness, depression.
The cups have fallen over.
An incomplete emotional
relationship. Divorce.
Grief, loss. The spilled sacrifice.
Betrayed or hurt confidence.
Marriage or friendly relationships
have become impossible.
A marriage without real love.
Disillusionment, disenchantment.
Bitterness and frustration about
matters in the past.
Useless repentance.
Regret and shame.
Apologies are not accepted.
An emotionally or spiritually
disappointing inheritance.
Everything seems transient and
hopeless; however, other alterna-
tives remain.
Identification with negative
emotions.

Meaning reversed:
More positive reversed than in
the "upright" position.

Reunion.

Hopeful expectations and future
perspectives.
The return of happier times.

Restoration of the relationship
with a loved one from the past.
The defeat of despair.

Apologies are accepted.
Forgiveness.

The questioner exchanges the
impure for the pure.

Cups Six: *Submission*

Meaning:
A finale with a clear overview of
what has happened.
All cups are filled once more, for
the last time.
Fortunate karma is experienced.
Looking back to all good things
from the past.
Affectionate memories.

The happiness of being a child is
rediscovered via grandchildren.
A work of life is completed.
One offers oneself as a gift.
Giving oneself away as a gift.
Total, loving servitude to the
other.

Soon something very worthy
will happen.
A beautiful, mild fantasy
becomes reality unexpectedly.
A new friendship, a new
encounter, a new environment.

Meaning reversed:
A finale with clouded images.
Not being able to live in the
present.
Living in a fantasy world.
Nostalgia blocks adjustment to
the present.

Escaping, from tough reality, into
the past.
Longing for the protected and
carefree times of childhood.

Hanging onto memories because
nothing else is left.
Bitterness about one's youth has
its impact and is worked through
in the present.
The inner child suffers misplaced
anger or jealousy.
Plans or fantasies in which fear of
failure plays a role.
Unhappy, difficult childhood.

Cups Seven: *Contemplation of life*

Meaning:
Farewell to the sacrifice.
Success is not pursued further.
Looking back upon life thus far, projected as a movie, with all its fascinations, obsessions, wishes, experiences, and duties.
The question arises: What, in fact, has been achieved?
Deep disappointment.
In the most favorable case, one sees that everything is imagination.
An inspiring vision appears in "the mirror of contemplation."
Departure of material life, power, greed, fantasies.
Surpassing one's own egoistic goals (if the spread is positive).
Modesty. Being confronted with the various options life has to offer, and facing them.

Meaning reversed:
Fantasy, imagination, and daydreaming.
Unrealistically obsessed and fascinated by the many options life offers.
Whims and fancies, illusions.
There is a danger that a personal fulfillment will become a goal in itself.
Too many and contradictory desires.
Danger of drifting away in an illusionary world.
Internal division about the decisions that have to be taken.
Fallacious success.
Self-deception.

Unfulfilled promises.

Shyness.

Cups Eight: *Setting free*

Meaning:
The questioner consciously turns his or her back to the cups: it has been enough.
Things are shoved aside as soon as they have been achieved.
The questioner breaks with ideals, values, and relationships because these have lost their meaning.
Searching for happiness.
There is clear judgment, because there are no illusions and things are seen at face value.
Modesty.
Being disappointed in something that has been commenced in the past—a hobby, job, relationship.
Rejection of the current situation.
Entering into an uncharted area.
Consciously parting from a particular style of life.
Possibly the start of a plan to migrate.
A mystical and metaphysical field is entered.
Spiritual loneliness.

Meaning reversed:
Disillusion and despair.
Giving up work.
Possible thoughts of, or actual, suicide attempts.

The questioner is not able to modify his or her life, because of fatigue and the unwillingness to put attainments in jeopardy.

Giving up.
Possibly a flight into using alcohol and/or other drugs.

Seeing the sun shine behind the moon.

Spiritual development is replaced by artificial material security.

This card may mean the demise of a particular enterprise.

Cups Nine: *Tied to earth*

Meaning:
The sacrifices have been brought.
Difficulties have been dealt with.
Prizes have been won.
Repudiation of further aspirations.
Resting on one's victories.
Contentment. Self-satisfaction.
Individuality. Inner certainty.
Good business deals have been
completed. Warranty for the
future.
Great sense of self-esteem.
A feeling of spiritual and physical
well-being. Good health.
Wishes are fulfilled.
Success in emotional and creative
endeavors.
A materialistic attitude prevails.
Attachments stagnate growth.
Possibility of vanity and
complacency.
Closed mind because of egoistic
focus on former successes.
Seeking material comforts.

Meaning reversed:
All good things in life are taken
for granted.
Difficulties only seem to have
been dealt with.
Illusive freedom.
Dissatisfaction. Quarrels.
Worries.
Depression, cynicism.
Threat of illness or material
hardship.
A too-big ego (blasphemy) or
excessive self-criticism and
self-hatred (suicide).
Wishes are not fulfilled.
Blunders and badly executed
plans. Mistakes.
Possibility of pursuing excessive
satisfaction. Bingeing, drinking,
sex.
It is all going too well.
Psychological or physical
poisoning; botulism; a stagnant
mind or body.

Cups Ten: *Augmented passage*

Meaning:
Liberation and happiness is near.
Letting go of the past
emotionally.
Serene comfort.
Peace. Love.
Tensions and internal and
relationship conflicts have
been resolved.
The feeling of coming home.
Realistic self-consciousness in
relation to the other.
Unity of the female and male
principles, anima and animus.
Psychological differences are
enriching the situation.
Longings of the heart will
become reality.
A fitting family life, a strong
friendship, and an enduring,
successful relationship beyond
expectations.
Good interpersonal relationships.
A good reputation.
Living in a virtuous way,
exercising Tao.

Meaning reversed:
Liberation in pain.
The answer has been found, but
the questioner has difficulties
detaching emotionally from the
past.
Uncontrolled anger is possible.
Certain ideas and friendships still
have to be dumped.

Within the (in principle) happy
family, there are differences of
opinion.

Possibly karmic loss of a
friendship or a child.
Difficulties with the raising or
educating of children. Difficult
children.

King of Swords

A man with gray hair and steel-blue eyes, a wise and penetrating mind, and a controlled dominance, with great analytical skills. Counselor and helper. A man of judgment. Has power over life and death.

KING OF SWORDS

Meaning:
Fair judgment and its consequences.
Authority, power, superiority.
A good and strong, empathic leader.
An authoritative person with acute intelligence.
A superior, analytical thinker.
Intellectual preponderance.
An active, experienced, and purposeful person.
A professional governor, judge, medical practitioner, lawyer, engineer.
Has to deal with laws and the judiciary system.
A positive judgment or command is received.
A lawyer is found. Honesty.
The spirit's sword pierces matter, clarifies affairs, and cuts the knots.

Meaning reversed:
Negative judgment.
Injustice.
Cruelty and sadism, barbarism.
A sickened form of justice.
Egoism. Bad intentions.
Perfidious behavior, vandalism.
A muddle-head in a position of power.

A dangerous man who, in the name of order, brings chaos.
A dictator of the worst kind.
A mean man who brings about unnecessary disturbances and sorrow.
An obliterating judgment.
Businesses may end in a disastrous persecution.
Subject to prejudice and condemnation.
Decadence.

Queen of Swords

A serious and sensitive woman with fair hair and gray-blue eyes, academic, with substantial individual power, a sharp mind, and noble composure.

QUEEN OF SWORDS

Meaning:
A subtle person who has been very fortunate but now has to deal with anxieties, setbacks, and misfortunes. This suffering is borne with dignity, which has a purifying effect.
Great female sorrow. Grieving.
Infertility.
Hardship and loneliness.
Misfortunes are borne with dignity.
Possibly widowed or divorced.

An intelligent woman who is purified through suffering.
Being embarrassed (by others).
Being sensitive to others.
Alertness, cleverness.

Academically formed intelligence, a sharp mind.

Meaning reversed:
Impeccable on the outside, but untrustworthy and deceitful.
Artificial behavior.
Continuous complaining and whining. Imaginary illnesses, seeking attention.
A femme fatale.
Narrow-mindedness and intolerance.
Bad temper.

Prudishness. A semblance of a relationship is kept alive.
A spurious, stupid, vain, and ostentatious woman.
Possibly treacherous, vile, secret enemies.
Psychological absence, not being "with it."
An ill-natured, evil-minded, vengeful, malicious person.

KNIGHT OF SWORDS

Knight of Swords

A man with light-blond hair and blue eyes. A master in well-considered action and demeanor. The perfect noble knight. Impetuously he carries the sword, the symbol of heavenly justice.

Meaning:
The self-confident, energetic drive of the young.
The unknown is encountered courageously.
Foes are defeated at full gallop.
Heroic action.
A moment of skillful and gallant comportment.
Victory over impediments and obstruction. Freedom and prosperity are regained; evil is destroyed.
Own rights are defended or won successfully.
The end of a frustrating situation.
Fulfillment of the Self.
Possible involvement in opposition, enmity, war.

Meaning reversed:
Inner resistance against fulfillment of the Self.
Rash actions.
Inward conflict.
Ups and downs.
Thoughtless and incompetent actions.
Overdone, vaunting, arrogant, inept attitude.
Ruin.
Vengeance.
Superfluous display of power, conflict.
Impulsive mistakes.
Possibly a dispute with, or annihilation by the opposite sex.
Colonization with dangerous consequences.

In general this is a very positive, awakened card. There are helpful forces with regard to incarnation. The surrounding cards will indicate which influences are impinging on the Knight of Swords.

Page of Swords

An active youthful person with blond hair and light-blue eyes and great alertness to unknown dangers. Has a clear mind, insight, and discretion.

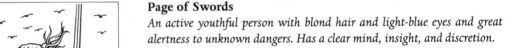

Meaning:
Messages about and judgment of conscience and inner growth.
Possesses the quality of insight.
Exercise in agility and self-mastery. Alertness.
Skillful in diplomatic work. Tact.
Having "the overview."
Careful search for eventual dangers.
Insight. Sensing and revealing.
Assessing well features of things, situations, and others.

Hidden weakness is revealed.
An impostor will be exposed.

Secret service.
Discretion.

Meaning reversed:
Messages are interpreted wrongly, which causes stagnation.
Lack of preparation.
A dreamer.

The questioner does not foresee and is not prepared, which are sources of danger.

Possibility of "clogging up."
Having no rebuttal when one is required.
Danger of alienation of own and others' feelings.
Through lack of preparation, running into the danger of being powerless when confronted with stronger people.
Danger of disclosure, infiltration, cunning pretense, calculation.

PAGE OF SWORDS

Swords One: *Power of the spirit*

Meaning:
Positive judgment.
Spiritual potency. Going through life honestly. Impressive conduct that commands respect.
Heavenly justice is administered and cannot be avoided.
Spirit of emulation and ambition.
Victory through willpower.
Success and energy. Triumph and power. All enterprises will succeed. Championship.
Many activities and movements in a positive direction. Prosperity.
An intellectual apex is reached.
Computational power.
Powerful, life-giving ideas, born from insight.
A liberating judgment takes place.
Great misery, possibly temporary.
Deep intellectual and emotional feelings.

Meaning reversed:
Negative judgment.
It is impossible to pull the sword out of the rock.
Back to the drawing board.
Improper use of power. Tyranny and disorder. Debacle.
Negative use of intellect.
Destruction on purpose.
Vandalism. Arguing someone or an idea to pieces.
Violence. Disaster. Loss on a grand scale.
The ego allows flattery.
Brutal temper.
Negative fulfillment of the ego.
Going through life dejected, low-spirited. Downfall.
Self destruction. Being abused by ruling superiors.
Possibly death.
Too empathic in matters of love.

This card depicts the archetypal sword, Excalibur. Arthur was able to extract it from the stone, thus establishing objective supremacy. Everyone deserves heavenly, objective justice, based on inner and karmic past.

Swords Two: *Inevitable judgment*

Meaning:
Heavenly justice is always executed rightly and in balance.

Purification of the soul.
Mental clarity. Tenacity.
Balanced and clear judgment.

Equanimity.
Counterbalanced powers.
An armistice that gives rest.

Peace is re-established.
Amnesty.
Liberation from the prison of past mind structures.
Insight into, and liberation from, own conditioning.
Making up the inner balance.

Meaning reversed:
The beginning of a painful change.
Negative judgment about oneself and the other.
Depression.
Being blocked in expression, speech, and breathing.
Stammering.
Double-dealing. Disloyalty, also of friends and associates.
Chance of treason. Lies. Shame. Exile.
An armistice full of tension.
The questioner is forced into a defensive position.
Misrepresentation of a matter.
Affairs start moving again . . . but in the wrong direction.
Impasse. Stalemate.

This card indicates influential protection for the one who seeks help.

Swords Three: *Grief*

Meaning:
Heavenly destiny (karma) is executed with great suffering. Immense grief about anything that is loved intensely, like the Virgin Mary's anguish for her son Jesus, condemned to death on the cross.
Deep inner pain and torture.
Grief and repentance.
Suppressed emotions are now liberated and expressed with vehemence.
Karmic causes enforce the absence or loss of a loved one.
Great loss. Divorce. Celibacy.
Entry into a convent.
Getting off on a tangent easily.
Intense and elevated emotions.
Learning through sympathy.

Meaning reversed:

Grief and mourning are experienced in a positive way.

Spiritual disquiet.
Thrown out of gear and alienated.
Inner disorder.

A meeting with someone who compromised the questioner.

Having to take a decision against one's own feelings.

The meanings of this card reversed are the same as upright, but the events indicated are less painful.

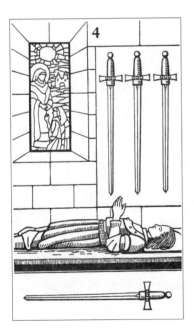

Swords Four: *Transmutation*

Meaning:
Psychological coma, apparent death, being stunned after a great loss or grief.
Reflection in isolation.
Giving in to a non-rational ability.
Patience. Waiting.
A period of rest after extensive spiritual and/or emotional exertions.
Recovery after a serious illness.
Voluntary retirement from the world.
Liberation from the duties and pressures of the system.
Self-chosen solitude to meditate and heal wound.
Temporary shelter.
Rest, peace, shelter.
May mean voluntary retreat, or admission to a rehab or psychiatric institution.
Voluntary exile.
Time to pamper oneself.
Transformation.

Meaning reversed:
Renewed activity.
There is an opportunity to regain what was lost.

Precautions are necessary.
It is necessary to exercise caution.
Renewed activity.

Circumstances and consequences are to be considered carefully.

Stringent bed rest is required.

Recovery through limitation.

Possibly forced admittance or incarceration.

Forced expulsion.

Swords Five: *Remembering the Self*

Meaning:
Heavenly justice is actualized.
Righteous victory and profit.
Mental struggle.
Eradication of identifications (role models, etc.) that one formerly believed in.
The questioner is promoted.
The objective is achieved.
Standing up for oneself with positive effect.
Settling with the negative aspects of oneself and the other.
A best friend or partner is castigated for their own good.
The necessity to let go of pride and face the inescapable.
Stormy positive developments in a situation full of conflicts.
Hope.
Verdict.
The soul is ready to incarnate.
Old mind structures dissolve.

Meaning reversed:
The negative aspects of heavenly justice are emphasized.
Righteous defeat. Loss of face.
Pride is broken. The questioner is defeated.

Demotion. Demotivation.
Conniving to gain a profit.
Dishonesty.
Seducement.
The deceiver is deceived.

Reciprocal political battle.

Lack of solidarity.

Despondency.

Despair.
An uncertain future. Treason.

Swords Six: *Crossing the great water*

Meaning:
"Crossing the great water."

Acquired justice is taken along.
Important changes in the conditions of life of the questioner and relatives.
Removal over a great distance.
Possible emigration to a foreign country.
Escape from the difficulties commences.
Responsibility and care are taken for a particular enterprise or a beloved person.
The difficulties are not completely over, but internally one takes one's distance.
Stepping aside. Flight.
The start of a new adventure in life. Asylum is acquired.
Success after fear.
A new perspective can become reality through action.
Start of a pregnancy, physically or metaphorically.

Meaning reversed:
No way out of the current difficulties, no solution.
A confession, statement.
A particular lawsuit goes profoundly wrong.
There is no renewal or growth.
The status quo continues.
Stalemate.
Stagnation and corruption.
Negative feelings.

Lack of diligence and entrepreneurship.

New plans run aground because of lack of commitment.

Asylum is sought, but its legalization has to wait.
Embarking on an illusion.

Delays with regard to letters or documents.

Swords Seven: *Loving growth*

Meaning:
In a clever way, heavenly justice is appropriated.
Physical and spiritual growth.
Success.
A new enterprise silently develops in a successful way.
Clever use of legal possibilities and subsidies.

Creative rascals are serving a beneficial cause.

Windfalls are not overlooked.
New plans are executed.
The pregnancy proceeds well.
The fetus (also metaphorically) develops successfully.

Sunny progress without much worry, after competence has been established.
Subtle energy exchange and communication.
Information exchange. Study.

Meaning reversed:

Partial success is likely.
A plan can go wrong.
There is a chance of treachery or fraud.
Avoid unlawful actions. Do not ignore worthwhile recommendations while working out a plan.
Being caught out.
Ideas pertaining to intended projects may be stolen by someone close by.
Some difficulties in developments or pregnancy.

Unfounded fear.

Possibly indiscreet behavior of friends who were trusted.

Swords Eight: *Bound to growth*

Meaning:
Being bound to, and accepting, heavenly justice.
A pregnancy is approaching delivery (also metaphorically).
Being bound in freedom.
Own possibilities are severely curtailed because of circumstances that, in principle, are self-chosen.
Decreasing power, due to labor put into a new development.
Energies are tapped.
Unable to do anything but carry out assignments patiently.
Being isolated from others; knowing that an important development is going on, but unable to see the development or its results.
Exercising acceptance, trust, and patience.
Possibilities now are limited.
Liberation from a binding situation is close, even though it does not seem that way.

Meaning reversed:
Somewhat the same as "upright" but with resistance or less acceptance.
If next to Death, The Devil, The Moon, or The Tower, possibly an aborted plan.

Emotional slavery or crisis.
Panic must be prevented.
Being in love. Puppy love.
Stagnation in the development of an important venture.
Endless "sitting on an egg."
The status quo is as firm as a rock.
Being depressed.
Scandal and slander.

Acceptance and trust are necessary to be freed from limitations and fear.

Swords Nine: *Awakening*

Meaning:
Lying awake over something with a perception of new perspectives.
The soul is subjected to the threat of the last, heavenly judgment as a consequence of the life that has been lived.
Waking up from a nightmare. The last intense contemplation on what has happened in the life.
Suffering, remorse, great despair, feelings of guilt, abhorrence, and inadequacy.
The realization of an unavoidable end of a period, life, relationship, love, project.
The last judgment threatens: great tension and fear are distorting the reality of life.
One does not realize yet that a new life, born from suffering, will manifest itself shortly.

Meaning reversed:
Lying awake over something, but with more perspective on the new that is becoming reality.

Fear based on reasoning that makes sense.
Force and conviction develop the ability to kiss things goodbye.

The same as "upright," but with more perspective on the new life that is becoming reality. The questioner accepts the inevitability of the reflections on his or her state.
Possibility of insinuation and doubt.

Traditionally, this card is a bad omen. The surrounding cards in the spread or a parallel card may shed light on it.

Swords Ten: *Birth*

Meaning:
The soul is subjected to and carries out the Last Judgment. It is now determined where and how the soul (plan, project) will start its new life.
The soul finds itself on a new shore. The previous life, obsession, plan, or structure is completely over.
Birth (also metaphorically). Now it not only can, but will, become better.
Rehabilitation. A positive, blank moment in the life of the questioner.
Now a new human being (idea, approach to life) is born.

Meaning reversed:
The same as the card "upright," but the indicated events happen in a difficult, plodding way. Saying goodbye and beginning anew. Woe.
A difficult "birth" with pain, complications, and a lot of tears.

Benefits, profit, improvements, and power may not be lasting.

A hesitant start.

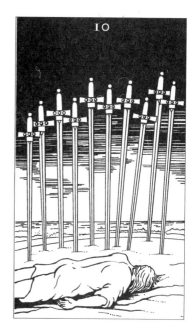

This card indicates an inexorable end and a new beginning. Now the new human being, idea, attitude to life, or relationship is born.

The ten swords place the soul in the land of the living—our world—by splitting eternity-space (space-time) into separate dimensions. They seal off the now-past life from intruding into and interfering with the soul's new incarnation. (The barrier of swords is not impenetrable like a wall of concrete. We may still see glimpses of that past life, but are unable to return to it.)

Appendices

CORRELATION TABLE

This correlation table summarizes and combines various concepts discussed in this book with the Major Arcana of the Tarot. The 3-6-12-24 part color circle was formulated by Johannes Goethe in *The Color Theory*, 1805–1810, and refined by Johannes Itten in *Kunst der Farbe*, 1960.

INVOC-ATION	#	MAJOR ARCANUM	ROYAL FAMILY	MINOR ARCANUM	ARCHETYPES	COLOR CIRCLE	MOON PHASE
TAOR	0	The Fool	Page of Pentacles	Pentacles 1 and 2		80% Yellow + 20% Blue	0 Postulate
TOAR	1	The Magician	Knight of Pentacles	Pentacles 3 and 4	Earth East	90% Yellow + 10% Blue	15 Observe
						YELLOW	
TORA	2	The Priestess	Queen of Pentacles	Pentacles 5 and 6	Spring Morning	90% Yellow + 10% Red	30 Experiment
TROA	3	The Emperor	King of Pentacles	Pentacles 7 and 8	Birth	80% Yellow + 20% Red	45 Oppose
TRAO	4	The Lovers		Pentacles 9	Belief	70% Yellow + 30% Red	60 Create
ATOR	(−)	Intuition		Pentacles 19		60% Yellow + 40% Red	75 Construct
						——— ORANGE ———	
ATRO	5	The Priest	King of Wands	Wands 1 and 2	Fire South	60% Red + 40% Yellow	90 Cure
OTRA	6	The Empress	Queen of Wands	Wands 3 and 4	Summer	70% Red + 30% Yellow	105 Expound
OTAR	7	The Chariot	Knight of Wands	Wands 5 and 6	Noon	80% Red + 20% Yellow	120 Explore
RTAO	8	The Hermit	Page of Wands	Wands 7 and 8	Production Hope	90% Red + 10% Yellow	135 Idealize
						RED	
RTOA	9	Justice		Wands 9		90% Red + 10% Blue	150 Reform
ROTA	10	The World		Wands 10		80% Red + 20% Blue	165 Reason
ORTA	11	Strength	Page of Cups	Cups 1 and 2		70% Red + 30% Blue	180 Combine
ARTO	12	The Hanged Man	Knight of Cups	Cups 3 and 4	Water West	60% Red + 40% Blue	195 Mediate
						VIOLET	
RATO	13	Temperance	Queen of Cups	Cups 5 and 6	Autumn Evening	60% Blue + 40% Red	210 Meditate
OATR	14	Death	King of Cups	Cups 7 and 8	Dying Love	70% Blue + 30% Red	225 Philosophize
AOTR	15	The Devil		Cups 9		80% Blue + 20% Red	240 Propagandize
ORAT	(+)	Truth		Cups 10		90% Blue + 10% Red	255 Lecture
						——— BLUE ———	
ROAT	16	The Tower	King of Swords	Swords 1 and 2	Air North	90% Blue + 10% Yellow	270 Command
RAOT	17	The Moon	Queen of Swords	Swords 3 and 4	Winter	80% Blue + 20% Yellow	285 Rule
AROT	18	The Star	Knight of Swords	Swords 5 and 6	Night	70% Blue + 30% Yellow	300 Preside
AORT	19	The Sun	Page of Swords	Swords 7 and 8	Transforming Knowledge	60% Blue + 40% Yellow	315 Pacify
					Gnosis	GREEN	
OART	20	The Last Judgment		Swords 9		60% Yellow + 40% Blue	330 Abstract
TARO	21	The Universe		Swords 10		70% Yellow + 30% Blue	345 Liquidate
		Common back of the cards			The Unearth	White Light	

CORRELATION TABLE

This correlation table includes important alphabets, characters or people, signs, and invocations in a number of occult and religious systems discussed in this book.

RUNE ALPHABET	GREEK ALPHABET	THE TWELVE NIDANAS OF BUDDHA	KNIGHTS OF THE ROUND TABLE	ZODIAC	APOSTLE	SUMMARY INVOCATION
Ur	Ω Omega	Avidya	Ector de Maris			
Odal	A Alpha	Avidya	Kay	Aries	Jacob the Younger	
Birka	B Beta	Samskara	Pellens			
Tiw	Γ Gamma	Samskara	Saser	Taurus	Bartholomeus	A — I am
Aquizi	Δ Delta	Vijnana	Bors de Ganys			
Feho	E Epsilon	Vijnana	Lamorak	Gemini	Andreus	
Gifu	Z Zeta	Nama-rupa	Palomides			
Ing	H Eta	Nama-rupa	Lucan	Cancer	Philippus	
Rit	Θ Theta	Sadytana	La Cote Mal Taillée			
Kaon	I Iota	Sadytana	Bleoberis de Ganis	Leo	Jacob the Elder	R — The way
Yer	K Kappa	Sparsa	Bedivere			
Wunna	Λ Lambda	Sparsa	Gareth of Orkney	Virgo	Thomas	
Naut	M Mu	Vedana	Tristan de Lyons			
Yr	N Nu	Vedana	Lyonell	Libra	Matthew	
Lagu	Ξ Xai	Trisna	Parcival			
Is	O Omicron	Trisna	Gawain	Scorpio	Taddeus	T — The truth
Thom	Π Pi	Upadana	Lancelot			
Os (Odin)	P Ro	Upadana	Galahad	Sagittarius	Simon	
Peorth	Σ Sigma	Bhava	Mordred			
Hagal	T Tau	Bhava	Alynore	Capricorn	Judas Iscariot	
Sig	Y Ypsilon	Jati	Lybyus Discophorus			O — The life
Eoh	Φ Phi	Jati	Brumeur	Aquarius	Simon Peter	
Dag	X Chi	Marana	Degore			
Man	Ψ Psi	Marana	Dagonet	Pisces	John	
Black Rune		Samsara/Nirvana	King Arthur		Jesus Christ	

TAROT DIVINATION WORK SHEET

THE BOW SPREAD

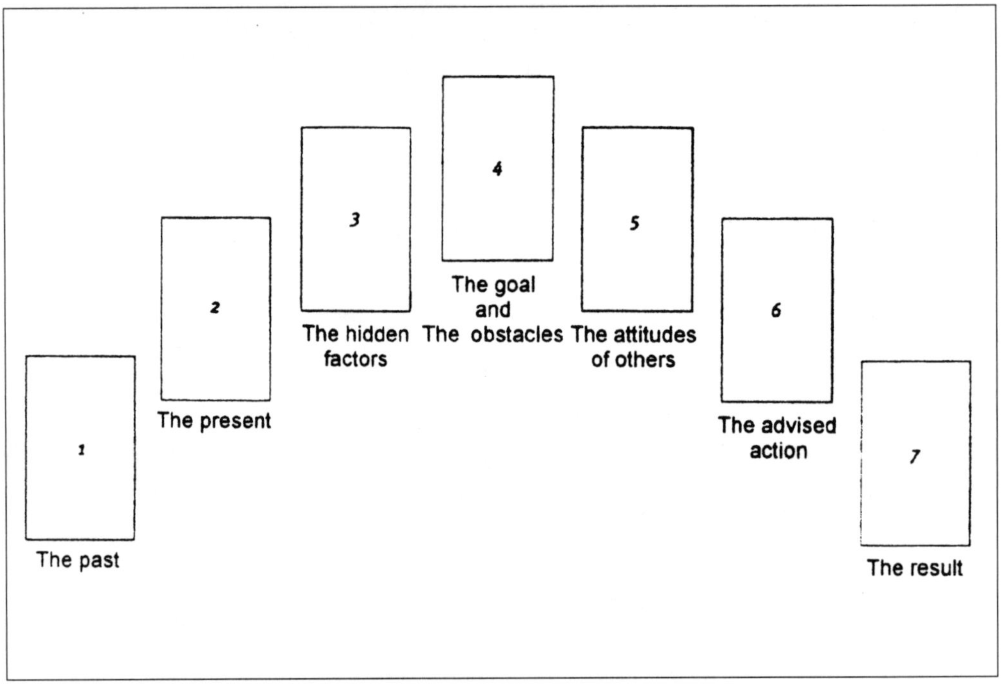

The Questioner: _____ Date: _____

The Situation: _____

The Question: _____

The Reading: _____

_____

_____

_____

This worksheet may be copied for the reader's own personal use

TAROT DIVINATION WORK SHEET

THE MIRROR SPREAD

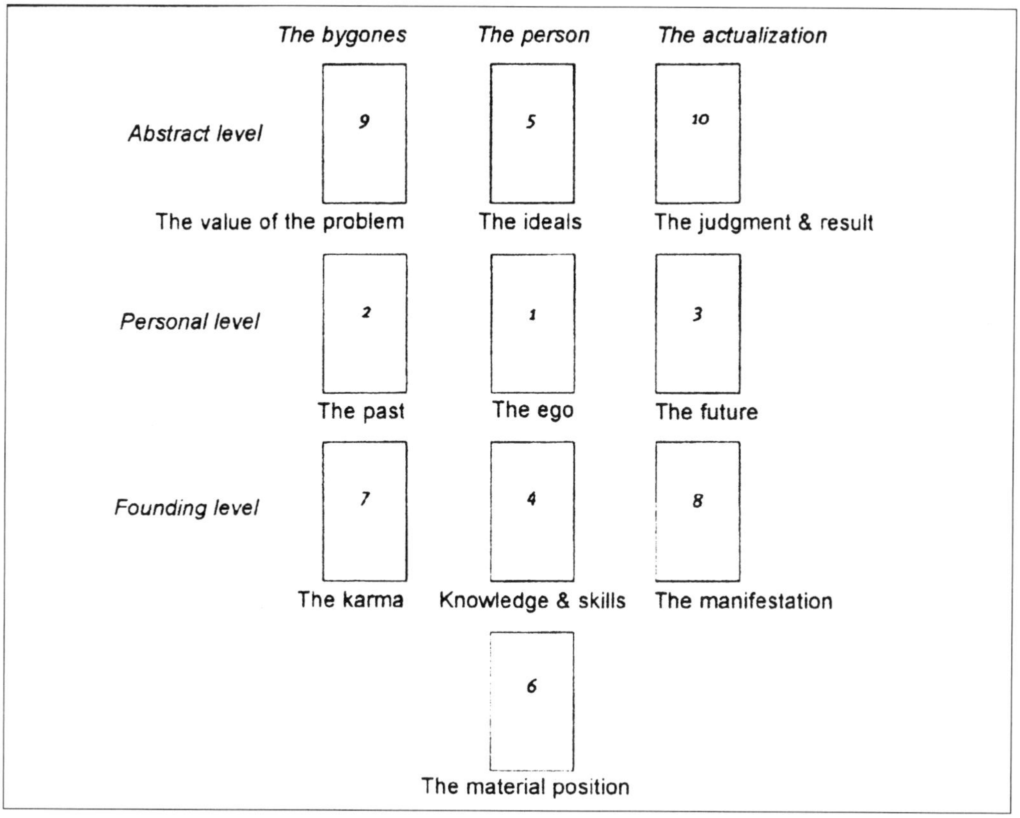

	The bygones	The person	The actualization
Abstract level	**9**	**5**	**10**
	The value of the problem	The ideals	The judgment & result
Personal level	**2**	**1**	**3**
	The past	The ego	The future
Founding level	**7**	**4**	**8**
	The karma	Knowledge & skills	The manifestation
		6	
		The material position	

The Questioner: _____ Date: _____

The Situation: _____

The Question: _____

The Reading: _____

_____

_____

_____

_____

This worksheet may be copied for the reader's own personal use

TAROT DIVINATION WORK SHEET

THE CELTIC CROSS SPREAD

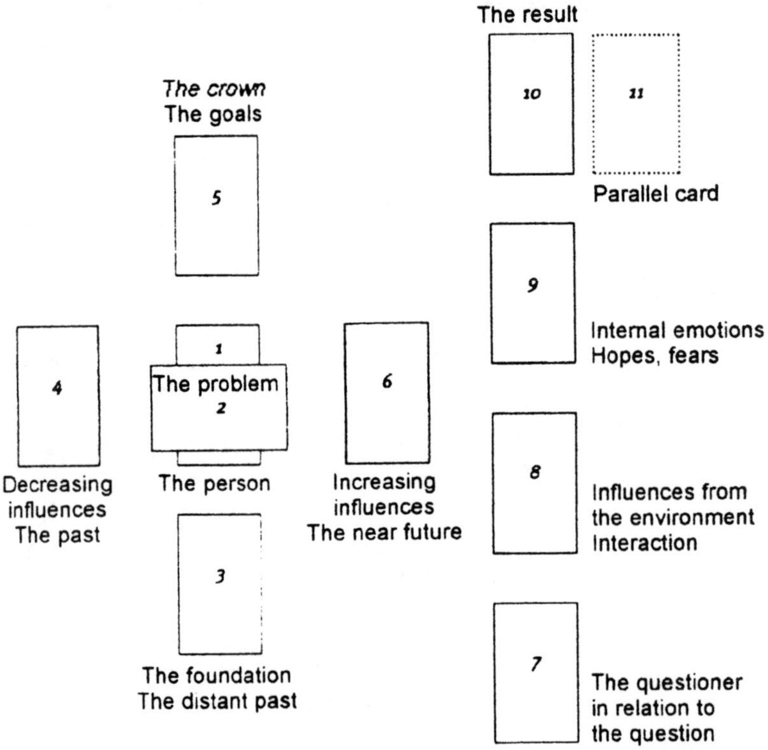

The result

10	11

Parallel card

The crown
The goals

5

9

Internal emotions
Hopes, fears

4		1		6
		The problem		
		2		

8

Decreasing
influences
The past

The person

Increasing
influences
The near future

Influences from
the environment
Interaction

3

7

The foundation
The distant past

The questioner
in relation to
the question

The Questioner: _____ Date: _____

The Situation: _____

The Question: _____

The Reading: _____

_____

_____

_____

This worksheet may be copied for the reader's own personal use

TAROT DIVINATION WORK SHEET

THE OUROBOROS SPREAD

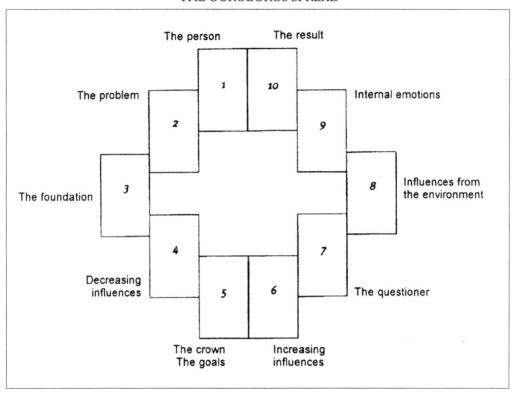

The Questioner: _____ Date: _____

The Situation: _____

The Question: _____

The Reading: _____

_____

_____

_____

This worksheet may be copied for the reader's own personal use

TAROT DIVINATION WORK SHEET

THE HOROSCOPE SPREAD

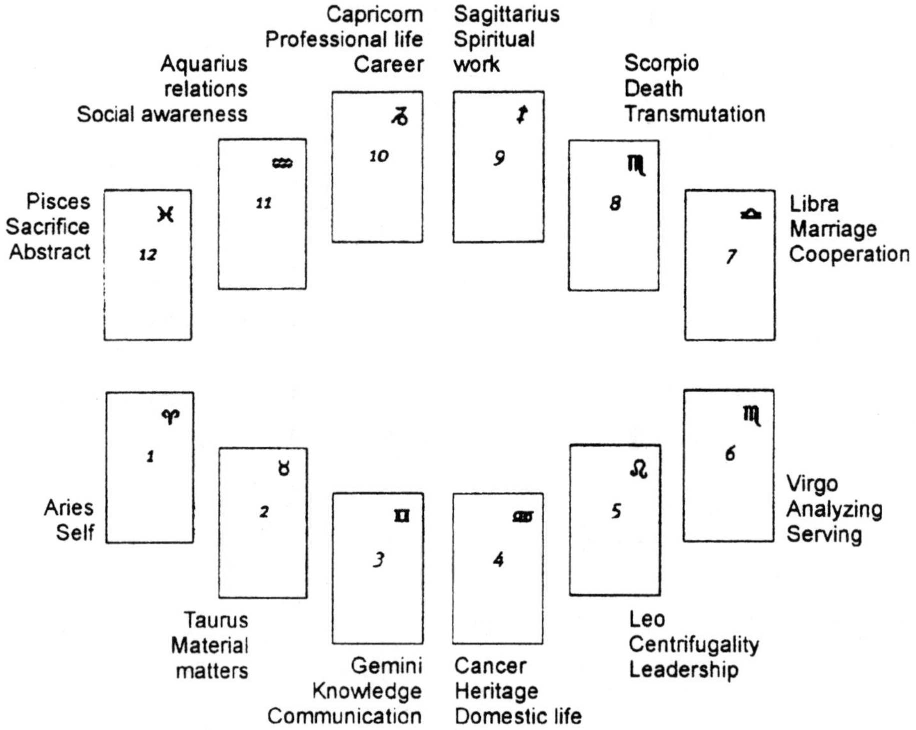

Capricorn
Professional life
Career

Sagittarius
Spiritual
work

Aquarius
relations
Social awareness

Scorpio
Death
Transmutation

♑
10

♐
9

♒
11

♏
8

Pisces
Sacrifice
Abstract

♓
12

♎
7

Libra
Marriage
Cooperation

♈
1

♍
6

Virgo
Analyzing
Serving

Aries
Self

♉
2

♌
5

♊
3

♋
4

Taurus
Material
matters

Leo
Centrifugality
Leadership

Gemini
Knowledge
Communication

Cancer
Heritage
Domestic life

The Questioner: _____ Date: _____

The Situation: _____

The Question: _____

The Reading: _____

_____

_____

_____

This worksheet may be copied for the reader's own personal use

TAROT DIVINATION WORK SHEET

THE CHAKRA SPREAD

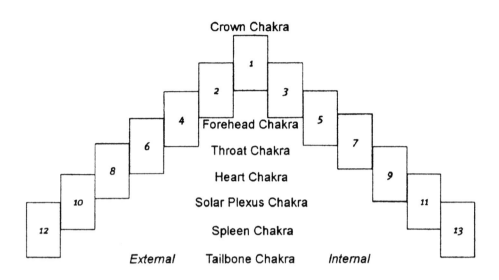

The Questioner: _____ Date: _____

The Situation: _____

The Question: _____

The Reading: _____

_____

_____

_____

This worksheet may be copied for the reader's own personal use

TARO INVOCATION PERMUTATION TABLE

INITIALIZATION

Place the four letters
of the word OART in
a circle, reading the
word counter-clockwise

OART → TARO *Permutation 1* Exchange the letter T with the one that follows it.	**TARO → TAOR** *Permutation 2* Exchange the letter opposite the letter T with the one that follows it.	**TAOR → TOAR** *Permutation 3* Exchange the letter opposite the letter T with the one that precedes it.	**TOAR → TORA** *Permutation 4* Exchange the letter opposite the letter T with the one that follows it.	**TORA → TROA** *Permutation 5* Exchange the letter opposite the letter T with the one that precedes it.	**TROA → TRAO** *Permutation 6* Exchange the letter opposite the letter T with the one that follows it.
TRAO → ATOR *Permutation 7* Swap all letters of the previously generated Tarot name.	**ATOR → ATRO** *Permutation 8* Exchange the letter opposite the letter T with the one that precedes it.	**ATRO → OTRA** *Permutation 9* Exchange the letter opposite the letter T with the one that follows it.	**OTRA → OTAR** *Permutation 10* Exchange the letter opposite the letter T with the one that precedes it.	**OTAR → RTAO** *Permutation 11* Exchange the letter opposite the letter T with the one that follows it.	**RTAO → RTOA** *Permutation 12* Exchange the letter opposite the letter T with the one that precedes it.
RTOA → ROTA *Permutation 13* Exchange the letter T with the one that follows It.	**ROTA → ORTA** *Permutation 14* Exchange the letter opposite the letter T with the one that follows it.	**ORTA → ARTO** *Permutation 15* Exchange the letter opposite the letter T with the one that precedes it.	**ARTO → RATO** *Permutation 16* Exchange the letter opposite the letter T with the one that follows it.	**RATO → OATR** *Permutation 17* Exchange the letter opposite the letter T with the one that precedes it.	**OATR → AOTR** *Permutation 18* Exchange the letter opposite the letter T with the one that follows it.
AOTR → ORAT *Permutation 19* Swap all letters of the previously generated Tarot name.	**ORAT → ROAT** *Permutation 20* Exchange the letter opposite the letter T with the one that precedes it.	**ROAT → RAOT** *Permutation 21* Exchange the letter opposite the letter T with the one that follows it.	**RAOT → AROT** *Permutation 22* Exchange the letter opposite the letter T with the one that precedes it.	**AROT → AORT** *Permutation 23* Exchange the letter opposite the letter T with the one that follows it.	**AORT → OART** *Permutation 24* Exchange the letter opposite the letter T with the one that precedes it.

Glossary

Abraxas

The god-idea Abraxas originated from the need of early Christian gnostics of the Alexandrian School to connect logically the irreconcilable antithesis of Absolute Spirit and Absolute Matter existing next to each other. Basilides, an Egyptian Christian living in the second century A.D. in Alexandria, and founder of the school of Gnosticism known as the Basilidians, claimed that he received his instructions direct from the apostle Matthew, and named this remarkable concept Abraxas. Basilidian teachings comprise Egyptian Hermeticism (a philosophy similar to Gnosticism), Eastern occultism, Chaldean astrology, and Persian philosophy. Basilides and his followers sought to combine the early Christian schools with the old pagan mysteries.

ABRAXAS is a word-symbol, the letters of which are numerically equal to the name of the god MITHRAS, and which signify his sevenfold radiating creative power.

Iconographically, Abraxas is symbolized as a complex creature with the body of a human, the head of a rooster, and each of his legs terminating as a snake. With his right hand he brandishes the symbol of Dyamis, the flagellum of power. His left arm carries the symbol of Sophia, the shield of wisdom. As victor he stands on a chariot that carries at the front the emblem of the sun-wheel with six spokes. The snake-heads of his legs drive four white horses at a gallop. Depicted in an ithyphallic manner he rides through the universe with the sun to his right and the moon to his left. C. G. Jung describes "the being" Abraxas extensively in his *Septem Sermones ad mortuos.*

Acausal influence

An influence that cannot be explained by means of cause and effect. Telepathy is an example. The arrival of nuclear physics around the 1930s, brought rigid causal thinking to an end, as it became clear that the position of an atom or nuclear particle cannot be predicted exactly.

Akashic records, Akasha chronicles

A Sanskrit concept for the cosmic registration of all events, thoughts, and feelings that have occurred since the beginning of time. They are said to be imprinted on *Akasha*, the astral light, of which it is said that it transmits waves of human will power, thought, feeling, and imagination. As such, the Akasha chronicles may be imagined as being a total hologram of all past, present, and future universes. Akasha then is the light that illuminates this hologram and thus creates the phenomenal world and makes it live. The Persian Sufis call the subtle matter of thought *Alam Almital*.

The Akashic records are accessible by certain individuals, making clairvoyance and prophecy possible. The collective unconscious and its archetypal structures, formulated by C. G. Jung, also belongs to the Akasha chronicles. Dr. Rupert Sheldrake compares the Akasha chronicles with the concept of the morphogenetic field, which he developed in his book, *A New Science of Life* (1984).

Al-Khwarizmi
Famous Arabic astronomer and mathematician (approx. A.D. 780–850). His name still lives in the term "algorithm" (to designate a rule or procedure). The term "algebra" was derived from the title of his compilation and further development of Mesopotamian mathematics, *Kitab al-jabr wa al-muqabalah*.

Alchemy, Alchemists
A system of knowledge that was developed in the early Middle Ages in the Western, Egyptian, and Arabic cultures. Broadly speaking, it is an attempt to understand the relationship between humankind and the cosmos. More specifically, it comprises thoughts and knowledge about the behavior of entities in the material and spiritual world. Alchemy therefore encompasses chemistry, psychology, astrology, and hermetic philosophy.

Under influence of the secularization of human spiritual life and the accompanying development of the natural sciences, the psychological and spiritual aspects of alchemy were gradually repudiated as unproductive ballast. The resulting chemistry and physics, also called classical chemistry and classical physics, have a strict logical structure built through inductive-scientific methods of reasoning.

In the beginning of the twentieth century, the discovery of radioactivity triggered research into the fundamental structure of matter, indicating that a strictly logical approach to the behavior of matter is impossible. As a result, modern chemistry, nuclear physics, quantum mechanics, quantum-chemistry, and quantum-physics developed. Important workers in these fields were Niels Bohr, Wolfgang Pauli, Werner K. Heisenberg, Max Planck, and Albert Einstein.

Over the ages, many alchemistic documents have been kept; possibly they also had practical chemical value. Although they were written in a cryptic fashion, they give us insight into early medieval symbolism and archetypal structures, and for that reason are important for research into the sources of the Tarot.

Alexander the Great
Son of Philippus II of Macedon and Olympia (daughter of Neoptolemus of Epirus), he was born in 356 B.C. and died in 323 B.C. His teacher was the philosopher Aristotle.

One of the greatest generals of all time, Alexander, in his short life conquered Asia Minor, Egypt, and the Middle East to the borders of India. The unification of Western Asia for which he strove resulted in an enormous expansion of trade and exchange of culture in this region.

Alexandria

Egyptian port on the Northwestern side of the Nile delta. Established by Alexander the Great in 332 B.C., it quickly became the most important city in Egypt, and, under his successors, the Ptolemaic kings, the capital city of Egypt.

It developed into the most important center of Hellenic and Semitic studies. Its current name is El Iskandariya.

Alphabet, Hebrew

There are two Hebrew alphabets, early Hebrew and classical Hebrew. Early Hebrew was used by the Jews before their exile in Babylon. Together with the Phoenician and Aramaic alphabets, it forms the group of North-Semitic alphabets. It consists of 22 letters that also have numerical values.

Algorithm

A systematic, unambiguous, logical procedure that produces—in a finite number of steps—the answer to a question or the solution to a problem. The term stems from Al-Khwarizmi, the name of an Arabic mathematician. The swing-algorithm in this book indicates the mathematical schema that generates and shows the logical order of the Tarot-invocations.

Antigone

In the three Theban plays by the Greek dramaturge Sophocles (born in 496 B.C. and deceased in 406 B.C.), Antigone is one of the two daughters of Oedipus and the niece of King Creon of Thebes (the successor to Oedipus). Antigone defied Creon's order to leave her dead brother Polynices to rot unburied on the battlefield by ritually burying Polynices. Creon's soldiers arrested Antigone and brought her to Creon. As she showed no remorse—knowing that she was right—he ordered her to be executed by having her immured in a cave. In this tale, Antigone represents the arcanum Intuition.

She fights for the rights that, according to her intuition are just, not fearing eventual downfall and ruin. We find a similar archetypal figure in Jeanne d'Arc.

Arcana

Plural of *arcanum*. From the Latin *arca*, "chest," the root of the word being *arc-*, meaning "completely closed." The expressions "ark of the Covenant" and "Noah's ark" bear the same meaning. The Latin verbs *arcere*, "locking up" or "encompassing," and *arcein*, "fending off," have the same root. In Sanskrit, the holy language of India in which the *Vedas* are written, *arcanâ* means "connecting of the senses in service of God."

Archetype

Archetype is a concept defined by the psychiatrist and philosopher Carl Gustav Jung (1875–1961) as a primordial image or collective pattern that is known to everyone because it is part of the human collective unconscious and supraconscious. "These collective patterns I have called archetypes, a term from St. Augustinus. An archetype means a typos (impression), a delineated group of human and divine soul structures of archaic nature, which contains mythological motives with a particular content and form" (C. G. Jung, Tavistock-readings, London, 1935).

Astarte

Phoenician fertility goddess, counterpart of the Babylonian and Assyrian goddess Ishtar.

Astrology, Chinese

Based on the moon calendar. A complete cycle takes 60 years to complete and is composed of five smaller cycles of 12 years each. Each year of these 12 is named after an animal, in this order: rat, oxen, tiger, rabbit, dragon, snake, horse, sheep, monkey, rooster, dog, and pig. The nature of the animal that belongs to a year has a profound influence on that year and the people born in it. Every sign is subjected to the influence of the five Chinese elements— Wood, Fire, Earth, Metal, and Water—which each have a positive and a negative pole (yin and yang).

Atlantis, Atlantids, Atlanteans

The earliest reference to Atlantis is found in the dialogues by Plato, *Timaeus* and *Critias*, from the fourth century B.C. Plato introduced Atlantis, in a discussion between Solon and priests from the Egyptian city Sais, as a large island that sank during a great volcanic explosion. Atlantis, as described by Plato, was a Bronze Age civilization. The two most gigantic eruptions in the Aegean Sea occurred in 25,000 B.C. and about 1500–1400 B.C. The second coincides with the catastrophic Thera eruptions. The Aegean Thera hypothesis about the location of Atlantis is thoroughly discussed by James W. Mayor in *Voyage to Atlantis*.

Another theory is that Atlantis was located somewhere in what now is called the Atlantic Ocean. Similarities between the cultures of the ancient Egyptian and Indian cultures of Central and South America—e.g., the 365-day calendar, the 24-letter alphabets, the pyramids, customs, and rites of balsa, and legends about the flood—are claimed to be remnants of a great culture that had its origins in an Atlantis that was positioned somewhere in the Atlantic Ocean and spread from there to the east and the west. Others believe that the legend of Atlantis was inspired by catastrophic events which may have destroyed the Minoan civilizations on Thera and Crete in the Mediterranean Sea.

Some esoterics claim that the Greek story is true in a sense, but like the early chapters of the Judeo-Christian Bible, is only a shadow of a former reality. According to these esoterics, the inhabitants of Atlantis—the Atlantids—were the distant descendants of the original settlers of that now vanished island continent. The Atlanteans, said to be non-corporeal mindstreams that landed about 50,000 years before, could project themselves into the material world and assume human shapes and bodies. It is proposed that the Atlanteans introduced to earth such advanced technologies as travel through time-space and gravity-control machines (which may have been used in the construction of the pyramids in Mexico and Egypt), as well as comprehensive philosophical machines such as the I Ching and the Tarot.

Autokinetic techniques
The imaginary movement of an object at rest. Autokinetic effect is used to study suggestion.

Baal
Also called Bel or Beel (Master). A god who was worshipped in many Eastern societies, especially by the Canaanites, who considered Baal a materialistic fertility god, and also by the Phoenicians and various Semitic peoples in the Middle East and North Africa. The Jews from the Old Testament knew Baal and dedicated a cult to him, much to the disapproval of their prophets. Baal was depicted in armor, with a lance in his right hand and a crown of sun rays. His voice was the thunder; his arrows were the lightning rays. He also sent rain to the earth. The Greeks identified Baal as Cronus or Zeus.

Babylon
Since about 1700 B.C., the capital of the southern part of Mesopotamia (Babylon) and one of the most famous ancient cities. Its original name was Babilan (Greek: Babylon, Hebrew: Babel). It was situated on the river Euphrates. Before the collapse of the Tower of Babel (Genesis 11:1–9), Babylon was one of the most important cultural, trade, and scientific centers in the world.

Bardo Thödol
Bardo is a Tibetan word that simply means transition or hanging in between. Bar = in between, do = hanging or being suspended. The word bardo became famous through the popularity of the Tibetan Book of the Dead, the translation of the original Tibetan-Buddhist text entitled Bardo Tödrol Chenmo, which means The Great Liberation Through Hearing in the Bardo. (Buddhism was transmitted into Tibet mainly from the seventh to the tenth centuries. Padmasambhava was one of the most illustrious Tantric masters in the eighth century).

Bardo teachings are very ancient and found in what are called the Dzogchen Tantras. Dzogchen was a monastic university founded in the seventeenth century in Kham, Eastern Tibet, and one of the largest and most influential centers of the tradition of Padmasambhava until its destruction in 1959 by the Chinese. With the blessing of the

Dalai Lama, this monastery was rebuilt in exile by the seventh Dzogchen Rinpoche in Mysore in the south of India.

The Great Liberation Through Hearing in the Bardo, or *The Tibetan Book of the Dead*, is a unique book of knowledge. It is a travel guide of after-death states designed to be read by a master or spiritual friend of a person who dies, after his death. The love for the deceased expressed during the reading opens a channel between the reader and the Akashic record (soul) of the deceased. The book divides the whole of our existence into four realities: life, dying and death, after-death, and rebirth. These four bardos (transition states) are:

> The natural bardo of this life;
> The painful bardo of dying;
> The luminous bardo of dharmata;
> The karmic bardo of becoming.

In the Tarot, the first bardo is represented by the day-arcana *The Fool*, up to and including *The Hanged Man*. The Tarot delineates the other three bardos from the night-arcana *Temperance* through to *The Universe*. Apart from the widely available direct translations of *The Tibetan Book of the Dead* in English, e.g., those by Francesca Fremantle and Chögyam Trungpa, it is very well discussed in an easily readable, involving, and very thorough way by Sogyal Rinpoche in his book *The Tibetan Book of Living and Dying*.

Beelzebub

Name of a Phoenician-Syrian god; in the Old Testament, the king of the devils. In the Philistine city Ekron, worshipped under the name Baalzebub (Chaldean: Baal-zebub, lord of the flies), in the New Testament (Matthew 12:24, Mark 3:22, and Lucas 11:15), known as Beelzebub, lord of dung. Gurdjieff used the name in the title of his book, *Beelzebub's Tales to His Grandson* (part of Gurdjieff's complete work, *All and Everything*), in a deliberate attempt to emphasize the terrible plight of humanity.

Blavatsky, Helena Petrovna

Russian occultist. Born Helena von Hahn in 1831 in Ekaterinoslav, the Ukraine. Author of *Isis Unveiled* (1877) and *The Secret Doctrine* (1888). Co-founder of the Theosophical Society (New York, December 13, 1875). She was a remarkable personality who has profoundly influenced today's thinking about the relationship between east and west, the unity of religion, and the divine origin of humankind. She died in 1891.

Bolt

The bolt or dorje is the Tibetan lama-scepter. In the shape of a stylized thunderbolt or lightning ray, it symbolizes the highest spiritual power.

Brahma

The most important god in Hinduism, also called the grandfather. Born out of a golden egg, after which he created the earth and everything in it.

Borobudur

Vast Buddhist sanctuary at Magelang in Middle Java (in Indonesia). This is a temple mountain in which the arrangement and symbolic forms of hundreds of stupas together form an enormous, three-dimensional mandala.

Cathari

From Greek *katharos*, meaning pure. In the eleventh century A.D., the Cathari, who guarded objective knowledge, formed a sect in southern France. The Cathari professed a Gnostic dualism, namely that there are two principles—especially of matter—one good and the other evil. A human had a pure soul and was an alien and sojourner in an evil world. Humankind's aim must be to free the spirit and restore it to communion with God.

In the first half of the eleventh century, isolated groups of Cathari appeared in western Germany, Flanders, and northern Italy. Similar views were held by the religious sects of the Paulicians and Bogomils in the Balkans and the Middle East. A period of rapid growth followed when Western dualists and Bogomil missionaries returned from the Second Crusade (1147–1149). From 1154 the Cathari were an organized church with a hierarchy of bishops, a liturgy, and a system of doctrines. Their main centers were in Toulouse, Provence, and the Pyrenées.

The Cathari were in constant opposition to the worldly and corrupt Roman Catholic Church. Their doctrines led them to rewrite the Biblical story. Jesus was merely an angel; his human sufferings and death were an illusion. The Cathar doctrines were Christian but, as they struck at the roots of orthodox Christianity, they were considered heresy. After Pope Innocent III attempted in vain (around 1200) to force the Count of Toulouse to put down the Cathar heretics, he prohibited the Catharic movement in 1215. Next, the Albigensian Crusade was proclaimed. An army led by a group of barons from northern France ravaged Toulouse and Provence and massacred hundreds of thousands. In 1244 the great fortress of Montségur in the Pyrenées was captured and destroyed. The Cathari went underground; many of them fled to Italy. The hierarchy faded out in the 1270s. Around 1412 the movement was almost completely eradicated by the Inquisition, and disappeared.

Chaldea

A country south of Babylon (currently Iraq) that is frequently mentioned in the Old Testament. Several ancient authors used the term "Chaldean" to denote priests and other persons educated in classical Babylonian literature, especially in the traditions of astronomy and astrology.

Celts

Old, Indo-European tribes with a unique music, art, and literature that invaded western-Europe starting around 1300 B.C. Being moved on by the Doric invasion in Greece from about 1000 B.C., they invaded Italy from Spain around 400 B.C. They finally settled in France and the British Isles. Celtic priests and priestesses (Druids) held high office as magicians and seers in the governments of their tribes. They believed in reincarnation and worshipped nature (the earth, trees, winds, fire, etc.).

Charon

Son of Erebus and Nyx (a deep hole in the earth, into which the souls of the deceased and the night disappear). In Greek mythology, the name of the ferryman who carried the souls of the deceased over the Styx, the river between our world and the underworld, to the abode of the dead, Hades. In the Minor Arcanum Six of Swords, Charon returns the soul to the land of the living.

Chiromancy

Interpretation of a person's character and the prediction of his or her future via reading and explaining lines and other features in the palms of the individual's hands.

Ciborium

Chalice made from gold or silver—gilded on the inside and with a lid—to keep the holy sacraments of the altar.

Clergy

The complete system of (especially Roman Catholic) ecclesiastical dignitaries.

Confucius

Chinese philosopher (approx. 551–479 B.C.). Next to Lao Tse, Confucius was China's greatest philosopher, political theoretician, and teacher, whose ideas have profoundly influenced eastern Asian civilization from 400 B.C. onwards, up to today.

Constantinople

The city that is now known as Istanbul. Largest city and port in Turkey. The city is situated on both sides of the Bosphorus, and is thus in both Europe and Asia. Being of great strategic importance since antiquity, it has been under Greek, Roman, and Turkish rule. Constantinople was the center of the eastern Roman or Byzantine Empire, and for the Crusaders, the bridge to Asia Minor. The most famous monument in the city is the Hagia Sofia, originally a Byzantine church, and currently a mosque.

Correlation Table

Matrix in which relationships between characteristics and/or behaviors are conveniently arranged. Used often in statistics to check test results, for example, in psychology.

Cosmology

The Greek word *kosmos* means "universe." A cosmology is the complex of teachings about what is known about the universe and the place of humankind therein. The term comprises philosophical and esoteric theories of old ages, as well as modern physical studies (as a part of astronomy) about the universe as a whole.

Court de Gébelin, Antoine

Minister and traveling preacher of the reformed Church, who lived from 1695 to 1760. Assisted in the restoration of Protestantism in France after a long period of religious persecution that started with the annulment of the Edict of Nantes in 1685 by Louis XIV. He also brought the Tarot into the open again.

Creon

King of Thebes in Greek sagas and in the play *Antigone* by Sophocles. Creon represents the archetype and psychology depicted in the arcanum King of Swords reversed. Sophocles portrays this archetype in *Antigone* as follows: after Oedipus blinds himself upon the discovery that he has unknowingly killed his father and married his mother, his daughters Antigone and Ismene guide him in exile to Athens. At the same time, Creon succeeds him as king of Thebes. Oedipus' sons, Eteocles and Polynices, fight for their rights to Thebes' throne, Eteocles at the side of Creon. But Polynices' attack is countered, and both Eteocles and Polynices die in the battle. Creon gives Eteocles a state funeral, but proclaims that Polynices' body must remain unburied on the battlefield to rot and be eaten by dogs and vultures. In Athens, this was an atrocious and immoral punishment: in Greek morals and ethos, the dead belong to the gods. The deceased could return to the gods, however, through burial and the appropriate rites. By decreeing this hideous punishment, (the archetypal) Creon transgresses existing morals in an attempt to establish his own values.

Antigone, who loved her brother dearly and was convinced that Creon's order was unjust, disregarded Creon's decree and buried Polynices according to ritual. Creon's soldiers reported Antigone's actions to Creon. Antigone was arrested. In front of Creon and her sister Ismene, she admitted her act without any remorse. Creon then ordered Antigone's execution by immuring her in a cave. Haemon, Creon's son, heard that his beloved Antigone was immured and sped to the cave to liberate her. He came too late. Antigone had already hanged herself. Haemon then committed suicide in Antigone's tomb. When Creon's spouse, Queen Euridyce heard about Haemon's death, she also committed suicide, cursing Creon for the loss of her son. Only then did Creon realize the mistakes he had made.

Crusades

A series of military expeditions from about A.D. 1100 to 1300. These expeditions aimed to end the occupation of Jerusalem and possession of the holy grave of Jesus Christ by the Islamic Turks.

During the first crusade, Jerusalem came under western rule for more than a hundred years, especially by the Order of Templars. The Templars were named after the temple of King Solomon, of which the Western Wall—now known in Israel as the "wailing wall"—is still visible. The fortifications that protected the old city are still present.

Cupid
The Roman god of love. *See also Water cupids.*

Dead Sea Scrolls
The common name for old religious texts, written on parchment and papyrus, discovered in Khirbat-Qumran, Israel, in caves in the hills around the Dead Sea.

A group of Essenes lived in Qumran, northwest of the Dead Sea, from 200 B.C. until A.D. 68. The scrolls found in the caves at Qumran belonged to the library of this community and were probably hidden in the caves when the Romans were about to subjugate the area (the Hebrew mountaintop fortress Masada, 31 miles [50km] south of Qumran fell into Roman hands in A.D. 72).

The Dead Sea Scrolls, dated from about 100 B.C. to A.D. 100, stayed unnoticed for about 2000 years. They were discovered in 1947. Initially they created a sensation, because their content has important religious and theological consequences, but this soon died out as the Dead Sea Scrolls remained for more than 40 years in the hands of a small, closed group of "scientists." In 1991 they were given free for translation to the public. The Dead Sea Scrolls give a unique perspective on the origins of Hebrew and Christian religion.

Demeter
Greek goddess, also called Mother Earth. She was the daughter of Cronus and Rhea and the sister of Zeus. She fostered agriculture and with it, an ordered life within the context of family and government, as opposed to the hunter-gatherer's life of constant flux. She is the white barley goddess who symbolizes the star constellation and zodiacal sign Virgo. Being an agricultural goddess, pigs were sacrificed to her. Demeter is portrayed as a stately woman with a crown of wheat stalks and a sickle. She is also the mother of Kore/Persephone. Her most important celebrations were the Eleusian and Thesmophorian mysteries. The Romans called her Ceres.

Dervishes
Members of an Islamic fraternity in Asia Minor that appeared in the twelfth century. The dervishes are famous for their mystical dances in which they imitate and try to unite with the cosmos through continuous whirling dance movements.

Difference between the moon phase and the length of the sun
In astrology the *difference* between the degree of the moon and the

degree of the sun determines the *essence* of a person. It is measured in absolute degrees. During an eclipse of the sun, the difference is nearly 0°; during an eclipse of the moon it is about 180°. A value of 50–300° indicates a traditionalist; 60°–170°, a critic and eclectic; 180°–290°, an innovator and planner. The astronomical length of the sun is measured in degrees along the Ecliptic, starting at the Spring equinox on the 21st of March at 0° Aries, and it increases during the year. For instance, the sun has a length of 270° on the 21st of December.

Divine Comedy
Poem of 33 songs, written in A.D. 1310–1314 by the Italian Dante Alighieri (1265–1321). It describes the journey of the soul after death through Hell, through Purgatory, and up to Paradise. It is considered one of the most important works in European literature.

Divination
Insight into the future or discovery of something that is hidden from normal perception by applying a philosophical machine and/or supernatural talents.

Dog of Death
In Egyptian religion the symbol of the god Anubis, who accompanies the deceased on his or her way to and through the afterworld.

Don Quixote
Main character in the eponymous novel by Cervantes. Don Quixote is the idealist who is purified through life, makes psychological changes, and starts to doubt the correctness of his ideals.

Druids
The learned class of the Celts (priests, judges, teachers). As a result of the christianizing of Western Europe, the clergy gradually took over the power of the Druids.

Edessa
After Pella, the most important stronghold of Macedonia.

Egyptian Book of the Dead
A collection of ancient Egyptian texts that gathers magical formulas and aphorisms. The texts were placed in graves and coffins to assist the soul on its journey to and through the afterworld.

Elemental beings
Also called "elementals." Natural sub-human beings that represent one or more of the Aristotelian elements earth, fire, water, and air. C. S. Lewis describes the elemental aspects of Morgause (in his commentary on Charles Williams' work *Lamorack and Queen Morgause of Orkney*) as follows: "Morgause is more like the spirit of stone itself—not, to be sure, of stone considered as a cold thing, but of stone considered as pressure, sharpness, ruthlessness: stone

the record of huge passions in Earth's depth . . ." Gareth Knight (in *The Secret Tradition of Arthurian Legend*) states about King Uriens of Gore, husband of Arthur's half-sister Morgana: "She is a creature at least half elemental, and she is a priestess of the Atlantean type, skilled in magic, whose powers relate at least as much to the inner worlds as to the outer"; and somewhat further, "Uriens of Gore is, in fact, an 'enlightened' elemental, or one seeking enlightenment. This, elementals can do, in relation to humans (who are) able to be aware of them, much as domestic animals can be enlightened by ordinary humanity."

Energy
In general, the power to produce a perceptible effect. In physics, energy is the property of a system that is a measure of its capacity to do work. Work then is defined as what is done when a force moves a point of application. Physical energy can be potential or kinetic and comes in a variety of forms. "Subtle energy," also called "psychological energy," cannot be measured in physical terms, but nonetheless may be sensed by, and produce effects in, humans.

Equinox
Either of the times twice yearly when the sun crosses the equator, and as a result, day and night everywhere on earth are of equal length.

Esoteric
The word esoteric is related to the Greek *esoterikos*, which is derived from *esoteros*, the comparative form of the adjective *eiso*, meaning within or part of the inner, spiritual world. The antonym is *exoteric*, meaning outside or belonging to the outside, physical world.

Essenes
Religious sect that flourished in Palestine from about the second century B.C. to the end of the first century A.D. The Essenes clustered in monasteries that, at least generally, excluded women. The Essenes meticulously observed the Law of Moses, ritual purity, and the Sabbath (during which they prayed and meditated on the Torah). They denied the resurrection of the body and shunned temple worship. Pliny fixed their number at some 4,000 in his day. The Dead Sea Scrolls, found in Khirbat-Qumran, are attributed to the Essenian community in that place.

Eternity
The cosmology we adhere to determines our understanding of eternity. Ouspensky, influenced by Einstein and De Sitter's time-space cosmology of the early twentieth century, defines eternity as "the endless existence of each and every moment in time" in his book, *In Search of the Miraculous: Fragments of an Unknown Teaching*. A hypothetical observer who would discuss an object in time-space such as a "moment in time," might conclude that such an object

has its own endless existence. In so doing, that observer mentally adds a fifth dimension to the four-dimensional object in question. In other words, eternity is time-space that has been allocated a fifth, temporal dimension.

Discussing objects or processes in four-dimensional time-space such as eternity points, time-lines, or synchronicity (the parallel running of time-lines through time-space), mentally isolates them from time-space and adds the fifth dimension. Another consequence is that any object in time-space that is discussed should be given the prefix "eternity." However, as it seems easier to comprehend and work with the concept "four-dimensional time-space" than with "five-dimensional eternity," in this book we generally use the terms "time-space" instead of "eternity" and "time-line" instead of the more correct "eternity-line."

It needs to be noted that each cosmology has its own way of "seeing" eternity. In Talbot's holographic-universal cosmology, eternity is the all-pervading omnipresent holographic (Akashic) record of everything in the implicate order.

Eternity-line
Concept formulated by Ouspensky. The life of an entity, person, business, or organization may mentally be represented by a string of events. Each of those events is an actualized eternity-moment in the Einstein-De Sitter time-space (eternity). The string of an entity's events consists of actualized eternity-moments and is that entity's *eternity-line*. An eternity-line is also called a *fate line*, an *evolution-line*, *evolutionary line*, or simply *time-line*.

Every human has his or her own eternity-line. When two people interact, they actualize that eternity-moment together and share karma—in other words, at such a moment (point), there is a confluence of the two persons' eternity-lines in time-space. One may expect that two married persons have eternity-lines that largely run parallel and have many junctions.

In a Tarot consultation, the diviner's and the questioner's eternity-lines temporarily coincide: the consultation is an actualized eternity-point and a jointly experienced occurrence. During the reading, by means of the symbolism in the drawn Tarot cards, the diviner clarifies the complex of eternity-planes or segments in the close vicinity of this eternity-point. Other divinatory systems work according to the same principle.

Eternity-moment
Singular point in time-space defined by four coordinates in Einstein-De Sitter time-space; also called "eternity-point." An eternity-moment is either potential or actualized. An actualized eternity-moment is called an *event*. A potential eternity-moment is named a *possibility*. In our life we actualize eternity-moments by making decisions and acting according to them: each actualized eternity-point is a reality. Most points remain unrealized and continue to stay forever potentialities or possibilities.

Events—actualized possibilities—do stay endlessly actualized in time-space, whereas possibilities may remain in the state of "not actualized." According to Ouspensky, once a potential eternity-moment is actualized, this actualization can never be undone: it can never be de-actualized or re-potentialized—in other words, it is entered forever in the Akashic record.

Possibilities do not exist in our reality, but may nevertheless be present in our minds as hypotheses (of course, they exist as potential eternity-moments in time-space).

Two potential eternity-moments may exclude each other from actualization. For example, an orange can be eaten or thrown on the floor, but not both. At some point in time, an entity's decision may lead to the actualization of a thus far potential eternity-moment.

Eternity-plane

Another concept formulated by Ouspensky. An *eternity-plane* is a collection of at least three points in four-dimensional time-space; these points may be actualized or potential. An entity's time-line, which consists of many eternity-points, is part of an eternity-plane as well. Time-space contains an endless number of eternity-planes.

The Tarot can be thought of as a classification of time-space in *eternity-planes* or *-segments*. Each arcanum symbolizes a selection of eternity-points in time-space that have important attributes in common. For example, the Major Arcanum The Priestess comprises eternity-points in which important learning takes place.

Starting from the time-space concept and its classification of similar eternity-moments into eternity-planes, we realize that all divinatory systems are related; it could not be otherwise. For example, in the I Ching, each hexagram circumscribes an eternity-plane. In this book, the zodiacal signs and the Scandinavian runes are correlated with the Tarot.

Eternity-segment

A group of related or similar eternity-points in the time-space continuum through which two or more eternity-planes can be drawn. Individual Tarot cards may be considered eternity-segments or eternity-planes. For example, The Fool represents all eternity-moments (actualized or potential) that comprise beginning situations.

Excalibur

The name of King Arthur's sword. According to a medieval British legend, Arthur was the only young man capable of drawing the sword out of the stone in which it was fixed. In this way he proved that he was to become the new (legendary) king of England. The sword Excalibur was invincible. When it broke in a battle between Arthur and Lancelot, a fairy fixed it by some secret means. Knowing he was dying, Arthur had Excalibur thrown into a nearby lake where a hand rose from the water, seized it, and drew it under.

Excalibur seems to have been derived from the name of a famous Irish sword called Caladbolg, and from Geoffrey of Monmouth's reference to Arthur's sword as Caliburn. Malory says that Excalibur means "cut-steel."

The sword Excalibur bears the same symbolism as the Tarot emblem Swords.

Fisher King

Person in the Grail legends who answers Parcival's questions about the illness of King Amfortas and the location of the Grail. In other legends, the Fisher King is the king of the Grail castle and is wounded in his thighs or genitals by one of Arthur's knights. During the period of his illness, his kingdom was called the Waste Land. Sir Galahad heals the Fisher King, paving the way for the resurrection in Spring to replace the barrenness of Winter.

Fractal

An irregular, fancy, often beautiful geometric figure, its most important characteristic being the recursive reproduction of its own form. Fractals are found in nature; for example, in the shape of clouds or cracks in dried claybeds. Artificially created fractals may show great similarity to such forms. Fractals can be created by calculating a large number of points using a mathematical formula, which is executed many times based on the result of its own previous calculations. The backs of the Tarot cards in the restored Tarot deck show a fractal that is based on the letter T, the Tau cross.

Freemasons

The largest, closed—and for a long time, secret—worldwide fraternity of the Free and Accepted Masons. It evolved from the guilds of stonemasons and cathedral builders of the Middle Ages. Around the year 1100, when new building principles were introduced in Europe under the influence of the Crusades, the Freemasons taught each other these principles. Gradually, their interests expanded into many esoteric knowledge systems that came from the east as well.

The Freemasons strive for spiritual and moral uplifting, mutual recognition, and assistance. The customs, rites, and symbols of the Freemasons are obtained from the Bible, the architecture of light.

Freemasonry is an intense, closed network with millions of members all over the world, bundled into fraternities that they call "lodges." In daily life, Freemasons greet and recognize each other through a secret symbolic gesture that the uninitiated will not pick up. Their inner hierarchical order indicates strong early influence from the order of the Knights Templar. It is likely that, when the Knights Templar were persecuted to death by the French King Phillip, many of them went undercover in Freemason fraternities. They enriched the Freemasons with the esoteric knowledge they had gained in the Near East. It is known that for centuries the Freemasons have had knowledge of the original 80-card Tarot. It is assumed that the Freemasons were given this knowledge by the Templars.

Freya

Also known as Freye. The main goddess of Scandinavian mythology. The sister and spouse of Wodan (Odin), she is also the goddess of love, fertility, battle, and death. The weekday Friday is named after her.

Fugue

Music with varying chords, written for any number of different voices or instruments, that imitate and follow each other. For this reason they are called fugues, as *fugue* literally means flight.

Galatians

Inhabitants of Galatia, a district in central Anatolia. Known for the letters described in the New Testament which the apostle Paul wrote to the early Christian community in Galatia.

Geomancy

Derived from the Greek words *gè*, meaning earth, and *manteia*, meaning the art of prediction, and the Latin word *manus*, meaning hand. Geomancy is a method of divination in which the diviner is manually active, for instance, by quickly pricking a number of holes in the earth. The number of holes or pebbles is counted. In case of an odd number, one circle is drawn, otherwise two circles. This procedure is repeated 16 times, so that four tetragrams result. The tetragrams that form—as well as the figures—have a particular meaning. Other geomantic methods of divination are grabbing a handful of pebbles from a brook's bed, or shuffling, selecting, and spreading out a set of cards.

Geomancy also is the art of arranging people, symbols, and/or objects built from natural elements, such as crystals, precious stones, and noble metals, and placing them in such a way that earth rays and mutual vibrations are connected, strengthened, and/or deflected. The arrangement of objects on an altar is determined by means of geomancy, as well as the floor plan and objects in pyramids, temples, cathedrals, and mosques. Geomancy is the oldest of four elemental mantic arts: geomancy, pyromancy, hydromancy, and aeromancy.

Gnomes

In European folklore, dwarfish subterranean-dwelling goblins or earth spirits who guard mines or precious treasures hidden in the earth. Gob, the king of the gnome race, ruled with a magic sword and is said to have influenced the melancholic temperament of humankind.

Gnosticism

Derived from the Greek word *gnostikos*—one who has gnosis or secret knowledge—which has the same root as the verb *gignoskein*, meaning learning to know. Gnosis is the knowledge that emerges from the individual insight that the total coherence of things is found in God, the cosmos, and humankind. Gnosis is meant to be for initiates in the temple and concerns the real language and facts of the inner nature of humankind.

Gnosis became especially known because of a group of spiritual Christians from the first centuries A.D. who were called "Gnostics" by the Church Fathers, such as Epiphanus in 375.

The key to gnosis is inscribed on the oracle of Apollo at Delphi: "know thyself." The development of self-knowing commences with introspection, building in the consciousness a resonance with our divine being, which we ultimately unite with and emanate. Gnostic revelation is distinguishable from philosophical enlightenment because it cannot be acquired by force of reason, and from Christian revelation, because it is not rooted in history and transmitted by scripture. It is rather the intuition of the mystery of the self. Jesus Christ called it "the knowledge of the depth of All."

In the Gnostic view, the unconscious self of humankind co-exists with God. But because of a tragic fall, it was thrown into a world that is completely alien to its being and alien to God. For the Gnostics, God is depth and silence beyond any name or predicate, the absolute, the source of good spirits who together form the "pleroma" or realm of light. These concepts are found in various myths that serve to express the idea that the unconscious self or spirit in humankind sleeps until awakened by the Savior. Through revelation from above, humankind becomes conscious of its origin, essence, and transcendent destiny.

Golden Dawn

A fin-de-siècle hermetic order in England, founded in the second half of the nineteenth century by the masonic Rosicrucians, Dr. William Wynn Westcott (1848–1925), Samuel Liddel MacGregor Mathers (1854–1925) and Dr. William Robert Woodman (1828–1891). The order's many prominent members studied western occultism based on hermeticism, including the Qabbala, astrology, theosophy, alchemistic symbolism, and the Tarot. The order gradually disintegrated because of clashes between its temperamental, gifted, and eccentric members. Sir Arthur Edward Waite took over management of the order and rewrote the Golden Dawn's teachings and rituals in the spirit of esoteric Christianity. He incorporated the knowledge he acquired about the Tarot in the Rider-Waite deck of cards.

Grail, Grail Legends

The Grail is the legendary chalice in which, during the crucifixion, Jesus Christ's blood was received. After the crucifixion, the rich tradesman Joseph of Arimathea gave his unused grave for the burial of Jesus. According to legend Joseph then took the Grail with Jesus' blood on a journey to the tin mines of Cornwall, England.

The Grail is the subject of many legends. The Knights of King Arthur received the assignment to find the Grail, in which the most pure knight would succeed. According to legend, this was Sir Galahad.

Gregorian Chants

Early medieval church music used to accompany the text of the Mass. Gregorian chants were sung a capella, i.e., without accompanying instruments.

Gringonneur, Jacquemin

This artist and cardmaker was asked by the French court in 1392 to paint three sets of Tarot cards for the French King Charles VI. He made the cards in beautiful colors on gilded parchment with a silver back. Seventeen of these cards are still in existence, displayed in the Bibliothèque Nationale in Paris.

Guaita, Marquis Stanislas de

Great magician in France. In 1888 he founded the Ordre Cabbalistique de la Rose Croix (at the same time in England, the Order of the Golden Dawn was founded). In 1890 Josephin Péladan, a dedicated member, left de Guaita and founded the Rose Croix Catholique du temple et du Graal. The battle between the Rosicrucians of de Guaita and of Péladan is called the battle of the Two Roses.

Gurdjieff, Georg Ivanovitch

Georg I. Gurdjieff (1877–1949) was born in Alexandropel in the district Kars in Trans-Caucasia. His father, mother, grandmother, and a number of old teachers convinced him that he had to work on himself in an uncompromising way. With extreme persistence he searched for people who could teach him. For 20 years he traveled through central Asia and the Middle East. There he found living sources (schools) of seemingly long lost traditions. Just before the start of the First World War, he returned to Moscow, where he assembled a group of students around him. He taught with conviction that humankind is in a state of sleep and slavery induced by a complex of hypnotic powers with exponential growth. Gurdjieff set himself to defuse these powers and "awaken" and liberate humankind. He sometimes used unpopular measures to confront people and for them to confront themselves.

At the outbreak of the Revolution in 1917, Gurdjieff went to the city of Essentuki in the Caucasus. In 1919 he established the Institute for the Harmonious Development of Man in Tiflis (now Tbilisi). Later, Gurdjieff and his students undertook an expedition through the Caucasus to Constantinople and then Berlin, arriving in 1922 in Paris. There, in the Chateau du Prieuré, he founded the Institut pour le Development Harmonieuse de l'Homme (the Institute for Harmonious Development of Humankind). There assembled an international gathering of people, who, under the guidance of Gurdjieff, worked out and disseminated his ideas. Among them were P. D. Ouspensky, J. G. Bennett, Thomas de Hartmann, and A. R. Orage. In many places around the world, groups emerged called "the Work."

When journalists asked Gurdjieff what kind of teachings he brought to the world, he answered: "esoteric (inner) Christianity."

The central concept of Gurdjieff's teachings is that humans are in a semi-sleeping state, that they have to wake up, become really aware of themselves, and start working on their spiritual development.

Halloween
Celtic feast on the evening prior to All Saints' Day (All Hallows), on the first of November. In Gaelic it is called *Samhain*. Halloween is an important celebration in the United States and Australia.

Hathor
Literally, house of Horus. Egyptian mother and fertility goddess, goddess of love, beauty, and joy, depicted as a cow or a female figure with cow horns. She also rules the afterworld and is therefore called "the woman of the west." In the negative sense, Hathor is the goddess of murder and manslaughter. In general, her archetype compares well with that of the Scandinavian goddess Freya (Freye).

Hebrews
Name for the inhabitants of Biblical Palestine.

Hecate
Goddess of the earth, fertility, and the magic powers of nature. Zeus acknowledged her power. Patron-goddess of wizards and witches. Best known as goddess of the underworld. Artemis, Persephone, and the moon goddess are identified with her as well.

Hector
Hector de Maris was an obscure but trusty vassal of King Uther Pendragon (the father of the future King Arthur) to whom the young Arthur was fostered out. Hector later became one of the Knights of the Round Table.

Heisenberg, Werner Karl
German physicist and philosopher (1901–1976) who developed the Heisenberg relations, a series of quantum-mechanical formulas to describe matter in a non-deterministic way.

Hera
Greek goddess of the heavens, daughter of the primordial god-pair Cronus and Rhea. Sister and spouse of Zeus. Goddess of marriage and all life phases of women. The peacock, crow, and cuckoo are dedicated to her. The Romans named her Juno. In general, as a female archetype, Hera is related to Freya, Hathor, and Mary.

Hermes
Greek god, son of Zeus and the nymph Maya (daughter of Atlas). Herald and messenger of the gods and therefore bearer of the herald's staff. God of the sciences. Legendary inventor of the lyre, writing, and the science of explanation of philosophical, theological, and later, Biblical writings (hermeneutics). He was also the

guardian of the education of youth and trade. The Romans called him Mercury. In occult writing Hermes is called Hermes Trismegistus. In Egyptian mythology, the god of wisdom, Thoth, has the same attributes.

Hermes' herald-staff is a straight baton with a globular knob at the top, wound with a double spiral of two polar snakes: the male, positive snake (yang) and the female, negative snake (yin), a symbol of the unification of counterparts. The snakes' seven coils are related to the seven planets, the seven tattvas, and the octave. These days the double snake (helix) is seen as the representation of the DNA molecule.

Hermes Trismegistus
Latin expression that literally means "Hermes the three times Great." It is the Greek name for the Egyptian god of wisdom, Thoth. Mythical source of holy books of wisdom, called *Hermetic Writings*, of which many were stored in the libraries of Alexandria and Pergamon. The study of these writings is called Hermeticism.

Hermetic
Alchemistic property named after Hermes Trismegistus, meaning completely, closed, sealed and impossible to open.

Hermetic Writings, Hermetica
Works of revelation of an occult, theological, and philosophical nature, ascribed to the Egyptian god of wisdom, Thoth, known in Latin as Hermes Trismegistus, meaning "Hermes the three times Great." The collection, written in Greek and Latin in the form of Platonic dialogues, probably dates from the middle of the first to the third century A.D. The works ascribed to Hermes Trismegistus were primarily on astrology; to these were later added treatises on medicine, alchemy, and magic. The underlying concept, namely that the cosmos constituted a unity and that all parts of it were interdependent, was also basic to the other occult sciences. The aim of hermeticism, like that of Gnosticism (a contemporary religious-philosophical movement), was the deification or rebirth of humans through the knowledge (gnosis) of the one transcendent God, the world, and humankind. The theological hermetic writings are represented chiefly by the 17 treatises of the *Corpus Hermeticum*. Although hermeticism is set in Egypt, its philosophy is Greek. The hermetic writings present a fusion of eastern religious elements with Platonic, Stoic, and Neo-Pythagorean philosophies. The Arabs extensively cultivated hermeticism and through them it reached and influenced the west. There are frequent allusions to Hermes Trismegistus in late medieval and Renaissance literature.

Hexagram
Name for a group of six (for which the Greek word is *hexa*) horizontal whole or broken line elements, which together form one of the 64 oracles described in the *I Ching, The Book of Changes*. A

hexagram is formed by a combination of two out of eight possible trigrams—Heaven, Earth, Thunder, Water, Mountain, Wind, Fire, and Lake. Obviously, each of these trigrams bears an archetypal content.

Hieroglyphs

Iconographic form of writing, developed by the Egyptians. In Hieratic writing, abstractions of the hieroglyphs are used to make the process of writing go faster.

Hildegard von Bingen

Hildegard von Bingen (pseudonym, Sibyl of the Rhine), theologian, musician, poet, dramatist, scientist, and physician, was born of aristocratic parents in 1089 and died in 1179 in Rupertsburg near Bingen. From the age of eight, she lived in a Benedictine convent, first in Disibodenberg, then, after 1136, as leader of her own community at Rupertsberg near Bingen. She experienced visions from the time she was a child. When she was 43, a committee of theologians confirmed the authenticity of her visions, which she subsequently recorded in writing and as drawings. Between 1151 and 1158, she wrote and collected musical compositions to be sung by the sisters at her convent at liturgical and other functions.

Hildegard also wrote treatises on medicine and natural history, and for amusement she contrived her own language. Though she was not canonized formally, she is listed as a saint in the Roman Martyrology.

Holy Land, The

Coastal area at the eastern part of the Mediterranean Sea; comprises parts of modern Israel, Lebanon, Jordan, and Egypt.

I Ching

Old Chinese text, subtitled *The Book of Changes*, one of the world's oldest books and one of the five classical works of Confucianism. The oldest parts seem to stem from the tenth century B.C.; it found its final shape in the last centuries B.C. The enigmatic *I Ching* has long fascinated Chinese as well as western philosophers. The book contains much wise advice and is still used for divination. C. G. Jung and many others have been convinced of the predicting power of the *I Ching*.

The *I Ching* is based on 64 hexagrams: combinations of six horizontal lines which can be whole or broken. Each hexagram is a stylized ideogram and consists of two trigrams—combinations of three whole or broken lines. The two types of lines indicate the fundamental duality of Chinese metaphysics. The broken line corresponds with the female principle *yin*; the complete line corresponds with the male principle *yang*.

The 64 hexagrams can be ordered in various ways. The oldest order is by King Fu Chi, the mythical founder of the Hsia dynasty (2205–1766 B.C.), and is based on the binary number system. The other—and most used—order is by King Wen, who established the Chou dynasty (1122–221 B.C.).

The *I Ching* is a book of wisdom and oracles with a complete cosmology and anthropology. As an oracle system it is related to the Tarot.

Ideogram

Abstract picture with a particular meaning. Chinese calligraphy concentrates on the artistic reproduction of the ideograms in Chinese writing. The earliest Chinese calligraphy was found on the shoulder blades of animals and on tortoise shells.

Individuation

Term described by C. G. Jung (1875–1961). Individuation is the process of becoming your own person, detached from all sorts of "isms" and mannerisms, collective and hypnotic worlds of influence, and masks. It is the process of bringing one's soul to the surface of one's existence. Jung used this term to point out the necessity of developing one's divine individuality and of waking up to real humanism. He stressed that individuation is the essential path to spiritual progress and the illumination of the world by one's own Divine Light.

Initiation

Ritual ceremony with the purpose of teaching someone the eternal order and the laws, rules, and taboos of life, as described in myths and/or religious writings. The word "initiation" is derived from the Latin verb *initiare*, meaning "to commence," "induct," or "lead into." The inclusion of young people in a tribe is a major initiation. In esoteric schools, societies, or orders, the acceptance of the new member (neophyte) is accompanied by occult ceremonies and rites. In primitive (illiterate) tribes initiation is often accompanied by ritually injuring the initiates, for example, circumcision. Apart from the formal inclusion in the group through the suffering that all group members have endured, a main reason for ritual injury is that the mythical teachings are better remembered through the association with the pain endured. Thorough inculcation is essential, as illiterate tribes cannot record their myths in writing. Often, primitive tribes use memorization schemas and stylized figures as an aid in memorizing tribal myths and laws. In the western world, physical initiation is replaced by psychological initiation through a complicated system of examinations.

Inquisition

In the Catholic Church, a judicial body to combat heresy, alchemy, witches, and wizardry. In the Middle Ages, the Inquisition had enormous power and committed countless executions and murders. It was not until the seventeenth century, about hundred years after the Reformation, that the influence of the Inquisition diminished.

Invocation

Literally, call (from the Latin word *vox*, or voice), often with a meditative, religious, or magical charge. Incantations and adjurations are invocations, too. The Tarot invocations are part of the mystical language Zenzar.

Ishtar

Best-known goddess in Mesopotamia (in name and character, related to the West Semitic goddess Astarte), originally a fertility figure. In her earliest manifestations she was associated with the storehouse and thus, personified as the goddess of dates, grain, wool, and meat. She evolved into a more complex character with contradictory connotations that included death, disaster, tears, fire, fair play, and enmity. Her most important attributes hence are youth, beauty, impulsiveness, fertility, readiness to fight, and procreation, but not motherhood. In Sumerian mythology, she is the daughter of the moon and wind goddess Nanna and the sun god Oroe Sjamasj and, as such, associated with Venus, the morning star. As a goddess of Venus, delighting in bodily love, Ishtar was the protectress of prostitutes and the alehouse. She was also the goddess of rain and thunderstorms and often pictured with a lion whose roar resembled thunder. Her holy symbol was the pentacle. As the morning star signals the advent of a new day, Ishtar's pentacle became a magical sign that protects against the evil eye, demons, and spirits that cause illnesses in humans and animals.

Isis

Egyptian goddess of motherhood. Protectress of mother, child, and the family. Later, she was worshipped as goddess-queen next to god-king Osiris. She is depicted with a cow's head or horns in her headdress. Isis, as mother goddess, personifies the throne. After Osiris is killed by his hostile brother Seth, and dismembered, Isis collects his body parts and brings him back from the dead. Later, Isis became the mother of the sun-god Horus, and thus the divine mother and protector of the dead. In the Holy Roman Empire, she was celebrated in the Isis mysteries. In Egypt, her worship continued until about 552 B.C., when Emperor Justinian ordered her temples to be closed. Mary Magdalene then took over the Isis-archetype.

Jeanne d'Arc

Jeanne d'Arc (in English, Joan of Arc) was a peasant girl born in 1412 in Domrémy, France. She felt herself guided by the voices of St. Michael, St. Catherine, and St. Margaret in her mission to unify France. As such, Jeanne d'Arc is a striking example of the archetype Intuition (Juno), especially with respect to this archetype's aspect of communication with one's inner being.

Jeanne d'Arc possessed many attributes characteristic of the female visionary: extreme personal piety, a claim to direct communication with the saints, and a consequent reliance upon the individual experience of God's presence beyond the ministrations of the priesthood and the institutional church. Jeanne also displayed remarkable mental and physical courage, as well as a robust common sense. As a result, she was a direct threat to the clergy who, in the end, had her burned at the stake.

On May 30, 1430, Jeanne d'Arc was arrested. A long series of trials followed, chaired by Bishop Cauchon of Beauvais and Jean Lemaître, the vice-inquisitor of France. She was charged with heresy, mainly based on the contention that her whole attitude and behavior showed blasphemous presumption: she claimed the authority of divine revelation for her pronouncements; she professed to be assured of salvation; and she wore men's clothing. On the question of her submission to the Church, she said that the Church could not err, but that it was to God and the saints that she held herself responsible for her words and actions. The trials continued into 1431. On May 29, it was decided that, being a heretic, she would have to be executed by burning at the stake, which took place on May 30, 1431.

Almost 20 years after that, Charles VII ordered an inquiry into her trial. After several years of proceedings, her sentence was annulled in 1456.

In the following centuries, Jeanne became a focus of unity for the French people, especially in times of crisis. Jeanne was canonized by Pope Benedict XV on May 16, 1920; her feast day is May 30. The yearly national festival in her honor is held on the second Sunday in May.

Jerusalem, the New
Also called the city of resurrection. John describes in detail (in Revelations 21:9–27): "Jerusalem, the holy city, coming down out of heaven from God with the glory of God." It is a transparent, cube-shaped city, floating free in space. The New Jerusalem has a systematic structure based on the numbers 3, 4, 6, 8, 12, and 12^2 (Revelation 21:9–27).

Joseph of Arimathea
A rich man, member of the Sanhedrin, who was secretly a follower of Jesus Christ. After Jesus' death, Joseph of Arimathea asked the Roman governor Pontius Pilate for the body of Jesus so as to bury it in his own tomb cut out in the rocks. According to legend, he also brought the Grail (the cup of the Last Supper, in which Jesus' blood was received during the crucifixion) to England.

Kali
Spouse of the Hindu god Shiva. Goddess of destruction and death. She is often portrayed as a black woman surrounded by snakes. She wears a necklace with skulls and her four arms are dripping blood. In Bengal for a long time humans were sacrificed to her. Some sculptures depict the divine couple as an androgynous individual.

Karma

Sanskrit, *karman*, meaning action. A universal law of cause and effect that provides the soul with opportunities for physical, mental, and spiritual growth. The law of karma is precise in the smallest detail of body, spirit, and environment. There are many kinds of karma: individual karma, the karma of a town, national karma, international karma. All these karmas are intricately inter-related. We cannot pin down one cause, because any event can be an extremely complicated mixture of many karmas ripening together.

Karma is both the power latent within actions, and the results of our actions and expressions of will power. The moral energy of any act is preserved (in the Akashic records) and manifests later in life, or in a next incarnation.

Negative karma suppresses growth. It is generated by incorrect belief in the existence of the ego, which sets off a chain reaction with the purpose of projecting the ego's territory and preserving the quasi-safety it offers. Virtuous actions will lead to better circumstances, but the chain reaction itself can be broken and surpassed through insight and discipline. The results of our actions are often delayed even into next incarnations, our future lifetimes, irrespective of whether we incarnate forward or backward in ordinary time. The kind of life we will have in the next incarnation is determined by the nature of our actions in the current one. This is so because our life is holographically "stored" in the implicate order, where ordinary time and matter do not exist, only information-consciousness-vibrations.

Karma is not fatalistic or predetermined. It gives us the ability to create and change. It is creative because we *can* determine how and why we act, we *can* change our behavior. The past is not in our grasp, but the future *is*: our thinking and acting change the future.

Karma, through its connection with reincarnation, is incorporated in the Tarot. The traveler, through the various stages in the Tarot life cycle, plays an active role in the creation of his or her (good or bad) karma by taking moral or immoral decisions in life.

Because of its logical structure via divinatory systems, effects of gathered karma can be predicted. This happens through symbolizing the main attributes of the segments of space-time that an individual's eternity-lines are passing through, using the archetypal, psychological, and managerial information present in the arcana.

In the otherworld or afterlife, the soul, unhindered by a physical body, extrapolates its eternity-lines through space-time and defines the new existence according to its karmic inheritance. According to Tibetan Buddhism, the soul is assisted in this complicated process by reading for the deceased *The Tibetan Book of the Dead*.

Khirbat-Qumran

East of Jerusalem, 1,312 feet (400m) below sea level, on the hill slopes in the northwest of the Dead Sea, are the ruins of the old fortress Qumran. Khirbat-Qumran is situated on a white limestone plateau, 1.24 miles (2km) from the Dead Sea. It is an area where battles for sanctuary and temple treasures have been fought for centuries. In this area, in 1947, a young Bedouin discovered the first, famous Dead Sea Scrolls.

King Arthur
Legendary king of England, who would have lived in the early Middle Ages. He assembled a group of knights around him, the Knights of the Round Table. They strove for virtue and tried to find the Holy Grail. The Arthurian legends represent life in those times vividly and well, but also give a good insight into important archetypes. The real King Arthur may have lived at the end of the fifth century in Cornwall. In about 410, Sir Thomas Malory wrote *Le Mort d'Arthur*, in which the stories about King Arthur and his knights were brought together.

Korè, korai
Greek, literally girl or virgin (plural *korai*). Freestanding statue of a maiden that appeared with the beginning of Greek monumental sculpture (600–500 B.C.). Korè sculptures were inspired by Egyptian art and, to a lesser degree, Mesopotamian art. Interpreters surmise that Korai were representations of young girls in the service of goddesses. Korè is also the name of the young Greek goddess Persephone who, before her abduction to the underworld by Hades, was a grain goddess.

Kundalini
Concept from yoga and tantric teachings. Vital life power that is coiled up like a snake at the base of the spine (tail bone), waiting to be awakened by a shock, meditation, or kundalini-yoga.

Kybalion, The
Mystic and occult writing from the Freemasons concerning the hermetic philosophy of ancient Egypt and Greece, and dedicated to Hermes Trismegistus.

Lammas
Celtic Sabbath, held on August 2.

Lao Tse (Lau Tsé)
"The Old Master," a legendary figure to whom is ascribed the *Tau Teh Tjing*, the holy book of the Taoists. Lao Tse was an older contemporary of Confucius. Later, he was celebrated as the founder of Taoism.

Lasloë, Elisabeth
French Tarotist and author of the book *The Secrets of the Tarot*. In this book she works with 22 Major Arcana of the Tarot of Marseilles and expands her texts with citations of holy books such as the *Bhagavad Gita* and the Bible. She also discusses the astrological aspects of each Major Arcanum.

Law of Three

Gurdjieff and Ouspensky formulated the Law of Three, which states that, contrary to the established sciences which normally work with two diverging or polar forces, or even only one force, there is a third force, which has a reconciling and stimulating character. For anything to happen, there must be three forces (active, passive, and neutral), each being equally important. If there are only active and passive forces, nothing can happen until a third force comes along, like a catalyst, to decide which of the other two forces wins.

The third principle is very fluid, transparent, and difficult to grasp. For example, a problem is not really solved by making a choice between two alternatives. The third alternative, often hard to find, usually bears the right solution. In Christian theology we find the Law of Three in the Holy trinity: the Father, the Son, and the Holy Ghost. The *I Ching* hints at the Law of Three in hexagram 12, P'i Standstill (Stagnation), in its comment on the line at the top: "The standstill does not last forever. However, it does not cease on its own accord, the right man (third force) is needed to end it. This is the difference between a state of peace and a state of stagnation. Continuous effort is necessary to maintain peace: left to itself it would change into stagnation and disintegration . . . ."

Lemuria

Lost continent that seems to have existed at about the same time as Atlantis, but at a different location: from east Africa and Madagascar in the west to the Sunda Islands in the east and India in the north. Most of Lemuria would have sunk into the Indian Ocean. Its existence would have been proved by the geographical dispersion of living beings and fossils, and through excavations. Among others, the authors J. Churchward and W. Scott Elliott have written books about it.

Levi, Eliphas

Pseudonym of the French occultist Alphonse Louis Constant (1810–1875), who wrote about many occult subjects. He was a Freemason of the lodge *Rose du Parfait Silence*.

Light of the Cosmos

Biblical concept and general archetype that is the foundation of the eternal life and way, used in many esoteric societies. Over time, many versions evolved from the original Tarot. The common back of the cards—a monochrome color and/or line structure—points to eternity, the infinite source and foundation of all things, the Self-radiating Light. The Tarot completed deck uses an eternal fractal on the common back of the cards to indicate the Light of the Cosmos.

Lilith

Hebrew for Night Monster, also called Lilit of Lilu. She is the Babylonian-Assyrian demon of gales, the night, and seduction. In

Qabbalistic writings, she symbolizes lust and sexual seduction. A superstitious Hebrew cult associated with Lilith survived as late as the seventh century A.D.

Lilith is a very seductive female figure who, as an archetypal vamp and black-magical witch, turns out to be an abomination who seduces and kills children because she is infertile herself. Lilith was the first woman of Adam Kadmon (*kadmon* means primeval). She listened neither to Adam, who complained about her to God, nor to God, who called her to account. She left Adam to live with the vultures on the rocks. Three angels tried in vain to force her to return. She is depicted with bird claws as feet, riding Adam, as described in the strictly forbidden, apocryphal book *Lilith*.

In incantations and magical texts, Lilith is often invoked. The evil she threatened, especially against children, was said to be counteracted by wearing an amulet bearing the names of the angels.

Logos

Greek for word, the human expression of a thought or meaning. The Greek concept *logos* has many meanings, including explanation, reason, story, teaching, proof, and statement. The Greek philosophers of the Stoa, the Stoicists, held that through reasoning, humankind can come to regard the universe (both physical and moral) as logical, and that, despite appearances, it is fundamentally rational in its order and coherence. According to the Stoicists, the universe was governed by fate. Virtue—the result of a wholesome state of mind—is always beneficial and the only thing needed for happiness.

Loops, eternal

An eternal loop is a process that returns to itself and therefore in principle continues forever. For this reason an eternal loop is a depiction of and pointer to infinity.

Eternal loops appear in numerous creative forms: in three dimensions as in the Möebius strip; in the graphics of Escher, as staircases that go up and down at the same time; in computer programs as recursive procedures; in music, for example, as *Das Musikalische Opfer (The Musical Offering)* by J. S. Bach; in occultism as Ouroboros; in the Tarot as the sequence of Major Arcana. Douglas Hofstadter discusses eternal loops extensively in his book *Gödel, Escher, Bach: an Eternal Golden Braid*.

Lullius, Raymond (Ramon Llull)

Spanish contemplative theologian, philosopher, and physicist who livd from 1235 to 1315. He was a mystic and poet whose writings (in Catalan, Arabic, and Latin) widely influenced Neoplatonic mysticism throughout medieval and seventeenth century Europe. He developed his ideas based more on reasoning than on the Bible and the Revelations. Influenced by the pacifist spirituality of St. Francis of Assisi, he traveled throughout North Africa and Asia Minor, attempting to convert Muslims to Christianity.

Lullius is best known as the inventor of the art of finding truth (*ars inveniendi veritatis*), that was primarily intended to support the Catholic faith in his missionary work, but was also designed to unify all branches of knowledge. After a mystical experience on Majorca's Mount Randa, he undertook to reduce all knowledge to what he called first principles, and determine their convergence point of unity. Lullius used logic and complex mechanical techniques (the *Ars Magna*) involving symbolic notation and combinatory diagrams to relate all forms of knowledge, including theology, philosophy, and the natural sciences, as analogues of one another and as manifestations of God in the universe. Charges of confusing faith with reason led to the condemnation of Lullius's teachings by Pope Gregory IX in 1376. In the nineteenth century, however, the Catholic Church showed more sympathetic interest and approved his veneration.

Machen, Arthur

Pseudonym of Arthur Llewelyn Jones (1863–1947), an Anglo-Welsh writer who, in his short stories, favored the supernatural and macabre. His work is the precursor of twentieth century Gothic science fiction.

Mandala

Sanskrit, meaning circle. In its most elevated form, a sacred circle that mirrors an illuminated state of consciousness through a strong symbolic pattern, making the invisible visible. Mandalas in beautiful colors and figures symbolize cosmologies concerning human nature, the universe, the construction of the world or universe, etc. By focusing on a mandala, both the mandala artist and meditator can open to divine energies and to their own spiritual and psychological selves. Mandalas, drawn and used in all cultures, are commonly used in Buddhism and Tantrism, and by the Navajo Indians.

Mantra

Sanskrit for means of transport. Word, syllable, sound, or sentence that contains the name of the Godhead, the principle, chakra, or arcanum. A mantra when spoken, sung, or repeated in silent meditation, transports a human to the highest regions of his or her being.

Marseilles Tarot

An often-used version of the Tarot of which the oldest cards date back to the sixteenth century. It consists of 78 cards, and is hence not restored (to number 80).

Materia Prima

The Latin word *materia,* meaning matter, is related to the word *mater*, which means mother. Prima is the feminine form of the word *primus*, meaning first. The Materia Prima is the foundation for the alchemistic pyramid (the seven chakras of humankind).

This foundation, which supports the first chakra, is formed by an individual's previous lives. In a cosmological sense, Materia Prima is the very heavy matter that was present at the beginning of creation.

Memento Mori
By means of the aphorism *Memento Mori*, meaning remember that you will die, sepulchral monuments from antiquity and the Middle Ages emphasize death and the impossibility of making up for mistakes after death, the irrevocable degradation (of the body) after death, and the judgment of the soul. The antonym of this aphorism is *Carpe Diem*, or seize the day.

Merlin
Legendary Celtic Druid and sage, seer and wizard in British sagas and novels from about A.D. 600–1200. In very old manuscripts Merlin is portrayed as a giant and builder of megalithic Stonehenge, but his name is better known from the legends about King Arthur and the Knights of the Round Table. In Welsh, *Myrrdin*.

Mesmer, Anton
Franz Anton Mesmer, Austrian medical practitioner (1734–1815). Developed a theory about a force, which he called "animal magnetism" with which he cured many illnesses. His method was called "mesmerism" and was the precursor of therapeutic hypnosis.

Mexican sundial (sunstone)
An Aztec astrological and mythological calendar and sacrificial table cut out of basalt in Mexico, which dates from the fifteenth century A.D. The circular stone has a diameter of 11.8 feet (3.6m), weighs 24 tons, and contains a large number of ornaments and hieroglyphs. The central ornament is the rules of the universe. Tonatiuh, the sun, is surrounded by the symbols of the four Aztec ante-worlds and their respective suns, and the 20 calendar days. It is remarkable that the symbols of the four ante-worlds and the 20 calendar days are depicted in a counterclockwise fashion. The Mexican sundial and the Tarot mandala are examples of pictorial, circular cosmologies.

Minoic writing
Also called linear A, the writing from the time of the Minoic kingdom on Crete (1600 B.C.) was preserved on clay tablets. Deciphering this writing is still very difficult because of the sudden, enigmatic disappearance of the Minoic culture, perhaps caused by the volcanic explosion of Thera, a volcanic island nearby.

Mithras
Sanskrit, *mitra*, old Aryan god of light, guardian of the cosmic order, and protector of treaties, who rode the life-bringing bull. The first written mention of Mitra in the *Vedas* dates to 1400 B.C.

He is mentioned also in the Persian Avesta (sacred book of Zoroastrianism, containing its account of the origin of the universe). In the Hellenic world, Mithras was identified with the sun-god Helios.

According to myth, Mithras was born bearing a torch and armed with a knife beside a sacred stream and under a sacred tree, a child of the earth itself. He soon rode, and later killed the life-giving cosmic bull, whose blood fertilizes all vegetation. Mithras' slaying of the bull was a popular subject of Hellenic art and became the prototype for a bull-slaying ritual of fertility in the Mithras cult.

Mithras cultures became widely distributed over India, Persia, the Celts, the Hellenic world, and the Roman Empire. Alexander the Great's ventures in Asia Minor and the Middle East spread the Mithras cult throughout the region. In the third and fourth centuries A.D., Roman soldiers carried and supported the cult as far West as Spain, Great Britain, and Germany.

It is inferred that the Spanish (and Italian) bullfights are reminiscent of Mithraic bull-slaying rituals. Interestingly, the mainly Roman Catholic Spanish people have integrated this aspect of Mithraic cult into their lives, whereas once, during the Roman Empire, the Mithras cult was the chief rival to the newly developing Christianity. The Celtic sun cult (the circle in the Celtic cross represents the sun's orbit around the sky) is also related to the Mithras cult.

Moon phase

The moon phase is the angle between the sun and the moon at the moment of birth. A person's moon phase is closely related to, and calculated in the same way as the *Pars Fortunae*, a Latin term meaning point of fortune. In a horoscope the *pars* marks the place where the moon would be if, at the moment of birth, the sun were rising at the horizon. (There is a corresponding *pars* for each planet but these are not normally calculated in a horoscope.)

Moon phase psychology

Moon phase psychology distinguishes 24 character types with regard to social involvement. The authors of this book have correlated these 24 types with the 24 Major Arcana. Moon phase psychology was developed in the 1950s by J. van Slooten and E. Parker. The moon phase is the angle measured from the earth in degrees between the sun and the moon. It expresses the general attitudes of individuals, what roles they play, and what missions they have in society. It does not express their talents or behavior towards others.

The 24 different societal types determined by moon phase psychology break down into people born around new moon (345° to 5°), who are analytically inclined, somewhat aloof, and sober. People born around full moon (175° to 195°) are romantic, warm-hearted, and gregarious. People born around the first quarter moon (85° to 105°) manifest by doing something themselves (for example, Albert Schweitzer); people born around the last quarter moon (255° to 285°) are working out what others have to do (for example, Winston Churchill).

The moon phases 0° to 180° represent the period of development until complete maturity (the first 12 Major Arcana). The moon phases 180° to 360° cover the decline and end of life (the second 12 Major Arcana).

Morphogenetic field

A term first proposed in the 1920s and now widely used by developmental biologists. A morphogenetic field is a region of influence capable of generating form, carrying information only (no detectable energy) and available throughout time and space without any loss of intensity after they have been created. In his book, *A New Science of Life* (1982), Rupert Sheldrake took what were fairly loose ideas about morphogenetic fields and formulated them into a testable theory. According to him, morphogenetic fields are created by patterns of physical forms, including biological systems as well as crystals, and help guide the formation of later, similar systems.

Mouseion, Museum

Mouseion is the Greek term for the seat of the Muses. It designated a philosophical institution or place of contemplation. The great legendary museum at Alexandria was founded around 280 B.C. by the Macedonian general Ptolemy I Soter who, after the death of Alexander the Great, concerned himself with the government of Egypt. With its college of scholars and its library, this museum probably was more a prototype university than an institution to preserve and interpret material aspects of heritage.

Neaniskos

Member of a special, initiated group to which belonged both Jesus Christ and Apollonius of Tyana (Appollonius was a mythical hero who lived in Tyana, Cappadocia, and who is said to have been much like Jesus in having performed miracles). Neaniskos would have been witness to the drama that took place after the Last Supper. During Jesus' capture in the Garden of Gethsemane, all the apostles fled, but Neaniskos stayed with Jesus with a white burial cloth wrapped around his naked body. When Neaniskos was caught, he fled naked, leaving the cloth in the hands of the soldiers (Mark 14:51–52). Later, at the grave of Jesus, he was a witness to Jesus' resurrection and told Mary Magdalene and Mary the mother of James about it (Mark 16:5–6). Waite chose the image of the mourning Neaniskos as the central person in the Minor Arcanum Five of Cups.

Nidanas, the Twelve

Nidana is Sanskrit for link. In Buddhism, the 12 Nidanas are the 12 links in an individual's process of becoming. The 12 states of a human caught in the chain of cause and effect are shown in famous paintings of the ego-demon holding the Wheel of Life.

The 12 Nidanas as concepts and as a cycle are closely related to the 24 Major Arcana of the Tarot:

1. *Avidya:* Innocence; existence in isolation (The Fool/ The Magician).
2. *Samskara:* Karmic formations are given form through striving (The Priestess/The Emperor).
3. *Vynana:* Development of feelings (The Lovers/Intuition).
4. *Nama-Rupa:* Feelings mature into personality; unity of body and soul (The Priest The Empress).
5. *Sadayatana:* Personality develops the five senses, and consciousness (The Chariot/The Hermit).
6. *Sparsa:* The five senses and consciousness are making contact with the outside world (Justice/The World).
7. *Vedana:* Contact intensifies perceptions (Strength/ The Hanged Man).
8. *Trisna:* Perceptions cause desire (Temperance/Death).
9. *Upadana:* Desire causes attachment (The Devil/Truth).
10. *Bhava:* Attachment strengthens the need for becoming-and-maintaining (The Tower/The Moon).
11. *Jati:* Holding one's own leads to regeneration and reincarnation (The Star/The Sun).
12. *Marana:* Regeneration maintains suffering and death and makes one return to the first phase of the life cycle (The Last Judgment/The Universe). Nirvana is reached by letting go of the Wheel of Life.

Nirvana

Sanskrit for blown out or extinct. In Buddhism it signifies the transcendent state of liberation and freedom achieved by the extinction of desire and of individual consciousness. According to the Buddhist analysis of the human situation, egocentricity and its resultant desires delude humankind and bind it to a continuous round of rebirths and consequent suffering. It is release of these bonds, complete non-identification with any worldly matters and the 12 causes of existence (the 12 Nidanas) that constitute Enlightenment, or Nirvana experience. This is a state of complete rest and perfect peace, in which every form of existence has been made impossible through termination of reincarnation. In most cases, nirvana can only be reached after death, but some holy persons achieve it during life.

Obsessor, obsession

A soul's eternity-line may become joined with another soul's eternity-line. In such a case, the soul to whom the second eternity-line belongs, invades and starts a symbiotic existence with the host, the soul and owner of the first eternity-line. The invading soul is called an *obsession* or *obsessor*. As the host-soul has accepted the symbiosis with the invading soul-obsessor, the host-soul is also the one who can end the symbiosis once it has identified the obsessor and qualified its influence as parasitic, unproductive, and destructive. Then, the host-soul can sever its own time-line from the other by a conscious mental act of politely sending the obsessor away.

Occultism

Derived from the Latin word *occultus*, which means hidden or secret. Occultism is the collective name for the teachings and practices of certain persons and groups of people who claim to have knowledge of a science or doctrine accessible only to its adepts or initiates. In antiquity there were mysteries and their initiations. In the Middle Ages, for example, the Qabbalists and alchemists were said to have a secret science. Modern forms of occultism are found in the Rosicrucians, anthroposophy, spiritism, theosophy, channeling, and classical homoeopathy.

Odin (Wodan)

The Scandinavian supreme god was Odin (the West Germans called him Wodan). He lived with his wife Freya in Valhalla (heaven). These deities can be compared with Zeus and Hera, and Jupiter and Juno, from Greek and Roman mythology, respectively. Odin is described extensively in *The Eddas*, an old Norwegian heroic saga that dates from about A.D. 800–1250. Best known is Odin's rune song, in which he sacrifices himself by nailing himself with his spear to the world-tree, Yggdrasil (like Jesus Christ on the cross). Over the next six days, he discovers the runes by observing the branches falling from Yggdrasil (an ash tree). Odin, not surprisingly, also was the god of wisdom and poetry.

Oedipus

In Greek, *oidipous* means swollen foot. Oedipus is the best-known hero in the sagas about the ancient Greek city, Thebes, and the central figure in three plays by the Greek playwright, Sophocles.

When Oedipus is born, it is prophesied that one day he will kill his father, the Theban king. His distraught father tries to stop this from happening by putting needles through Oedipus' feet, so that he cannot walk, and then giving his son to a shepherd with an order to kill him. However, the shepherd fails to kill the child. After growing up as the foster-child of another king, Oedipus, under attack by a group of travelers, unknowingly kills his father, a member of the attacking group. Next, he solves the riddle proposed by the Sphinx to each traveler on the way to Thebes; at this, the Sphinx kills itself. Eventually, Oedipus becomes the king of Thebes and unknowingly marries his widowed mother. He has four children with her and rules Thebes for many years. When prompted by the blind seer Tiresias, Oedipus ultimately discovers the crimes he has unknowingly committed. He resigns the throne, blinds himself with pins, and departs Thebes, guided by his daughter Antigone.

Ondine

Female water spirit, also called Undine. Derived from the Latin word *unda* (French *onde*), which means wave.

Onvlee, Jo

Dutch Gurdjieff worker, Tarotist, astrologer and Tai Chi master.

Orare

Latin verb meaning to speak or to pray, related to the Latin word for mouth, *ora*. The word oracle is derived from the verb *orare*.

Osiris

The most important king-god in the old Egyptian religion. Osiris was the father-god and the personification of the spontaneous creating power of all life that arises from death. Osiris combined features of several older gods. With the advent of (written) history, he was connected to the goat shepherd god Anedti from Boesiris in the Nile delta from whom he took over the shepherd's staff and whip (flagellum). The whip was also an attribute of the god-idea Baal, Hammon, Iawahh, and Abraxas. Both staff and whip became attributes of the kings of Egypt, who were said to represent Osiris in the world of the living. Later, Osiris was worshipped next to his sister and spouse, Isis. Iconographically, he was depicted as an ithyphallic mummy, thus marking the conservation of his procreative powers after death. Osiris also symbolized the beginning of Egyptian culture.

In primordial times, when gods and half-gods (extra-terrestrial beings) were among the beings on this planet, Osiris, as one of them, would have brought the Egyptians their civilization. On a wooden coffin in the third pyramid of Giza (the fourth dynasty, 2930–2750 B.C.) is written: "Hail, Osiris King of the North and the South Men-Kau-Ra, who lives eternally. The heavens have brought you forth. You were born from Nut (the sky). You are the fruit of Geb (the earth). Your mother Nut, a being of divine mystery, expands herself over you. She has allowed you to be a god, you will never have enemies, king of the North and the South, Men-Kau-Ra, who lives forever."

Ouroboros

Emblematic serpent of ancient Egypt and Greece, represented with its tail in its mouth, continually devouring itself and being reborn from itself. This is one of the oldest symbols of the universe, eternity and *materia prima*. This Gnostic and alchemistic symbol expresses the unity of all things, material and spiritual, which never disappears, but perpetually changes form in an eternal cycle of destruction and recreation. A beautiful picture of the Ouroboros with the text "the one who hides the hours" is found in the second coffin of Tutankhamun (1330 B.C.).

Ouspensky, P. D.

Piotr Demianowitsch Ouspensky (1878–1947) was born in Moscow. The first book of this philosophical and psychological writer, *The Fourth Dimension* (1909), offered a contribution to mathematical theory. It was in *Tertium Organum* (1912) and *A New Model of the*

Universe (1914) that he revealed his stature as a thinker and his deep preoccupation with the problems of human existence. His meeting with G. I. Gurdjieff in 1915 was a turning point in his life. From this time on, his interest centered on the practical study of methods for the development of consciousness in humankind. Ouspensky worked with Gurdjieff for many years as a student and close follower.

Ouspensky has recorded and commented with astounding precision and clarity on numerous discussions between Gurdjieff and his students. In his book, *A New Model of the Universe*, first published in 1931, Ouspensky dedicated chapter five entirely to a discussion of the symbolism in the Tarot. Both Gurdjieff and Ouspensky died at the end of the 1940s.

Panta Rhei
Aphorism of the early Greek philosopher Heraclitus, stating that everything flows or is in perpetual movement, representing the briefest summary of his teachings. Heraclitus lived in Ephesus from the sixth to fifth century B.C.

Papus
Pseudonym of the French doctor and prominent occultist Gérard Encausse (1865–1916). Author of *Le Tarot des Bohémiens* (1889), he was a member of the Ordre Qabbalistique du Rose Croix.

Parcival
One of the knights of King Arthur and the person who, in the Grail legends, finds the Holy Grail.

Pauli, Wolfgang
Swiss physicist (1900–1958). He wrote the first standard work about the theory of relativity. In 1945 he received the Nobel Prize for his contribution to the development of quantum mechanics. Pauli is famous for his formulation of the *exclusion principle* in 1925, which asserts that no two fermions in a closed system (e.g., an atom) can be at the same time in the same state or configuration (way and speed of rotation). Fermions are a particular class of sub-atomic particles to which electrons also belong.

Pentacle
Figure formed by the diagonals of a regular pentagram (the Greek word *penta* means five, *grammè* is line), that of a five-pointed star. It is also called *pentalpha*, as the letter "A" can be read in it five times.

The pentacle is a very old symbol. In Babylon it was the holy symbol of the goddess of war and sexual love, Ishtar. Ishtar was associated with Venus and the morning star, which signals the advent of a new day when demons lose their power. The pentacle became a magical sign protecting against the "evil eye" that causes illness in humans and animals, and in general expresses rulership of the spirit over air-demons, fire-ghosts, water-spooks, and earth shades.

The pentacle is also known as the *Signum Pythagoricum* (sign of the Pythagoreans). Because of its pure mathematical—thus sound—construction, it became the symbol of spiritual and physical health. In the Renaissance, the archetypal pentacle, being the sign of the Pythagoreans as well as Ishtar's holy sign against demons and illnesses, developed into a general medical emblem symbolizing health, widely used by medical guilds and pharmacists until well into the nineteenth century. The Pentacle, as a "blueprint" of the human body and soul, summarizes physical and spiritual movements in and around its existence.

Pergamon

Town in Mysia, 16 miles from the Aegean Sea on a lofty, isolated hill on the northern side of the valley of the Caicus River. Its present name is Bergama (in the province of Izmir in Turkey). Pergamon existed from at least the fifth century B.C. It became important in the Hellenistic Age, from 323 until 130 B.C., when it was the capital city of the kingdom of the Attalides. Pergamon was one of the most important and beautiful of all Greek cities, and is one of the most outstanding examples of city planning of that period. Its library was excelled only by that of Alexandria. After Rome fell, the Byzantines ruled it. In 716, the city and its library with 200,000 parchment rolls were destroyed by the Arabs. In the fourteenth century, it passed into Ottoman hands.

Persephone

Greek goddess of the underworld; in her youth also called Korè, the young grain goddess, daughter of Zeus and Demeter, the goddess of agriculture. In Homer's work, *Hymn to Demeter*, the story is told of how young Persephone was gathering flowers when she was seized by Hades and abducted to the underworld of which she was, from then on, the queen. After learning of her abduction of her daughter, Demeter became so oblivious to the harvest in her misery that widespread famines ensued. Zeus then commanded Hades to release Persephone to her mother. But Persephone could not return full-time to the living because she had eaten in Hades' realm, reflecting a very old idea that strictly divided the food of the dead from that of the living. So Zeus decided that Persephone could live with her mother for two-thirds of the year (Spring, Summer, and part of Autumn) and for one third with Hades (the remaining part of Autumn and Winter).

The story of Persephone's abduction, disappearance, and return parallels fertility myths of western Asia. She may well have been a pre-Greek goddess, worshipped by early settlers in the country, and only later incorporated into the religion. Persephone's transformations are the cornerstone of the Eleusian mysteries about the supra-conscious and unconscious.

Phaeton

Phaeton was the son of the Greek sun-god Helios. When at last Phaeton was allowed to drive his father's sun cart across the sky, he rode so fast that he lost control, causing droughts and heat waves on earth. Zeus stopped him with a thunderbolt that sent Phaeton crashing to earth. His sisters wept for him and metamorphosed into poplars; their tears became drops of amber.

Pharisees
A fundamentalist Hebrew sect from about 100 B.C. until A.D. 100. As did the Essenes, the Pharisees meticulously observed the Law of Moses and the Torah. However, contrary to the Essenes' ascetic life, the Pharisees worshipped in temples and lived a public life. The New Testament describes in several places the verbal battle of Jesus Christ with the Pharisees concerning their shortsighted fundamentalism.

Phoenix
Legendary ancient Egyptian bird said to have lived five centuries in the desert, then to be consumed in fire of its own making, and subsequently rising in youthful freshness from its own ashes. Often regarded as an emblem of immortality, eternal life, and of (Christ's) resurrection.

Priest-Scientist
At one time science was considered priestly and royal, as priest-scientists ruled over souls and had the skills and inclination to study others. The real priest guides the fellow human to liberation.

Psychokinesis
Movement of objects without material interference. From the Greek words *psychè*, meaning spirit, and *kinèsis*, movement. Para-psychological phenomenon of influencing matter by thoughts and feelings.

Pyramid, the Great
Of Mesopotamian origin, the Chaldean-Hebrew name for the Great Pyramid aptly is *parim-middin*, meaning light-measures. Pyramids are monumental structures, built mostly for funerary purposes. The Great Pyramid of Khufu at Giza is a beacon of reflections and a monument of measures. It demonstrates an astounding number of mathematical, geometrical, astronomical, and geological facts. One of the secrets of the Great Pyramid is in its form: a geometrical shape that has a square base measuring 755 by 755 feet (230 by 230m); the planes on the sides coming together at the angle of 51° 49' 38," following the Golden Rule of Proportions, or the Golden Mean.

Pyrrhic victory
Pyrrhus was a Hellenistic king of Epirus (319–272 B.C.). Driven by ambition to establish a great empire in the western part of the Mediterranean Sea, he fought many battles against the Romans. In 280 he crossed to Italy with 25,000 soldiers and defeated the

Romans decisively at Heraclea, but at great cost. In 279 he defeated the Romans again, this time at Ausculum in Apulia, again suffering heavy casualties. In 278 he conquered most of Sicily. In 275 he suffered heavy losses in a battle against Rome at Benevento. He was killed in a night skirmish in the streets of Argos. Pyrrhus' costly military successes gave rise to the phrase "Pyrrhic victory."

Pythagoreans

A philosophical school and religious brotherhood, believed to be founded by Pythagoras around 525 B.C. Their main contribution is their theory of numbers, which holds that at its deepest level, reality is mathematical in nature. They applied number relationships to music theory, acoustics, geometry, and astronomy, and prescribed certain secret cultic practices. Pythagoreanism deeply influenced the development of classical Greek philosophy and medieval European thought.

Qabbala

Hebrew secret teaching that presents itself as a very old revelation, handed down via an unbroken chain of initiations since the second century B.C. The Qabbala teaches, among other things, that all that lives is the expression of a great process of divine self-expression. According to the Qabbala, each letter of the Hebrew alphabet (which also has a numerical power) has a divine meaning. An important Qabbalistic mandala is the Tree of Life, a two-dimensional arrangement of ten centers depicting divine forces.

Quantum mechanics

Theory about physical phenomena that happen on a very small (sub)atomic scale. Today's quantum mechanics was developed in the years 1923–1927, but its origins date back to about 1900. Max Planck theorized that the transfer of energy between matter and electromagnetic radiation happens in discrete quantities. Einstein expanded this hypothesis to the theory that radiation itself consists of energy quanta. Since then, the quantum principle has been applied in all fields of the natural sciences that concern themselves with processes on a (sub)atomic scale, such as quantum chemistry. Together, these applications of quantum mechanics are called quantum theory.

One of the philosophical consequences of quantum theory is the notion that the universe in essence is paradoxical and alogical in nature: matter may behave as, and change into, energy waves, and energy waves may change into matter. Both processes happen on a grand scale everywhere. For instance, in an atomic bomb and nuclear reactor, matter is transformed into energy; the same conversion takes place in the sun and the stars.

Quichés

A tribe belonging to the Mayas in the highlands of Guatemala. The Quichés are the only Mayas who have a written literature. Their holy book is *Popul Vuh*, written in Quiché.

Recursion

Latin, meaning a course that runs backwards or a back reference. A process or function in which a rule refers to that same process itself. If no precautions are taken or no limits are set, a recursion will repeat endlessly. Recursive structures are applied in music (such as in J. S. Bach's fugues), visual arts (many of Escher's drawings), and in computer programs. When a recursive procedure is executed in a computer program, an endless loop is prevented from happening by writing into the recursion a command to terminate itself after a variable has reached a particular value.

Reiki

Derived from the Japanese words *rei*, meaning universal, and *ki*, or life energy. A Japanese method of healing in which universal life energy is transferred to the patient via the hands. By spiritually tuning into this life energy, the healer is filled with it, after which the healing energy can be transferred to the patient.

Reincarnation

From the Latin words *re*, meaning return, and *incarnare*, or becoming flesh. Also called transmigration or metempsychosis. In religion and philosophy, the rebirth of the soul after death in another body to live another life. While belief in reincarnation is most characteristic of Asian religions and philosophies, it also appears in ancient African and Middle Eastern religions, the Greek orphic mysteries, Manichaeism, and Gnosticism, as well as in modern religious movements, such as theosophy.

Among the ancient Greeks, orphism held that a pre-existent soul survives bodily death and is later reincarnated in a human or mammalian body, eventually being released from the cycle of birth and death and regaining its former, pure state. Plato, in the fifth and fourth centuries B.C., believed in an immortal soul that undertakes frequent incarnations.

The main Asian religions that believe in reincarnation all arose in India and have in common the universal law of karma. Karma is inevitable and infallible. Whenever we harm others, we are directly harming ourselves. Whenever we bring happiness, we are bringing ourselves future happiness. The belief in reincarnation implies that there is progress, ultimate justice, and goodness in the universe. Reincarnation and karma are directly related. "There is no need for temples; no need for complicated philosophy. Our brain, our own heart, is our temple; my philosophy is kindness" (the Dalai Lama).

Rosicrucian Order

Fraternity of Rosicrucians, named after a small group of Lutheran scientists founded by Christian Rosenkreutz (1378–1484). During the seventeenth and eighteenth centuries, many Rosicrucian fraternities emerged. They were alchemistically inclined, but also had humanitarian and Christian interests. The German order of Geld und Rosenkreutzer was one of the most important, especially in middle Europe. The order was organized in nine degrees and kept close links with the Freemasons; it was dissolved, however, by the end of the eighteenth century. In the United States, the order revived after 1909, thanks to the efforts of Spencer Lewis. Since then, the movement has had many members all over the world.

Runes, runes alphabet

The Gothic word *rune* means secret or mystery. Runes was a writing system of uncertain origin used by Scandinavian, Icelandic, Germanic, Old English, and Celtic tribes in northern Europe from the third until the sixteenth century.

There are two basic types of runes, Nordic and Celtic. Although the letter symbols of both Nordic and Celtic runes are built up from straight lines, they symbolize different letters and sounds and have different names. The systems of runic writing have different histories. Nonetheless, they were both derived from the Phoenician alphabet that evolved in the first millennium B.C.

Nordic runes were developed from the Etruscan alphabet of northern Italy by the Goths, a Germanic tribe. The letters after the first six are also called *futhark*. There are at least three main types of Nordic runes: Germanic runes were used in northern Europe before A.D. 800; Anglian runes were used in Britain from the fifth until the twelfth century A.D., and Nordic runes were used from the eighth until the thirteenth century in Scandinavia and Iceland. The three types have different numbers of letters.

Nordic and Celtic runes were—and still are—used for signs, poems, and predictions, but have never been a spoken language.

Scientism

Positivistic movement that became prominent especially in the second half of the nineteenth century. Scientism rejects religion and metaphysics and the possibility of divine revelation. During the first half of the twentieth century, interest in scientism receded strongly because of renewed interest in metaphysics. This interest was triggered by quantum-mechanical and nuclear-physical discoveries, which forced rethinking of the foundations of the natural sciences and their methods of investigation and conjecture.

Self-hypnosis

Hypnotic state generated by the individual. Also called autohypnosis.

Serapeum

Name of the temple of the Hellenistic-Egyptian god Serapis. The burial place of the holy Apis bulls at Memphis is also called Serapeum. In the Serapea lived hermits whose oracle dreams and predictions were very highly valued. The famous Serapeum of Alexandria was destroyed by Christians in A.D. 391.

Shiva

From Sanskrit, the Auspicious One. An important, ambiguous Indian godhead from the Vedanta who combines contradictory opposites. On the one hand, he is unpredictable and destructive; on the other, the creator. He is both the ascetic and the symbol of sensuality. He rides the cosmic bull Nanda. Dancing, he maintains the universe. The archetype that Hinduism regards as Shiva is also the central figure in the Major Arcanum The Universe. The female consort of Shiva is the goddess Kali.

Sirius, the Dog Star (in Canis Major)
Brightest star visible from earth. Also called the Dog Star because of its location in the stellar constellation Canis Major (the Dog). Due to the archetypal relationship of the dog/jackal with death, Sirius has long been associated with death and reincarnation. In the Tarot, Sirius is present in the arcana The Chariot and The Star.

Sirius consists of the very bright star Sirius A, and a very small, heavy, white dwarf star, Sirius B (also called Digitaria). Sirius B is invisible to the naked eye, and was not discovered until the nineteenth century. It is remarkable that both stars and their orbits were known by the old African Dogon tribes and the Egyptian and Sumerian civilizations. It is alleged that these civilizations received their knowledge from living beings from Sirius, or one of its planets.

Smith, Pamela Coleman
Friend of Sir Arthur Edward Waite and member of the Order of the Golden Dawn. In close cooperation with Waite, Pamela drew a new, modernized set of Tarot cards, the Rider-Waite Tarot deck, in 1910. This deck is the most used Tarot deck in the world.

Solar Plexus
The third chakra. The Latin word plexus means braided. The solar plexus is a network of blood vessels and nerves that have an important role in conveying sensations to the brain. It is located just above the navel.

Solomon
Hebrew Shlomo, son and successor of David, and traditionally regarded as the greatest king of Judea, who lived around the tenth century B.C. It is believed that he received his wisdom directly from God so that he would judge in the best possible way.

Sophia
From the Greek word sophos, meaning wisdom. Sophia was the personification of the female aspect of God. Initially, Christianity's main emphasis was on inner life and development. When the Church in the later centuries became power hungry, this knowledge was hidden so that people would not strive for unity with the Supreme Being and had to use the Church as the highest mediator between God and sinning humankind. The obfuscation of the yin-yang and animus-anima principles, in the Tarot represented by the two Major Arcana Jupiter (Truth) and Juno (Intuition), was a direct consequence.

Sophocles

Sophocles (born in 496 B.C. in Colonus and deceased in 406 B.C. in Athens) was a playwright, philosopher, and general. Of the 123 plays attributed to him, only seven have remained intact. Three of these are set in mythical Thebes, the city with seven gates. In chronological order they are: *Antigone, Oedipus the King,* and *Oedipus at Colonus. Oedipus the King* is the best-known drama; it deals with the irreconcilable guilt and innocence of King Oedipus. The blind seer Tiresias plays a key role in it. Even today, Sophocles' mystical and psychological plays invite analysis at a level that has occurred only with the plays *Hamlet* and *Faust.*

Space-Time

Another word for four-dimensional space. All events that have happened, are to happen, or may happen in creation—all universes together—form space-time. Ouspensky points out that, strictly speaking, since space-time exists by itself endlessly, it must have a fifth dimension as a parameter to indicate its existential position. Space-time and its fifth dimension together are *eternity.*

In our world our consciousness perceives time and space as being separated. To a soul after death or in a near-death experience, this separation ceases. People who have gone through a near-death experience (such as Stefan von Jankovich, described by P. Andreas in *Die phantastische wissenchaft*), say they have experienced four-dimensional space, but are unable to represent it with earthly tools or instruments.

Most of us cannot create a mental picture of space-time, the main problem being the lack of a well-defined time perspective. An analogy that may help is a CD on which a musical piece is condensed in space-time in such a linear way that we can "see" the recorded piece in one glance. In this analogy, a CD player is a device that splits up the linear-recorded music into a series of material and spatial airwaves that progress through space and time and reach our eardrums one after another. Our mind recreates the music the way the composer heard it in his or her mind the first time.

Regarding the nature of space-time: Einstein stated that matter is a form of energy. Therefore, it seems logical to conjecture that space-time is some form of energy as well.

It is surmised that every human's soul perceives space-time without actually separating time and space. Most humans have a (very) limited capacity to be conscious of their soul's perceptions of space-time. Intuition is the filtering through of the soul's perceptions of space-time into our consciousness. Psychics are considered to have enhanced space-time perception, or rather, a more open channel for the soul's perceptions of space-time to pass through.

Time-travel, being an instantaneous repositioning of an entity in space-time, likely involves sudden changes in energy levels. Dean Koontz, in his fascinating novel *Lightning* (1988), describes the sudden energy changes that presumably accompany time-travel.

The Tarot can be considered a mental classification of similar eternity points in space-time. Psychics and diviners use the Tarot and other divinatory systems to verbalize their perceptions of space-time.

Stone, the Philosopher's
Alchemistic concept, in Latin called *Lapis Philosophum*. To the Philosopher's Stone were attributed enormous powers: it could give eternal youth as well as turn common compounds into gold. Alchemists tried all sorts of combinations of materials to find the Philosopher's Stone so as to produce gold. Often mercury and lead were involved, both because of their heaviness and the colorful red, orange, and yellow compounds that these elements produced when heated (oxidized). Though the alchemists did not succeed in discovering the Philosopher's Stone nor a way of making gold, on the way, they discovered many important chemical processes. So in a way, the failure to produce the Philosopher's Stone led to the discoveries that formed the cornerstones of modern chemistry. The Philosopher's Stone is also seen as a mystical entity that could improve human nature; in alchemistic writings, mostly written as allegory, the two meanings were often intertwined.

Stonehenge
Megalithic cosmological structure on the Salisbury Plains in the south of England. The megalithic monument itself was built in three distinct phases over a period of about 1,700 years. This long time span is astounding in itself and clearly indicates that high intelligences must have managed the construction. From 2800 to 2000 B.C., several concentric circular banks of earth were built, as well as a straight wide roadway to the Avon River, now called The Avenue. Phase 2 began around 2100 B.C. and was carried out by the Beaker folk. They erected 80 large bluish stones in two incomplete rings in the center of the monument. These stones came from the Preseli mountains in southwest Wales, 130 miles (209km) away. They were brought most of the way by water through a network of rivers and then overland from Amesbury to Stonehenge via The Avenue. Phase 3 was carried out by early Bronze Age people; it took them from about 2000 until 1100 B.C. They removed the bluestone circle and put up in the center five very tall trilithons weighing over 45 tons each. Then, they set up a ring of about 30 sandstone uprights (each averaging 30 tons in weight), linked by stone lintels around the central edifice. Finally, they re-erected the bluestones in two groups, one inside the horseshoe of five trilithons and the other outside it.

J. J. Hurtak states in *The Keys of Enoch* (1977) that Stonehenge was built by a group of high intelligences named the priesthood of On. Their purpose was to create ". . . geophysical time models linking the destiny of the earth with specific programs of higher intelligence. It is a place where the soul is fed a taste of the infinite source of Light." It is asserted that the priesthood of On also guided the construction of the great pyramids.

Today it is assumed that Stonehenge was a Druidic temple for sky and fertility worship, as well as a calendar and astronomical instrument. On Midsummer Day, the shadow of the Heel stone (positioned outside the outer ring) formed by the rising sun penetrates right into the womb-shaped center of Stonehenge.

Swastika

Derived from the Sanskrit word *svastika*, meaning conducive to well-being or happiness. The swastika as a symbol of prosperity and good fortune is widely distributed throughout all ancient and modern cultures in Europe and Asia, as well in North, Central, and South America.

The swastika places a cross, symbolizing the spirit and light, inside a circle, symbolizing the universe and matter. Through revolution, matter is elevated to spirit.

According to Churchward, the swastika was originally a Lemurian symbol that was spread over the world via Atlantis. "Stolen" by the German Thule Society, this divine symbol was abused by the national socialists from 1930 to 1945.

Sufism

This word is linked to the Greek word *sophia*, which means wisdom, and the Arabic word *suf*, meaning wool. This refers to the pure white woolen garment worn by some sufis.

Sufism is very old. It arose as a movement in Persia in the seventh century A.D. among pious Muslims as a reaction against the worldliness of early Islam. In its yearning for a personal union with God, Sufism found Islamic law too divorced from a personal theology. In the thirteenth century A.D., Sufism spread from Persia and the Middle East to India. Sufism has since synthesized religious elements from the east and the west. Religious and mystical influences which it has incorporated spring from many traditions, among them, Neoplatonism, Hermeticism, Byzantine Christianity, Zoroastrianism, Buddhism, and Vedanta.

After 1910, Sufism became a substantial world movement through the efforts and travels of the musician and Sufi mystic Hazrat Inayat Khan (born 1882 in Baroda, India, died in Delhi, India, 1927). The international Sufi Movement was incorporated in Geneva in 1923.

Sufism positions itself as universal: the various forms of the religion are all based on the same true wisdom, notwithstanding their external differences in some aspects. Sufism emphasizes being human—the ideal is love, harmony, and beauty. Its formal goals are:

• to actualize and spread universal knowledge and the religion of love and wisdom, so prejudices may fall away, the human heart may be filled with love, and all hatred may be eradicated;
• to discover the light and power that slumber in humankind; the power of mysticism and the essence of philosophy;
• to assist in bringing the two poles of the world, east and west, closer together.

Tai chi

Chinese concept, from the words *tai*, or final, and *chi*, breath or energy, hence meaning "ultimate life energy." Tai chi is represented by a circle that is divided into two (yin-yang) and is the continuation of *wu chi*, the empty circle from which tai chi follows. *Tai chi chuan* (*chuan* = fist) is a stylized martial art in which one can actualize the ultimate life power in oneself by means of specific movements.

Taoism

The philosophical-religious teaching of Tao—the way the universe evolves—to which mankind must comply in order not to suffer unnecessary difficulties.

Tao Teh Ching

Written by the legendary philosopher Lao Tse, a contemporary of Confucius, the *Tao Teh Ching* consists of 81 chapters (verses) that profoundly yet accessibly explain the philosophy of Taoism.

Tarocchi

Italian for Tarot game or deck.

Tarot, the

The Russian philosopher G. I. Gurdjieff (1872–1949) described the Tarot as an objective system that hermetically unifies magic symbolism, astrology, alchemy, and numerology, as well as letter and word symbolism. It has been passed on to us from mythical times. As this collection of pictures on cards is loose-leaf, it is not static like a book, but dynamic and synchronous with the changing universe. The Tarot contains arcane teachings; at the same time, it is the instrument to enter into this living science.

Tarot, the Magical

Aleister Crowley (1875–1947) derived the Magical Tarot card deck from *The Book of Thoth, a Short Essay on the Tarot of the Egyptians*, which he wrote and published in 1896. The design of the cards is rigid and schematic. The Major Arcana are correlated to the Hebrew alphabet.

Tarot of Marseilles, the

The Tarot of Marseilles is one of the oldest and best-known Tarot decks. The deck was designed first in 1713 by cartier Jean Payens. That edition is very rare and incomplete. A complete deck exists dated 1761, from Nicolas Conver. It was reprinted for the general public in 1930.

Tarot by Wirth, the

The Tarot by Oswald Wirth dated 1889 is very beautiful and is still in use, like the Tarot of Marseilles and the Tarot by Waite. Wirth based his Tarot on elements from Freemasonry and theosophy, being a dedicated member of both. His book *Le Tarot des Imagiers du Moyen Age*, dedicated to the memory of the Marquis Stanislas de Guita, is very well known.

Tarot helix
A spiraled evolutionary representation of the 24 Major Arcana. One winding cycle of the 12 Principal Arcana doubles itself into a spiral with two coils, of which the coil with the second 12 Major Arcana is one "octave" higher than the coil with the first 12 Major Arcana.

Tarot in the Restored Order, the
The literal translation of the title of the Dutch edition of *The Complete New Tarot*.

Tarot invocation
One of the 24 permutations of the word TARO. These words are also called Tarot names.

Tarotists
People who study and divine with the Tarot.

Tarotists, reformed
A group of Tarotists who have tried to liberate themselves from the occult, and study the Tarot as scientifically as possible.

Tarot mandala
A mandala (a pictorial geometrical structure for the purpose of meditation) constructed from the arcana in the Tarot.

Telekinesis
Movement of objects in a paranormal way, that is, without apparent physical cause. Also called psychokinetics.

Templars
Also called Knights Templar, members of the Poor Knights of Christ and the Temple of Salomon. This order was founded during the early days of the Kingdom of Jerusalem, when the Crusaders controlled only a few strongholds and pilgrims were often attacked by Muslim bands. The order was established by the crusaders Hugo van Payen and Bisol of St. Omer, together with six others.

The order was headed by a grandmaster who had a royal rank and was responsible directly to the pope. They performed courageously and grew in numbers quickly. The order was well managed, established many monasteries, and acquired many properties throughout western Europe. They adopted absolute secrecy over all their internal activities.

After the fall of Akko in 1291, the order moved to the island of Cyprus. Clerical and secular kings sought and found ways to appropriate the order's enormous wealth and property, and break its spiritual power. In this way, the order lost its right of existence. In a major trial around 1307, the Inquisition falsely accused the

Templars of immorality and heresy. Almost all the Templars were murdered. In 1312 Pope Clemens V dissolved the order. Two years later, the grandmaster Jacques de Molnay was burned at the stake. The Templars are considered the precursors of various closed and secret groups—notably the Freemasons, who also emerged around that time.

Temple of Solomon
Solomon was king of Judea from 972–932 B.C., during the heyday of the Hebrew civilization. The wisdom of Solomon is still proverbial. The design of the temple was given to him in a divine revelation, in which God gave the king instruction about what were to be the materials, measures, proportions, and geomancy of the Lord's dwelling.

Theosophy
Derived from the Greek words *theos*, meaning god, and *sophia*, or wisdom. A religious philosophy with mystical concerns that can be traced to the ancient world. All theosophical thought is based on the mystical premise that God must be experienced directly to be known at all. Theosophical aspects can be found in thinkers such as Pythagoras and Plato; the Gnostic teachers Simon Magus and Valentinus; the Neoplatonists Plotinus and Proclus; the medieval mystics Meister Eckhart and Nicolas of Cusa; the Renaissance mystics Paracelsus and Giordano Bruno; and Jakob Böhm. The richest and most profound source of theosophical views, however, has been Indian thought, from the earliest *Vedas* through the *Upanishads* and the *Bhagavad Gita*, and on to modern times.

Since 1875 theosophy has been largely identified with Helena Petrovna Blavatsky (1831–1891), who founded the Theosophical Society in 1875 in New York. Its main philosophical concerns are:

- emphasis on mystical experience and perfection of humankind through subsequent incarnations;
- esoteric doctrine: deciphering the hidden meaning concealed in sacred texts; and
- occult phenomena: experiencing and studying extraordinary occurrences with higher psychic and spiritual powers.

The Theosophical Society has countless branches all over the world, each working rather independently. In the United States, it has influenced a series of other religious movements.

Therapeutai
Greek word meaning healers, servants, or worshippers. The Therapeutai were a Hellenistic-Hebrew community of ascetic hermits resembling the Essenes. It is believed that they were living in scattered houses on the shores of Lake Mareotis in the vicinity of Alexandria in Egypt during the first century B.C. The sect was unusually severe in discipline and mode of life. The main difference between the Therapeutai and the Essenes is that the latter

were anti-intellectual, while wisdom was the main objective of the Therapeutai. The Therapeutai shared with the Essenes a dualistic view of body and soul.

Thoth
Egyptian god of wisdom; protector of writers, magic and science; and messenger of the gods, often depicted as an ibis or baboon. The Greeks identified Thoth with Hermes. He guarded the laws, institutions, and temple rites, and had insight into the law of cosmic life that arises from death. The creative powers of Thoth could revive Osiris and any other deceased from death.

Thule
Island in the Atlantic Ocean now called Greenland. In the Middle Ages, Thule was identified with Iceland, and thought to be a remnant of Atlantis. An ultra-secret pre-World War II fraternity of German, Polish, and Russian nobility appropriated the island's name. After World War II, it was discovered that the Thule Fraternity had been the ideological forerunner of Adolf Hitler's National Socialism.

Tibetan Book of the Dead
The ancient Tibetan-Buddhist text entitled *Bardo Tödrol Chenmo*, a literal translation of which is *The Great Liberation Through Hearing in the Bardo*. *Bar* means in between and *do* means hanging or being suspended. The concept of bardo is central to the *Tibetan Book of the Dead*.

Tiresias
In Greek mythology, the blind seer who advised many heroes. Some listened to him, such as Odysseus (Tiresias advised Odysseus that he would never return home if he harmed the cattle of the sun-god Helio). Others ignored him, to their cost, such as the hard-headed Creon. Tiresias was so wise that even his ghost kept his wits and and did not become forgetful.

One of the tales about Tiresias explains his blindness as the punishment for seeing the goddess Athena bathing.

In Sophocles' plays, Tiresias (of Thebes) served both King Oedipus and King Creon. He is an example of the archetype depicted in the Major Arcanum Justice.

Torah
The Hebrew word for teaching, the term denotes the five written books of Moses, which together form the first part of the Old Testament. In the shape of a double scroll, the Torah is read in the synagogue. In a wider sense, the laws and rules of Judaism.

Transmutation
From Latin, meaning change-over. The change of one chemical element into another. The metamorphosis of a caterpillar into a butterfly is also a transmutation.

Tree of Life

A tree that is mentioned in most mythologies and (old) religions as a symbol of (eternal) life and resurrection. The Tree of Life was, and still is, worshipped as such. It is placed in Paradise or in the center of the cosmos. In Jewish mysticism, it is also called the sephirothic tree. This mandala consists of ten interconnected sephiroth, centers or divine forces.

1	Kether	The Crown
2	Hokmah	Wisdom
3	Binah	Understanding
4	Hesed	Mercy, Love
5	Geburah	Severity, Power
6	Tifereth	Beauty
7	Netsah	Victory, Endurance
8	Hod	Splendor, Majesty
9	Yesod	Foundation
10	Matkuth	The Kingdom

Whoever eats the fruits of the Tree of Life (in a spiritual sense) will attain insight into the Self and ultimately, eternal life.

In the Paradise described in the Biblical Book of Genesis were two trees: the Tree of Life and the Tree of Good and Evil. Both trees are depicted in the Major Arcanum The Lovers.

Troyes, Chrétien de

French writer and composer who lived in the second half of the twelfth century. He wrote five novels about knighthood. His work was translated from the thirteenth century onward.

Time, directionality of

According to Ouspensky's model of the universe, points in space-time are either potential or actual. Potentialities that have been actualized can never be "de-actualized." When a mistake is corrected, the situation after the correction is different from before, because we have learned something. At an esoteric level, the principle of unidirectionality of time, for example, follows from the asynchronous appearance of positive and negative forces in our everyday world where time and space are separated. When objective processes are invoked, the negative forces appear first, the positive forces later.

Quantum theory of the atom, however, states that positive and negative directions in time are equally probable. Hence, it is difficult to understand how microphysical, statistical mechanics can make possible macrophysical thermodynamics, in which the entropy grows with time.

In astronomy, the generally accepted "big bang" theory, formulated in 1929 by Edwin Powell Hubble (1889–1953), states that the universe was created in a big bang, about 10 to 20 billion years ago, and from then on has been expanding. The big bang theory, however, is not universally accepted. In Buddhist circles it is believed that the universe itself goes through an endless series of development and expansion, followed by contraction and implosive destruction, and then re-emergence.

Stephen Hawking, when he applied the theory of general relativity to black holes, realized that the sub-atomic singularity in the middle of a black hole with its infinite gravity field would make time stop. "Falling through the wormhole in space-time created by a black hole" would mean traveling backwards in time once the singularity had been passed. As it may be possible that in the vicinity of a black hole, space-time time is negative, some processes in space-time may be running backward in time, and thus be bidirectional. If, in space-time, time can run forward as well as backward, it is possible for a black hole to *explode*. As such, an explosion is only possible under the influence of anti-gravitational forces that push matter violently apart; logically, negative time could be related to anti-gravity.

Unidirectional time seems to be the case only in situations where time and space are separated—in our physical world. At higher levels of existence, as in our psychological world, time does not exist in its "ordinary" unidirectional way. It comprises both events in the future and in the past as one great, multidimensional holographic record. Psychological time, which has its reference points in the mind, can run forward and backward. It is believed that a soul can incarnate forward and backward in time as well. At the interface of supernal existence and time-space separated existence, such as in dreams and incarnational regressions, we translate supernal, holographic time as bidirectional and are able to envisage events running forward as well as backward.

Unearth
Concept formulated by the mystics Marcel Messing and Jakob Böhm. The shortest possible paradox to indicate heaven.

Urania
In Greek mythology, the muse of astronomy, portrayed as a young woman holding in her left hand a globe and in the right a pointer, looking into the sky.

Uriel
One of the four archangels who watches the lights in the sky and is connected with the element water. He was the one who warned Henoch of the materialization of the earth.

Vedanta
One of the six orthodox systems of Indian philosophy, and the one that forms the basis of most modern schools of Hinduism. In Sanskrit, *Vedanta* means the conclusion (*anta*) of the *Vedas*.

The three fundamental Vedanta texts are the *Upanishads*, the *Brama-sutras*, which are brief interpretations of the *Upanishads*, and the famous poetic dialogue, the *Bhagavad Gita* (the *Song of the Lord*).

The influence of the Vedanta on Indian thought and philosophy has been profound. Although different interpretations of the Vedanta texts emerged over the centuries, the Vedanta schools hold in common these beliefs: (1) transmigration of the Self (*samsara*) and the desirability of release from the cycle of reincarnations; (2) the authority of the *Veda* on the means of release; (3) that *Brahman* is the cause of the world; (4) that the Self (*Atman*) is the agent of its own acts (karma) and therefore the recipient of the fruits of these actions (*phala*).

Vedas

Veda is Sanskrit, meaning knowing. The *Vedas* are sacred hymns composed in archaic Sanskrit, some of which possess great literary merit. They seem to stem from 2000–1200 B.C. and form a liturgical body that in part grew up around the soma ritual. The priest responsible for the sacrificial fire and for carrying out the related ceremony, recited sacred formulas known as mantras. The *Rigveda*, the *Veda of the Hymns*, is the oldest and most important. It contains 1,028 hymns divided into ten books and is correlated with Pentacles in the Tarot. The *Samaveda*, the *Veda of Melodies*, emerged from the *Rigveda*. It consists of two parts and is correlated with Wands. The *Vajoerveda*, the *Veda of Blessed Formulas*, gives among other things, instructions for human sacrifices (which have been carried out for centuries, seemingly also by the Aztecs). It is correlated with Cups in the Tarot. The *Atharveda*, the *Veda of Magic Formulas*, comprises 20 books and is correlated with Swords in the Tarot.

The entire body of Vedic literature and the expositions that became attached to them, such as the *Upanishads*, was considered the product of divine revelation. The whole of the works seems to have been preserved orally. Even today, the *Vedas*, notably the three oldest, are recited with intonations and rhythms that have been handed down from the earliest days.

Visconti

Name of a Ghibellian Milanese family prominent in the thirteenth to fifteenth centuries. Several members were of ill fame because of their cruelty against adversaries, but the Visconti were also important patrons of the arts and sciences. The Visconti-Sforza Tarocchi game from about 1430 is still complete and in excellent condition.

Wace, Robert

Anglo-Normandian poet, born about 1115 on the island of Jersey, deceased about 1183. In his poems he covers the history of the inhabitants of Britain and Normandy. His 15,000-verse-long *Roman de Brut*, written about 1155, is very well known.

Walpurgis, Walpurgia

St. Walpurgis (also called Walburga) was born about 710 in Wessex, England, and died in 779 in Heidenheim, Germany. An abbess and missionary who played an important role in St. Boniface's organization of the Frankish Church, she was buried at Heidenheim. Her body was later moved and interred in the Church of the Holy Cross at Eichstätt. Soon after her death, her memory seems to have become confused with that of Waldborg, a pre-Christian fertility goddess.

On Walpurgis Night—the eve of May 1 (the day her relics were taken to Eichstätt)—a Celtic Sabbath is celebrated in which witches are believed to rendezvous and have free play in the Harz mountain group in Germany.

Water cupids

The Latin verb *cupere*, meaning to desire. Cupid is the young companion and assistant of the Roman goddess of love, Venus. Depicted as a toddler with wings, bow, and arrows, he flies through the air looking for targets for his love arrows. Water cupids, portrayed on the throne of the Queen of Cups in the Tarot, live in water and swim with tridents, searching for candidates to make fall in love. They are always male.

Work, The

Concept from G. I. Gurdjieff's teachings, by which is meant working on yourself. According to Gurdjieff, humans are in a "sleeping" state even when they are awake. They have to wake up, become really aware of themselves, and start working on their own spiritual development.

The Work is a spiritual discipline. It carries a core of great ideas and practices, which are at the heart of all religions. This way of inner development, to be pursued by ordinary people in everyday life, has been passed down by word-of-mouth from ancient times to our own through many generations of teachers and students. The Work requires great self-discipline. It is built on several principles, three of the chief being:

- know yourself;
- nothing too much; and
- verify everything for yourself.

By going against one's "own will," using a continuing stream of exercises, dance, and meditation, the individual endeavors to achieve a state of self-remembrance in which the person becomes aware of the fact that he or she is "sleeping." This can also be understood from the New Testament (II Peter 1:13–16).

The Work also points to the Great Work (*Magnum Opus*) of the alchemists. To them this meant searching for the Philosopher's Stone and making gold, as much as working on oneself and thus actualizing oneself (with the result that death is overcome).

Yang

Chinese concept of the active, male principle in the Cosmos (for example, the sun).

Yin

Chinese concept of the passive, female principle in the Cosmos (for example, the moon). Yin passively attracts. Yang actively responds to and follows yin's attraction.

Zenzar

Also called Senzar or Sensar. A mystical, universal language spoken by holy persons, and immediately understood. It consists of objective sound structures and graphical symbols. The 24 Tarot invocations are part of the Zenzar language. Some Zenzar words are phonetically easy to understand in ordinary language. Two examples are:

1. The sound *ATOR*. This sound structure represents and bears the same meaning as the invocation for the Major Arcanum Intuition. The same sound structure is found in the words Hathor, Ishtar, and Astarte, all names for the ancient female, independent, strong-willed archetypal goddess of love.
2. The sound *ARTO*. This sound stands for the concepts embodied in the Major Arcanum The Hanged Man. The same sound is found in the English word "art" and between higher and lower worlds through self-sacrifice.

As the Major Arcana together form a cosmology that universally describes all developments, Tarot invocations can be used for white-magic purposes.

It is speculated that in crop circles, aliens use Zenzar symbols to convey messages to us.

Zeus

The chief deity in ancient Greek religion, a sky and weather god identified with the Roman god Jupiter. According to a Cretan myth later adopted by the Greeks, Cronus, king of the Titans, upon learning that one of his children would dethrone him, swallowed his children as soon as they were born. Rhea, his wife, saved the infant Zeus by substituting a stone wrapped in Zeus' swaddling. She hid Zeus in a cave. After Zeus grew to manhood, he succeeded in dethroning Cronus, perhaps with the assistance of his brothers Poseidon (god of the sea) and Hades (god of the underworld), with whom he divided the governorship of the world. Zeus rules the lot of humans. He is the Greek god of law and order, protector of guests. In the *Iliad* he collects clouds and makes rain, hail, and snow. He hurls lightning bolts and makes the thunder roll. Swaying his shield, he causes darkness and storms; he can order the sun and moon to stop. The change of seasons is his work. He mediates conflicts between the gods in heaven, and guards with parental interest the actions of all mortals. The oak and the eagle are dedicated to him.

Index